Rop.

D1824963

Financial Accounting

Maintaining Financial Records and Accounts

Unit 5, NVQ Level 3, AAT, CAT

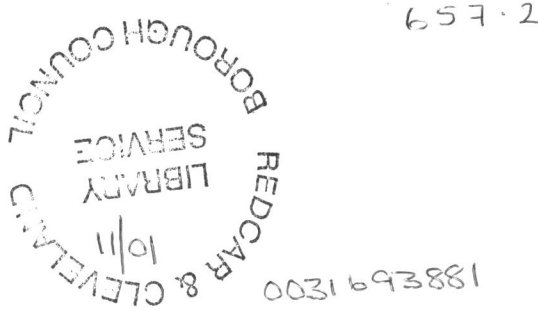

657.2

REDCAR & CLEVELAND BOROUGH COUNCIL
LIBRARY SERVICE
11/01

0031693881

Frank Wood and Sheila Robinson

FINANCIAL TIMES
Prentice Hall

An imprint of **Pearson Education**

Harlow, England · London · New York · Reading, Massachusetts · San Francisco
Toronto · Don Mills, Ontario · Sydney · Tokyo · Singapore · Hong Kong · Seoul
Taipei · Cape Town · Madrid · Mexico City · Amsterdam · Munich · Paris · Milan

0031693881

Pearson Education Limited
Edinburgh Gate
Harlow
Essex CM20 2JE, England
and Associated Companies throughout the world

Visit us on the World Wide Web at:
www.pearsoneduc.com

© Pearson Education Limited 2001

The right of Frank Wood and Sheila Robinson to be identified as authors of this work has been asserted by them accordance with the Copyright, Designs and Patents Act 1988.

All rights reserved; no part of this publication may be reproduced, stored in a retrieval system, or transmitted in any form or by any means, electronic, mechanical, photocopying, recording or otherwise without either the prior written permission of the Publishers or a licence permitting restricted copying in the United Kingdom issued by the Copyright Licensing Agency Ltd., 90 Tottenham Court Road, London W1P 0LP.

ISBN 0 273 63980 3

British Library Cataloguing-in-Publication Data
A catalogue record for this book is available from the British Library.

Set by 35 in 10.5/13pt Caslon 224
Printed in Malaysia, KVP

Contents

Preface x
Acknowledgements xi

1 Financial management of a business 1

1.1 Introduction 1
1.2 Definition of accounting 1
1.3 Importance and need for accounting 2
1.4 Planning and decision making 2
1.5 Types of organisation 3
1.6 Regulatory Accounting System 3

2 The accounting cycle 6

2.1 The accounting cycle 6
2.2 Source documents 8
2.3 Books of original entry 9
2.4 Double entry book keeping system .9
2.5 Worked example of double entry 11
2.6 The ledgers 12
2.7 Classification of accounts 13
2.8 Balancing off accounts and the trial balance 13
2.9 Final accounts 15
2.10 Summary of the accounting cycle 17

3 The trial balance 20

3.1 Introduction 20
3.2 Definition 20
3.3 Total debit entries = Total credit entries 20
3.4 Errors not revealed by a trial balance 24
3.5 Correction of errors 25
3.6 Steps to take if the trial balance does not balance 25
3.7 Casting 25
3.8 The uses of the trial balance 26

4 Trading and profit and loss accounts:
an introduction 29

4.1 Purpose of trading and profit and loss accounts 29
4.2 The format of the trading and profit and loss account 30
4.3 Horizontal and vertical trading and profit and loss accounts 30
4.4 Information required before preparation of the trading and
profit and loss accounts 30
4.5 Effect on the capital account 34
4.6 The vertical layout for trading and profit and loss accounts 34
4.7 The balances still in the books 35

5 Balance sheets 40

5.1 Definition and content of a balance sheet 40
5.2 Preparing a balance sheet (horizontal layout) 40
5.3 No double entry in balance sheets 41
5.4 Balance sheet layout 42
5.5 A properly drawn up balance sheet (horizontal style) 43
5.6 Vertical style balance sheets 44
5.7 Examinations and vertical and horizontal style final accounts . . .45

6 Trading and profit and loss accounts and
balance sheets: further considerations 46

6.1 Returns outwards and returns inwards 46
6.2 Carriage 48
6.3 The second year of a business 50
6.4 Model layout of final accounts 54

7 Accounting concepts and the regulatory
framework of accounting 60

7.1 Introduction 60
7.2 Objectivity and subjectivity 61
7.3 Definition of an accounting concept 61
7.4 SSAP 2: Disclosure of Accounting Policies 62
7.5 Accounting standards and the Financial Reporting Standards 67
7.6 Accounting standards and the legal framework 67
7.7 Accounting standards: requirements of NVQ Level 3
in Accounting 68
7.8 Confidentiality 73

8   Capital and revenue expenditure 77

8.1   Introduction 77
8.2   Capital expenditure 77
8.3   Revenue expenditure 78
8.4   Differences between capital and revenue expenditure 78
8.5   Joint expenditure 79
8.6   Incorrect treatment of expenditure 79
8.7   Treatment of loan interest 79
8.8   Capital and revenue receipts 80

9   Methods of depreciation and the acquisition of fixed assets 83

9.1   Introduction 83
9.2   Depreciation of fixed assets 83
9.3   Causes of depreciation 84
9.4   Land and buildings 86
9.5   Appreciation 86
9.6   Provision for depreciation as allocation of cost 86
9.7   Methods of calculating depreciation charges 87
9.8   Choice of method 88
9.9   Depreciation provisions and assets bought or sold 89
9.10   SSAP 12: Accounting for Depreciation 90
9.11   Authorisation for the acquisition and disposal of fixed assets 90
9.12   Disposal of fixed assets 91
9.13   Fixed asset register 91
9.14   Checking and verifying fixed assets 92
9.15   Funding the purchase of fixed assets 93

10   Double entry records for depreciation and the disposal of assets 98

10.1   Recording depreciation 98
10.2   The disposal of an asset 99
10.3   Further examples of disposal of assets 105
10.4   Accounting for VAT on fixed assets 110
10.5   Depreciation provisions and the replacements of assets 112
10.6   Step-by-step guide to dealing with depreciation in the final accounts 112

11   Bad debts and provisions for bad debts 117

11.1   Bad debts 117
11.2   Provisions for bad debts 118

11.3 Provisions for bad debts: estimating provisions 119
11.4 Accounting entries for provisions for bad debts 120
11.5 Increasing the provision 121
11.6 Reducing the provision 122
11.7 A worked example 123
11.8 Bad debts recovered 124
11.9 Step-by-step guide to dealing with bad debts and
provisions for bad debts 125

12 Other adjustments for final accounts 129

12.1 The final accounts so far 129
12.2 Adjustments needed for expenses owing or paid in advance 129
12.3 Accrued expenses (i.e. expenses owing) 130
12.4 Prepaid expenses 131
12.5 Revenue owing at the end of period 132
12.6 Expenses and revenue account balances and the
balance sheet 133
12.7 Expenses and revenue accounts covering more than
one period 134
12.8 Goods for own use 136
12.9 Distinctions between various kinds of capital 136
12.10 Final accounts in the services sector 137

13 Stock valuation 143

13.1 Different valuations of stocks 143
13.2 First In/First Out method (FIFO) .144
13.3 Last In/First Out method (LIFO) .144
13.4 Average cost method (AVCO) 145
13.5 Stock evaluation and the calculation of profits 145
13.6 Reduction to net realisable value .146
13.7 Some other bases in use 147
13.8 Factors affecting the stock valuation decision 147
13.9 The conflict of aims 148
13.10 Work in progress 149
13.11 Goods on sale or return 149
13.12 Stocktaking and the balance sheet date 149
13.13 Stock levels 150
13.14 SSAP 9: Stocks and long-term contracts 150

14 The journal 154

14.1 The journal: a book of original entry 154
14.2 Typical uses of the journal 155
14.3 Journal entries in examination questions 155
14.4 Purchase and sale on credit of fixed assets 156

14.5 Correction of errors 157
14.6 Bad debts 168
14.7 Opening entries 169
14.8 Other items 171
14.9 Examination questions involving the journal and
         control accounts 173

15 Control accounts and reconciliation of ledger accounts 178

15.1   Need for control accounts 178
15.2   Principle of control accounts 179
15.3   Information for control accounts .180
15.4   Form of control accounts 181
15.5   Other transfers 184
15.6   A more complicated example 185
15.7   Other advantages of control accounts 185
15.8   Other sources of information for control accounts 186
15.9   Control accounts as part of double entry 186
15.10 Examination questions involving control accounts and
          journal entries 188
15.11 Reconciliation of control accounts 190
15.12 Reconciliation of ledger accounts .191

16 The extended trial balance 196

16.1 Introduction 196
16.2 The extended trial balance 196
16.3 Preparing the extended trial balance 198
16.4 A worked example 198
16.5 Other considerations 204
16.6 A more complicated example 206
16.7 Skeleton trial balance 210

17 Bank reconciliation statements 217

17.1 Completing entries in the cash book 217
17.2 Where closing balances differ 218
17.3 The bank balance in the balance sheet 220
17.4 Other terms used in banking 220
17.5 Bank overdrafts 220
17.6 Dishonoured cheques 221
17.7 Bank reconciliation statements: business practice and
         examination questions 222

18 Single entry and incomplete records 233

18.1	Accounting ratios covered in this unit	.233
18.2	Mark-up and margin	.233
18.3	Calculating missing figures	.234
18.4	The relationship between mark-up and margin	.236
18.5	Why double entry is not used	.237
18.6	Profit as an increase in capital	.237
18.7	Drawing up the final accounts	.240
18.8	Incomplete records and missing figures	.243
18.9	Where there are two missing pieces of information	.245
18.10	Cash sales and purchases for cash	.245
18.11	Goods stolen or lost by fire, etc.	.245
18.12	Step-by-step guide to incomplete records	.247

19 Club and society accounts 257

19.1	Non-trading organisations	.257
19.2	Receipts and payments accounts	.257
19.3	Income and expenditure accounts	.258
19.4	Profit or loss for a special purpose	.258
19.5	Accumulated fund	.258
19.6	Drawing up income and expenditure accounts	.259
19.7	Subscriptions	.260
19.8	Outstanding subscriptions and the prudence concept	.262
19.9	Donations	.262
19.10	Entrance fees	.262
19.11	Life membership	.263
19.12	Treasurers' responsibilities	.263

20 Partnerships 272

20.1	The need for partnerships	.272
20.2	Nature of a partnership	.273
20.3	Limited partners	.273
20.4	Partnership agreements	.273
20.5	Contents of partnership agreements	.274
20.6	An example of the distribution of profits	.276
20.7	The final accounts	.277
20.8	Fixed and fluctuating capital accounts	.278
20.9	Where no partnership agreement exists	.280
20.10	The balance sheet	.281
20.11	A fully worked exercise	.281

21 Manufacturing accounts 289

21.1 Introduction to manufacturing accounts 289
21.2 Divisions of costs 289
21.3 Direct and indirect costs 290
21.4 Factory overhead expenses 290
21.5 Administration expenses 290
21.6 Selling and distribution expenses 290
21.7 Format of final accounts 290
21.8 A worked example of a manufacturing account 292
21.9 Work in progress 292
21.10 Another worked example of a manufacturing account 293
21.11 Apportionment of expenses 294
21.12 Full set of final accounts 295
21.13 Market value of goods manufactured 297
21.14 Finished stocks at market price 298

Appendix 1: Practice assessments 303
Appendix 2: Useful names and addresses 316
Answers 318
Index 377

Preface

This textbook has been written with three main objectives.

First, to meet the requirements of the Accounting National Training Organisation (ANTO), formerly Lead Body for Accounting, at NVQ Level 3 in financial accounting. It is intended to develop the student's skills and to provide knowledge and understanding required in the following unit:

- **Unit 5**. Maintaining Financial Records and Preparing Accounts. The unique NVQ number for this unit is 1050488.

The Association of Accounting Technicians (AAT) requires students to demonstrate competence in this unit as part of their Intermediate Certificate. Edexcel (formerly BTEC) also requires demonstration of competence in the unit as part of their Accounting qualification at NVQ Level 3.

Second, to provide knowledge and understanding for students undertaking the following courses.

- AAT, Diploma in Accounting (non-UK students only)
- Association of Chartered Certified Accountants (ACCA): Certified Accounting Technician (CAT)

Third, for other accounting courses where students need to acquire knowledge and understanding in keeping financial records and preparing accounts. This book can also be used for training accountancy staff and would be a valuable reference for people working in financial departments.

The AAT education and training scheme requires that students undertake assessments at intermediate level. These involve devolved assessments and a central assessment. They can be thought of as case studies which simulate situations which can be found in everyday accounting work.

Appendix 1 contains practice assessments which have been devised to simulate the AAT central assessment and the ACCA:CAT examination. Students attempting these will gain a valuable indication as to their competence and readiness for undertaking either the AAT or ACCA assessments.

Each chapter includes a list of new terms followed by a series of Student Activities which can be used by students to assess their progress. Answers are provided at the end of the book, but where questions have been marked with the suffix X (e.g. 3.4X), the answers to such questions will be found in a separate answer book, *Financial Accounting Lecturer's Guide*, which will be supplied free to lecturers on request to the publishers.

Acknowledgements

The authors are grateful to the following for their permission to use past assessment papers in the case of the Association of Accounting Technicians (AAT) and to use past examination papers in the case of the Association of Chartered Certified Accountants (ACCA).

Thanks also to Michelle Wood for her keen interest and diligent work in preparing the draft manuscript.

Author's note

Frank Wood sadly died during the preparation of this book. I have been privileged to work with Frank for many years as co-author of a number of books. His contribution to accounting through his many books has been exceptional and he has had a major influence on the way accountancy has been taught world-wide over the last 30 years. I shall miss him but shall continue to develop the wonderful legacy he has been able to pass on.

Sheila Robinson

Financial management of a business

AIMS

- **To understand the need for accounting and its importance in business management.**

- **To know the main users of accounting information.**

- **To distinguish between the different business organisations.**

- **To be aware of the regulatory accounting system.**

1.1 Introduction

A vital aspect of any business is proper financial management. The owners of the business would have invested money in, what they considered to be, a viable enterprise based on a particular expertise. They may also have borrowed money to help to finance the business. This investment needs to be used carefully so that the business can flourish and generate a profit. Most businesses start with a sound idea and great enthusiasm by the owners who commit much time and effort to establishing a customer base. To ensure that the effort and financial commitment are not wasted it is essential that proper financial control is used as part of good management practice. Too many businesses fail in the early stages due to the lack of sound financial control. Well-established and successful businesses will undoubtedly have good accounting procedures and financial management which not only keep the owners aware of the financial status of the business but generate information for external parties such as the Inland Revenue. These interested parties are discussed below, but before examining the need for accounting it is appropriate to consider a definition for accounting.

1.2 Definition of accounting

A number of definitions have been put forward over the years but the following one is concise and coincides with the aim of this book and the Accounting National Training Organisation.

A skill or practice of maintaining accounts and preparing reports to aid the financial control and management of a business.

1.3 Importance and need for accounting

As stated earlier, businesses must operate profitably otherwise they will cease to exist. The financial statements, which are produced by the accounting department, will clearly show the profit or loss which has been made and the financial position of the business.

The two most important statements are:

1. Trading and profit and loss account
2. Balance sheet

Both these statements will have been checked and verified by a firm of auditors as part of the legal requirements for correct financial reporting. It is essential that accurate financial information is available to the auditors to enable them to fulfil their functions properly.

There are, however, others who are keenly interested in the activities of the business. These include:

- Inland Revenue – they collect employees' tax and national insurance contributions and tax on the profits of the business.
- Customs and Excise – they are responsible for the collection or refund of monies for a value added tax (VAT) registered business.
- Investors – these may be private individuals, companies or banks who will want to monitor the performance of the business to ensure that they will get a return for their investment.
- Suppliers – they will need to be sure of the financial stability of the business before accepting orders.
- Customers – they will need to be sure of the financial stability of the business before placing orders.

In order that the business can satisfy all these interested parties it must follow certain accounting procedures and practices in a formal sequence. Essentially this sequence can be stated as:

1. Collecting and recording accounting data
2. Classifying and analysing the data
3. Communicating financial information in the form of final accounts and the business report

This sequence is shown in the form of a diagram, 'The accounting cycle' (see Chapter 2, Exhibit 2.1).

1.4 Planning and decision making

The major reason for producing financial accounts and statements is to provide management with the means to monitor the financial performance of the business. They will have the information to enable them to make rational decisions and to formulate revised plans as necessary. For example, the statements might show an unexpected rise in the cost of purchased goods which is likely to affect the profits and cash flows of the business, and action would be needed to deal with this situation. Financial plans are usually known as budgets. Both planning and budgeting are dealt with in a later NVQ unit.

1.5   Types of organisation

Organisations are classified according to their structure and financial make-up and are mainly classified as shown below. The classification will determine its legal status and the financial reporting that is required of the organisation.

- **Sole trader**   An individual trading alone in his or her own name, or under a recognised trading name. He or she is solely liable for all business debts but when successful takes all the profits.
- **Partnership**   A group of more than two people and a maximum of twenty, carrying on a particular business with a view to making a profit. This topic will be covered later in Chapter 20.
- **Limited companies** (both private and public):
  - (a)   A *private* company is a legal entity with at least 2 shareholders. The liability of the shareholders is limited to the amount that they have agreed to invest.
  - (b)   A *public* company is, again, a legal entity with limited shareholder liability, but, unlike a private company, a public company can ask the public to subscribe for its shares.
- **Non-trading organisations**   Clubs, associations and other non-profit-making organisations are normally run for the benefit of their members to engage in a particular activity and not to make a profit. Their financial statements will take the form of income and expenditure accounts (to be covered in a later chapter).

The Accounting Standards at NVQ Level 3 do not cover the financial reporting with which limited companies must comply, and are thus dealt with in later books.

1.6   Regulatory Accounting System

The accounting profession is subject to the regulatory requirements of The Accounting Standards Board, which was set up by the accountancy bodies in 1990, and took over from the previous regulator, The Accounting Standards Committee (ASC). Over a period of about twenty years, prior to 1990, the ASC issued many Statements of Standard Accounting Practice. These are normally referred to as SSAPs; new standards developed by the board are called Financial Reporting Standards, abbreviated as FRSs.

Unit 5: *Maintaining Financial Records and Preparing Accounts* requires that candidates have knowledge and understanding of the following SSAPs, except for certain aspects as stated below.

SSAP 2: *Disclosure of Accounting Policies*

SSAP 5: *Accounting for VAT*

SSAP 9: *Stocks and Long-Term Contracts*

- except for the valuation of long-term contracts and the calculation of production overheads.

SSAP 12: *Accounting for Depreciation*

- except the revaluation of assets and the revision of estimates of useful life.

SSAP 13: *Accounting for Research and Development*

- candidates to know definitions of:
  - Pure research
  - Applied research
  - Development

as they apply to the standard.

NEW TERMS

Accounting   A skill or practice of maintaining accounts and preparing reports to aid the financial control and management of a business.

Accounting cycle   A diagram showing the procedure for collecting, recording, analysing and communicating financial information (see Chapter 2, Exhibit 2.1).

Auditors   A specialist firm of accountants appointed by an organisation to examine and verify that its financial statements have been presented fairly, comply with accounting practice and meet legal requirements.

Budget   A financial plan produced by an organisation.

Financial statements   Formal documents produced by an organisation to show the financial status of the business at a particular time. These include trading and profit and loss account and balance sheet. See later chapters for more details.

Financial Reporting Standards (FRSs)   Standards of accounting practice which are issued by the Accounting Standards Committee to ensure fair and consistent financial reporting.

Limited company (private)   A legal entity with at least two shareholders where the liability of the shareholders is limited to the amount of their investment. The public cannot subscribe for its shares.

Limited company (public)   A legal entity with many shareholders since the public can subscribe for its shares. Shareholder liability is limited to the amount of their investment.

Non-trading organisations   Include clubs, associations and other non-profit-making organisations which are normally run for the benefit of their members to engage in a particular activity.

Partnership   A group of more than two people and a maximum of twenty, carrying on a particular business with a view to making a profit.

Sole trader   A business owned by one person only.

Statements of Standard Accounting Practice (SSAPs)   Regulatory accounting requirements issued by the previous Accounting Standards Board.

Student Activities

1.1 State briefly the importance of good financial control to the owners of a business.

1.2 There are a number of bodies or individuals, other than the owners, who will have an interest in the financial performance statements of a business. List these interested parties and explain briefly the reasons for their interest.

1.3 List the main types of business organisation and explain their basic structure and financial make-up.

1.4 The accounting profession is subject to financial regulatory requirements in the form of SSAPs and FRSs. Give the full title of these abbreviations and state the name of the body which issues the requirements.

The accounting cycle

AIMS

- This chapter aims to provide an overview of the accounting cycle within an organisation's financial year. It aims to provide an understanding of the source documents used within the firm's trading activities, the recording of the documents into the books of original entry and posting to the appropriate account in the ledger.

- The chapter provides an introduction to the trial balance and the final accounts of an organisation, including the trading and profit and loss account and the balance sheet.

2.1 The accounting cycle

Traditionally businesses operate on a twelve-month cycle which may be the same as the calendar year January to December or perhaps the same as the tax year which, in the United Kingdom, runs from 6 April of one year to 5 April of the next year. Alternatively, some businesses operate from the date the business first began to trade, for example 1 July of one year to 30 June of the next year.

During the twelve-month period the business receives many documents of a financial nature which have to be entered in the books of account using either a manual or a computer system.

At the end of each month the books are usually balanced up and a trial balance prepared from which the final accounts (to be discussed later) may be prepared. Also, at the end of each month, outstanding accounts are usually settled, wages and salaries are paid and money received during the month from the organisation's debtors are all recorded.

If the organisation uses a computer system of accounting then, at the end of each month, a great deal of useful information can also be obtained such as outstanding debtors and creditors and the length of time the debt has been owing, plus financial information which is useful to management in their appraisal of the business and to assist in forward planning.

It is usual for the final accounts of a business to be prepared on an annual basis since they are required for taxation purposes and for the use of the owner(s) of the business.

This textbook will show how the final accounts of a businesses are prepared, including making necessary adjustments and complying with the regulatory system of accounting. The basic principles of book keeping – including double entry, the documents used in buying and selling and the books of original entry – have been covered extensively in a previous book by the same authors, *Transaction Accounting*, Units 1 and 2: Recording and Accounting for Cash and Credit Transactions. Students studying accounting for the first time are recommended to study this text, especially Part 1 – Introduction to Accounting.

Exhibit 2.1 shows the accounting cycle of a profit-making organisation. This should be referred to as each part of the cycle will now be discussed, starting with the source documents.

Exhibit 2.1

The accounting cycle for a profit-making organisation

Source documents	
Where original information is to be found	■ Sales and purchases invoices ■ Debit and credit notes for returns ■ Bank paying-in slips and cheque counterfoils ■ Receipts for cash paid out and received ■ Correspondence containing other financial information

Original entry	
What happens to the information	Classified and then entered in books of prime entry: ■ Sales and purchases day books (journals) ■ Returns inwards and outwards day books (journals) ■ Cash books* ■ The journal

Double entry	
How the dual aspect of each transaction is recorded	Double entry accounts

General ledger	Sales ledger	Purchases ledger	Cash books*
Real and nominal accounts	Debtors' accounts	Creditors' accounts	Cash book and petty cash book

(*Note*: Cash books fulfil both the roles of books of prime entry and double entry accounts)

Check arithmetic	
Checking the arithmetical accuracy of double entry accounts	Trial balance

Profit or loss	
Calculation of profit or loss for the accounting period	Trading and profit and loss accounts

Closing financial position	
Financial statement showing liabilities, assets and capital at the end of the accounting period	Balance sheet

2.2 Source documents

Source documents are documents where original information is found, for example, sales and purchase invoices and credit notes. All businesses and organisations which are involved in either trading activities or providing a service use these important documents.

- **Invoice**   An invoice is a document prepared by the seller whenever he or she sells goods or provides services on credit. The invoice contains the following information: the seller's name and address and value added tax registration number, the purchaser's name and address plus an order number and date, details of the goods and services supplied including quantity and relevant reference numbers, the date of delivery and finally details of the total amount due including VAT. (The book keepers of both the supplier and purchaser will use the invoice to record details of the transaction in the books of account.)

- **Credit note**   This document is raised by the supplier when goods have been returned by the purchaser due to their being damaged, faulty or supplied to the wrong specification, or when an overcharge has been made on an invoice. The amount owed by the customer (the debtor) will be reduced by the amount of the credit note. Credit notes are sometimes printed in red to distinguish them from invoices. (Again, credit notes are important documents which need to be entered in the books of both the supplier and purchaser.)

- **Bank paying-in slips**   These are forms used for paying money into a bank account. The recipient of the money must record on the counterfoil of the paying-in slip details of the amount paid and by whom so that the details may be recorded in the firm's cash book.

- **Cheque counterfoils**   When a cheque is made out it is important to complete the counterfoil entering details of the amount paid and to whom together with any other relevant details. The payment will also be recorded in the cash book.

- **Receipts**   This document acknowledges the receipt of money from a customer and is often issued when a customer purchases goods for cash rather than on credit. Again counterfoils are completed and used to enter the details of the receipt of cash in the cash book.

- **Correspondence**   Occasionally correspondence from a customer may be used as a source document to record a financial transaction that may be out of the ordinary, for example, when a debtor is unable to pay an outstanding amount and offers to settle the debt by giving the supplier an asset. Such a transaction would be entered in the journal proper (refer to Chapter 14). Internal documents such as a memorandum from a senior member of the organisation may be used in the same way.

It must be noted that all information of a financial nature must be supported by a source document and it is from this document that the details are entered in the business's book keeping system. Source documents are also referred to as **prime documents**.

2.3 Books of original entry

These are books in which the transaction is first entered. There are separate books for different types of transaction, as follows:

- **Sales day book** (also called **sales journal**) A book used for listing sales invoices; it gives details of the date of the sale, to whom and the amount of the sale. Sales day books may also contain analysis columns to give details of the amount charged for the goods, the VAT charged and, finally, the total amount due. Columnar sales day books may also be extended to analyse sales between different goods, departments and so on.

- **Returns inwards day book** (also called **sales returns day book** or **journal**) This is used to list any returns made by customers. This will lead to a credit note being issued to them.

- **Purchase day book** (also called **purchases journal**) This is similar to the sales day book, but contains lists of purchase invoices received from suppliers of goods or services. The purchases day book may also contain analysis columns depending upon the accounting system.

- **Returns outwards day book** (also called **purchases returns day book** or **journal**) This is used to record goods returned to suppliers.

- **Cash book** This is another book of original entry used to enter cash and bank receipts and payments. The cash book provides a record of the business's bank account and also provides details of the amount of cash in hand. It is both a book of original entry and part of the double entry system as it contains the balances of both cash in hand and cash at bank.

- **Petty cash book** A cash book used for making small (petty) payments, details of which are entered from petty cash vouchers supported if possible by a receipt.

- **The journal** This is used to record items that are much less common and sometimes complicated and are not recorded in any other book of original entry. The journal will be covered later, in Chapter 14.

2.4 Double entry book keeping system

The system of double entry book keeping is a method of recording transactions in the books of account of a business. In the sections above, source documents, which provide all the relevant information, were discussed fully followed by the books of *original* entry. The next important stage is to understand the double entry system of book keeping.

Business transactions deal with money or money's worth and each transaction always affects *two* things. For example, if a firm buys goods valued at £500 and pays for them by cheque, two things will have occurred: first, the stock of goods is increased; second, the money in the firm's bank account will have decreased by £500. If the firm then pays cash for a motor van, then, first, the money in the cash account will be reduced and, second, the motor van will have been acquired for the business. The dual aspect of treating each transaction is then recorded in 'an account'. An account shows us the 'history of' a particular business transaction, for example, the bank account or motor van account. If manual records are kept, then each account is usually shown on a separate page; if a computerised system is used, then each account is given a separate code number. Exhibit 2.2 shows an example of an account.

Exhibit 2.2

				Name of Account			Reference No.
Dr							Cr
Date	Details	Folio	£	Date	Details	Folio	£
	Debit side				Credit side		

The left-hand side of the account is known as the **debit side** and is abbreviated **Dr** while the right-hand side is known as the **credit side** and is abbreviated **Cr**. You will notice that the account looks rather like a letter 'T' and indeed accounts are often referred to as 'T accounts'. The words *debit* and *credit* in book keeping terms do not mean the same as in normal language and should be viewed differently from the start to avoid confusion. Students new to studying double entry may find it useful to use 'IN' and 'OUT' initially, in addition to debit and credit (see below).

Rules for double entry

Double entry is relatively easy to learn and understand if the following rules are learnt and understood:

1. Double entry means that every transaction affects two things and should, therefore, be entered twice: once on the **debit side** of an account and once on the **credit side** of an account.
2. The order in which the items are entered does not matter, the debit entry could be entered first or the credit entry could be entered first.

To help students having difficulty deciding on which side of each account the items should be entered, a useful hint is to think of the debit side being 'IN' to the account and the credit side being 'OUT' of the account. The following examples show the use of this approach:

1. 'Paid cash £50 to buy stationery.' The double entry for this transaction would be as follows:
    (a) Cash goes 'OUT' – a credit entry in the cash account.
    (b) Stationery comes 'IN' – a debit entry in the stationery account.
2. 'Paid £1,000 cash out of the cash till into the bank account of the business.' The double entry for this transaction would be as follows:
    (a) Money is paid 'IN' to the bank account – a debit entry in the bank account.
    (b) Cash goes 'OUT' of the cash till – a credit entry in the cash account.

2.5 Worked example of double entry

Consider the following example:

2003
Jan 1 Robert Ashley decides to start his own business and puts his savings of £6,000 into a business bank account.
   3 Robert decides to rent some premises and pays £500 by cheque for rent.
   5 Bought joinery machinery paying by cheque £2,000.
   6 Bought timber, nails, glue etc. on credit from Wood Supplies valued £1,000.
   7 Withdrew £200 from the bank for personal use (drawings).

The effect of these transactions is shown below:

	Transactions	*Effect*	*Action*
2003			
Jan 1	Started business with £6,000 paid into the bank account	Increases the asset of bank Increases the capital	Debit the bank account – money goes IN Credit the capital account – money comes OUT of the owner's money
Jan 3	Paid rent of premises, £500, by cheque	Decreases the asset of bank Increases the expense of rent	Credit the bank account – money comes OUT Debit the rent account – the benefit goes IN
Jan 5	Bought machinery, £2,000, paid by cheque	Increases the asset of machinery Decreases the asset of bank	Debit the machinery account – machinery comes IN Credit the bank account – money goes OUT
Jan 6	Bought timber, etc., on credit from Wood Supplies, £1,000	Increases the asset of purchases Increases the amount owed to the creditor (a liability)	Debit the purchases account – the purchases come IN Credit Wood Supplies account – the goods have come OUT of Wood Supplies
Jan 7	Withdrew £200 from the bank for own use	Decreases the asset of bank Capital is decreased by £200	Credit the bank account – money comes OUT Debit the drawings account – money goes IN

The above example can now be shown in account form:

Dr			Bank Account		Cr
2003			*2003*		
Jan 1	Capital	6,000	Jan 3	Rent	500
			Jan 5	Machinery	2,000
			Jan 7	Drawings	200

Dr	Capital Account		Cr
		2003	
		Jan 1 Bank	6,000

Dr	Rent Account		Cr
2003			
Jan 3 Bank	500		

Dr	Machinery Account		Cr
2003			
Jan 5 Bank	2,000		

Dr	Purchases Account		Cr
2003			
Jan 6 Wood Supplies	1,000		

Dr	Wood Supplies Account		Cr
		2003	
		Jan 6 Purchases	1,000

Dr	Drawings Account		Cr
2003			
Jan 7 Bank	200		

You will notice that in each account the date is entered followed by a description, which cross indexes to the corresponding account, followed by the amount.

As mentioned previously, double entry is covered fully in the previous book, *Transaction Accounting*, and students studying accounting for the first time would be advised to refer to Part 1 of that text.

2.6   The ledgers

In the above worked example all the transactions were entered in an 'account' – each account being kept in a ledger. If the business is very small then only one ledger may be used, but once the business expands it is better to have more than one ledger to allow different members of staff to be able to record transactions at the same time.

Once details from the source documents are entered in the books of original entry then the next stage of the book keeping procedure is to show the effect of the transactions by putting them into double entry accounts, as illustrated in the above worked example. The different types of ledger used are as follows (their alternative names are shown in brackets):

Sales Ledger (Debtors Ledger)	Purchases Ledger (Creditors Ledger)	General Ledger (Nominal Ledger)
Shows records of customer's personal accounts	*Shows records of suppliers' personal accounts*	*Contains the remaining double entry accounts, such as expenses, income, assets, capital*

2.7 Classification of accounts

Accounts are divided into **personal accounts** and **impersonal accounts**. Personal accounts are accounts that deal with people and firms – in other words, the debtors and creditors, *debtors* being people who owe money to the firm and *creditors* being people or firms to whom money is owed. The debtors' accounts are maintained in the sales ledger which may also be referred to as the debtors' ledger, the creditors' accounts are kept in the purchases ledger also referred to as the creditors' ledger.

Impersonal accounts are divided into *real* and *nominal* accounts.

- **Real accounts** are those which deal with possessions of the business, for example, buildings, machinery, computer equipment, fixtures and fittings, stock, etc.
- **Nominal accounts** are those in which expenses and income are recorded, for example, sales, purchases, wages, electricity, commissions received, etc.

The diagram illustrates the classification of accounts.

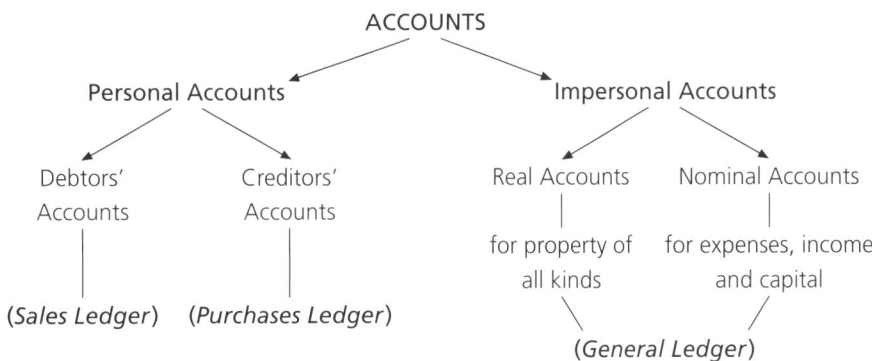

2.8 Balancing off accounts and the trial balance

Usually businesses balance off their accounts at the end of each month and prepare a trial balance for several reasons. First of all it is important to check periodically that the transactions have been entered correctly in the books of account; second, it is useful to know how much is outstanding from the debtors and how much the business owes to its creditors. Also, with the use of computer accounting packages, the business can easily prepare draft financial statements showing the profit or loss to date and the financial position of the firm at a specific date. These financial statements will be dealt with in Section 2.9.

Balancing off accounts

Each ledger account will require balancing off at the end of the period (usually monthly). Balancing off simply means finding the difference between the total of the debit entries and the total of the credit entries in a particular account. The 'difference' between the two sides is known as the 'balance' and this figure is inserted on the side of the account that shows the least amount of money. If both sides of the account are then totalled up, they should agree, having inserted the 'balance'; if they do not add up correctly, then an error may have been made in the calculation of the balance or perhaps in adding up the account. The calculations then need to be rechecked.

Once the account has been balanced off the balance is brought down to the opposite side of the account ready for the following month's transactions to take place. If we refer back to the worked example in section 2.5 and look at the 'Bank Account', this would be balanced off as follows:

Dr		Bank Account			Cr
2003			*2003*		
Jan 1	Capital	6,000	Jan 3	Rent	500
			Jan 5	Machinery	2,000
			Jan 7	Drawings	200
		____	Jan 31	Balance c/d	3,300
		6,000			6,000
Feb 1	Balance b/d	3,300			

Once balanced off, the account shows that the amount of money in the bank at the beginning of February is £3,300.

You will notice that next to the word 'Balance' the letters c/d appear; these stand for 'carried down' and the letters b/d stand for 'brought down'. If the balance is being transferred from one page of the ledger to a new page, then the letters c/f and b/f may be used, standing for 'carried forward' and 'brought forward'. When the account has been balanced off then the balance is inserted in a 'trial balance' along with all the other balances at the end of the period (see below).

The trial balance

Already you have seen that the method of book keeping in use is the double entry system, which means:

■ for each debit entry there is a corresponding credit entry, and
■ for each credit entry there is a corresponding debit entry.

Therefore it follows that all the items recorded on the debit side of the accounts should equal **in total** all the items recorded on the credit side. As mentioned above, the accounts are balanced off periodically to ensure that items have been correctly recorded and that the accounts balanced off accurately. To ensure that the books 'balance' a **trial balance** may be drawn up at the end of the period.

A trial balance is a list of all the balances on double entry (the ledgers) accounts and the cash book at a particular point in time. The trial balance lists the name of each account together with the balance shown in either the debit or credit columns. Provided no errors have occurred, the two columns should agree when totalled.

It is important to note that the trial balance is not part of the double entry system; it is merely a list of balances drawn up to check the arithmetical accuracy of the book keeping entries. It does, however, serve two purposes:

- It checks the accuracy of the double entry transactions.
- It facilitates the preparation of the final accounts of the business.

If a trial balance was drawn up from the worked example in Section 2.5 it would appear as shown.

Robert Ashley
Trial Balance as at 31 January 2003

	Dr	Cr
	£	£
Bank	3,300	
Capital		6,000
Rent	500	
Machinery	2,000	
Purchases	1,000	
Wood Supplies		1,000
Drawings	200	
	7,000	7,000

It may at first sight appear that the balancing of a trial balance proves that the books are correct. This, however, may not be true. It means that certain types of error have not been made, but there are several types of error that will not affect the balancing of a trial balance, such as omitting a transaction altogether. Examples of the errors which could be revealed, provided there are no compensating errors which would cancel out each other, are errors in addition, using one figure for the debit entry and another figure for the credit entry, entering only one aspect of a transaction, and so on. We shall consider these in greater detail in later chapters.

As stated earlier, one of the purposes of the trial balance is to facilitate the preparation of the final accounts of the business. An extension to this function is the use of an extended trial balance which is similar to the one shown above but includes analysis columns to facilitate dealing with the adjustments necessary when preparing final accounts. This will be covered fully in Chapter 16.

2.9 Final accounts

Final accounts are the financial statements that a business prepares at the end of its financial year (accounting period). They include the **trading and profit and loss account** which shows the gross and net profits or losses made during the period and the **balance sheet** which indicates the financial position of the business at a particular point in time. As the name implies, the final accounts are the end product of the recording of all the business transactions throughout the financial year. Once prepared they are used by the owners of the business for information, interpretation and planning purposes.

Trading and profit and loss account

The trading and profit and loss account is a combined account which shows both the gross profit and net profit. The **trading account** is shown first and gives the **gross profit**, which is the excess of sales over the cost of goods sold in the period. The **net profit** is found when the **profit and loss account** is prepared and consists of the gross profit plus any revenue other than that from sales, such as discounts received or commissions earned, less the total costs used up during the period. Where the cost of goods sold is greater than the sales, the result would be a **gross loss**, but this is a relatively rare occurrence. Where the costs used up exceed the gross profit plus other revenue then the result would be a **net loss**.

Balance sheet

The **balance sheet** is a financial statement that sets out the book value of assets, liabilities and capital 'as at' a particular point in time. In simple terms it shows what a business 'owns' and 'owes' and what a business is worth at a specific date.

Assets, liabilities and capital are further explained below:

- **Assets** Assets are resources that are owned by the business, they are classified between fixed assets and current assets:
  - **Fixed assets** are of a more permanent nature, such as land and buildings, plant and machinery, motor vehicles, computer equipment etc. They have a long life and are expected to be used in the operation of the business and not primarily bought for resale.
  - **Current assets** include cash in hand, cash at bank, stock and debtors. They are assets that can reasonably be converted into cash or sold within a short period of time, usually within one year.
- **Liabilities** A liability is something that is owing and for which the business is liable to pay at some point in time. A liability can be divided into either a current liability or a long-term liability as follows:
  - **Current liabilities** have to be paid for in the near future, usually within one year. They include payments due to creditors and a bank overdraft, which is a temporary loan facility offered by banks.
  - **Long-term liabilities** do not have to be repaid in the near future and include loans from people or other organisations which, it has been agreed, do not need repayment within the next twelve months.
- **Capital** This is the amount of money invested in the business by its owner(s) plus profits which have been reinvested into the business.

Examples of the final accounts of a business, including the trading and profit and loss account and balance sheet, will be shown throughout this textbook.

2.10 Summary of the accounting cycle

This chapter has shown how the accounting procedures of a business are recorded and the information that is derived from those records. It may be useful to list them once again at this point:

Initially *source documents* are received as follows:

Documents	Entered into book of original entry
Sales invoices	Sales day book (also called sales journal)
Credit notes (sent to customers)	Returns inwards day book (also called sales returns day book)
Purchases invoices	Purchases day book (also called purchases journal)
Credit notes (received from suppliers)	Returns outwards day book (also called purchases returns day book)
Cash and cheques received	Cash book (also a ledger account)
Cheques paid out	Cash book (also a ledger account)
Small cash payments	Petty cash book (also a ledger account for cash in hand)
Miscellaneous correspondence	The journal

Once the details of the transaction have been entered into the books of original entry, the information is then entered into the ledgers by means of the double entry system. This procedure is often referred to as 'posting'.

Sales transactions are posted to the *sales ledger*, purchases transactions are posted to the *purchases ledger* and items involving the real and nominal accounts are posted to the *general ledger*.

At the end of each month the books are balanced off and a *trial balance* prepared to check the arithmetical accuracy of the book keeping entries. At the end of the accounting period the final trial balance is used to prepare the year-end accounts, i.e. the *trading and profit and loss account* and the *balance sheet*. The accounts are then presented to the owner(s) of the business for their information, interpretation and action in the form of planning and budgeting for the next accounting period.

NEW TERMS

Accounting cycle   The period in which a business operates, its financial year. It involves recording all the trading activities from source documents to the preparation of the final accounts.

Assets   Resources that are owned by the business.

Balance sheet   A financial statement that sets out the book value of assets, liabilities and capital 'as at' a specific date.

Balancing off   Finding the difference between the total of the debit entries and the total of the credit entries in a particular account. The difference between the two sides is known as the 'balance'.

Bank paying-in slip   Form used for paying money into a bank account.

Books of original entry   Books where the first entry of a transaction is made.

Capital   The amount of money invested in the business by its owner(s) plus profits that have been reinvested into the business.

Cash book   Book of original entry for cash and bank receipts and payments. It is also a ledger account for the balance of cash and bank balances.

Cheque counterfoil   Part of the cheque which is retained by the person making out the cheque to provide a record of the transaction, often referred to as the cheque book stub.

Credit note   This document is issued by the supplier when goods have been returned by the purchaser due to their being damaged, faulty or to the wrong specification, or when an overcharge has been made on an invoice. The amount owed by the customer (the debtor) will be reduced by the amount of the credit note.

Creditor   A person to whom money is owed for goods or services.

Current assets   Assets which change from day to day and include cash in hand, cash at bank, stock and debtors. They are assets that can reasonably be converted into cash or sold within a short period of time, usually within one year.

Current liabilities   Liabilities that have to be paid for in the near future, usually within one year; they include payments due to creditors and a bank overdraft, which is a temporary facility offered by banks.

Debtor   A person who owes money to the business for goods or services supplied.

Double entry book keeping   A system of book keeping where transactions are recorded twice in the books of account.

Fixed assets   Assets which are of a more permanent nature such as land and buildings, plant and machinery, motor vehicles, computer equipment, etc. They have a long life and are expected to be used in the operation of the business and are not primarily bought for resale.

General ledger   The general (nominal) ledger contains the remaining double entry accounts such as expenses, income, assets and capital.

Gross loss   A gross loss occurs when the cost of goods sold exceeds the sales figure.

Gross profit   This is found by deducting the cost of goods sold from the sales figure.

Impersonal accounts   All accounts other than debtors' and creditors' accounts.

Invoice   This is a document prepared by the seller whenever goods or services are provided on credit. It tells the business receiving the goods or services that money is now owed to the supplier.

Journal   Book of original entry for all items other than those for cash or goods.

Ledger   Book used to enter book keeping transactions. There are several types of ledger, see 'general or nominal ledger', 'sales ledger' and 'purchases ledger'.

Liabilities   A liability is something that is owing and for which the business is liable to pay at some point in time.

Long-term liabilities   Long-term liabilities are liabilities that do not have to be repaid in the near future and include long-term bank loans.

Net loss   This is where the cost of goods sold plus expenses is greater than the revenue.

Net profit   Gross profit less expenses.

Nominal accounts   Accounts in which expenses, income and capital are recorded.

Personal accounts   Accounts for both creditors and debtors.

Petty cash book   A cash book used for making small (petty) payments. Payments are usually analysed and the totals of each column later posted to the various accounts in the general ledger.

Profit and loss account   Account in which net profit is calculated.

Purchases day book   Book of original entry for credit purchases (also called purchases journal).

Purchases ledger   A ledger for suppliers' personal accounts.

Real accounts   Accounts which deal with possessions of the business, for example buildings, machinery, fixtures and fittings, etc.

Receipts   Documents which acknowledge the receipt of money from a customer.

Returns inwards day book   Book of original entry for goods returned by customers.

Returns outwards day book   Book of original entry for goods returned to suppliers.

Sales day book   Book for original entry for credit sales (also called sales journal).

Sales ledger   A ledger for customers' personal accounts.

Source document   Original documents which contain details of business trading activities for example, invoices, credit notes, paying-in slips, etc.

Trading account   Account in which the gross profit is calculated.

Trading and profit and loss account   Combined account in which both gross and net profits are calculated.

Trial balance   A list of all the balances on double entry (the ledgers) accounts and the cash book at a particular point in time. The trial balance lists the name of each account together with the balance shown in either debit or credit columns.

Student Activities

2.1   Source documents in accounting are very important.

(a)   Describe the contents of both an invoice and a credit note.
(b)   State when each of these would be used.

2.2X   The books of original entry are used to record initial accounting information and separate books are used for different types of transactions. List the various books used and give a brief explanation of their use.

2.3   For what purpose would you use the following ledgers:

(a)   General or nominal ledger?
(b)   Sales ledger?
(c)   Purchases ledger?

2.4X   Distinguish between personal and impersonal accounts giving examples of what each might contain.

2.5   State the purpose in drawing up a trial balance.

2.6   Describe how fixed assets differ from current assets.

2.7   State what a balance sheet is and its purpose.

2.8   Describe clearly the difference between a current liability and a long-term liability.

CHAPTER 3

The trial balance

AIMS

- To be able to understand why trial balance totals should equal one another.

- To be able to draw up a trial balance from a given set of accounts.

- To appreciate that some kinds of error can be made but the trial balance totals will still equal one another.

3.1 Introduction

In Chapter 2, an overview of the accounting cycle was discussed from entering source documents into the books of account and following them through to the trial balance and finally to the preparation of the final accounts. This chapter will look in more detail at the preparation of the trial balance, steps to take if it does not balance and how errors can still be made but yet do not affect the balancing of the trial balance.

3.2 Definition

As mentioned in the previous chapter, the trial balance is a list of all the balances on the double entry (the ledgers) accounts and the cash book at a particular point in time. The trial balance lists the name of each account together with the balance shown in either the debit or credit columns. It is a statement prepared to prove the arithmetical accuracy of the book keeping entries.

3.3 Total debit entries = Total credit entries

As discussed previously, the method of book keeping used is the double entry system which means:

- for each debit entry there is a corresponding credit entry, and
- for each credit entry there is a corresponding debit entry

Once all the transactions have been entered into the books of account the books are then 'balanced off' at the end of the particular period, usually monthly. Provided no errors have been made, all the items recorded in the books of account on the debit side should equal in *total* all the items recorded on the credit said of the books. It is necessary to check that for each debit entry there is also a credit entry. To check that the two totals are equal – usually known as seeing if the two sides of the books 'balance' – a **trial balance** may be drawn up at the end of a period. Exhibit 3.1 shows a worked example.

Exhibit 3.1

A worked example

G Allen started a new business on 1 May 2001. He entered the following transactions in his books and balanced them off at the end of the month.

2001

May	1	Started the business with £30,000 capital which was placed into a bank account.
	1	Bought a motor van for £5,000, paying by cheque.
	2	Paid three months rent £1,500 by cheque.
	3	Bought £2,700 goods on credit from D Green.
	4	Bought £750 goods on credit from P Hall.
	5	Cash sales £540.
	6	Returned goods £120 to P Hall.
	10	Sold goods for £1,770 on credit to R Shaw.
	12	Cash sales £440.
	14	Purchased stationery £55 and paid by cash.
	18	Bought £570 goods on credit from P Hall.
	21	Bought office machinery £1,650 paying by cheque.
	22	Sold goods for £600 on credit to T Morris
	23	R Shaw returned £420 goods to G Allen.
	25	T Morris returned goods £100 to G Allen.
	28	Returned goods £195 to P Hall.
	29	Paid D Green £2,700 by cheque.
	30	Paid P Hall £630 by cheque.
	31	R Shaw paid us a cheque amounting to £1,350.

Books of G Allen

Dr			Bank Account				Cr
2001			£	*2001*			£
May	1	Capital	30,000	May	1	Motor van	5,000
	31	R Shaw	1,350		2	Rent	1,500
					21	Office machinery	1,650
					29	D Green	2,700
					30	P Hall	630
					31	Balance c/d	19,870
			31,350				31,350
Jun	1	Balance b/d	19,870				

Dr			Cash Account				Cr
2001			£	*2001*			£
May	5	Sales	540	May	14	Stationery	55
	12	Sales	440		31	Balance c/d	925
			980				980
Jun	1	Balance b/d	925				

Exhibit 3.1 (continued)

Dr			Sales Account			Cr
2001		£	*2001*			£
May 31	Balance c/d	3,350	May 5	Cash		540
			10	R Shaw		1,770
			12	Cash		440
			22	T Morris		600
		3,350				3,350
			Jun 1	Balance b/d		3,350

Dr			Returns Inwards Account		Cr
2001		£	*2001*		£
May 23	R Shaw	420	May 31	Balance c/d	520
25	T Morris	100			
		520			520
Jun 1	Balance b/d	520			

Dr			Purchases Account		Cr
2001		£	*2001*		£
May 2	D Green	2,700	May 31	Balance c/d	4,020
4	P Hall	750			
18	P Hall	570			
		4,020			4,020
Jun 1	Balance b/d	4,020			

Dr			Returns Outwards Account			Cr
2001		£	*2001*			£
May 31	Balance b/d	315	May 6	P Hall		120
			28	P Hall		195
		315				315
			Jun 1	Balance b/d		315

Dr			Office Machinery Account		Cr
2001		£	*2001*		£
May 21	Bank	1,650			

Dr			Motor Van Account		Cr
2001		£	*2001*		£
May 1	Bank	5,000			

Dr			Rent Account		Cr
2001		£	*2001*		£
May 2	Rent	1,500			

Dr			Stationery Account		Cr
2001		£	*2001*		£
May 14	Cash	55			

Exhibit 3.1 (continued)

Dr	Capital Account		Cr
2001	£	*2001*	£
		May 1 Bank	30,000

Dr	T Morris Account		Cr
2001	£	*2001*	£
May 22 Sales	600	May 25 Returns inwards	100
		31 Balance c/d	500
	600		600
Jun 1 Balance b/d	500		

Dr	R Shaw Account		Cr
2001	£	*2001*	£
May 10 Sales	1,770	May 23 Returns inwards	420
		31 Bank	1,350
	1,770		1,770

Dr	D Green Account		Cr
2001	£	*2001*	£
May 29 Bank	2,700	May 2 Purchases	2,700

Dr	P Hall Account		Cr
2001	£	*2001*	£
May 6 Returns outwards	120	May 4 Purchases	750
28 Returns outwards	195	18 Purchases	570
30 Bank	630		
31 Balance c/d	375		
	1,320		1,320
		Jun 1 Balance b/d	375

G Allen
Trial Balance as at 31 May 2001

	Dr	Cr
	£	£
Bank	19,870	
Cash	925	
Sales		3,350
Returns inwards	520	
Purchases	4,020	
Returns outwards		315
Office machinery	1,650	
Motor van	5,000	
Rent	1,500	
Stationery	55	
Capital		30,000
T Morris	500	
P Hall		375
	34,040	34,040

You will notice that the totals on the above trial balance agree with each other, which means that the trial balance is arithmetically correct; however, it is possible that certain errors may have been made which have not affected the balancing of a trial balance. This possibility will be discussed later in the chapter.

3.4 Errors not revealed by a trial balance

It may at first sight appear that the balancing of a trial balance proves that the books are correct but this, however, may be wrong. It means that certain types of error have not been made, but there are several types of error that will not affect the balancing of a trial balance. These will now be considered.

1. **Errors of omission** Where a transaction is completely omitted from the books, for example, if a business purchases goods on credit from A Chadwick for £500 but did not enter it in the accounts there would be neither a debit nor a credit entry. The trial balance would still balance but would be inaccurate since the purchases account should have been debited with £500 and A Chadwick's account credited with £500.

2. **Errors of commission** This type of error is where the correct amount is entered but in the wrong person's account, e.g. where a sale of goods £4,000 to H Robinson is entered in the account of H Robertson. If such an error is made it must be noted that the correct class of account was used, both the accounts concerned being personal accounts.

3. **Error of principle** This is where a transaction is entered in the wrong class of account. For instance, the purchase of a fixed asset should be debited to a fixed asset account; if, in error, it is debited to an expense account, then it has been entered in the wrong class of account. For example, the purchase of a motor vehicle is debited in error to the motor expenses account when, in fact, it should have been debited to the motor vehicle account.

4. **Compensating error** These are errors which cancel each other out. For example, if the sales account was added up to be £1,000 too much and the purchases account was also added up to be £1,000 too much, then these two errors would cancel out in the trial balance because the totals of both the debit side and credit side of the trial balance will be £1,000 too much.

5. **Errors of original entry** This occurs when an incorrect figure is posted to the correct sides of the correct accounts. For example, if sales of £700 to G Duffy had been entered in the accounts as £70 then the trial balance would still balance even though this error had been made. Another common error is where figures are transposed – for example, an amount of £78 might have been entered as £87, and again this type of error would not be revealed by the trial balance as it would still balance if £87 is entered on both sides of the account.

6. **Complete reversal of entries** The correct amounts are entered in the correct accounts, but each item is shown on the wrong side of each account. For example, a purchase of stationery for cash has been entered in error on the debit side of the cash book and the credit side of the stationery account. The entries should have been credit cash book, debit stationery account.

3.5 Correction of errors

When errors have been found they have to be corrected. The corrections need to be made in the double entry accounts and, in addition, an entry should also be made in the journal to explain the correction.

Correction of errors will be covered in greater detail in Chapter 14, the journal.

3.6 Steps to take if the trial balance does not balance

If the trial balance does not balance, i.e. the two totals are different, then this is evidence that at least one error has been made in either the double entry book keeping or in the preparation of the trial balance itself. In this case the following steps should be taken to locate the error(s):

1. If the trial balance is badly written and contains many alterations, then rewrite.

2. Add each side of the trial balance up again; if you added 'upwards' the first time then start at the top and work 'downwards' the second time, and vice versa.

3. Find the amount of the discrepancy and check in the accounts for a transaction of this amount; if located, ensure that the double entry has been carried out correctly.

4. Halve the amount of the discrepancy and check to see if there is a transaction for this amount; if located, ensure that the double entry has been carried out correctly. This type of error may have occurred if an item had been entered on the wrong side of the trial balance.

5. If the amount of the discrepancy is divisible by nine then this indicates that when the figure was originally entered it may have been transposed – for example, £63 entered in error as £36, or £27 entered as £72.

6. Check that the balance on each account has been correctly calculated and entered onto the trial balance in the right column using the correct amount.

7. Ensure that every outstanding balance from all the ledgers and the cash book has been included in the trial balance and tick each balance ensuring that it is entered correctly.

8. If the error has still not been identified then the error must be sought in the accounts themselves. It may be necessary to check all the entries from the date of the last trial balance.

3.7 Casting

The term 'casting' or 'to cast' means to add up figures. Overcasting means incorrectly adding up a column of figures to give an answer which is *greater* than it should be while undercasting means incorrectly adding up a column of figures to give an answer which is *less* than it should be.

3.8 The uses of the trial balance

The trial balance may be used for the following purposes:

- To check that the books 'balance', i.e. that every debit entry has been accompanied by a credit entry.

- To ascertain the number of errors that have been made and make the necessary corrections.

- As a basis from which the final accounts of a business are prepared, i.e. the trading account, the profit and loss account and the balance sheet. This will be covered in the next chapter.

NEW TERMS

Casting   Adding up figures.

Compensating error   Where two errors of equal amounts, but on opposite sides of the accounts, cancel out each other.

Complete reversal of entries   Where the correct accounts are used but each item is shown on the wrong side of the account.

Errors of commission   Where a correct amount is entered, but in the wrong person's account.

Error of omission   Where a transaction is completely omitted from the books.

Error of original entry   Where an item is entered, but both debit and credit entries are of the same incorrect amount.

Error of principle   Where an item is entered in the wrong type of account, e.g. a fixed asset entered in an expense account.

Student Activities

3.1

(a) Of the following which *best* describes a trial balance? A trial balance
   (A) is the final account in the books.
   (B) shows all the asset balances.
   (C) is a list of balances on the books.
   (D) shows the financial position of a business.

(b) When should the trial balance totals differ?
   (A) Only when it is drawn up by an accountant.
   (B) When it is drawn up before the profit and loss account is prepared.
   (C) If it is drawn up half way through the financial year.
   (D) None of the above.

(c) Which of the following do not affect the trial balance agreement?
   (i)   Purchases of £105 from B Hand entered in D Hand's account.
   (ii) Sales £87 to T Moore entered in both accounts as £78.
   (iii) Cheque payment to S Taylor of £240 entered only in the cash book.
   (iv) Motor van purchased £12,000 entered in motor expenses account.
   A (i) and (ii)   B (ii) only   C (ii) and (iv)   D (i), (ii) and (iv)

(d) What would be the totals on a trial balance given the following balances: Loan from father £6,000; stock £11,865; bank overdraft £1,104; debtors £9,276; motor car £16,500; cash in hand £363; creditors £8,298; plant and machinery £11,700; capital?
(A) £34,482   (B) £43,884   (C) £49,704   (D) £50,988

(e) Which of the following do **not** affect trial balance agreement?

    (i) Purchases £130 from J Smith completely omitted from the books.
    (ii) Sales £767 to M Morris entered in his account as £76.
    (iii) Rent account added up £100 too much.
    (iv) Sales to T Marley £177 entered as £170 on both the debit and credit sides of the account.
    (A) (i) and (iv)   (B) (i) and (ii)   (C) (i) and (iii)   (D) (iii) and (iv)

3.2 State whether the following accounts would be either a debit or a credit balance.

(a) Capital	**(b)** Sales
(c) Stationery	**(d)** Bank overdraft
(e) Day & Co (creditor)	**(f)** Machinery
(g) Rent and rates	**(h)** Drawings
(i) Bank loan	**(j)** Purchases

3.3 State what type of error has occurred in the following examples.

(a) Purchases account has been debited with the purchase of office furniture costing £950 paid by cheque.

(b) Sale of goods to J Clarkson £660, has been entered in J Clark's account.

(c) Sale of goods £3,000 to N Ward has been completely omitted from the books of account.

(d) A sale of goods to K Kirkham for £49 was entered in the books as £94.

(e) A payment of cash £58 to M Dawson was entered on the receipts side of the cash book in error, and credited to M Dawson's account.

(f) A second-hand motor van bought for £4,000 was entered in the motor expenses account.

(g) Interest received £800 had been entered in error in the sales account.

3.4X In the following examples state what type of error has occurred:

    (i) A sale of goods £300 to B Johnson had been entered in B Johnstone's account.

    (ii) The purchase of a computer on credit from Business Products Ltd had been completely omitted from the books.

    (iii) A sale of £442 to E Franklin had been entered in the books as £402 for both the debit and credit entries.

    (iv) Commission received of £750 had been entered in error in the sales account.

    (v) The purchase of paper for the photo-copier £400 had been entered in error in the office equipment account.

    (vi) A receipt of cash from Croft & Son had been entered on the credit side of the cash book and the debit side of Croft & Son's account.

    (vii) A purchase of goods costing £670 had been entered in error on the debit side of the drawings account.

3.5 Record the following transactions for J Jenkins for the month of January 2004, balance off all the accounts and extract a trial balance as at 31 January 2004.

2004

Jan 1 Started in business with £10,000 in the bank.

2 Paid rent for premises £500 by cheque

4 Bought office furniture and fittings on credit from Baileys Ltd £1,200.

5 Bought goods on credit from H Pickford & Son £320, J Jackson Ltd £460 and Plastic Ware Ltd £980.

6 Cash sales £480.

8 Bought second hand motor van £3,500 paying by cheque.

10 Bought stationery for cash £45.

12 Bought goods on credit £527 from J Jackson Ltd.

14 Sold goods on credit to Cornerways & Co. £96, McGilvery Mfr. £64 and Rogers & Brown £1,820.

15 Paid wages in cash £128.

16 Cash sales £340.

18 Paid the following by cheque H Pickford & Son £320 and Plastic Ware Ltd on account £460.

23 Bought motor van on credit £4,500 from Park Car Sales.

25 Bought goods on credit from Plastic Ware Ltd £720.

26 Sold goods on credit to Cornerways & Co. £300 and Rogers & Brown £515.

28 Received cheques from McGilvery Mfr. £64 and Rogers & Brown £1,820.

29 Paid for petrol by cash £25.

30 Paid in cash wages £320 and stationery £92.

30 Paid electricity account by cheque £52.

31 Paid the following by cheque: telephone account £94 and Baileys Ltd £1,200.

31 Received cheque from Cornerways & Co. £96.

3.6X Mark Adams opened a book shop on 1 April 2003 and his transactions for the first month's trading are shown below. Note that Mark is not registered for valued added tax.

April Transactions

Apr 1 Started in business with £22,000 in the bank.

1 Paid three months' rent on premises £1,800 by cheque.

7 Bought shop fittings and shelving paying by cheque £3,230.

7 Bought books paying by cheque £5,000.

9 Took £1,000 out of the bank and put it into a cash account.

9 Bought stationery £163 paying by cash.

10 Bought more books this time on credit from Book Supplies £4,200.

14 Book sales paid into the bank £980.

16 Paid sundry expenses £28 in cash.

20 Book sales paid direct into the bank £1,300.

25 Purchased further books on credit from Delta Books £1,500.

28 Books sales paid direct into the bank £2,000.

30 Paid salaries by cheque £2,100.

Required

(a) To enter the transactions for April 2003 and balance off the accounts at the end of the month (day books are not required).

(b) Prepare a trial balance as at 30 April 2003.

Ensure that you leave enough space between each account especially the bank, cash, purchases and sales accounts.

Trading and profit and loss accounts: an introduction

AIMS

- To be able to understand the difference between gross profit and net profit.

- To be able to draw up a trading and profit and loss account from information given in a trial balance.

- To be able to recognise that an adjustment is required for the closing stock at the end of the period.

- To be able to enter up the capital account after the trading and profit and loss accounts have been drawn up.

- To be able to draw up trading and profit and loss accounts using both the horizontal and vertical layouts.

4.1   Purpose of trading and profit and loss accounts

The main reason why people decide to start their own business is to make profits. Of course, if they are not successful they may well incur losses. The calculation of such profits and/or losses is probably the most important objective of the accounting function. The owner(s) of the business will want to know how the actual profits compare with the profits they had aimed to achieve. They may also want to know their profits for such diverse reasons as: to assist them in planning and budgeting for future trading periods; to help them to obtain a loan from a bank or a private individual; and to show a prospective partner or a person to whom they may wish to sell the business. They will also need to know their profits or losses for income tax purposes.

If a business is only involved with buying and selling, the profits are calculated by drawing up a **trading and profit and loss account**. For a manufacturer it is also useful to prepare a **manufacturing account** – a topic that will be dealt with in a later chapter.

4.2 The format of the trading and profit and loss account

One of the most important uses of the trading and profit and loss account is that of comparing the results obtained with the results expected. In a trading organisation much attention is paid to how much profit is made, before deducting expenses, for every £100 of sales. To enable this to be easily seen in the profit calculations, the account in which profit is calculated is divided into two sections: one in which the **gross profit** is found and the other in which the **net profit** is calculated.

KEY TERMS   **Gross profit** (calculated in **trading account**)   This is the excess of sales over the cost of goods sold in the period.

Net profit (calculated in the **profit and loss account**)   This is what is left of the gross profit after all other expenses have been deducted.

The *gross profit* is the excess of the sales over the cost of goods sold and is found by the use of the *trading account*. The *net profit*, found when the *profit and loss account* is prepared, consists of the gross profit plus any revenue other than that from sales, such as discounts received or commissions earned, less the total costs used up during the period. Where the cost of goods sold is greater than the sales the result would be a **gross loss**, but this is a relatively rare occurrence. Where the costs used up exceed the gross profit plus other revenue then the result is a **net loss**. By taking the figure of sales less the cost of goods sold, it can be seen that the accounting custom is to calculate a trader's profits only when the goods have been disposed of, and not before.

4.3 Horizontal and vertical trading and profit and loss accounts

In the next section the preparation of the trading and profit and loss accounts using the horizontal layout will be shown. The left-hand side of these accounts shows the debit amount, while the right-hand side shows the credit amount. These accounts can, therefore, be seen as part of the double entry system and students should be able to understand why entries in the accounts are shown as a debit or a credit entry.

In Section 4.6 the trading and profit and loss account will be shown using the vertical layout.

4.4 Information required before preparation of the trading and profit and loss accounts

Before drawing up a trading and profit and loss account a trial balance should be prepared since this contains almost all the information required for the preparation of the account. (Later in this book you will see that certain adjustments have to be made to these accounts, but for the present these will be ignored.)

The trial balance of M Clark (Exhibit 4.1), which was drawn up on 31 December 2005 after completion of his first year of trading, can now be considered.

Exhibit 4.1

M Clark
Trial Balance as at 31 December 2005

	Dr £	Cr £
Sales		38,500
Purchases	29,000	
Rent	2,400	
Lighting expenses	1,500	
General expenses	600	
Fixtures and fittings	5,000	
Debtors	6,800	
Creditors		9,100
Bank	5,100	
Motor car	10,000	
Cash	200	
Drawings	7,000	
Capital		20,000
	67,600	67,600

Usually some of the goods bought (purchases) may not have been sold by the end of the accounting period. It has already been shown that gross profit is calculated as follows:

 Sales – Cost of goods sold = Gross profit

However, purchases only equal cost of goods sold if there is no stock at the end of a period. Calculation of the cost of goods sold is as follows:

Goods bought in the period	= Purchases
Less: Goods bought but not sold in the period	= Closing stock
	= Cost of goods sold

As there is no record in the books of the value of the unsold stock on 31 December 2005 for M Clark, the only way that Clark can find this figure is by stock taking on 31 December 2005 at the close of business. To carry out this task he would have to make a list of all the unsold goods and then find out their value. The value that he would normally place on them would be the cost price of the goods. It is assumed that the unsold stock at 31 December 2005 was £3,000.

The cost of goods sold figure would be:

	£
Purchases	29,000
Less: Closing stock	3,000
Cost of goods sold	26,000

Given the figure of sales £38,500, the gross profit can be calculated:

Sales – Cost of goods sold	= Gross profit
£38,500 – £26,000	= £12,500

This, however, is not performing the task by using the double entry accounts. In double entry the following entries must be made.

The balance of the sales account is transferred to the trading account by:

1. Debiting the sales account (thus closing the account).
2. Crediting the trading account.

The balance of the purchases account is transferred to the trading account by:

1. Debiting the trading account.
2. Crediting the purchases account (thus closing this account).

There is as yet no entry for the closing stock in the double entry accounts. This is achieved as follows:

1. Debit a stock account with the value of the closing stock.
2. Credit the trading account (thus completing the double entry).

It is now usual for the trading account and profit and loss accounts to be shown under one combined heading, the trading account being the top section and the profit and loss account being the lower section of this combined account.

M Clark
Trading and Profit and Loss Account
for the year ended 31 December 2005

	£		£
Purchases	29,000	Sales	38,500
Gross profit c/d	12,500	Closing stock	3,000
	41,500		41,500
		Gross profit b/d	12,500

The balance shown on the trading account is shown as gross profit rather that being described as a balance. When found the gross profit is carried down to the profit and loss section of the account. The accounts so far used appear as follows:

Dr		Sales Account		Cr
2005		£	2005	£
Dec 31	Trading account	38,500	Dec 31 Balance b/d	38,500

Dr		Purchases Account		Cr
2005		£	2005	£
Dec 31	Balance b/d	29,000	Dec 31 Trading account	29,000

Dr		Stock Account		Cr
2005		£		
Dec 31	Trading account	3,000		

The entry of closing stock on the credit side of the trading account and profit and loss account is in effect a deduction from the purchases on the debit side. In present-day accounting it is usual to find the closing stock actually shown as a deduction from the purchases on the debit side, and the figure then disclosed being described as 'cost of goods sold'. This is illustrated in Exhibit 4.2.

It must be remembered in this example that it is M Clark's first year of trading and there is no opening stock. Accounting for stock in the ensuing years of a business will be considered later in this book.

The profit and loss account can now be drawn up. Any revenue accounts, other than sales which have already been dealt with, would be transferred to the credit side of the profit and loss account. Typical examples are commissions received and rent received. In the case of M Clark there are no such revenue accounts.

The costs used up in the year – in other words, the expenses of the year – are transferred to the debit side of the profit and loss account. It may also be thought, and quite rightly, that as the fixtures and fittings and motor car have been used during the year with the subsequent deterioration of the assets, something should be charged for their use. The methods for doing this are left until Chapters 9 and 10.

The revised trading account with the addition of the profit and loss account will now appear as shown in Exhibit 4.2.

Exhibit 4.2

M Clark
Trading and Profit and Loss Account
for the year ended 31 December 2005

	£		£
Purchases	29,000	Sales	38,500
Less Closing stock	3,000		
Cost of goods sold	26,000		
Gross profit c/d	12,500		
	38,500		38,500
Rent	2,400	Gross profit b/d	12,500
Lighting expenses	1,500		
General expenses	600		
Net profit	8,000		
	12,500		12,500

The expense accounts closed off will now appear as:

Dr		Rent Account			Cr
2005		£	*2005*		£
Dec 31	Balance b/d	2,400	Dec 31	Profit and loss	2,400

Dr		Lighting Expenses Account			Cr
2005		£	*2005*		£
Dec 31	Balance b/d	1,500	Dec 31	Profit and loss	1,500

Dr	General Expenses Account		Cr
2005		£	
Dec 31 Balance b/d		<u>600</u>	
	2005		£
	Dec 31 Profit and loss		<u>600</u>

4.5 Effect on the capital account

Although the net profit has been calculated at £8,000, and is shown as a debit entry in the profit and loss account, no credit entry has yet been made. This now needs to be done. As net profit increases the capital of the proprietor, the credit entry must be made in the capital account.

The trading and profit and loss accounts, and indeed all the revenue and expense accounts, can thus be seen to be devices whereby the capital account is saved from being concerned with unnecessary detail. Every sale of a good at a profit increases the capital of the proprietor, as does each item of revenue such as rent received. On the other hand, each sale of a good at a loss, or each item of expense, decreases the capital of the proprietor. Instead of altering the capital afresh after each transaction the respective items of profit and loss and of revenue and expense are collected together using suitably described accounts. Then the whole of the details are brought together in one set of accounts, the trading and profit and loss account, and the increase to the capital, i.e. the net profit, is determined. Alternatively, the decrease in the capital as represented by the net loss is ascertained.

The fact that a separate drawings account has been in use can now also be seen to have been in keeping with the policy of avoiding unnecessary detail in the capital account. There will thus be one figure for drawings which will be the total of the drawings for the whole of the period, and will be transferred to the debit of the capital account.

The capital account, showing these transfers, and the drawings account now closed are as follows:

Dr		Capital Account			Cr
2005		£	2005		£
Dec 31	Drawings	7,000	Jan 1	Cash	20,000
31	Balance c/d	21,000	Dec 31	Net profit from	
				profit and loss	8,000
		———			———
		30,000			30,000

Dr		Drawings Account			Cr
2005		£	2005		£
Dec 31	Balance b/d	<u>7,000</u>	Dec 31	Capital	<u>7,000</u>

4.6 The vertical layout for trading and profit and loss accounts

In Exhibit 4.3 the vertical layout for drawing up a trading and profit and loss account will be shown, using the information in Exhibit 4.2.

It can be seen that the figures are exactly the same whether the horizontal or vertical method of display is used.

Exhibit 4.3

M Clark
Trading and Profit and Loss Account
for the year ended 31 December 2005

	£	£
Sales		38,500
Less Cost of goods sold:		
Purchases	29,000	
Less Closing stock	3,000	26,000
Gross profit		12,500
Less Expenses:		
Rent	2,400	
Lighting expenses	1,500	
General expenses	600	4,500
Net profit		8,000

A model layout of a trading and profit and loss account is shown in Chapter 6.

This is a more modern method of presentation. It would make more sense to someone who knew very little about accounting, as it does not show it in a debit/credit way.

However, showing the horizontal style first probably makes it easier for students to see how the double entry system is used to calculate profits.

4.7 The balances still in the books

It should be noticed that not all the items in the trial balance have been used in the trading and profit and loss account. The remaining balances are assets or liabilities or capital, they are not expenses or sales. These will be used up later when a balance sheet is drawn up. As illustrated in Chapter 2, assets, liabilities and capital are shown in balance sheets.

It is not normally necessary to redraft the trial balance after the trading and profit and loss accounts have been prepared, but it will be useful to do so in order to establish which balances still remain in the books (see Exhibit 4.4).

Exhibit 4.4

M Clark
Trial Balance as on 31 December 2005
(after Trading and Profit and Loss Accounts completed)

	Dr	Cr
	£	£
Motor car	10,000	
Fixtures and fittings	5,000	
Debtors	6,800	
Creditors		9,100
Stock	3,000	
Bank	5,100	
Cash	200	
Capital		21,000
	30,100	30,100

The first thing to notice is that the stock account, not originally in the trial balance, is in the redrafted trial balance, as the item was not created as a balance in the books until the trading account was prepared. These balances will be used by us when we start to look at the balance sheets.

NEW TERMS

Horizontal layout of final accounts   The old way of showing final accounts, following the principles of double entry.

Manufacturing account   Normally prepared by a manufacturer prior to drawing up a trading and profit and loss account (see Chapter 21).

Vertical layout of final accounts   Accepted current presentation of final accounts (refer to text).

Student Activities

! *All answers should show the vertical layout of the trading and profit and loss accounts.*

4.1 From the following trial balance of C Rowlands, extracted after one year's trading, prepare the trading and profit and loss account for the year ended 31 December 2006. A balance sheet is not required.

C Rowlands
Trial Balance as at 31 December 2006

	Dr £	Cr £
Sales		73,848
Purchases	58,516	
Wages	8,600	
Motor expenses	2,080	
Rates	2,680	
Insurance	444	
General expenses	420	
Premises	20,000	
Motor vehicle	12,000	
Debtors	7,800	
Creditors		6,418
Cash at bank	6,616	
Cash in hand	160	
Drawings	8,950	
Capital		48,000
	128,266	128,266

Stock at 31 December 2006 was valued at £10,192

! *Retain your answer. It will be used later in Question 5.1.*

4.2 From the following trial balance of S Jennings after his first year's trading, you are required to draw up a trading and profit and loss account for the year ended 30 June 2004.

S Jennings
Trial Balance as at 30 June 2004

	Dr £	Cr £
Sales		99,082
Purchases	71,409	
Rates	2,000	
Printing and stationery	562	
Electricity	1,266	
Wages	9,492	
Insurance	605	
Premises	145,000	
Computer equipment	8,000	
Debtors	9,498	
Sundry expenses	1,518	
Creditors		3,618
Cash at bank	6,541	
Drawings	12,200	
Motor vehicle	16,500	
Motor expenses	3,109	
Capital		185,000
	287,700	287,700

Stock at 30 June 2004 was valued at £11,498.

 Retain your answer. It will be used later in Question 5.2.

4.3X From the following trial balance of M Beet drawn up on the conclusion of her first year in business, draw up a trading and profit and loss account for the year ended 31 December 2001.

M Beet
Trial Balance as at 31 December 2001

	Dr £	Cr £
Capital		100,602
Premises	46,000	
Office equipment	2,000	
General expenses	1,575	
Rates	3,000	
Motor expenses	2,513	
Salaries	30,700	
Insurance	1,940	
Purchases	157,887	
Sales		201,113
Motor vehicles	21,000	
Creditors		40,100
Debtors	30,675	
Cash at bank	10,312	
Cash in hand	188	
Drawings	32,625	
Electricity	1,400	
	341,815	341,815

Stock at 31 December 2001 was valued at £37,200.

Retain your answer. It will be used later in Question 5.3X.

 4.4X Prepare a trading and profit and loss account for the year ended 30 June 2004 for P Jackson. The trial balance as at 30 June 2004 after his first year of trading was as follows:

P Jackson
Trial Balance as at 30 June 2004

	Dr £	Cr £
Rates	5,360	
Insurance	1,830	
Lighting and heating expenses	3,096	
Motor expenses	6,760	
Salaries	38,100	
Sales		213,600
Purchases	185,820	
Sundry expenses	4,836	
Motor vans	21,000	
Creditors		19,500
Debtors	40,860	
Storage equipment	23,760	
Premises	68,000	
Cash at bank	6,804	
Drawings	37,668	
Capital		210,794
	443,894	443,894

Stock at 30 June 2004 was valued at £59,760.

 Retain your answer. It will be used later in Question 5.4X.

4.5 Mrs P Stewart commenced trading as a card and gift shop with a capital of £6,855 on 1 April 2007. At the end of her first year's trading on 31 March 2008 she was able to identify from her accounting records that she had received £24,765 from cash sales in the year. Goods bought had cost her £13,545 to purchase, and she still had £2,345 cards and gifts at cost, in stock on 31 March 2008. In the year she had also spent £2,100 on staff wages, and taken cash drawings of £5,500. Other overhead costs incurred were:

	£
Rent and rates	1,580
Electricity	565
Motor expenses	845
Insurance	345
General expenses	245

Exam hint: Before you attempt to draw up the trading and profit and loss account, it would be a good idea to extract the trial balance at 31 March 2008 from the information given.

On 31 March 2008 Mrs P Stewart had cash in hand of £135, a bank balance of £2,675, and owed £3,285 to creditors. Mrs Stewart's business owned a car which had a value of £5,875 at 31 March 2008. She had also bought shelving and fixtures and fittings in the year to the value of £1,495.

You are required to draw up the trading and profit and loss account for the first year's trading.

! *The closing stock figure should be shown as a note at the foot of the trial balance.*

Retain your answer. It will be used later in Question 5.5.

4.6X Miss R Burgess has just completed her first year of trading for the year ended 30 April 2008, as a retailer of model railway accessories. Her initial capital was £9,025.

At 30 April 2008, she was owed £5,600 by customers, and owed £4,825 to suppliers. She calculated she had stock on hand, at cost, at the year end of £7,670, and her bank account was overdrawn by £2,560. The petty cash float held £25 at 30 April 2008.

From her records, she calculated the following figures for the year ended 30 April 2008:

	£
Total of cash and credit sales during the year	56,540
Total of cash and credit purchases during the year	34,315
Rent	6,000
Drawings	10,000
Motor expenses	1,735
Insurance	345
General expenses	780
Salaries	7,550

Miss R Burgess had fixtures to the value of £3,750 and a van worth £2,850 at 30 April 2008.

Required

(a) Draw up a trial balance as at 30 April 2008.
(b) Draw up the trading and profit and loss account for the first year's trading.

! *Retain your answer. It will be used later in Question 5.6X.*

CHAPTER 5

Balance sheets

AIMS

- To be able to draw up a balance sheet from information given in the trial balance.

- To understand that balance sheets are not part of the double entry system.

- To appreciate the need for showing balances under the headings 'fixed assets', 'current assets', 'current liabilities' and 'capital'.

- To be able to draw up balance sheets using both the horizontal and the vertical layouts.

5.1 Definition and content of a balance sheet

A **balance sheet** is a financial statement setting out the book values of assets, liabilities and capital 'as at' a particular point in time. As already stated in Chapter 2, in simple terms it shows what a business 'owns' and 'owes' at a specific date.

Details of the assets, liabilities and capital have to be found in the records of the business and then written out as a balance sheet. It is easy to find these details as they consist of all the balances remaining in the records once the trading and profit and loss account for the period have been completed. All balances remaining have to be assets, liabilities or capital since the other balances should have been closed off when the trading and profit and loss account was completed.

5.2 Preparing a balance sheet (horizontal layout)

The trial balance of M Clark is shown in Exhibit 5.1 (from Exhibit 4.4) as on 31 December 2005 *after* the trading and profit and loss account had been prepared.

Exhibit 5.1

M Clark
Trial balance as at 31 December 2005
(after Trading and Profit and Loss Account completed)

	Dr £	Cr £
Motor car	10,000	
Fixtures and fittings	5,000	
Debtors	6,800	
Creditors		9,100
Stock	3,000	
Bank	5,100	
Cash	200	
Capital		21,000
	30,100	30,100

The balance sheet as at 31 December 2005 can now be drawn up using the horizontal layout as in Exhibit 5.2 (the vertical layout will be shown later in Section 5.6). Note that the assets are shown on the left-hand side with capital and liabilities on the right-hand side.

Exhibit 5.2

M Clark
Balance Sheet as at 31 December 2005

Assets	£	Capital and liabilities	£
Fixtures and fittings	5,000	Capital	21,000
Motor car	10,000	Creditors	9,100
Stock	3,000		
Debtors	6,800		
Bank	5,100		
Cash	200		
	30,100		30,100

5.3 No double entry in balance sheets

It may seem strange to learn that balance sheets are *not* part of the double entry system. If accounts are drawn up for such things as the cash account, rent account, sales account, trading and profit and loss account and so on, then they are part of the double entry system as entries will have been made on the debit sides and credit sides of these accounts.

When a balance sheet is drawn up nothing is entered in the various accounts nor is any balance actually transferred from the account (such as the balance in the fixtures account or the stock balance, or any of the other accounts) to the balance sheet.

When preparing a balance sheet it is only necessary to *list* the assets, capital and liabilities balances in order to form a balance sheet. This means that none of these accounts has been closed off, **nothing is entered in the accounts**.

At the start of the next accounting period, these accounts are still open containing balances. As a result of business transactions, entries for the next period are then made in these accounts such as adding to, or deducting from, the amounts shown in the accounts using normal double entry.

When the word 'account' is used, this indicates that it is part of the double entry system and will include debit and credit entries. If the word 'account' cannot be used, it is not part of the double entry system. For instance, the following items are not 'accounts', and are therefore *not* part of the double entry system:

- **Trial balance**   This is simply a proof of the equality of debit and credit balances in the accounts.
- **Balance sheet**   A list of balances arranged according to whether they are assets, capital or liabilities, to depict the financial situation on a specific date.

5.4   Balance sheet layout

When visiting a department store one would not expect to see goods for sale all mixed up and not laid out properly. One would expect that the goods would be displayed in such a way that the customer could easily find the specific goods required. Similarly, in balance sheets one does not want all the items shown in random order. The information should be displayed so that it can easily be seen and understood.

For people such as bank managers, accountants and investors who look at many different balance sheets, it is necessary to keep to one method of presentation to enable easier comparison. The method for presenting items in a balance sheet will now be shown.

Assets

First, consideration will be given to assets, which are shown under two headings: **Fixed assets** and **Current assets**.

Assets are called *fixed assets* when they:

(a)   are of long life;

(b)   are to be used in the business; and

(c)   were not bought only for the purpose of resale.

Examples: Land and buildings, plant and machinery, motor vehicles, fixtures and fittings.

Fixed assets are listed in the balance sheet, starting with those the business will keep the longest, and ending with those that will not be kept so long. For instance:

Fixed assets

1.   Land and buildings
2.   Fixtures and fittings
3.   Plant and machinery
4.   Motor vehicles

Current assets are cash in hand, cash at bank, items held for resale at a profit or items that have a short life. These are listed starting with the asset that is least likely to be turned into cash, finishing with cash itself. The accepted order is listed as:

Current assets

1. Stock
2. Debtors
3. Cash at bank
4. Cash in hand

Students tend to disagree with this order because stock has appeared before debtors. On first sight stock would appear to be more easily realisable than debtors. In fact, however, debtors could normally be more quickly turned into cash by factorising them, i.e. selling the rights to the amounts owing to a finance company for an agreed amount. On the other hand, disposing of all the stock of a business is often a long and difficult task. Another advantage is that the method follows the order in which full realisation of the assets takes place. First, before any sale takes place there must be a stock of goods which, when sold on credit, turns into debtors, and when payment is made by the debtors it turns into cash.

Capital and liabilities

The order on the other side of the horizontal style balance sheet is:

- **Capital**
- **Long-term liabilities**   For instance, loans which do not have to be repaid in the near future, this being taken to be the next twelve months.
- **Current liabilities**   Items to be paid for in the near future.

In Section 5.6 capital and liabilities will be shown in a vertical style balance sheet.

5.5 A properly drawn up balance sheet (horizontal style)

Exhibit 5.3 shows Exhibit 5.2 drawn up in a better style using the various headings as discussed above. Also read the notes following the exhibit.

Exhibit 5.3

M Clark
Balance Sheet as at 31 December 2005

Fixed assets	£	£	Capital	£	£
Furniture and fittings		5,000	Cash introduced	20,000	
Motor car		10,000	Add Net profit for		
		15,000	the year	8,000	
Current assets				28,000	
Stock	3,000				
Debtors	6,800		Less Drawings	7,000	

Exhibit 5.3 (continued)

Current assets	£	£		£	£
Bank	5,100				21,000
Cash	200		Current liabilities		
		15,100	Creditors		9,100
		30,100			30,100

Notes

(a) A total for capital and for each class of liabilities should be shown. An example of this is the £15,100 total of current assets. To do this the figures for each asset are listed, and only the total is shown in the end column.

(b) It is not necessary to write the word 'account' after each item.

(c) The owner will be most interested in his capital. To show only the final balance of £21,000 means that the owner will not know how it was calculated. So full details of his capital account are shown.

(d) Look at the date on the balance sheet. Now compare it with the dates put on the top of the trading and profit and loss account. The balance sheet is a position statement – it is shown as being at one point in time, i.e. as at 31 December 2005.

The trading and profit and loss account is different. It is for a period of time, in this case for a whole year.

5.6 Vertical style balance sheets

Exhibit 5.4 is now shown using the more modern vertical layout.

Exhibit 5.4

M Clark
Balance Sheet as at 31 December 2005

	£	£
Fixed assets		
Furniture and fittings		5,000
Motor car		10,000
		15,000
Current assets		
Stock	3,000	
Debtors	6,800	
Bank	5,100	
Cash	200	
	15,100	
Less Current liabilities		
Creditors	9,100	
Net current assets		6,000
		21,000
Capital		
Cash introduced		20,000
Add Net profit for the year		8,000
		28,000
Less Drawings		7,000
		21,000

A model layout of a balance sheet is shown in Chapter 6.

Examinations and vertical and horizontal style final accounts

Many examiners will prefer answers to be given using vertical style final accounts. However, questions are often asked in which the information given in the question uses horizontal style final accounts.

As examinations vary world wide, it is advisable for students follow the advice given to them by their teacher or lecturer.

NEW TERM   **Factoring**   A method for a business to improve its cash flow by 'selling' its debtors to a factoring company.

Student Activities

All answers should show the vertical layout of the balance sheets.

5.1   Complete Question 4.1 by drawing up a balance sheet as at 31 December 2006 for C Rowlands.

5.2   Complete Question 4.2 by drawing up a balance sheet as at 30 June 2004 for S Jennings.

5.3X   Complete Question 4.3X by drawing up a balance sheet as at 31 December 2001 for M Beet.

5.4X   Complete Question 4.4X by drawing up a balance sheet as at 30 June 2004 for P Jackson.

5.5   Complete Question 4.5 by drawing up a balance sheet as at 31 March 2008 for Mrs P Stewart.

5.6   Complete Question 4.6X by drawing up a balance sheet as at 30 April 2008 for Miss R Burgess.

CHAPTER 6

Trading and profit and loss accounts and balance sheets: further considerations

AIMS

■ To be able to record returns inwards and returns outwards in the final accounts.

■ To understand that carriage inwards on goods purchased is treated as part of the cost of goods sold.

■ To realise that carriage outwards is an expense to be entered in the profit and loss account.

■ To be able to adjust the final accounts properly for both the opening and closing stocks of the period.

■ To appreciate that costs of putting goods into a saleable condition should be charged to the trading account in a merchandising firm.

6.1   Returns outwards and returns inwards

When firms deal with the purchase and sale of goods it is inevitable that there are occasions when goods have to be returned by the purchaser to the supplier because they are damaged, faulty or perhaps not to the specification ordered. The goods will be returned to the supplier accompanied by a returns note which gives details of the goods being returned and the reason together with details of the order number, date, etc.

Returns outwards (also called purchases returns)

When a business returns goods to a supplier for one of the above-mentioned reasons they are known as **returns outwards** or **purchases returns**. The book keeping entries are as follows:

> *Debit* supplier's account (i.e. the creditor)
> *Credit* the returns outwards (or purchases returns) account

The returns outwards account is kept separate from the purchases account to enable a check to be made on the amount of goods being returned.

Returns inwards (also called sales returns)

If goods are returned by a customer (debtor) then they are referred to as **returns inwards** or **sales returns**. The book keeping entries would be as shown below:

Debit returns inwards (sales returns) account
Credit customer's (debtors') account

The returns inwards are again kept separate from the sales account to enable a check to be made on the amount of goods being returned to the firm.

Treatment in the trading account

In Chapter 4 the returns outwards and returns inwards accounts were deliberately omitted so that the first sight of the trading and profit and loss accounts would not be too difficult. Since a large number of firms will return goods to their suppliers (returns outwards), and have goods returned to them (returns inwards), then these returns must be taken into consideration when calculating the gross profit. Suppose that in Exhibit 4.1, the Trial Balance of M Clark, the balances showing stock movements had instead been as follows:

M Clark
Trial Balance as at 31 December 2005

	Dr £	Cr £
Sales		40,000
Purchases	31,200	
Returns inwards	1,500	
Returns outwards		2,200

Looking at Exhibit 4.1 it can be seen that originally the example used was sales of £38,500 and purchases of £29,000. If it had been as now shown in the above trial balance then the trading account for the year would be shown as follows using both the horizontal and vertical methods of presentation.

Exhibit 6.1

Horizontal style

M Clark
Trading and Profit and Loss Account
for the year ended 31 December 2005

	£	£		£	£
Purchases	31,200		Sales	40,000	
Less Returns outwards	2,200	29,000	*Less* Returns inwards	1,500	38,500
Less Closing stock		3,000			
Cost of good sold		26,000			
Gross profit		12,500			
		38,500			38,500

The trading and profit and loss account will now be shown using the vertical style of presentation.

Exhibit 6.2

Vertical style

M Clark Trading and Profit and Loss Account for the year ended 31 December 2005		
	£	£
Sales	40,000	
Less Returns inwards	1,500	38,500
Less Cost of goods sold:		
Purchases	31,200	
Less Returns outwards	2,200	
	29,000	
Less Closing stock	3,000	26,000
Gross profit		12,500

Comparing the original trial balance with the new trial balance it can be seen that the figure of gross profit is the same. Sales were £38,500 in the original example. In the new example returns inwards should be deducted to arrive at the correct figure for goods sold to customers and *kept* by them, i.e. £40,000 – £1,500 = £38,500. Purchases were £29,000: in the new example returns outwards should be deducted to arrive at the correct figure of purchases *kept* by Clark, i.e. £31,200 – £2,200 = £29,000. The gross profit will remain at £12,500 as shown in Exhibits 6.1 and 6.2.

6.2 Carriage

Carriage (cost of transport of goods) into a firm is called **carriage inwards**. Carriage of goods out of a firm to its customers is called **carriage outwards**.

When goods are bought the cost of carriage inwards may be included as part of the price, or the firm may have to pay separately for it. Suppose the firm was buying exactly the same goods from different suppliers. One supplier might sell them for £100 and would deliver the goods and not send a bill for carriage. Another supplier might sell the goods for £95, but not deliver and you would have to pay £5 to a haulage firm for carriage inwards, i.e. a total cost of £100.

To keep the cost of buying goods being shown on the same basis, carriage inwards is always added to the purchases in the trading account.

Carriage outwards to customers is not part of a firm's expenses in buying goods, and is always entered in the profit and loss account.

Suppose that, in the illustration shown in this chapter, the goods had been bought for the same total figure of £31,200 but in fact £29,200 was the figure for purchases and £2,000 for carriage inwards. The trial balance and trading accounts using both horizontal and vertical styles appear as Exhibit 6.3.

Exhibit 6.3

Trial balance as at 31 December 2005

	Dr £	Cr £
Sales		40,000
Purchases	29,200	
Returns inwards	1,500	
Returns outwards		2,200
Carriage inwards	2,000	

Horizontal style

M Clark
Trading and Profit and Loss Account
for the year ended 31 December 2005

	£	£		£	£
Purchases	29,200		Sales	40,000	
Less Returns outwards	2,200	27,000	*Less* Returns inwards	1,500	38,500
Carriage inwards		2,000			
		29,000			
Less Closing stock		3,000			
Cost of goods sold		26,000			
Gross profit c/d		12,500			
		38,500			38,500
			Gross profit b/d		12,500

Vertical style

M Clark
Trading and Profit and Loss Account
for the year ended 31 December 2005

	£	£
Sales	40,000	
Less Returns inwards	1,500	38,500
Less Cost of goods sold:		
Purchases	29,200	
Less Returns outwards	2,200	
	27,000	
Carriage inwards	2,000	
	29,000	
Less Closing stock	3,000	26,000
Gross profit		12,500

It can be seen that Exhibits 4.1, 6.1 and 6.3 have been concerned with the same overall amount of goods bought and sold by the firm, at the same overall prices. Therefore, in each case the same gross profit of £12,500 is shown.

 Before you proceed further you are advised to attempt Questions 6.1 and 6.2X.

The second year of a business

At the end of his second year of trading, on 31 December 2006, M Clark extracts another trial balance.

Exhibit 6.4

M Clark
Trial balance as at 31 December 2006

	Dr £	Cr £
Sales		67,000
Purchases	42,600	
Lighting and heating expenses	1,900	
Rent	2,400	
Wages: shop assistant	5,200	
General expenses	700	
Carriage outwards	1,100	
Buildings	20,000	
Fixtures and fittings	7,500	
Debtors	12,000	
Creditors		9,000
Bank	1,200	
Cash	400	
Drawings	9,000	
Capital		21,000
Stock (at 31 December 2005)	3,000	
Motor car	10,000	
Loan from D Jones		20,000
	117,000	117,000

Adjustments needed for stock

Previously the accounts have been prepared for a new business only. The business started without stock and, therefore, had closing stock only when the accounts for the first year were drawn up.

When preparing the trading and profit and loss accounts for the second year the difference can now be seen. Referring to Exhibits 5.1 and 6.4 for M Clark, the stock figures needed for the trading accounts are shown as:

Trading account for the period	Year to 31 December 2005	Year to 31 December 2006
Opening stock 1.1.2005	None	
Closing stock 31.12.2005	£3,000	
Opening stock 1.1.2006		£3,000
Closing stock 31.12.2006		£5,500

This means that calculations for the first year of trading, to 31 December 2005, had only one stock figure included in them. This was the closing stock of £5,500 (see Exhibit 6.5). For the second year of trading, to 31 December 2006, both opening and closing stock figures will be in the calculations.

The stock shown in the trial balance, Exhibit 6.4, is that brought forward from the previous year on 31 December 2005; it is, therefore, the opening stock of 2006. The closing stock at 31 December 2006 can only be found by stock-taking. Let us assume that, at cost, it amounts to £5,500.

First, the calculation of the cost of the goods sold for 2006 is shown to be:

	£
Stock of goods at start of the year	3,000
Add Purchases	42,600
Total goods available for sale	45,600
Less What remains at the end of the year:	
i.e. stock of goods at close	5,500
Therefore cost of goods that have been sold	40,100

A diagram illustrating the above example is shown in Exhibit 6.5.

Exhibit 6.5

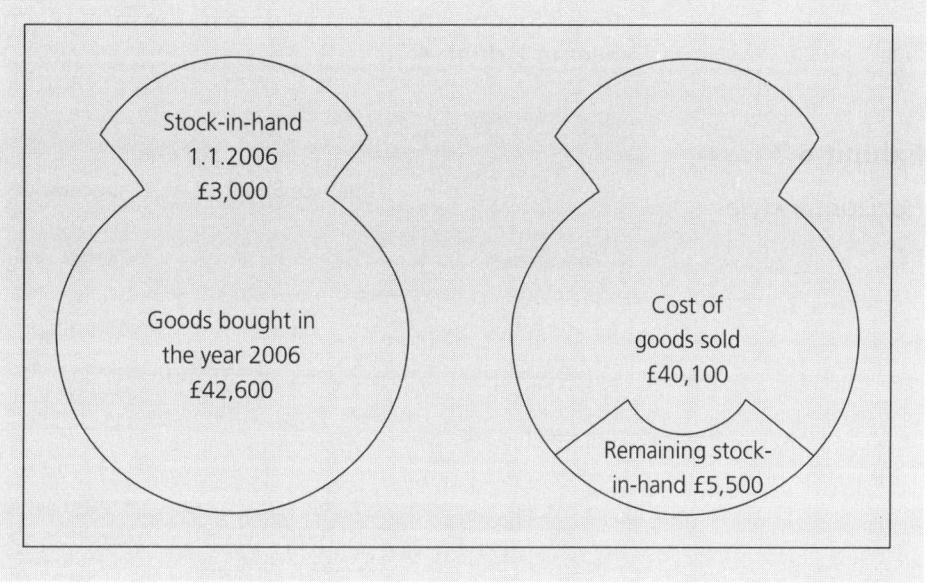

The sales were £67,000, so

Sales £67,000 − Cost of goods sold £40,100 = Gross profit £26,900.

Now the trading and profit and loss accounts can be drawn up in the horizontal style using double entry (see Exhibit 6.6). They are shown in the vertical style in Exhibit 6.8.

Exhibit 6.6

Horizontal style

M Clark
Trading and Profit and Loss Account
for the year ended 31 December 2006

	£		£
Opening Stock	3,000	Sales	67,000
Add Purchases	42,600		
	45,600		
Less Closing stock	5,500		
Cost of goods sold	40,100		
Gross profit c/d	26,900		
	67,000		67,000
Wages	5,200	Gross profit b/d	26,900
Lighting and heating expenses	1,900		
Rent	2,400		
General expenses	700		
Carriage outwards	1,100		
Net profit	15,600		
	26,900		26,900

The balances remaining in the books, including the new balance on the stock account, are now drawn up in the form of a horizontal style balance sheet in Exhibit 6.7.

Exhibit 6.7

Horizontal style

M Clark
Balance Sheet as at 31 December 2006

Fixed assets	£	£	*Capital*	£	£
Buildings		20,000	Balance 1 Jan	21,000	
Fixtures and fittings		7,500	*Add* net profit for year	15,600	
Motor car		10,000		36,600	
		37,500	*Less* Drawings	9,000	27,600
Current assets			*Long-term liability*		
Stock	5,500		Loan from D Jones		20,000
Debtors	12,000		*Current liabilities*		
Bank	1,200		Creditors		9,000
Cash	400	19,100			
		56,600			56,600

Exhibits 6.8 and 6.9 show the same items using the vertical style.

Stock account

It is perhaps helpful if the stock account covering both years can now be seen:

Dr		Stock Account			Cr
2005		£	*2006*		£
Dec 31	Trading account	3,000	Jan 1 Trading account		3,000
2006					
Dec 31	Trading account	5,500			

Exhibit 6.8

Vertical style

<table>
<tr><td colspan="3">M Clark
Trading and Profit and Loss account
for the year ended 31 December 2006</td></tr>
<tr><td></td><td>£</td><td>£</td></tr>
<tr><td>Sales</td><td></td><td>67,000</td></tr>
<tr><td>Less Cost of goods sold:</td><td></td><td></td></tr>
<tr><td>Opening stock</td><td>3,000</td><td></td></tr>
<tr><td>Add Purchases</td><td>42,600</td><td></td></tr>
<tr><td></td><td>45,600</td><td></td></tr>
<tr><td>Less Closing stock</td><td>5,500</td><td>40,100</td></tr>
<tr><td>Gross profit</td><td></td><td>26,900</td></tr>
<tr><td>Less Expenses:</td><td></td><td></td></tr>
<tr><td>Wages</td><td>5,200</td><td></td></tr>
<tr><td>Lighting and heating expenses</td><td>1,900</td><td></td></tr>
<tr><td>Rent</td><td>2,400</td><td></td></tr>
<tr><td>General expenses</td><td>700</td><td></td></tr>
<tr><td>Carriage outwards</td><td>1,100</td><td>11,300</td></tr>
<tr><td>Net profit</td><td></td><td>15,600</td></tr>
</table>

Exhibit 6.9

Vertical style

<table>
<tr><td colspan="3">M Clark
Balance Sheet as at 31 December 2006</td></tr>
<tr><td></td><td>£</td><td>£</td></tr>
<tr><td>*Fixed assets*</td><td></td><td></td></tr>
<tr><td>Buildings</td><td>20,000</td><td></td></tr>
<tr><td>Fixtures and fittings</td><td>7,500</td><td></td></tr>
<tr><td>Motor car</td><td>10,000</td><td>37,500</td></tr>
<tr><td>*Current assets*</td><td></td><td></td></tr>
<tr><td>Stock</td><td>5,500</td><td></td></tr>
<tr><td>Debtors</td><td>12,000</td><td></td></tr>
<tr><td>Bank</td><td>1,200</td><td></td></tr>
<tr><td>Cash</td><td>400</td><td></td></tr>
<tr><td></td><td>19,100</td><td></td></tr>
<tr><td>*Less Current liabilities*</td><td></td><td></td></tr>
<tr><td>Creditors</td><td>9,000</td><td></td></tr>
<tr><td>Net current assets</td><td></td><td>10,100</td></tr>
<tr><td></td><td></td><td>47,600</td></tr>
<tr><td>*Less Long-term liability*</td><td></td><td></td></tr>
<tr><td>Loan from D Jones</td><td></td><td>20,000</td></tr>
<tr><td></td><td></td><td>27,600</td></tr>
<tr><td>*Financed by*</td><td></td><td></td></tr>
<tr><td>Capital: Balance at 1 January 2006</td><td>21,000</td><td></td></tr>
<tr><td>Add Net profit for the year</td><td>15,600</td><td></td></tr>
<tr><td></td><td>36,600</td><td></td></tr>
<tr><td>Less Drawings</td><td>9,000</td><td>27,600</td></tr>
</table>

Final accounts

The term **final accounts** is often used to mean collectively the trading and profit and loss account and the balance sheet. The term can be misleading as the balance sheet is not an account.

Other expenses in the trading account

The costs of putting goods into a saleable condition should be charged in the trading account. In the case of a trader these are relatively few. An example might be a trader who sells clocks packed in boxes. If he bought the clocks from one source, and the boxes from another source, both of these items would be charged in the trading account as purchases. In addition, if a person is paid wages to pack the clocks, then such wages would be charged in the trading account. The wages of shop assistants who sold the clocks would be charged in the profit and loss account. The wages of the person packing the clocks would be the only wages in this instance concerned with 'putting the goods into a saleable condition'.

For goods imported from abroad it is usual to find that the costs of import duty, marine insurance, freight, etc., are also treated as part of the cost of goods sold and are therefore debited to the trading account.

6.4 Model layout of final accounts

Exhibits 6.10 and 6.11 show model layouts of a trading and profit and loss account and a balance sheet respectively. Students may find it useful to use the layouts when carrying out the student activities at the end of this chapter.

The treatment of *returns inwards* and *outwards* and *carriage inwards* and *outwards* is often confusing and a step-by-step guide to deal with these is shown below:

1. *Returns inwards and returns outwards*
    - (a) Returns inwards – deduct from sales in trading account.
    - (b) Returns outwards – deduct from purchases in trading account.
2. *Carriage inwards and carriage outwards*
    - (a) Carriage inwards – add to purchases in trading account.
    - (b) Carriage outwards – charge as an expense in profit and loss account.

Exhibit 6.10

Model layout of a trading and profit and loss account

NAME OF PROPRIETOR
TRADING & PROFIT & LOSS A/C
FOR THE YEAR ENDED. . . .

	£	£
Sales	xxx	
Less Returns inwards	xx	xxx
Less Cost of goods sold:		
Opening stock	x	
Add Purchases	x	
Add Carriage inwards	x	
Add Wages (occasionally – depends on question)	x	
	xx	
Less Returns outwards	x	
	xx	
Less Closing stock	x	xxx
GROSS PROFIT		xxx
Add Income		
Discounts + interest received	x	
Reductions in provision for bad debts	x	xx
		xxx
Less Expenses:		
Wages & salaries	x	
Rates	x	
Insurance	x	
Rent	x	
General expenses	x	
Postages	x	
Stationery	x	
Carriage outwards	x	
Discounts allowed	x	
Electricity	x	
Depreciation	x	
Bad debts (written off)	x	
Increase in provision for bad debts	x	xxx
NET PROFIT		xxx

❗ *Bad debts (written off), depreciation, and provision for bad debts, while shown above, will be fully dealt with in Chapters 9 to 11.*

Exhibit 6.11

Model layout of a balance sheet

NAME OF PROPRIETOR
BALANCE SHEET
AS AT. . . .

	Cost £	Total depreciation £	Net book value £
Fixed assets			
Premises	x	x	x
Office furniture	x	x	x
Office equipment	x	x	x
Machinery	x	x	x
Motor vehicle	x	x	x
	xx	xx	x
Current assets			
Stock (closing)	x		
Debtors (*Less* Provision for bad debts)	x		
Prepayments	x		
Cash at bank	x		
Cash in hand	x	xx	
Less Current liabilities			
Creditors	x		
Expenses owing	x		
Bank overdraft	x	xx	
Net Current assets			xx
			xxx
Less Long-term liabilities			
Long-term loan			x
			£xxx
Financed by			
Capital			xxx
Add Profit			x
			xxx
Less Drawings			x
			£xxx

 Prepayments and expenses owing, while shown above, will be dealt with in a later chapter.

NEW TERMS

Carriage inwards   Cost of transport of goods into a business.

Carriage outwards   Cost of transport to the customers of a business.

Final accounts   Term that includes the trading and profit and loss accounts and balance sheet.

Returns inwards   Goods returned to the supplier by the customer because they are damaged, faulty or perhaps not to the specification ordered. (Also known as 'sales returns'.)

Returns outwards   Goods originally purchased for resale, which are returned by a business to its suppliers. (Also known as 'purchases returns'.)

🛑 *All answers should show the vertical layout of the trading and profit and loss accounts.*

6.1 From the following details draw up the trading account of T Clarke for the year ended 31 December 2003, which was his first year in business:

	£
Carriage inwards	670
Returns outwards	495
Returns inwards	890
Sales	38,742
Purchases	33,333
Stock of goods: 31 December 2003	7,489

6.2X The following details for the year ended 31 March 2008 are available. Draw up the trading account of K Taylor for that year.

	£
Stock: 31 March 2008	18,504
Returns inwards	1,372
Returns outwards	2,896
Purchases	53,397
Carriage inwards	1,122
Sales	54,600

6.3 From the following trial balance of R Graham draw up a trading and profit and loss account for the year ended 30 September 2006, and a balance sheet as at that date.

	Dr	Cr
	£	£
Stock 1 October 2005	2,368	
Carriage outwards	200	
Carriage inwards	310	
Returns inwards	205	
Returns outwards		322
Purchases	11,874	
Sales		18,600
Salaries and wages	3,862	
Rent	304	
Insurance	78	
Motor expenses	664	
Office expenses	216	
Lighting and heating expenses	166	
General expenses	314	
Premises	5,000	
Motor vehicle	1,800	
Fixtures and fittings	350	
Debtors	3,896	
Creditors		1,731

	Dr	Cr
	£	£
Cash at bank	482	
Drawings	1,200	
Capital		12,636
	33,289	33,289

Stock at 30 September 2006 was £2,946.

6.4 The following trial balance was extracted from the books of B Jackson on 30 April 2007. From it, and the note regarding stock, prepare his trading and profit and loss account for the year ended 30 April 2007, and a balance sheet as at that date.

	Dr	Cr
	£	£
Sales		18,600
Purchases	11,556	
Stock 1 May 2006	3,776	
Carriage outwards	326	
Carriage inwards	234	
Returns inwards	440	
Returns outwards		355
Salaries and wages	2,447	
Motor expenses	664	
Rent	576	
Sundry expenses	1,202	
Motor vehicle	2,400	
Fixtures and fittings	600	
Debtors	4,577	
Creditors		3,045
Cash at bank	3,876	
Cash in hand	120	
Drawings	2,050	
Capital		12,844
	34,844	34,844

Stock at 30 April 2007 was £4,998.

6.5X The following is the trial balance of J Smailes as at 31 March 2006. Draw up a set of final accounts for the year ended 31 March 2006.

	Dr	Cr
	£	£
Stock 1 April 2005	18,160	
Sales		92,340
Purchases	69,185	
Carriage inwards	420	
Carriage outwards	1,570	
Returns outwards		640
Wages and salaries	10,240	
Rent and rates	3,015	
Communication expenses	624	
Commissions payable	216	

	Dr	Cr
	£	£
Insurance	405	
Sundry expenses	318	
Buildings	20,000	
Debtors	14,320	
Creditors		8,160
Fixtures	2,850	
Cash at bank	2,970	
Cash in hand	115	
Drawings	7,620	
Capital		50,888
	152,028	152,028

Stock at 31 March 2006 was £22,390.

6.6X L Stokes drew up the following trial balance as at 30 September 2008. You are to draft the trading and profit and loss account for the year to 30 September 2008 and a balance sheet as at that date.

	Dr	Cr
	£	£
Capital		30,955
Drawings	8,420	
Cash at bank	3,115	
Cash in hand	295	
Debtors	12,300	
Creditors		9,370
Stock 30 September 2007	23,910	
Motor van	4,100	
Office equipment	6,250	
Sales		130,900
Purchases	92,100	
Returns inwards	550	
Carriage inwards	215	
Returns outwards		307
Carriage outwards	309	
Motor expenses	1,630	
Rent	2,970	
Telephone charges	405	
Wages and salaries	12,810	
Insurance	492	
Office expenses	1,377	
Sundry expenses	284	
	171,532	171,532

Stock at 30 September 2008 was £27,475.

CHAPTER 7

Accounting concepts and the regulatory framework of accounting

AIMS

- To appreciate the assumptions which are made when recording accounting data.

- To realise one set of accounts is used for several different purposes.

- To understand what is meant by objectivity and subjectivity.

- To appreciate the basic concepts of accounting.

- To understand how the regulatory framework of accounting operates and provides 'rules' which are used in the preparation of final accounts.

- To know that there are accounting standards.

7.1 Introduction

In your studies of book keeping and accounting at NVQ Level 2, and the previous chapters in this book, concentration has been placed mainly on the recording of financial transactions in the books of account. Recording of these transactions has been based on certain **assumptions** which have deliberately not been discussed in detail previously. The reason for leaving this discussion until now is because it is much easier to look at them with a greater understanding **after** basic double entry has been covered and you have knowledge of the final accounts of a business. These assumptions are known as the **accounting concepts**.

The trading and profit and loss accounts and balance sheets shown in the previous chapters were drawn up for the owner of the business. As shown later in the book, businesses are often owned by more than just one person and the financial statements for those businesses are for the use of all owners.

An owner of a business may not be the only person to see the final accounts. As mentioned in Chapter 1, the owners may have to show a copy to the bank manager if they wish to borrow money. The Inspector of Taxes will also require a copy for the calculation of taxes. Then there may be other interested parties, such as prospective investors, suppliers, customers, and so on.

7.2 Objectivity and subjectivity

It is especially important in accounting that the procedures or methods used are agreed and understood by everyone. This approach is said to be **objective**. When the approach is **subjective**, it means that the owners wish to use their own method, even though no one else may agree to it. This concept is easier to understand if we consider the following situation. Assume that you are in a class of students and that you have the problem of valuing your assets, which consist of 10 textbooks. The first value you decide upon is how much you could sell them for. You estimate that they are worth £90, but other members of the class may give figures from £60 to £100.

Suppose you now decide to put a value on the use of the books to you. You may well think that the use of these books will enable you to pass your examinations and enable you to get a good job. Another person may have the opposite idea concerning the use of the books. The use value placed on the books by others in the class will be quite different.

Finally, you decide to value them by reference to cost. You refer to the receipts for the books, which show that you paid a total of £200. If the rest of the class do not think that you have altered the receipts, then they may all agree that the value expressed as cost is £200. Since this is the only value that you can all agree to, then each of you decides to use the idea of showing the value of the asset of books at the cost price.

The desire to provide the same set of accounts for many different parties, and thus to provide a measure that gains their consensus of opinion, means that objectivity is sought in financial accounting. If you are able to understand this desire for objectivity, then many of the apparent contradictions can be understood because it is often at the heart of the financial accounting methods in use at the present time.

Financial accounting seeks objectivity and, of course, it must have rules which lay down the way in which the activities of the business are recorded. These rules are known as **accounting concepts**.

7.3 Definition of an accounting concept

Over the years accounting systems have developed more for practical than for theoretical reasons. Consequently, several basic procedures have evolved which form the **basic rules of accounting**. These are often referred to as **accounting concepts and conventions**.

A **concept** may be defined as an idea. Thus, an **accounting concept** is an assumption that underlies the preparation of the financial statements of the organisation.

Previously, accountants had a great deal of freedom when preparing and presenting financial information. However, in the United Kingdom since 1971, the accounting profession has introduced accounting requirements via the Accounting Standards Committee which, in 1990, was replaced by the Accounting Standards Board, and professional accountants are expected to follow these requirements when preparing financial statements. The earlier requirements issued by the Accounting Standards Committee were known as Statements of Standard Accounting Practice (SSAPs). Those issued by the Accounting Standards Board are known as Financial Reporting Standards (FRSs). This topic will be discussed later in Sections 7.5 and 7.6. However, let us first look at the accounting standards that formally identified accounting concepts, SSAP 2: Disclosure of Accounting Policies.

7.4   SSAP 2: Disclosure of Accounting Policies

Users of financial statements will wish to analyse and evaluate the accounts. They cannot do this effectively unless they know which methods have been used when the accounts were prepared. SSAP 2, which refers to companies, was issued to help to bring about an improvement in the quality of financial reporting.

This SSAP begins by distinguishing between three terms, namely **fundamental accounting concepts, accounting bases** and **accounting policies**.

Fundamental accounting concepts

These are the broad basic assumptions used in preparing the periodic financial accounts of a business. The accounting standard identifies four fundamental accounting concepts:

- Going concern concept
- Accrual concept
- Consistency concept
- Prudence concept

Going concern concept

This concept implies that the business will continue to operate for the foreseeable future. In other words, it is assumed that the business will continue for a long period of time.

Accrual concept

This concept says that net profit is the difference between revenues and expenses rather than the difference between cash received and paid. Remember, businesses operate more often on credit than on cash.

Sales are **revenues** when the goods are sold and *not* when the money is received, which can be in a later period. Purchases are **expenses** when goods are bought, *not* when they are paid for. As we shall see in Chapter 12, items such as rent, insurance and motor expenses are treated as expenses when they are incurred, not when they are paid for. Adjustments are made when preparing financial statements for expenses owing and those paid in advance. Other adjustments that you will read about in Chapters 10 and 11 include adjusting for depreciation of fixed assets and for probable bad debts.

Determining the expenses used up to obtain the revenues is referred to as **matching** expenses against revenues, which is why this concept is also called the 'matching concept'.

By showing the actual expenses 'incurred' in a period matched against revenues 'earned' in the same period, a correct figure of net profit will be shown in the profit and loss account.

Consistency concept

This concept requires that the same treatment be applied when dealing with similar items not only in one period but in all subsequent periods.

The concept is important since it assists in analysis of the financial information and decision making, and it is vital that the organisation uses the same accounting principles each year. If the organisation was constantly changing its methods then this would result in misleading profits being calculated and inaccurate analyses, hence the reason why the convention of consistency is used. The convention states that when a firm has adopted a method for the accounting treatment of an item, it should treat all similar items that follow in exactly the same way.

However, this does not mean that the firm must always use a particular method; the firm may make changes provided it has good reason to do so and each change is declared in the notes to the financial statements.

Examples of when the consistency concept is used include:

- methods of depreciation (see later chapter)
- stock valuation (see later in this chapter).

Prudence concept

Accountants often have to use their judgement to decide which figure to use for a particular item; for example, suppose a debt has been outstanding for a long time and it is not certain that it will ever be paid. Should the accountant be an optimist in thinking that it will be paid, or should he or she be more pessimistic?

It is the accountant's duty to ensure that the financial accounts are prepared as accurately as possible in disclosing the proper facts about a business. Therefore, the accountant should make certain that assets are not valued too highly. Similarly, liabilities should not be shown at values that are too low, otherwise people might inadvisedly lend money to a firm, which they would not have done had they known the proper facts.

The accountant should always be on the side of safety. This is known as **prudence**. The prudence concept means that normally he or she will take the figure which will understate, rather than overstate the profit. Thus, the accountant should choose the figure which will cause the capital of the firm to be shown at a lower amount rather than at a higher one. The accountant will also make sure that all losses are recorded in the books and, at the same time, ensure that profits are not anticipated by recording them before they have been gained.

The term 'conservatism' was widely used until it was generally replaced by 'prudence'.

The SSAP states that where there is a conflict between the use of the accruals concept and the prudence concept, then observance of the prudence concept must be followed.

Accounting bases

These are the methods for applying fundamental accounting concepts to financial transactions and items in financial accounts. In particular they must be used for:

- determining the periods in which revenue and costs should be recognised in the profit and loss account;
- determining the amounts at which material items should be shown in the balance sheet.

Instances where accounting bases are important include:

- The basic methods of valuing stock and work in progress. (Methods available include First-In/First-Out, Last-In/First-Out and the Average Cost Method, to be discussed in Chapter 13.)
- Depreciation of fixed assets. (The methods which may be used to depreciate fixed assets include the straight line method and the reducing balance method – see Chapters 9 and 10.)

Accounting policies

These constitute the bases which have been consistently used by a business. One example might be a business which has used the straight line method of depreciation for several years. This, therefore, has become its accounting policy for depreciation.

Other accounting concepts and conventions

There are several other accounting concepts and conventions which are followed when preparing the financial accounts of a business, all of which you may require to know when taking an examination.

Business entity concept

The concept implies that the affairs of a business are to be treated as being quite separate from the personal activities of its owner(s). The items recorded in the books of the business are, therefore, restricted to the transactions of the business. No matter what activities the proprietor(s) are involved in outside the business, they are completely disregarded in the books kept by the business.

The only time that the personal resources of the proprietor(s) affect the firm's accounting records is when they introduce new capital into the business or take drawings out of it.

Realisation concept

This concept holds the view that profit can only be taken into account when realisation has occurred – in other words, until it is reasonably certain of being earned. Profit is normally said to be earned when:

- goods or services are provided to the buyer, and
- the buyer incurs liability for them.

This concept of profit is known as the **realisation concept**. Notice that it is *not*

- when the order is received, or
- when the customer pays for the goods

as this can give a false record. Profit that is brought into account in this way may, in a later period, be found to have been incorrectly taken as profit due to the goods having been returned. Also any services that are provided can result in an allowance being given in a later period owing to poor performance. If the allowance or returns can be reasonably estimated, an adjustment may be made to the calculated profit in the period when realisation occurred.

Historical cost concept

This concept means that the assets of the business are recorded in the accounts at cost price. For example, if a building is purchased at a cost price of £50,000 it will appear in the balance sheet at that value.

The advantages of using the cost method of valuation is that the assets can be easily verified since there will be a source document (invoice) which can be used to check the amount entered in the books of account. Second, no valuations need be carried out on certain assets such as motor vehicles whose values can be very subjective. The motor vehicle will be entered in the balance sheet at cost price. This cost will again be shown on the source document, the invoice.

The money measurement concept

Accounting is concerned only with these facts:

- it can be measured in money; and
- most people will agree to the money value of the transaction.

This means that accounting can never tell you everything about a business. For example, accounting does not show the following:

- whether the firm has good or bad managers;
- that there are serious problems with the workforce;
- that a rival product is about to take away many of the firm's best customers;
- that the government is about to pass a law which will cost the business a great deal of expense in the future.

The reason that these four points, or similar items, are not recorded is that it would be impossible to work out a money value for them to which most people could agree.

Some people think that accounting tells you everything you want to know, but the above shows that this is not true.

Materiality concept

This concept applies when the value of an item is relatively insignificant such that it does not warrant separate recording. That is, it is not 'material'. Whether or not an item is of material value and importance depends upon the individual item.

For example, if a firm purchases a box of paper-clips for use over a period of time, then this cost is used up every time someone uses a paper-clip. While it would be possible to record this as an expense, the price of a box of paper-clips is so little that it is not worth recording in this fashion. The box of paper-clips is not a material item, and therefore would be charged as an expense in the period it was bought, irrespective of the fact that it could last for more than one accounting period. *In other words, do not waste time in the elaborate recording of trivial items.*

Similarly, the purchase of such items as metal waste paper bins, calculators and a small clock would be charged as expenses in the period it which they were bought because they are not material items, even though they may last for many years. A motor lorry, would, however, be deemed to be a material item, and so, as will be seen in a later chapter on depreciation, an attempt is made to charge each period with the cost consumed in each period of its use.

Materiality is not subject to laws or rules and the decision as to what is material and what is not largely depends upon each individual business. A firm may well decide that all items under £100 should be treated as expenses in the period in which they were bought, even though they may well be in use in the firm for the following ten years. An example would be an office chair costing £65. Another firm, perhaps a larger organisation, may fix its limit at £1,000. Different limits may be set for different types of items. The decision as to what is material and what is not depends on judgement and on the individual firm.

The dual aspect concept

This states there are two aspects of accounting, one represented by the assets of the business and the other by the claims against them. The concept states that these two aspects are always equal to each other. In other words:

Assets = Capital + Liabilities

Double entry is the name given to the method of recording the transactions under the **dual aspect** concept.

The time interval concept

One of the underlying principles of accounting is that final accounts are prepared at regular intervals of one year. For internal management purposes they may even be prepared on a monthly or weekly basis.

Substance over form

The legal form of a transaction can differ from its real substance, and, where this happens, accounting should show the transaction in accordance with its real substance, which is basically how the transaction affects the economic situation of the firm. This means that accounting in this instance will not reflect the exact legal position concerning that transaction. An example would be when a business rented a car under a lease that allowed it to purchase the car at the end of 3 years for £1. The substance of the agreement is hire purchase, but the form is rental. It should be treated as if it were a hire purchase.

7.5 Accounting standards and the Financial Reporting Standards

At one time there were quite wide differences in the ways that accountants calculated profits, but in the late 1960s a number of high profile cases in the United Kingdom led to a widespread outcry against the lack of uniformity in financial reporting.

To reduce the possibility of very large variations in reported profits under different methods, the UK accounting bodies formed the Accounting Standards Committee (ASC) in 1971. Over a period of approximately twenty years, this committee issued many Statements of Standard Accounting Practice (SSAPs) and accountants and auditors were expected to comply with these SSAPs. If an SSAP was not complied with, the audit report had to give the reasons why the SSAP had been ignored.

The use of SSAPs did not mean that two identical businesses would show exactly the same profits year by year. It did, however, considerably reduce the possibilities of very large variations in such profit reporting.

In 1990, the accountancy bodies replaced the ASC with the Accounting Standards Board (ASB). It took over the practices that were still in use at that time, and these continue to be known as SSAPs. Standards developed by the ASB are called Financial Reporting Standards (FRSs). The ASB may issue pronouncements other than FRSs announcing, as each one appears, what authority, scope and applications it will have.

In November 1997, the ASB issued a third category of standard: the Financial Reporting Standard for Smaller Entities (FRSSE). SSAPs and FRSs had, generally, been developed with the larger company in mind. The FRSSE was the ASB's response to the view that smaller companies should not have to apply all the cumbersome rules contained in the SSAPs and FRSs. It is, in effect, a collection of some of the rules from virtually all the other accounting standards. Small companies can choose whether to apply the FRSSEs or, as seems unlikely, continue to apply all the other accounting standards.

7.6 Accounting standards and the legal framework

Accounting standards are drafted so that they comply with the laws of the United Kingdom and the Republic of Ireland. They also comply with European Union Directives. This is done to ensure that there is no conflict between the law and accounting standards. Anyone preparing financial statements for publication must observe the rules laid down in the accounting standards.

As mentioned in Chapter 1, knowledge and understanding of the following SSAPs is required for the NVQ Level 3 in Accounting:

SSAP 2: Disclosure of Accounting Policies

Refer to Section 7.4.

SSAP 5: Accounting for Value Added Tax (VAT)

Introduction

This accounting standard was first issued in 1974 prior to the introduction of value added tax, usually abbreviated to VAT. VAT is a tax charged on the supply of most goods and services in the United Kingdom. It is collected by traders and borne by the final consumer. Once the tax is collected it is paid to the government's Customs and Excise Department which is responsible for the administration of VAT. Some goods and services are not taxable, for example postal services. In addition some persons and firms are exempted (see below).

Rate of value added tax

The standard rate of VAT is decided by Parliament. It has been changed from time to time and at the time of writing it is 17.5%. There is also currently a reduced rate of 5% on domestic fuel and power and one of 5% on the installation of some energy-saving materials, and a zero rate.

In the following example the rate of VAT will be shown as 10%, simply because it is easy to calculate.

Taxable firms

Imagine that Firm A takes raw materials it has produced and sells some to the general public and some to traders.

1. **Sale to the general public**
    Firm A sells goods to Jones for £100 + VAT.

		£
The sales invoice is for:	Price	100
	+ VAT 10%	10 = Total price £110

    Firm A will then pay the £10 it has collected to the Customs and Excise.

2. **Sale to another trader, who then sells to the general public**
    Firm A sells goods to Firm B for £100 + VAT.

		£
The sales invoice is for:	Price	100
	+ VAT 10%	10 = Total price £110

    Firm B sells the raw materials to a member of the general public for £140 + VAT.

	£
The sales invoice is for: Price	140
+ VAT 10%	14 = Total price £154

In this case Firm A will pay the Customs and Excise £10 for VAT collected. Firm B will pay the Customs and Excise a cheque for £4, being the amount collected (£14) less the VAT paid to A (£10).

In the above cases you can see that the full amount of VAT has fallen on the person who finally buys the goods. Firms A and B have merely acted as collectors of the tax.

The value of goods sold by us or of services supplied by us is known as our 'outputs'. Thus VAT on such items is called **'output tax'**. The value of goods bought by us or of services supplied to us is known as inputs. The VAT on these items is, therefore, **'input tax'**.

Exempted firms

Some firms do not have to add VAT to the price at which they sell their products or services. Firms will not get a refund of the VAT they have themselves paid on goods and services bought by them. The types of firms exempted can be listed under two headings:

1. **Nature of business**   Various types of business do not have to add VAT to charges for goods or services. A bank, for instance, does not have to add VAT on to its bank charges.
2. **Small firms**   If small firms do register for VAT then they will have to keep full VAT records in addition to charging out VAT. To save very small businesses the costs and effort of keeping such records the government allows them not to register unless they want to, provided that their turnover is below a certain amount (currently £52,000). They can also deregister if their turnover falls below a certain level (currently £50,000).

Zero-rated firms

This special category of firm:

1. does not have to add VAT to the selling price of products, and
2. can obtain a refund of all VAT paid on the purchase of goods or services.

If, therefore, £100,000 of goods are sold by the firm, nothing has to be added for VAT but, if £8,000 VAT had been paid by it on goods or services bought, then the firm would be able to claim a full refund of the £8,000 paid.

It is (2) above which distinguishes it from an exempted firm. A zero-rated firm is, therefore, in a better position than an exempted firm. Examples of zero-rated firms are firms selling food.

Partly exempt traders

Some traders will find that they are selling some goods which are exempt and some which are zero rated and others which are standard rated. These traders will have to apportion their turnover accordingly, and follow the rules already described for each separate part of their turnover.

Different methods of accounting for VAT

We can see from what has been said already that the accounting treatment will vary between:

1. **Firms which can recover VAT paid** All firms except exempted firms do not suffer VAT as an expense. They either:

   - get a refund of whatever VAT they have paid, as in the case of a zero-rated firm; or
   - collect VAT from their customers, deduct the VAT paid on goods and services bought by the firm, and simply remit the balance owing to the Customs and Excise.

2. **Firms which cannot recover VAT paid** This applies to all firms which are treated as exempted firms and, therefore, suffer the tax because they cannot get it refunded.

VAT and cash discounts

Where a cash discount is offered for speedy payment, VAT is calculated on an amount represented by the value of the invoice less such a discount. Even if the cash discount is lost because of late payment, the VAT will not change.

One of the main aims of SSAP 5 was to obtain consistency of the accounting treatment and presentation of VAT in the financial statement of a business, as follows:

- Turnover shown in the profit and loss account should exclude VAT on taxable outputs (sales).
- If VAT is paid on an item, e.g. purchases, motor repairs or a fixed asset such as machinery, and the firm cannot reclaim VAT, then the VAT paid is included as part of the cost of the item. For example, machinery bought for £1,000 plus VAT at 17.5% of £175 would be shown in the balance sheet at a figure of £1,175.
- Any amount due to, or from, Customs and Excise should be included in creditors, or in debtors, as appropriate and need not be disclosed as a separate item.

SSAP 9: Stocks and Long-term Contracts

Due to the many different types of businesses and conditions within them, there simply cannot be one system of valuation for stocks and work-in-progress. All the standard can do is narrow the different methods that can be used.

Stock should be valued at the total of the '**lower of cost or net realisable value**' of the separate items of stock or groups of similar items. Profit *should not*, except in case of long-term contracts such as constructing a very large bridge or a motorway, be recognised in advance, but immediate account should be made of anticipated losses.

In the balance sheet, stocks should be subclassified according to the different kinds of stock held. For example, in manufacturing accounts (to be covered later) there are usually three types of stock, including: stock of raw materials, stock of work-in-progress, and stock of finished goods. Showing the value of the different types of stock in the balance sheet is in compliance with the Companies Act 1985.

Net realisable value consists of the expected selling price *less* any expenses necessary to sell the product. This may be below cost because of obsolescence, deterioration and similar factors.

SSAP 9 defines 'cost' as being:

> *That expenditure which has been incurred in the normal course of the business in bringing the product or service to its present location and condition. This expenditure should include, in addition to the cost of purchase, such costs of conversion as are appropriate to that location and condition.*

Cost of purchase comprises the purchase price including import duties, transport and handling costs and any other directly attributable costs, less trade discounts, rebates and subsidies.

Cost of conversion comprises:

- Costs which are specifically attributable to units of production, i.e. direct labour, direct expenses and subcontracted work.
- Production overheads based on the normal level of activity, taking one year with another, should all include fixed production overheads. Selling and administration costs should not, however, be included in these costs.
- Other overheads, if any, attributable in the particular circumstances of the business to bring the product or service to its present location and condition.

Note that abnormal costs (i.e. exceptional spoilage and idle capacity) are not included since they should not have the effect of increasing stock valuation.

The valuation of stock

There are several methods of valuing stock including:

- **First-In/First-Out**, usually known as FIFO, the first letters of each word. This method says that the first goods to be received are the first to be issued.
- **Last-In/First-Out**, usually known as LIFO. As each issue of goods is made they are said to be from the last batch of goods received before that date. Where there is not enough left of the last batch of goods received, the balance of goods needed is said to come from the previous batch still unsold, and so on.
- **Average cost**, abbreviated to AVCO. Using this method, with each receipt of goods the average cost for each item of stock is recalculated. Further issues of goods are then costed at that figure until a further batch of goods is received, necessitating another recalculation.

Whichever method of stock valuation a business decides to use, it should continue to use the same method unless there are particular reasons for a change, thus complying with the 'consistency concept of accounting'.

It should be noted that the LIFO method of stock valuation should not be used since it does not provide an up-to-date valuation. Although accepted by the SSAP and the Companies Act 1985, LIFO is not considered likely to be appropriate.

Long-term contracts

Stock valuation is covered more fully in Chapter 13.

The valuation of long-term contracts and the calculation of production overheads is not required at NVQ Level 3.

SSAP 12: Accounting for Depreciation

This standard applies to all but a few fixed assets. Freehold land is not normally depreciated as land usually lasts forever unless it is subject to depletion or loss of value for reasons which may be applicable in certain circumstances, such as land erosion, extraction of minerals, dumping of toxic waste etc.

KEY TERMS **Depreciation** The measure of wearing out, consumption or other reduction in the useful economic life of a fixed asset whether arising from use, passage of time or obsolescence through technological or market changes.

Useful economic life This is the period over which the present owner will derive economic benefit from the use of an asset.

Residual value This is the realisable value of the asset at the end of its economic life (i.e. the scrap value), based on prices prevailing at the date of acquisition or revaluation, where this has taken place. Realisation costs should be deducted in arriving at residual values.

Depreciation should be applied in respect of all fixed assets which have a finite useful economic life. It should be provided by allocating the cost less net realisable value over the periods expected to benefit from the use of the asset being depreciated. No particular method of depreciation is prescribed. However, the method selected should be that which produces the most appropriate allocation of depreciation to each period in relation to the benefit being received in that period through use of the asset. The depreciation should be calculated on the value as shown on the balance sheet and charged against the profit and loss account for the particular period. (This topic will be covered more fully in Chapters 9 and 10.)

SSAP 13: Accounting for Research and Development

Many organisations spend vast amounts of income on research and development projects. Examples include those engaged in producing drugs in the pharmaceutical industry and companies producing high technological products. The accounting treatment of these large amounts of expenditure is therefore important as it affects both the profits of the business and the balance sheet valuations.

SSAP 13 divides research and development expenditure into three sections:

- **Pure (or basic) research** Experimental or theoretical work undertaken primarily to acquire new scientific or technical knowledge for its own sake rather than directed towards any specific aim or application.
- **Applied research** Original or critical investigation undertaken in order to gain new scientific or technical knowledge and directed towards a specific practical aim or objective.
- **Development** Use of scientific or technical knowledge in order to produce new or substantially improved materials, devices, products, services or systems.

This accounting standard states that expenditure incurred on pure and applied research can be regarded as part of a continuing operation required to maintain a company's business and its competitive position. As a result, these costs should be written-off as they are incurred (i.e. shown as an expense in the profit and loss account).

The development of new and improved products is, however, distinguishable from pure and applied research. Expenditure incurred on such development is normally undertaken with a reasonable expectation of specific commercial success and of future benefits arising from the work, either from increased revenue and related profits or from reduced costs. However, development expenditure should be written-off in the year of expenditure, except in the following set of circumstances when it may be deferred to future periods.

1. There is a clearly defined project.
2. The related expenditure is separately identifiable.
3. It is feasible and commercially viable.
4. Overall profits are expected.
5. Resources exist to complete the project.

 If the expenditure is capitalised it must be 'amortised' (i.e. depreciated).

Therefore, in summary, for expenditure on *pure basic research* and *applied research*, all costs may be written off as incurred in the profit and loss account; while *development expenditure* may be written off in the profit and loss account or may be 'capitalised' and shown in the balance sheet as an asset provided the above requirements are met. If capitalised it must be *amortised* (another name for depreciation).

7.8 Confidentiality

Although it is not a concept of accounting, employees who work in the financial department of an organisation, and those who have access to its financial information, should recognise that this information is confidential. It should not be disclosed to anyone within the organisation except to those authorised to receive it.

It should only be disclosed 'outside' the organisation to such bodies as the Inland Revenue or Customs and Excise, as required by government legislation.

The organisation's auditors will also require access to the financial records in order to prepare its financial statements.

NEW TERMS
Accounting bases   The methods which have been developed for applying fundamental accounting concepts to financial transactions and in the preparation of financial statements.

Accounting concept   Accounting procedures developed over the years to form the 'basic rules of accounting'.

Accounting policies   The specific accounting bases selected and consistently used by an organisation.

Accounting principles   Rules and conventions which ought to be followed when preparing financial statements.

Accounting standards   These have statutory recognition and must, therefore, be complied with when preparing financial statements intended to give a true and fair view.

Accounting Standards Board (ASB)   A UK body formed in 1990, responsible for issuing Financial Reporting Standards (FRSs) and other pronouncements. It replaced the ASC.

Accounting Standards Committee (ASC)   The original committee which produced Statements of Standard Accounting Practice (SSAPs) and related professional pronouncements between 1976 and 1990.

Accruals concept   The concept that profit is the difference between revenue and expenses (*see also* Matching concept).

Amortisation   A term used instead of depreciation when assets are used up simply because of the time factor.

Applied research   Original research undertaken to gain new scientific or technical knowledge directed at a specific practical aim or objective.

AVCO   A method by which goods used are priced out at average cost.

Business entity concept   Assumption that only transactions that affect the firm, and not the owner's private transactions, will be recorded.

Consistency concept   Keeping to the same method of recording transactions.

Cost concept   Assets are normally shown at cost price.

Cost of conversion   Costs specifically attributable to units of production including production overheads and other specific overheads, if applicable, but excluding selling and distribution costs.

Cost of purchase   Comprises the purchase price including import duties, transport and handling costs and any other directly attributable costs, less trade discounts, rebates and subsidies.

Depletion   The wasting away of an asset as it is used up.

Depreciation   The part of the cost of the fixed asset consumed during its period of use by the firm.

Development expenditure   Use of scientific or technological knowledge to produce new or substantially improved products, services or systems, etc.

Dual aspect concept   The concept of dealing with both aspects of a transaction.

Exempted firms   Firms which do not have to add VAT to the price of goods and services supplied by them and which cannot obtain a refund of VAT paid on goods and services purchased by them.

FIFO   A method by which the first goods to be received are said to be the first to be sold.

Going concern concept   Assumption that a business is to continue for a long time.

Inputs   The value of goods and services purchased by a business.

Input tax   The VAT charged to a business on its purchases and expenses (inputs).

LIFO   A method by which the goods sold are said to have come from the last batch of goods received.

Matching concept   Actual expenses 'incurred' in a particular period should be matched against revenues 'earned' so that a correct figure of net profit is shown in the profit and loss account (*see also* Accruals concept).

Materiality concept   Recording something in a special way only if the amount is not a small one.

Money measurement concept   The concept that accounting is concerned only with facts measurable in money.

Net realisable value   The value of goods calculated as the selling price less expenses before sale.

Objectivity   Using a method that everyone can agree to.

Outputs   The value of goods and services sold to a business.

Output tax   The VAT charged by a business on its supplies (outputs).

Partly exempt traders   Traders selling goods which are exempt, some of which are zero rated and others which are standard rated.

Prudence concept   Ensuring that profit is not shown as being too high, or that assets are shown at too high a value.

Pure (or basic) research   Experimental or theoretical work undertaken to acquire new scientific or technical knowledge.

Realisation concept   The concept of profit as being earned at a particular point.

Residual value   This is the realisable value of the asset at the end of its economic life.

Subjectivity   Using a method that other people may not agree to, possibly derived from one's own personal preferences.

Substance over form   Where the true nature of a transaction takes precedence over its legal form.

Time interval concept   Final accounts are prepared at regular intervals.

Useful economic life   The useful economic life of an asset is the period over which the present owner will derive economic benefit from its use.

Value added tax (VAT)   A tax charged on the supply of most goods and services. The tax is borne by the final consumer of the goods or services, not by the business selling them to the consumer. VAT is administered by the government's department of Customs and Excise.

7.1 Objectivity is important in analysing and preparing accounting information. Explain the term 'objectivity' giving an example as to how it might be applied.

7.2X Accounting concepts are used in preparing financial accounts of a business.

(a) Briefly explain any three of the following concepts:

   (i) Going concern concept
   (ii) Accrual concept
   (iii) Consistency concept
   (iv) Prudence concept

(b) Identify the Statement of Standard Accounting Practice which refers to the above concepts.

7.3 As an accounts technician you have just checked the aged debtors list and have found an account which has been unpaid for more than 6 months, that of the Priory Paper Co., for £187.00. No response is gained from enquiries by letter or telephone and a visit is made to their last known address by one of your sales representatives. She finds that the premises are now occupied by a printing company whose owner tells her that the owner of Priory Paper Co. is rumoured to have gone abroad.

Which accounting concept would you follow and what action would you recommend your company take in dealing with this matter?

7.4 (a) Explain briefly what you understand by the 'historical cost concept'.

(b) Give an advantage in using the cost method of valuation.

7.5X Melissa Dunn and her husband started a business and leased some premises. Melissa purchased various small value items for the office including a calculator, stapler, waste-paper bin, etc.

(a) Explain briefly why the purchase of these items would normally be treated as revenue rather than capital expenditure.

(b) Which accounting concept deals with this situation?

7.6 The Accounting Standards Board came into being in 1990 to replace the Accounting Standards Committee. State its role and the type of standards it issues.

7.7 SSAP 5 refers to the requirements for dealing with value added tax. State what these requirements are in the presentation of VAT in the financial statements of a business.

7.8X Referring to SSAP 9 (Stocks and Long-term Contracts) state the various methods of valuing stock.

7.9 Expenditure on pure (or basic) research is required to be shown as an expense in the profit and loss account by SSAP 13. Explain why this is done.

CHAPTER 8

Capital and revenue expenditure

AIMS

- To be able to distinguish between expenditure that is capital and expenditure that is revenue, including items that are part capital and part revenue expenditure.

- To realise the effect on the final accounts, and the profits shown there, if revenue expenditure is wrongly treated as being capital expenditure, and vice versa.

8.1 Introduction

This chapter will deal with the distinction between capital and revenue expenditure and show the importance of careful classification which can ultimately affect the recorded profits and the balance sheet valuations of a business.

8.2 Capital expenditure

This is expenditure on the purchase of fixed assets or buying additions to existing fixed assets. Fixed assets are those assets which have an expected life of greater than one year and are used in the business to enable it to generate income and, ultimately, profit. Examples include:

- Premises, land and buildings
- Machinery, plant and equipment
- Office and computer equipment
- Furniture and fittings.

Additions to existing fixed assets should also be classified as **capital expenditure**, examples include:

- Purchasing a scanner for the computer
- Adding extra storage capacity to a mainframe computer
- Expenses incurred in updating machinery to increase production
- Additional shelving and fittings in a retail store.

It is important to include the following items of expenditure when fixed assets are purchased:

- The cost of acquiring the fixed assets
- The cost of delivery to the firm
- Legal costs of buying premises, land and buildings
- Installation costs
- Architects' fees for building plans and for supervising the construction of buildings
- Demolition costs to remove obsolete buildings before new work can begin.

8.3 Revenue expenditure

Expenditure which does not increase the value of fixed assets but is incurred in the day-to-day running expenses of the business is known as **revenue expenditure**.

The difference can be seen when considering the cost of running a motor vehicle for a business. The expenditure incurred in acquiring the motor vehicle is classed as **capital expenditure** while the cost of the petrol used to run the vehicle is **revenue expenditure.** This is because the revenue expenditure is used up in a few days and does not add to the value of the fixed asset.

8.4 Differences between capital and revenue expenditure

A few examples are listed in Exhibit 8.1 demonstrating the difference between capital and revenue expenditure. It can be seen that revenue expenditure is that chargeable to the trading and profit and loss account, while capital expenditure results in increased figures for fixed assets in the balance sheet.

Exhibit 8.1

Difference between capital and revenue expenditure

Capital	Revenue
Premises purchased	Rent of premises
Legal charges for conveyancing	Legal charges for debt collection
New machinery	Repairs to machinery
Installations of machinery	Electricity costs of using machinery
Additions to assets	Maintenance of assets
Motor vehicles	Current Road Fund Tax
Delivery charges on new assets	Carriage on purchases and sales
Extension costs of new offices	Redecorating existing offices
Cost of adding air-conditioning to room	Interest on loan to purchase air-conditioning

8.5 Joint expenditure

In certain cases an item of expenditure will need to be divided between capital and revenue expenditure. Suppose a builder was engaged to carry out some work on your premises, the total bill being £30,000. If one-third of this was for repair work and two-thirds for improvements, then £10,000 should be charged to the profit and loss account as revenue expenditure, and £20,000 identified as capital expenditure and, therefore, added to the value of premises and shown as such in the balance sheet.

8.6 Incorrect treatment of expenditure

If one of the following occurs:

- capital expenditure is incorrectly treated as revenue expenditure, or
- revenue expenditure is incorrectly treated as capital expenditure

then both the balance sheet figures and trading and profit and loss account figures will be incorrect. This means that the net profit figure will also be incorrect.

If capital expenditure is incorrectly posted to revenue expenditure – for example, if the purchase of a photo-copier is posted in error to the stationery account instead of the office equipment account – then:

> **net profit** would be understated
> *and*
> **balance sheet** values would not include the value of the asset.

If revenue expenditure is incorrectly posted to capital expenditure, for example if stationery is posted to office equipment instead of the stationery account, then:

> **net profit** would be overstated
> *and*
> **balance sheet** values would be over-valued.

If the expenditure affects items in the trading account, then the **gross profit** figure will also be incorrect.

8.7 Treatment of loan interest

If money is borrowed to finance the purchase of a fixed asset then interest will have to be paid on the loan. The loan interest, however, is *not* a cost of acquiring the asset, but is simply a cost of financing it. This means that loan interest is revenue expenditure, *not* capital expenditure, and should be charged to the profit and loss account.

8.8 Capital and revenue receipts

When an item of capital expenditure is sold, the receipt is called a **capital receipt**. Suppose a motor van is bought for £10,000, and sold five years later for £2,000. The £10,000 was treated as capital expenditure, therefore, the £2,000 received is treated as a capital receipt.

Revenue receipts are sales or other revenue items, such as rent receivable or commissions receivable.

NEW TERMS **Capital expenditure** When a business spends money to buy or add value to a fixed asset.

Revenue expenditure Expenses needed for the day-to-day running of the business.

Student Activities

8.1 (a) What is meant by 'capital expenditure', and 'revenue expenditure'?

(b) Some of the following items should be treated as capital and some as revenue. For each of them state which classification applies:

(i) The purchase of machinery for use in the business.
(ii) Carriage paid to bring the machinery in (i) above to the works.
(iii) Complete redecoration of the premises at a cost of £1,500.
(iv) A quarterly account for heating.
(v) The purchase of a soft drinks vending machine for the canteen with a stock of soft drinks.
(vi) Wages paid by a building contractor to his own workmen for the erection of an office in the builder's stockyard.

8.2X Indicate which of the following would be revenue items and which would be capital items in a wholesale bakery:

(a) Purchase of a new motor van.

(b) Purchase of replacement engine for existing motor van.

(c) Cost of altering interior of new van to increase carrying capacity.

(d) Cost of motor taxation licence for new van.

(e) Cost of motor taxation licence for existing van.

(f) Cost of painting firm's name on new van.

(g) Repair and maintenance of existing van.

8.3 Explain clearly the difference between capital expenditure and revenue expenditure. State which of the following you would classify as capital expenditure, giving your reasons:

(a) Cost of building extension to factory.

(b) Purchase of extra filing cabinets for sales office.

(c) Cost of repairs to accounting machine.

(d) Cost of installing reconditioned engine in delivery van.

(e) Legal fees paid in connection with factory extension.

8.4X The data which follows was extracted from the books of account of H Kirk, an engineer, on 31 March 2006, his financial year end.

		£
(a)	Purchase of extra milling machine (includes £300 for repair of an old machine)	2,900
(b)	Rent	750
(c)	Electrical expenses (includes new wiring £600, part of premises improvement)	3,280
(d)	Carriage inwards (includes £150 carriage on new cement mixer)	1,260
(e)	Purchase of extra drilling machine	4,100

You are required to allocate each or part of the items above to either 'capital' or 'revenue' expenditure.

8.5X **(a)** Star Fashions Ltd, who manufacture children's clothing, are planning to purchase a new cutting machine costing £20,000. Would the following items of expenditure be classed as capital or revenue expenditure?

  (i) The purchase price of the cutting machine.
  (ii) The cost of installing the machine.
  (iii) The cost of initial training for the staff to operate the new machine (this cost is quite significant).
  (iv) The cost of future repairs and maintenance of the machine.

(b) If capital expenditure is treated as revenue expenditure, then:

  (i) How would the total expenses and the net profit for the period be affected?
  (ii) What effect would the error have on the value of the fixed assets in the balance sheet?

8.6 T Taylor has drawn up his final accounts for the year ended 31 December 2008. On examining them, you find that:

(a) Taylor has debited the cost of office equipment £311 to the purchases account.

(b) Taylor has debited the cost of repairing office equipment £290 to the motor repairs account.

(c) Sale of a building for £10,000 has been credited to the sales account.

(d) Repayment of a loan £500 has been debited to the loan interest account.

From his figures he has calculated gross profit as £95,620 and net profit as £28,910.

Ignoring any adjustments for depreciation, calculate revised figures of gross and net profits after taking (a) to (d) into account.

8.7X S Simpson has calculated his gross profit for the year to 30 June 2000 as £129,450 and net profit as £77,270. You find that Simpson's books show:

(a) Sale of a motor vehicle for £4,100 has been credited to the sales account.

(b) Fixtures, bought for £750, have been debited to the repairs account.

(c) Receipt of a loan for £6,000 has been credited to the sales account.

(d) Repairs to motor vehicles of £379 have been debited to the general expenses account.

Ignoring any adjustments for depreciation, calculate the revised figures of gross and net profits.

8.8X A business has incorrectly charged some of its expenditure in its final accounts. You are to show, for each of the following, the effects on the calculations of (a) gross profit, (b) net profit, (c) fixed assets in the balance sheet and (d) current assets in the balance sheet. (Ignore depreciation.)

(i) Motor van costing £5,500 debited to motor expenses account.

(ii) Carriage outwards £77 debited to fixtures account.

(iii) Rent £2,000 debited to buildings account.

(iv) Machinery £6,000 debited to fixtures account.

(v) Office equipment £790 debited to purchases account.

(vi) Discounts allowed £2,380 debited to machinery account.

The incorrect figures already shown were as follows:

(a) Gross profit £216,290.

(b) Net profit £110,160.

(c) Fixed assets £190,000.

(d) Current assets £77,600.

Methods of depreciation and the acquisition of fixed assets

CHAPTER 9

AIMS

- To understand the need for charging depreciation and the causes of depreciation.

- To be able to calculate depreciation using either the straight line or reducing balance methods, including depreciation calculations when assets are bought or sold within an accounting period.

- To understand the importance of obtaining authorisation for the acquisition/disposal of fixed assets, recording them in the fixed assets register and maintaining control.

- To understand the financing of capital acquisitions.

9.1 Introduction

In the previous chapter we considered the distinction between capital and revenue expenditure. Capital expenditure involves the purchase of fixed assets. This chapter covers the need for charging depreciation on these assets and the causes of depreciation.

The methods of calculating depreciation usually involve either the straight line or reducing balance method. The chapter also discusses the acquisition of fixed assets including authorisation, recording transactions in the fixed assets register, the verification procedures and obtaining resources for financing the purchase.

The double entry aspect of recording the transaction of purchase, disposal and charges for depreciation will be shown in Chapter 10.

9.2 Depreciation of fixed assets

As mentioned in Chapter 8, fixed assets are those of material value which are:

- of long life
- to be used in the business
- not bought with the main purpose of resale.

83

However, fixed assets such as machinery, equipment, motor vehicles and even buildings do not last for ever. If the amount received (if any) on disposal is deducted from the cost of buying them, the difference is called **depreciation**.

The only time that depreciation can be calculated accurately is when the fixed asset is finally disposed of, and the difference between the cost to its owner and the amount received on disposal is then calculated. If a motor van was bought for £15,000 and sold four years later for £3,000, then the amount of depreciation would be £15,000 less £3,000 = £12,000.

Depreciation is the part of the original cost of the fixed asset consumed during its period of use by the firm. It is an expense for services consumed in the same way as expenses for such items as wages, rent or electricity. Since depreciation is an expense it will be charged to the profit and loss account and will, therefore, reduce the net profit.

9.3 Causes of depreciation

The main causes of depreciation are as follows:

- Physical deterioration
- Economic factors
- The time factor
- Depletion.

These are shown in greater detail below.

Physical deterioration

Wear and tear

When a motor vehicle or machinery or fixtures and fittings are used they eventually wear out. Some last many years, others last only a few years. This is true of buildings, although some may last for a long time.

Erosion, rust, rot and decay

Land may be eroded or wasted away by the action of wind, rain, sun and other elements of nature. Similarly, the metals in motor vehicles or machinery will rust away. Wood will rot eventually. Decay is a process which will also be present due to the elements of nature and the lack of proper attention.

Economic factors

These may be said to be the reasons for an asset being put out of use even though it is in good physical condition. The two main factors are usually **obsolescence** and **inadequacy**.

Obsolescence

This is the process of becoming out of date. For instance, over the years there has been great progress in the development of synthesisers and electronic devices used by leading commercial musicians. The old equipment will therefore have become obsolete, and much of it will have been taken out of use by such musicians.

This does not mean that the equipment is worn out. Other people may well buy the old equipment and use it, possible because they cannot afford to buy new up-to-date equipment.

Inadequacy

This arises when an asset is no longer used because of the growth and changes in the size of the firm. For instance, a small ferryboat that is operated by a firm at a coastal resort will become entirely inadequate when the resort becomes more popular. Then it will be found that it would be more efficient and economical to operate a large ferryboat, and so the smaller boat will be put out of use by the firm.

In this case it does not mean that the ferryboat is no longer in good working order. It may be sold to a firm at a smaller resort.

The time factor

Obviously time is needed for wear and tear, erosion, etc., and for obsolescence and inadequacy to take place. However, there are fixed assets to which the time factor is connected in a different way. These are assets which have a legal life fixed in terms of years.

For instance, you may agree to rent some buildings for 10 years. This is normally called a lease. When the years have passed the lease is worth nothing to you, since it has finished. Whatever you paid for the lease is now of no value.

A similar asset is where you buy a patent with complete rights so that only you are able to produce something. When the patent's time has run out it then has no value. The usual length of life of a patent is 16 years.

 Instead of using the term 'depreciation', the term 'amortisation' is often used for these assets.

Depletion

Other assets are of wasting character, perhaps due to the extraction of raw materials from them. These materials are then either used by the firm to make something else, or sold in their raw state to other firms. Natural resources such as mines, quarries and oil wells come under this heading. Providing for the consumption of an asset of a wasting character is called a **provision for depletion**.

9.4 Land and buildings

Prior to SSAP 12, which applied after 1977, freehold and long leasehold properties were very rarely subject to a charge for depreciation. It was contended that, as property values tended to rise instead of fall, it was inappropriate to charge depreciation.

However, SSAP 12 requires that depreciation be written off over the property's useful life, with the exception that freehold land will not normally require a provision for depreciation, because land does not normally depreciate. Buildings do, however, eventually fall into disrepair or become obsolete and must be subject to a charge for depreciation each year. When a revaluation of property takes place, the depreciation charge must be on the revalued figure.

Exceptions to all this are **investment properties**. These are properties owned not for use but simply for investment. In this case investment properties will be shown in the balance sheet at their open market value.

9.5 Appreciation

At this stage of the chapter readers may well begin to ask themselves about the assets that increase (appreciate) in value. The answer to this is that normal accounting procedure would be to ignore any such appreciation, as to bring appreciation into account would be to contravene both the cost concept and the prudence concept as discussed in Chapter 7. Nevertheless, in certain circumstances appreciation is taken into account in partnership and limited company accounts, but we will leave that discussion until partnerships and limited companies are considered.

9.6 Provision for depreciation as allocation of cost

Depreciation in total over the life of an asset can be calculated quite simply as cost less amount receivable when the asset is put out of use by the firm. If the item is bought and sold within the one accounting period, then the depreciation for that period is charged as a revenue expense in arriving at that period's net profit. The difficulties start when the asset is used for more than one accounting period, and an attempt has to be made to charge each period with the depreciation for that period.

Even though depreciation provisions are now regarded as allocating cost to each accounting period (except for accounting for inflation), it does not follow that there is any 'true' method of performing even this task. All that can be said is that the cost should be allocated over the life of the asset in such a way as to charge it as equitably as possible to the periods in which the asset is used. The difficulties involved are considerable and some of them are now listed.

1. Apart from a few assets, such as a lease, how accurately can a firm assess an asset's useful life? Even a lease may be put out of use if the premises leased have become inadequate.

2. How does one measure use? A car owned by a firm for two years may have been driven one year by a very careful driver and another year by a reckless driver. The standard of driving will affect the motor car and also the amount of cash receivable on its disposal. How should such a firm apportion the car's depreciation costs?

3. There are other expenses besides depreciation, such as repairs and maintenance of the fixed asset. As both of these affect the rate and amount of depreciation should they not also affect the depreciation provision calculations?

4. How can a firm possibly know the amount receivable in x years' time when the asset is put out of use?

These are only some of the difficulties. Therefore, the methods of calculating provisions for depreciation are mainly accounting customs.

9.7 Methods of calculating depreciation charges

The two main methods in use are the **straight line method** and the **reducing balance method**. Most accountants think that, although other methods may be needed in certain cases, the straight line method is one that is generally most suitable.

Straight line method

By this method, sometimes also called the fixed instalment method, the number of years of use is estimated. The cost is then divided by the number of years, to give the depreciation charge each year.

For instance, if a motor lorry was bought for £22,000 and we estimated that we would keep it for four years then sell it for £2,000, the depreciation to be charged would be:

$$\frac{\text{Cost (£22,000)} - \text{Estimated disposal value (£2,000)}}{\text{Number of expected years of use (4)}} = \frac{£20,000}{4}$$

= £5,000 depreciation each year for four years.

If, after four years, the motor lorry had no disposal value, the charge for depreciation would have been:

$$\frac{\text{Cost (£22,000)}}{\text{Number of years use (4)}} = \frac{£22,000}{4}$$

= £5,500 depreciation each year for four years.

Reducing balance method

By this method a fixed percentage for depreciation is deducted from the cost in the first year. In the second or later years the same percentage is taken of the reduced balance (i.e. cost *less* depreciation already charged). This method is also known as the **diminishing balance** method.

If a machine is bought for £10,000, and depreciation is to be charged at 20%, the calculations for the first three years would be as follows:

	£
Cost	10,000
Year 1: depreciation (20%)	2,000
	8,000
Year 2: depreciation (20% of £8,000)	1,600
	6,400
Year 3: depreciation (20% of £6,400)	1,280
Cost not yet apportioned, end of Year 3	5,120

The percentage to be applied, assuming a significant amount for residual value, is usually between two and three times greater for the reducing balance method than for the straight line method.

The advocates of this method usually argue that it helps to even out the total charged as expenses for the use of the asset each year. They state that provisions for depreciation are not the only costs charged, that there are also running costs and that the repairs and maintenance element of running costs usually increase with age. Therefore, to equate the total costs for each year of use, the depreciation provisions should fall as the repairs and maintenance element increases. However, as can be seen from the figures of the example already given, the repairs and maintenance element would have to be comparatively large to bring about an equal total charge for each year of use.

To summarise, the people who favour this method say that:

In the early years		In the later years
A higher charge for depreciation	will tend to be fairly equal to	A lower charge for depreciation
+		+
A lower charge for repairs and upkeep		A higher charge for repairs and upkeep

9.8   Choice of method

The purpose of a charge for depreciation is to spread the total cost of the asset over the periods in which it is available to be used. The method chosen should be that which allocates cost to each period in accordance with the amount of benefit gained from the use of the asset in the period.

If, therefore, the main value is to be obtained from the asset in its earliest years, it may be appropriate to use the reducing balance method which charges more in the early years. If, on the other hand, the benefits are to be gained evenly over the years, then the straight line method would be more appropriate.

The repairs and maintenance factor has also to be taken into account – an argument that has already been mentioned in the previous section.

Exhibit 9.1 gives a comparison of the calculations if the same cost is given for the two methods.

Exhibit 9.1

A firm has just bought a machine for £8,000. It will be kept in use for four years, then it will be disposed of for an estimated amount of £500. They ask for a comparison of the amounts charged as depreciation using both methods.

For the straight line method a figure of (£8,000 − £500) ÷ 4 = £7,500 ÷ 4 = £1,875 per annum is to be used. For the reducing balance method a percentage figure of 50% will be used.

	Straight line method £		Reducing balance method £
Cost	8,000		8,000
Depreciation: Year 1	1,875	(50% of £8,000)	4,000
	6,125		4,000
Depreciation: Year 2	1,875	(50% of £4,000)	2,000
	4,250		2,000
Depreciation: Year 3	1,875	(50% of £2,000)	1,000
	2,375		1,000
Depreciation: Year 4	1,875	(50% of £1,000)	500
Disposal value	500		500

This illustrates the fact that the reducing balance method has a much higher charge for depreciation in the early years, and lower charges in the later years.

9.9 Depreciation provisions and assets bought or sold

There are two main methods of calculating depreciation provisions for assets bought or sold during an accounting period.

1. To ignore the dates during the year that the assets were bought or sold and merely calculate a full period's depreciation on the assets in use at the end of the period. Thus, assets sold during the accounting period will have had no provision made for depreciation for that last period irrespective of how many months they were in use. Conversely, assets bought during the period will have a full period of depreciation provision charged even though they may not have been owned throughout the whole of the period.

2. Provision for depreciation made on the basis of one month's ownership equals one month's depreciation. Fractions of months are usually ignored. This is obviously a more scientific method than the method described above.

For examination purposes, where the dates on which assets are bought and sold are shown, the reducing balance method is the method expected by the examiner. If no such dates are given, then obviously the straight line method will have to be used.

9.10 SSAP 12: Accounting for Depreciation

This SSAP was discussed in Chapter 7, Section 7.7, and it may be useful at this point to recap on the main points which the SSAP states:

1. Depreciation is a measure of the wearing out, consumption or other reduction of a fixed asset arising from use, time or obsolescence through technological or market changes.

2. Depreciation should be provided in respect of all fixed assets which have a definite life by allocating the costs, less the residual value, over the expected useful life of the asset. (See also Section 9.4 concerning land and buildings.)

3. While no particular method of depreciation is prescribed, a suitable method should be selected and the method and percentages used for each type of asset noted in the accounts.

4. It is possible to change the method of depreciation used but the change must be noted in the accounts.

9.11 Authorisation for the acquisition and disposal of fixed assets

All authorisation starts at the highest level in companies with the decision by the directors to follow a clear strategy in the company's development. Strategic plans cover a reasonably long period, usually five years, and form the basis for action to be taken. These plans will consider potential sales, profitability, financial resources, productivity, staffing implications and training.

For example, owing to increased competition, the directors may decide to substantially alter an existing factory which uses out-of-date machinery and install technically advanced automated equipment. The process for implementing these changes would involve the drawing up of budgets to control both the acquisition and disposal of assets. In this example, the budgets might take the form of:

- *Disposal budget*   Removal of all out-of-date machinery
- *Factory refurbishment budget*   Modification to the factory to prepare for new automated equipment
- *New equipment budget*   Purchase of automated machinery.

These budgets would probably be under the control of the directors and their authorisation would be needed for the company to place contracts due to their high monetary value.

The company will have other budgets showing departmental managers what monies are available for them to maintain the efficiency of the departments. Senior managers might have a budget of £100,000 with the authority to make a single capital acquisition/disposal up to £5,000. Less senior managers might have a budget of £20,000 with a single capital acquisition limit of £1,000.

Company authorisation procedures regarding the acquisition and disposal of fixed assets varies from one organisation to another, but a specific form is normally in use (see Exhibit 9.2).

Exhibit 9.2

Form for the authorisation and purchase of a fixed asset

Fixed Asset Purchase Authorisation

Please complete and return to financial director

Budget Name: _____

Brief specification of item: _____

_____

_____

Supplier: _____ Cost: _____

Payment terms and date due: _____

Authorised by: _____ Position: _____

Approved by: _____ Position: _____

(if over authorisation limit)

State if: Company Purchase/Hire Purchase/Lease/Part Exchange

When Lease, state terms: _____

When Part Exchange, state Fixed Asset Disposal Ref.: _____

9.12 Disposal of fixed assets

This is a very important aspect of fixed assets management and the following steps need to be taken:

1. Authorisation should be obtained to dispose of the asset – a specific form would normally be completed.
2. Amend the register of fixed assets to show the disposal date and value (if any) of the disposed item.

The authorisation for disposals is normally clearly defined and could include chief executive/directors, factory/department manager or in some large organisations a special department may deal with disposals. The object in the process is to gain the maximum value for the company in terms of resale/scrap prices or lowest cost of removal.

9.13 Fixed asset register

It is essential for all organisations to compile and maintain a full record of fixed assets in the form of a register which would be held by the finance or specialist department. A typical register might include the items shown in Exhibit 9.3.

Exhibit 9.3

Fixed asset register

Fixed Asset Register

Item No.: G296
Description: York Box Van 1,500 kg capacity, W241 XDR
Purchase Date: 6.4.2001
Cost: £15,000
Estimated Life: 3 years   Location: Transport

Purchase date	Cost (excl. VAT) £	Estimated life	Residual value £	Dep'n method SL or RB	% Age per annum	Dep'n for year £	Total dep'n to date £	NBV £	Disposal proceeds (ex VAT) £	Profit/ loss on sale £

Note: SL = Straight line method of depreciation
RB = Reduced balance method of depreciation } Refer to Section 9.7.
NBV = Net book value, that is the cost or valuation of a fixed asset less the accumulated
        depreciation, often referred to as 'written down value'.

 Recording of the fixed assets in the books of account will be dealt with in Chapter 10.

9.14   Checking and verifying fixed assets

The value of fixed assets has to be stated fairly in the balance sheet, thus the accuracy of the fixed assets register needs to be verified at regular intervals. A physical check of these assets should be carried out similar to that used when stocktaking.

The check should be made to ensure that each item on the register

- still exists
- has an Item No. that matches its description
- is in the correct location
- is still used.

Any item that cannot be found may have been stolen, discarded due to obsolescence or damage or errors have been made in entering the details in the register. Some new assets may have been acquired but have not yet been recorded.

Following the physical check, the total value of the items should be reconciled with the asset accounts in the general ledger.

9.15 Funding the purchase of fixed assets

As can be seen from Exhibit 9.2, the form shows that there are various means of financing fixed asset purchase.

- **Company funds** paid out of the company bank account, without recourse to outside agencies.
- **Loans** usually money borrowed from the bank who will require interest and security for the loan.
- **Hire purchase** a credit agreement requiring a deposit and regular payments. Ownership of the item passes to the company on final payment.
- **Leasing** again a credit agreement requiring regular payment but the company does not gain ownership on final payment.
- **Part exchange** the value of a fixed asset disposal is used to offset the cost of an acquisition.

Loans, hire purchase and leasing are useful when a company wants to maintain good liquidity or when funds are not available for the purchase of capital items.

NEW TERMS

Authorisation of assets When a company director or senior manager authorises the purchase or disposal of a fixed asset.

Depletion The wasting away of an asset as it is used up.

Depreciation The part of the cost of the fixed asset consumed during its period of use by the business.

Fixed Asset Register Register used to record details of fixed assets purchased and disposed of, plus details of depreciation charges.

Hire purchase An agreement between the business and hire purchase company which enables the business to enjoy the use of the asset. The hirer pays regular instalments for the use of the asset. Ownership passes on payment of the last instalment.

Leasing This is an agreement whereby the business enjoys the use of the asset for which they pay a regular hire charge.

Loans Money borrowed from a bank or finance company who may require security. Interest is charged on the loan and the borrower repays the loan, plus interest, by making regular repayments.

Net book value (NBV) The cost (or valuation) of a fixed asset less depreciation to date, often referred to as 'written down value' (WDV).

Obsolescence Becoming out of date.

Reducing balance method Depreciation calculations which is at a lesser amount every following period.

Straight line method Depreciation calculation which remains at an equal amount each year.

9.1 K Richardson runs a small manufacturing business and purchases a new machine for £40,000. It has an estimated life of five years and a scrap value of £5,000. Richardson is not sure whether to use the straight line or reducing balance method of depreciation for the purpose of calculating depreciation on the machine.

You are required to calculate the depreciation on the machine using both methods, showing clearly the balance remaining in the machine account at the end of the five years for each method. (Assume that 40% per annum is to be used for the reducing balance method.)

9.2 A printing press costs £37,500 and will be kept for four years when it will be traded in at an estimated value of £15,360. Show the calculations of the figures for depreciation (to the nearest £) for each of the four years using (a) the straight line method and (b) the reducing balance method, using a depreciation rate of 20%.

9.3X A motor vehicle costs £19,200 and will be kept for four years, and then sold for an estimated value of £1,200. Calculate the depreciation for each year using (a) the reducing balance method, using a depreciation rate of 50%, and (b) the straight line method.

9.4X A photo-copier costs £5,120. It will be kept for five years, and then sold at an estimated figure of £1,215. Show the calculations of the figures for depreciation for each year using (a) the straight line method, and (b) the reducing balance method, using a depreciation rate of 25%.

9.5X A tractor cost £72,900 and has an estimated life of five years after which it will be traded in at an estimated value of £9,600. Show your calculations of the amount of depreciation each year using (a) the reducing balance method at a rate of $33\frac{1}{3}$% and (b) the straight line method.

9.6 A dumper is brought for £6,000. It will last for three years and will then be sold back to the supplier for £3,072. Show the depreciation calculations for each year using (a) the reducing balance method with a rate of 20%, and (b) the straight line method.

9.7X On 1 January 2001 a business purchased a laser printer costing £1,800. The printer has an estimated life of four years after which it will have no residual value. It is expected that the output from the printer will be:

Year	Sheets printed
2001	35,000
2002	45,000
2003	45,000
2004	55,000
	180,000

Required

(a) Calculate the annual depreciation charges for the years 2001, 2002, 2003 and 2004 on the laser printer using the following bases:

   (i) the straight line basis,

   (ii) the reducing balance method at 60% per annum, and

   (iii) the units of output method.

   Note: Your workings should be to the nearest £.

(b) Identify four factors which can cause fixed assets to depreciate.

(c) Which of these four factors is the most important for each of the following fixed assets?

   (i) a 90-year lease on a building

   (ii) land

   (iii) a forest of mature trees to be felled for timber

   (iv) replacing an old stamping press after the launch of an improved press capable of increasing output of higher quality at lower cost.

(Association of Accounting Technicians)

9.8X You are required to investigate and analyse your own employer's procedures for the acquisition of items of capital expenditure. Include such things as the procedures for the purchase and recording the details in the company's fixed asset register. You may obtain original documents, provided your employer has no objections, and present your findings in a brief report.

9.9 Extracts from the fixed asset register of The Moreland Machine Company are shown below. The company's accountant asks you to complete the extracts for the years ended 31 December 2003 and 2004 by calculating the amount of depreciation to be charged each year on both assets.

Fixed Asset Register										

Item No: OF 27318
Description: Office Furniture
Purchase Date: 1 January 2001
Cost: £5,000
Estimated Life: 5 years   Location: Main Office

Purchase date	Cost (ex VAT) £	Estimated life	Residual value £	Dep'n method SL or RB	% per annum	Dep'n for year £	Total dep'n to date £	Net book value £	Disposal proceeds (ex VAT) £	Profit/ loss on sale £
2001										
1 Jan	5,000	6 years	500	RB	20%					
31 Dec						1,000	1,000	4,000		
2002										
31 Dec						800	1,800	3,200		

Fixed Asset Register

Item No: TL 34109
Description: Pressing Machine
Purchase Date: 1 January 2000
Cost: £25,000
Estimated Life: 4 years   Location: Machine Shop

Purchase date	Cost (ex VAT) £	Estimated life	Residual value £	Dep'n method SL or RB	% per annum	Dep'n for year £	Total dep'n to date £	Net book value £	Disposal proceeds (ex VAT) £	Profit/ loss on sale £
2000 1 Jan	25,000	4 years	NIL	SL	25%					
2000 31 Dec						6,250	6,250	18,750		
2001 31 Dec						6,250	12,500	12,500		

9.10 The Moreland Machine Company is considering replacing the company vehicles and is wondering whether to pay for them immediately or buy them on hire purchase. Discuss these two options giving the advantages and disadvantages of each.

9.11X The Information Technology section of your firm is developing a software package to replace the fixed asset register which is currently maintained manually. You have received the following memo requesting your assistance.

MEMO

From: Information Technology Section
To: Trainee accountant
Re: Development of computerised fixed asset register

We are in the process of developing a software package to replace the existing fixed asset register. Could you assist us by clarifying the purpose of a fixed asset register and the information to be recorded in it?

It would be helpful if you could illustrate how the information is currently recorded in the ledger using the following data and assumptions:

The year end is 31 July 2009, and the depreciation policy is that assets are depreciated at a rate of 15% per annum on the reducing balance basis. A full year's depreciation is provided in the year of acquisition of an asset, and no depreciation is provided in the year of disposal.

ASSET 1
Acquired   May 2007
Cost   £22,000
Sold   31 May 2009 in part exchange for Asset 2
Part exchange value   £13,700

ASSET 2   Amount paid by cheque: £15,800

Thank you.

Required

(i) Write a memo to the IT section which:
   (a) states the purpose of a fixed asset register;
   (b) indicates four items of information which would normally be included in a fixed asset register and states the purpose of each of these items of information.

(ii) As an appendix to your memo prepare:
   (a) the asset cost account for the year to 31 July 2009;
   (b) the provision for depreciation account for the year to 31 July 2009;
   (c) the asset disposal account for the year to 31 July 2009.

(ACCA.CAT)

Students reading the above question may imagine at first sight that this is a question on Information Technology. However, as you can see, the question simply asks you to give some basic information.

CHAPTER 10

Double entry records for depreciation and the disposal of assets

AIMS

- To incorporate depreciation calculations into the accounting records.

- To record the disposal of fixed assets and the adjustments needed to the provision for depreciation accounts.

- To appreciate the accounting requirement of recording fixed assets on which VAT has been charged for registered and unregistered businesses.

10.1 Recording depreciation

Looking back a number of years, the charge for depreciation was always shown in the fixed asset accounts; this method, however, has now fallen into disuse. In the method used today, the fixed assets accounts show the assets at cost price, the depreciation being shown separately accumulating in a 'provision for depreciation account'.

The following example illustrates the accounting records:

Exhibit 10.1

A business purchases a stamping machine for use in the firm's workshop for £2,000 (ignore VAT) on 1 January 2005. The company uses the reducing balance method of depreciation using a rate of 20% per annum. The financial year end is 31 December. The records for the first three years are shown below:

Dr		Machinery Account		Cr
2005		*£*		
Jan 1	Bank	2,000		

		Cash Book (payments side)		Cash	Bank
				£	*£*
2005					
Jan 1	Machinery				2,000

Exhibit 10.1 (continued)

No entry is made in the asset account for depreciation, instead the depreciation is shown accumulating in a separate account. The accounting entries are as follows:

Dr	Provision for Depreciation – Machinery Account		Cr
2005	£	*2005*	£
Dec 31 Balance c/d	400	Dec 31 Profit and loss	400
2006		*2006*	
Dec 31 Balance c/d	720	Jan 1 Balance b/d	400
		Dec 31 Profit and loss	320
	720		720
2007		*2007*	
Dec 31 Balance c/d	976	Jan 1 Balance b/d	720
		Dec 31 Profit and loss	256
	976		976
		2008	
		Jan 1 Balance b/d	976

Profit and Loss Account (extracts) for the year ended 31 December

	£
2005 Provision for depreciation: Machinery	400
2006 Provision for depreciation: Machinery	320
2007 Provision for depreciation: Machinery	256

Now the balance on the machinery account is shown on the balance sheet at the end of each year less the balance on the provision for depreciation account.

Balance Sheet (extracts) as at 31 December

	Cost	Depreciation to date	Net book value
	£	£	£
2005 Machinery	2,000	400	1,600
2006 Machinery	2,000	720	1,280
2007 Machinery	2,000	976	1,024

10.2   The disposal of an asset

Reason for accounting entries

Upon the sale of an asset, we will want to delete it from our accounts. This means that the cost of that asset needs to be taken out of the asset account. In addition, the depreciation of the asset which has been sold will have to be taken out of the depreciation provision. Finally, the profit and loss on sale, if any, will have to be calculated.

When we charge depreciation on a fixed asset we have to make estimates. We cannot be absolutely certain how long we will keep the asset in use, nor can we be certain, at the date of purchase, how much the asset will be sold for on disposal. Nor can we always estimate correctly. This means that, when the asset is disposed of, the cash received for it is usually different from our original estimate.

Accounting entries needed

On the sale of a fixed asset – for instance, machinery – the following entries are needed:

(A) Transfer the cost price of the asset sold to an assets disposal account (in this case a machinery disposals account):

>   *Debit* machinery disposals account.
>   *Credit* machinery account.

(B) Transfer the depreciation already charged to the assets disposal account:

>   *Debit* provision for depreciation: machinery.
>   *Credit* machinery disposals account.

(C) For remittance received on disposal:

>   *Debit* cash book.
>   *Credit* machinery disposals account.

(D) Transfer difference (amount to balance the account) to the profit and loss account. If the machinery disposals account shows a credit balance, it is a profit on sale:

>   *Debit* machinery disposals account.
>   *Credit* profit and loss account.

(E) If the machinery disposals account shows a debit balance, it is a loss on sale:

>   *Debit* profit and loss account.
>   *Credit* machinery disposals account.

These entries can be illustrated by looking at those needed if the machinery already shown in Exhibit 10.1 was sold. The records to 31 December 2007 show that the cost of the machine was £2,000 and a total of £976 has been written off as depreciation, leaving a net book value of £2,000 − £976 = £1,024. If, therefore, the machine is sold on 2 January 2008 for *more than* £1,024, a profit on sale will be made. If, on the other hand, the machine is sold for *less than* £1,024, then a loss on disposal will be incurred.

Exhibit 10.2 shows the entries needed when the machine has been sold for £1,070 and therefore a profit on sale has been made. Exhibit 10.3 shows where the machine has been sold for £950, thus incurring a loss on sale. In both cases the sale is on 2 January 2008 and no depreciation is charged for the two days' ownership in 2008.

While it is normal for journal entries to be shown first, followed by the double entry transactions, many students have difficulty dealing with journal entries. The authors, having experienced their own students meeting this problem, believe that the difficulty arises because students often think in terms of the debits and credits in accounts. Instead, they should think of the journal simply as a form of written instruction stating which account is to be debited and which account is to be credited, with a description of the transaction involved.

To try to help you to avoid this sort of problem with journal entries, we will first show the double entry then write up the journal for those entries. In all cases the letters (A) to (E) relate to the entries given above.

Exhibit 10.2

Assets sold at a profit

Machinery Account GL1

2005		£	2008			£
Jan 1	Bank	2,000	Jan 2	Machinery disposals (A)		2,000

Provision for Depreciation: Machinery Account GL2

2008			£	2008		£
Jan 2	Machinery disposals	(B)	976	Jan 1	Balance b/d	976

Machinery Disposals Account GL3

2008				£	2008				£
Jan 2	Machinery	(A)		2,000	Jan 2	Provision for			
Dec 31	Profit and loss					depreciation	(B)		976
	(Profit on disposal)	(D)		46	Jan 2	Bank	(C)		1,070
				2,046					2,046

Cash Book (receipts side) CB1

			Cash £	Bank £
2005				
Jan 1	Machinery	(C)		1,070

Profit and Loss Account for the year ended 31 December 2008

		£
Gross profit		xxx
Add Profit on sale of machinery	(D)	46

The following are the journal entries for Exhibit 10.2.

The Journal

Date	Details			Folio	Dr	Cr
					£	£
2008 Jan 2	(i) Machinery disposals	(A)	GL3		2,000	
	Machinery	(A)	GL1			2,000
	Being transfer of cost of machine to machinery disposals account.					
Jan 2	(ii) Provision for depreciation: Machinery	(B)	GL2		976	
	Machinery disposals	(B)	GL3			976
	Being transfer of depreciation to date to machinery disposals account.					
Jan 2	(iii) Bank	(C)	CB1		1,070	
	Machinery disposals	(C)	GL3			1,070
	Being cheque received of £1,070 on sale of machinery.					
Jan 2	(iv) Machinery disposals	(D)	GL3		46	
	Profit and loss	(D)				46
	Being profit on disposal of machinery £46 transferred to profit and loss account.					

Exhibit 10.3

Assets sold at a loss

The double entry is shown first, followed by the journal entries.

Machinery Account   GL1

2005		£	2008			£
Jan 1	Bank	2,000	Jan 2	Machinery disposals (A)		2,000

Provision for Depreciation: Machinery Account   GL2

2008		£	2008		£
Jan 2	Machinery disposals (B)	976	Jan 1 Balance b/d		976

Machinery Disposals Account   GL3

2008			£	2008			£
Jan 2	Machinery	(A)	2,000	Jan 2	Provision for depreciation	(B)	976
				2	Bank	(C)	950
				Dec 31	Profit and loss (loss on disposal)	(D)	74
			2,000				2,000

Cash Book (receipts side)   CB1

2008			Cash £	Bank £
Jan 2	Machinery	(C)		950

Exhibit 10.3 (continued)

Profit and Loss Account for the year ended 31 December 2008

		£
Gross profit		xxx
Less Loss on sale of machinery	(D)	74

The journal entries are given below.

The Journal

Date	Details		Folio	Dr	Cr
2008				£	£
Jan 2	(i) Machinery disposals	(A)	GL3	2,000	
	Machinery	(A)	GL1		2,000
	Being transfer of cost of machine to machinery disposals account.				
Jan 2	(ii) Provision for depreciation: Machinery	(B)	GL2	976	
	Machinery disposals	(B)	GL3		976
	Being transfer of depreciation to date to machinery disposals account.				
Jan 2	(iii) Bank	(C)	CB1	950	
	Machinery disposals	(C)	GL3		950
	Being cheque received of £950 on sale of machinery.				
Jan 2	(iv) Profit and loss	(D)		74	
	Machinery disposals	(D)	GL3		74
	Being loss on disposal of machinery £74 transferred to profit and loss account.				

In many cases the disposal of an asset will mean that the asset has been sold; however, this may not always be the case. A car may be put in part exchange against the purchase of a new car. Here the disposal value is the exchange value. If a new car costing £10,000 was to be paid for by cash £6,000 and £4,000 for the old car put in exchange, then the disposal value of the old car is £4,000.

A further example is shown in the following exhibit.

Exhibit 10.4

On 1 January 2005, Langham Co. bought a Ford motor car costing £10,000 to be used by their personnel manager. It was decided to depreciate the car at 25% per annum using the reducing balance method. In January 2007 the car was contantly breaking down and was traded in and replaced by a new Renault vehicle. The garage allowed them a part exchange price of £5,000 for the Ford car. The new Renault vehicle cost £12,000 and the balance of £7,000 was paid for by cheque on 1 January 2007.

The book keeping entries are shown below, followed by the journal entries needed in January 2007 for the disposal and acquisition of the cars.

Motor Car Account   GL1

2005		£	2007		£
Jan 1	Bank: Ford car	10,000	Jan 1	Motor car disposals (A)	10,000
2007					
Jan 1	Motor car disposals (C)	5,000	Dec 31	Balance c/d	12,000
Jan 1	Bank: Renault car (E)	7,000			
		12,000			12,000
2008					
Jan 1	Balance (Renault) b/d	12,000			

Provision for Depreciation – Motor Car Account   GL2

2007		£	2007		£
Jan 1	Motor car disposals (B)	4,375	Jan 1	Balance b/d	4,375

Motor Car – Disposals Account   GL3

2007			£	2007			£
Jan 1	Motor car	(A)	10,000	Jan 1	Provision for depreciation	(B)	4,375
				Jan 1	Motor car (part exchange value)	(C)	5,000
				Jan 1	Profit and loss	(D)	625
			10,000				10,000

Profit and Loss Account

			£
Gross profit			xxx
Less Loss on motor car		(D)	625

Cash Book (payments side)   CB1

			Cash	Bank
			£	£
2007				
Jan 1	Motor car – Renault	(E)		7,000

The journal entries are as follows:

The Journal

Date	Details		Folio	Dr	Cr
2007				£	£
Jan 1	(i) Motor car disposals	(A)	GL3	10,000	
	Motor car	(A)	GL1		10,000
	Being transfer of cost price of Ford motor car to motor car disposals account.				
Jan 1	(ii) Provision for depreciation: Motor car	(B)	GL2	*4,375	
	Motor car disposals	(B)	GL3		4,375
	Being transfer of depreciation to date to motor car disposals account.				
Jan 1	(iii) Motor car account	(C)	GL1	5,000	
	Motor car disposals account	(C)	GL3		5,000
	Being part exchange value of Ford motor car traded in for new Renault car.				
Jan 1	(iv) Profit and loss	(D)		625	
	Motor car disposals account	(D)	GL3		625
	Being loss on part exchange of Ford motor car.				
Jan 1	(v) Motor car	(E)	GL1	7,000	
	Bank	(E)	CB1		7,000
	Being balance of money due on purchase of Renault motor car, cost price £12,000, less part exchange allowance of £5,000.				

* Workings: Depreciation Ford car cost £10,000, depreciate at 25% per annum using the reducing balance method:

	£
Year 2005 = 25% of 10,000	2,500
Year 2006 = 25% of (10,000 − 2,500) = 25% of 7,500	1,875
Depreciation to date	4,375

Similarly, a car may have been in an accident and now be worthless. If insured, the disposal value will be the amount received from the insurance company. If an asset is scrapped, the disposal value is that received from the sale of scrap, which may be nil.

10.3 Further examples of disposal of assets

So far the examples shown have deliberately been kept quite simple. Only one item of an asset has been shown in each case. In Exhibits 10.4 and 10.5, which give examples of more complicated cases, the journal entries will *not* be shown, only the double entry accounting records will be illustrated.

Exhibit 10.5

A machine is bought on 1 January 2005 for £1,000 and another on 1 October 2006 for £1,200. The first machine is sold on 2 January 2007 for £720. The firm's financial year ends on 31 December. The machinery is to be depreciated at 10%, using the straight line method and based on assets in existence at the end of each year, ignoring items sold during the year.

Dr		Machinery Account			Cr
2005		£	*2005*		£
Jan 1	Cash	1,000	Dec 31	Balance c/d	1,000
		1,000			1,000
2006			*2006*		
Jan 1	Balance b/d	1,000	Dec 31	Balance c/d	2,200
Oct 1	Cash	1,200			
		2,200			2,200
2007			*2007*		
Jan	Balance b/d	2,200	Jan 2	Disposals	1,000
			Dec 31	Balance c/d	1,200
		2,200			2,200
2008					
Jan 1	Balance b/d	1,200			

Dr		Provision for Depreciation – Machinery Account			Cr
2005		£	*2005*		£
Dec 31	Balance c/d	100	Dec 31	Profit and loss	100
		100			100
2006			*2006*		
Dec 31	Balance c/d	320	Jan 1	Balance b/d	100
			Dec 31	Profit and loss	220
		320			320
2007			*2007*		
Jan 2	Disposals of machinery		Jan 1	Balance b/d	320
	(2 years × 10% × 1,000)	200	Dec 31	Profit and loss	120
Dec 31	Balance c/d	240			
		440			440
			2008		
			Jan 1	Balance b/d	240

Dr		Disposals of Machinery Account			Cr
2007		£	*2007*		£
Jan 2	Machinery	1,000	Jan 2	Cash	720
			Jan 2	Provision for depreciation	200
			Dec 31	Profit and loss	80
		1,000			1,000

Profit and Loss Account (extracts) for the year ended 31 December

		£
	Less Expenses:	
2005	Provision for depreciation: Machinery	100
2006	Provision for depreciation: Machinery	220
2007	Provision for depreciation: Machinery	120
	Loss on machinery sold	80

Exhibit 10.5 (continued)

Balance Sheet (extracts) as at 31 December

		Cost	Depreciation to date	Net book value
		£	£	£
2005	Machinery	1,000	100	900
2006	Machinery	2,200	320	1,880
2007	Machinery	1,200	240	960

Another example can now be given. This is somewhat more complicated, first owing to a greater number of items, and second because the depreciation provisions are calculated on a proportionate bases, i.e. one month's depreciation for every one month's ownership.

Exhibit 10.6

A business whose financial year end is 31 December buys two motor vans on 1 January 2001, Van No. 1 for £16,000 and Van No. 2 for £10,000. It also buys another motor van, Van No. 3, on 1 July 2003 for £18,000 and another, Van No. 4, on 1 October 2003 for £14,400.

The first two motor vans are sold: Van No. 1 for £4,580 on 30 September 2004, and Van No. 2 for scrap £100 on 30 June 2005.

Depreciation is on the straight line method applied on a month by month basis, using 20% per annum, ignoring scrap value in this particular case when calculating depreciation per annum.

Show the extracts from the asset account, provision for depreciation account, disposal account and profit and loss accounts for the years ended 31 December 2001, 2002, 2003, 2004 and 2005 and the balance sheet extracts as at those dates.

Dr			Motor Vans Account		Cr
2001		£	**2001**		£
Jan 1	Cash – Van No. 1	16,000	Dec 31	Balance c/d	26,000
Jan 1	Cash – Van No. 2	10,000			
		26,000			26,000
2002			**2002**		
Jan 1	Balance b/d	26,000	Dec 31	Balance c/d	26,000
		26,000			26,000
2003			**2003**		
Jan 1	Balance b/d	26,000	Dec 31	Balance c/d	58,400
Jul 1	Cash – Van No. 3	18,000			
Oct 1	Cash – Van No. 4	14,400			
		58,400			58,400
2004			**2004**		
Jan 1	Balance b/d	58,400	Sep 30	Transfer to disposals (Van No. 1)	16,000
			Dec 31	Balance c/d	42,400
		58,400			58,400

Exhibit 10.6 (continued)

Dr		Motor Vans Account				Cr
2005		£	**2005**			£
Jan 1	Balance b/d	42,400	Jun 30	Transfer to disposals		
				(Van No. 2)		10,000
			Dec 31	Balance c/d		32,400
		42,400				42,400
2006						
Jan 1	Balance b/d	32,400				

Dr		Provision for Depreciation: Motor Vans Account				Cr
2001		£	**2001**			£
Dec 31	Balance c/d	5,200	Dec 31	Profit and loss		5,200
		5,200				5,200
2002			**2002**			
Dec 31	Balance c/d	10,400	Jan 1	Balance b/d		5,200
			Dec 31	Profit and loss		5,200
		10,400				10,400
2003			**2003**			
Dec 31	Balance c/d	18,120	Jan 1	Balance b/d		10,400
			Dec 31	Profit and loss		7,720
		18,120				18,120
2004			**2004**			
Sep 30	Transfer to disposals		Jan 1	Balance b/d		18,120
	(Van No. 1)	12,000	Dec 31	Profit and loss		10,880
Dec 31	Balance c/d	17,000				
		29,000				29,000
2005			**2005**			
Jun 30	Transfer to disposals		Jan 1	Balance b/d		17,000
	(Van No. 2)	9,000	Dec 31	Profit and loss		7,480
Dec 31	Balance c/d	15,480				
		24,480				24,480
			2006			
			Jan 1	Balance b/d		15,480

Dr		Disposals of Motor Vans Account				Cr
2004		£	**2004**			£
Sep 30	Transfer motor van	16,000	Sep 30	Provision for		
Dec 31	Profit and loss			depreciation		12,000
	(Profit on disposal)	580	Sep 30	Cash		4,580
		16,580				16,580
2005			**2005**			
Jun 30	Transfer motor van	10,000	Jun 30	Provision for		
				depreciation		9,000
			Jun 30	Cash		100
			Dec 31	Profit and loss		
				(Loss on disposal)		900
		10,000				10,000

Exhibit 10.6 (continued)

Workings:
Depreciation
provision

		£	£
2001	20% of £26,000		5,200
2002	20% of £26,000		5,200
2003	20% of £26,000 × 12 months	5,200	
	20% of £18,000 × 6 months	1,800	
	20% of £14,000 × 3 months	720	7,720
2004	20% of £42,400 × 12 months	8,480	
	20% of £16,000 × 9 months	2,400	10,880
2005	20% of £32,400 × 12 months	6,480	
	20% of £10,000 × 6 months	1,000	7,480

Workings: Transfers
of depreciation
provisions to
disposals account

Van No. 1   Bought 1 Jan 2001 Cost £16,000
Sold 30 September 2004
Period of ownership $3^3/4$ years
Depreciation provisions $3^3/4 \times 20\% \times £16,000 = £12,000$

Van No. 2   Bought 1 January 2001 Cost £10,000
Sold 30 June 2005
Period of ownership $4^1/2$ years
Depreciation provisions $4^1/2 \times 20\% \times £10,000 = £9,000$

Profit and Loss Account (extracts) for the year ended 31 December

		£
Gross profit (each year 2001, 2002, 2003)		xxx
Less Expenses:		
2001	Provision for depreciation: Motor vans	5,200
2002	Provision for depreciation: Motor vans	5,200
2003	Provision for depreciation: Motor vans	7,720
Gross profit for 2004		
2004	Gross profit	xxx
	Add Profit on sale of motor van sold	580
		xxx
	Less Expenses:	
	Provision for depreciation: Motor vans	10,880
		xxx
Gross profit for 2005		
2005	Gross profit	xxx
	Less Expenses:	

		£	£
	Provision for depreciation: Motor vans	7,480	
	Loss on sale of motor van	900	8,380
			xxx

Balance Sheet (extracts) as at 31 December

	Cost	Depreciation to date	Net book value
	£	£	£
2001 Motor vans	26,000	5,200	20,800
2002 Motor vans	26,000	10,400	15,600
2003 Motor vans	58,400	18,120	40,280
2004 Motor vans	42,400	17,000	25,400
2005 Motor vans	32,400	15,480	16,920

10.4 Accounting for VAT on fixed assets

Businesses not accountable for VAT

If a business is not VAT registered then it will suffer VAT on any goods or services that the business purchases (i.e. its **inputs**). In other words, the VAT will increase the cost of any goods purchased or services received and should be included in any such costs. With regard to the purchase of fixed assets any VAT charged should be added to the cost of the asset. Thus when entering the asset in the asset account the cost should include VAT, for example:

Exhibit 10.7

On 1 January 2003 Instant Printers & Co. purchased a new photocopier model No. Superior LT 957 at a cost of £3,000 plus VAT at 17.5%, making a total cost of £3,525. The book keeping entries, including the entries in the journal, would be as follows.

Note the double entry is shown first followed by the journal entries.

		GL1
Dr	Office Machinery Account	Cr

2003		£	
Jan 1	Bank	3,525	

Cash Book (payments side)			CB1

		Cash £	Bank £
2003			
Jan 1	Office machinery		3,525

The Journal

Date	Details	Folio	Dr	Cr
2003			£	£
Jan 1	Office machinery	GL1	3,525	
	Bank	CB1		3,525
	Being purchase of photocopier model No. Superior LT 957 at a cost of £3,525 including VAT. Authorised by company secretary – Authorisation No. Admin. 2003/45.			

Businesses registered for VAT

Businesses registered for VAT have to pay VAT on items of revenue expenditure and items of capital expenditure, except for certain specified items on which no one pays VAT – for example, books are free of VAT. However, although a VAT registered business has to pay VAT on its revenue and capital expenditure, the VAT can be reclaimed from the governmental authority (Customs and Excise in the UK).

This means that if a business buys a machine with a basic cost of £10,000, it will have to pay £10,000 + £1,175 (VAT at 17.5% on £10,000) = £11,750 for the machine. However, the business can claim a refund of the VAT paid: £1,750. Thus the actual cost to the business is the amount paid, £11,750, less refund claimed, £1,750 = £10,000. Exhibit 10.8 shows the journal and accounting entries.

Exhibit 10.8

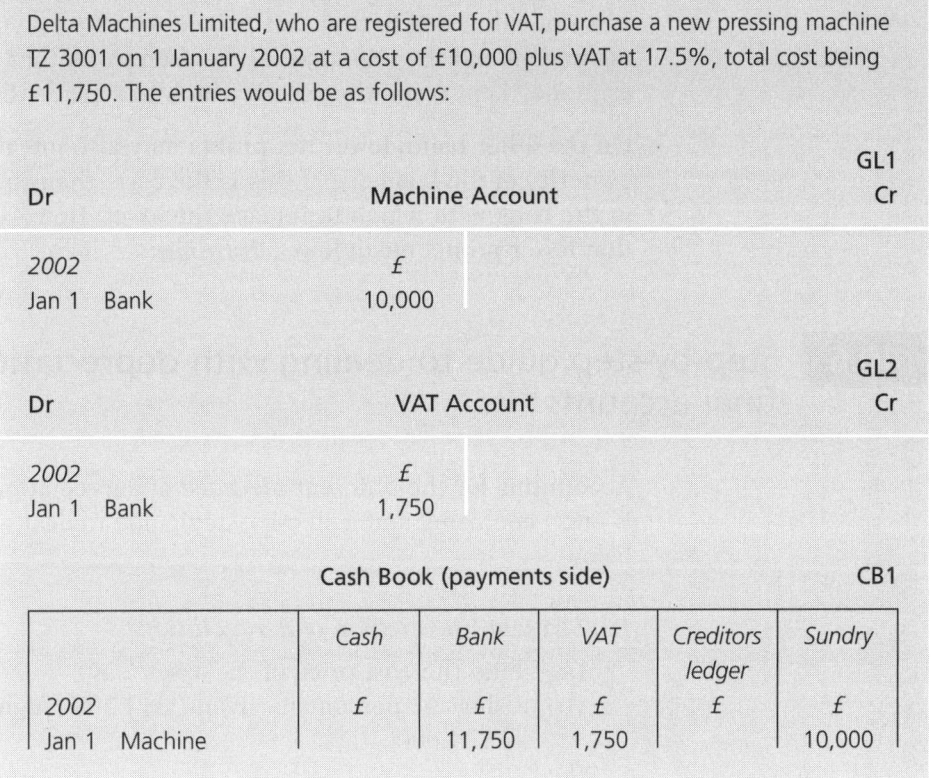

Delta Machines Limited, who are registered for VAT, purchase a new pressing machine TZ 3001 on 1 January 2002 at a cost of £10,000 plus VAT at 17.5%, total cost being £11,750. The entries would be as follows:

		GL1
Dr	Machine Account	Cr

2002		£	
Jan 1	Bank	10,000	

		GL2
Dr	VAT Account	Cr

2002		£	
Jan 1	Bank	1,750	

Cash Book (payments side)　　　　CB1

		Cash	Bank	VAT	Creditors ledger	Sundry
2002		£	£	£	£	£
Jan 1	Machine		11,750	1,750		10,000

Since Delta Machines Limited are registered for VAT you will notice that their VAT Account has been debited with £1,750, this amount will then be added to any VAT paid on purchases and expenses and offset against VAT charged on the company's sales.

The Journal

Date	Details	Folio	Dr	Cr
2002			£	£
Jan 1	Machine	GL 1	10,000	
	VAT	GL 2	1,750	
	Bank	CB 1		11,750
	Being purchase of pressing machine No. TZ 3001 for use in the machine shop. Note: Capital expenditure budget authorisation 2002/21.			

❗ *VAT is covered fully in Transaction Accounting, Chapter 23.*

10.5 Depreciation provisions and the replacements of assets

Making a provision for depreciation does not mean that money is invested somewhere to finance the replacement of the asset when it is put out of use. It is simply a book keeping entry, and the end result is that lower net profits are shown because the provisions have been charged to the profit and loss account.

It is not surprising to find that people who have not studied accounting misunderstand the situation. They often think that a provision is the same as money kept somewhere with which to replace the asset eventually.

On the other hand, lower net profits may also mean lower drawings by the owner(s) of the business. If this is the case, then there will be more money in the bank with which to replace the asset. However, there is no guarantee that lower profits mean lower drawings.

10.6 Step-by-step guide to dealing with depreciation in the final accounts

Accounting for the different methods of depreciation in the final accounts is often confusing and a step-by-step guide to deal with this topic is shown below.

1. *Straight line method of depreciation*
   - **(a)** Find the cost price of the asset (say)   £24,000
   - **(b)** Using the percentage given (say) 20% calculate 20% of £24,000   = £4,800

   then
   - **(c)** Charge £4,800 as an expense in the profit and loss account.
   - **(d)** In the balance sheet deduct the *total* depreciation (i.e. £4,800 from this year plus any depreciation deducted in previous years – see figure on the credit side in the trial balance (provision for depreciation account)) – from the cost price of the asset (£24,000) to arrive at the net book value (NBV): £24,000 *minus* £4,800 = £19,200 NBV.

2. *Reducing balance method of depreciation*
   - **(a)** Find the cost price of the asset (say)   £10,000
   - **(b)** Find the total amount of depreciation deducted to date (see credit side of the trial balance), say   £4,000
   - **(c)** Find the difference   £6,000
   - **(d)** Using percentage given (say 10%), calculate 10% of £6,000   £600

   then charge £600 as an expense in the profit and loss account.

In the balance sheet deduct the *total* depreciation (i.e. £600 from this year *plus* any depreciation deducted in previous years, i.e. £4,000 from the cost price (£10,000 less depreciation to date £4,600)) to arrive at the net book value of £5,400.

NEW TERM   **Provision for depreciation account**   The account where depreciation is accumulated for balance sheet purposes. In the balance sheet the cost price of the asset is shown less the depreciation to date to give the NBV.

10.1 The Boyd Delivery Service started in business on 1 January 2001 and on that date purchased two motor vans at a cost of £12,000 each; a further motor van was also purchased for £14,000 on 1 July 2001.

You are required to write up the motor vans account and the provision for depreciation account for the years ended 31 December 2001 and 2002. The straight line method of depreciation is used at a rate of 20% per annum, ignore scrap value in this case, and depreciation should be apportioned on the basis of one month's ownership needs one month's depreciation. (Ignore VAT.)

10.2 The Apex Production Company started business on 1 January 2003 and their financial year end was 31 December. The company purchased machinery over the following years:

2003	1 January	1 Machine costing £8,000
2004	1 July	2 Machines costing £5,000 each
	1 October	1 Machine costing £6,000
2006	1 April	1 Machine costing £2,000

Depreciation is at the rate of 20% per annum, using the straight line method and the machines are to be depreciated for each proportion of a year. (VAT is to be ignored.)

You are required to show:

(a) The machinery account.

(b) The provision for depreciation account.

(c) The balance sheet extracts for each of the years 2003, 2004, 2005 and 2006.

10.3X A company maintains its fixed assets at cost and also uses depreciation provision accounts, one for each type of asset in use. The following transactions in assets have taken place over the last few years:

2005	1 January	Bought machinery £6,400; fixtures £1,000
	1 July	Bought fixtures £2,000
2006	1 October	Bought machinery £7,200
	1 December	Bought fixtures £500

Machinery is to be depreciated at the rate of 25% per annum, and the fixtures at the rate of 20% per annum, using the reducing balance method. Depreciation is to be calculated on assets in existence at the end of the year, giving a full year's depreciation even though the asset was bought part way through the year. The company's financial year ends on 31 December and VAT is to be ignored.

You are required to show:

(a) The machinery account.

(b) The fixtures account.

(c)　The two separate provision for depreciation accounts.

(d)　The fixed asset section of the balance sheet at the end of each year, for the years ended 31 December 2005 and 2006.

10.4　Swift Secretarial Services decides to purchase computer equipment at a total cost of £28,000 on 1 April 2002. The computer equipment is to be depreciated at a rate of 50% per annum using the reducing balance method and charging a full year's depreciation in the year of purchase but none in the year of disposal. The company's financial year end is 31 December.

On 1 July 2005 the company decides to use the service of a computer consultancy to do all its computer work and sells the old equipment for £4,000.

(a)　You are required to show the book keeping entries recording the purchase, depreciation and disposal of the computer equipment. (Cash book not required and ignore VAT.)

(b)　Describe three causes of depreciation.

10.5X　A company's financial year runs from 1 January to 31 December. It decides to depreciate its plant at the rate of 20% per annum using the straight line method. Depreciation is charged for each month of ownership including the year of disposal. The following transactions in assets have taken place:

2004	1 January	Purchased plant costing £9,000
	1 October	Purchased plant costing £6,000
2006	1 July	Purchased plant costing £5,500
2007	30 September	Sold plant which had been bought for £9,000 on 1 January 2004 for the sum of £2,750

You are required to show:

(a)　The plant account.

(b)　The provision for depreciation account.

(c)　The plant disposal account.

(d)　The balance sheet extracts at the end of each year, namely, 2004, 2005, 2006 and 2007.

(*VAT is to be ignored.*)

10.6　A company maintains its fixed assets at cost. Depreciation provision accounts for each asset are kept. At 31 December 2008 the position was as follows:

	Total cost to date	Total depreciation to date
Machinery	£52,590	£25,670
Office furniture	£2,860	£1,490

The following additions were made during the financial year ended 31 December 2009:

Machinery £2,480, office furniture £320.
Some old machines bought in 2005 for £2,800 were sold for £800 during the year.

The rates of depreciation are:

Machinery 10%, office furniture 5%, using the straight line basis, calculated on the assets in existence at the end of each financial year irrespective of date of purchase.

You are required to show the asset and provision for depreciation accounts for the year ended 31 December 2009, the machinery disposals account and the balance sheet entries at that date.

10.7 On 1 April 2002 Jessop Printing Company commenced business and purchased the following assets:

2002

April 1	Computer equipment	£12,000
April 1	Machinery	£20,000
October 1	Furniture and fittings	£8,000

All the above purchases were subject to an addition of VAT at 17.5% (note that the company is registered for VAT and will be able to obtain a refund of VAT paid).

It was decided to depreciate the computer equipment at 50% per annum using the reducing balance method, and the machinery and furniture and fittings at 20% per annum using the straight line method. Assets are to be depreciated from the date of purchase and the company's financial year ends on 31 March.

You are required to enter the journal and accounting records as follows:

(a) Journal entries for the above transactions for the first year only. (*Narratives not required.*)

(b) The computer equipment account, machinery account, furniture and fittings account and VAT account for the years ended 31 March 2003 and 2004.

(c) The provision for depreciation – computer account; the provision for depreciation – machinery account; and the provision for depreciation – furniture and fittings account for the years ended 31 March 2003 and 2004.

(d) Balance sheet extracts of the fixed assets as at 31 March 2003 and 2004. (*Entries in the bank account are not required.*)

10.8X Hawkins Manufacturing Services started in business on 1 January 2002 and purchased the following assets:

2002

January 1	Plant and equipment	£24,000
January 1	Office equipment	£12,500

Both the above purchases were subject to an addition of VAT at 17.5%. (Note that the company is registered for VAT and will be able to claim a refund of VAT paid.)

The following year further assets (subject to VAT at 17.5%) were purchased as follows:

2003
October 1   Computer Equipment   £14,000
December 1   Plant and Equipment   £5,000

It was decided to depreciate the plant and equipment and the office equipment at 20% per annum and the computer equipment at 25% using the reducing balance method. Depreciation is to be calculated on assets in existence at the end of each year irrespective of the date of acquisition. The financial year end of the business is 31 December.

You are required to show the accounting entries for the years ended 31 December 2002 and 2003. (Note that journal entries are not required, nor is the bank account.) As no other entries concerning VAT are available to you, the VAT account is not to have its balances carried down.

10.9X
(i)   Explain what is meant by the term 'depreciation' and describe two methods of depreciation.

(ii) In what ways do you consider the concept of consistency applies to depreciation?

(iii) What are the main accounting requirements of SSAP 12 'Accounting for Depreciation'?

(iv) Explain the procedure for reclaiming VAT charged on fixed assets if a business is registered for VAT.

10.10X
The financial year of Muldane plc ended on 31 May 2009. At 1 June 2008 the company owned motor vehicles costing £124,000 which had been depreciated by a total of £88,000. On 1 August 2008 Muldane plc sold motor vehicles which had cost £54,000 and which had been depreciated by £49,000 for £3,900 cash and purchased new motor vehicles costing £71,000.

It is the policy of Muldane plc to depreciate its motor vehicles at 35% per annum using the reducing balance method. A full year's depreciation is charged on all motor vehicles in use at the end of each year. No depreciation is charged for the year on assets disposed of during the year.

Show the following accounts as they would appear in the ledger of Muldane plc for the year ended 31 May 2009 only:

(i)   The motor vehicles account

(ii) The provision for depreciation – motor vehicles account, and

(iii) The assets disposal account.

(Association of Accounting Technicians)

CHAPTER 11

Bad debts and provisions for bad debts

AIMS

■ To understand how bad debts can be written off.

■ To make provisions for possible bad debts.

■ To understand the accounting entries for bad debts recovered.

■ To show an aged debtors schedule.

11.1 Bad debts

If a firm finds that it is impossible to collect a debt, then that debt should be written off as a **bad debt**. This could happen if the debtor is suffering a loss in his business, or may even have gone bankrupt and is thus unable to pay the debt. A bad debt is, therefore, an expense of the firm.

An example of debts being written off as bad is shown in Exhibit 11.1.

Exhibit 11.1

We sold £50 goods to K Lee on 5 January 2005, but he became bankrupt. On 16 February 2005 we sold £240 goods to T Young. He managed to pay £200 on 17 May 2005, but it became obvious that he would never be able to pay the final £40.

When drawing up our final accounts to 31 December 2005, we decided to write these off as bad debts. The accounting entries are:

Accounting entries	Explanation
Debit: Bad debts account	To transfer the amount of unpaid debt to the bad debts account.
Credit: Debtor's account	To reduce the liability of the debtor who is unable to settle the debt.
Debit: Profit and loss account	To record the amount of bad debts of the period concerned.
Credit: Bad debts account	To transfer the amount of bad debts to profit and loss account.

The accounts would appear as follows:

Dr		K Lee Account			Cr
2005		£	2005		£
Jan 5	Sales	50	Dec 31	Bad debts	50

Dr		T Young Account			Cr
2005		£	2005		£
Feb 16	Sales	240	May 17	Cash	200
			Dec 31	Bad debts	40
		240			240

Dr		Bad Debts Account			Cr
2005		£	2005		£
Dec 31	K Lee	50	Dec 31	Profit and loss a/c	90
31	T Young	40			
		90			90

Profit and Loss Account (extract) for the year ended 31 December 2005

		£
Gross profit		xxx
Less Expenses:		
Bad debts	90	90

11.2 Provisions for bad debts

Let us look at the accounts of K Clark who started in business on 1 January 2000 and has just completed his first year of trading on 31 December 2000.

He has sold goods for £50,000 which cost him £36,000, so his gross profit was £50,000 − £36,000 = £14,000. However, included in the £50,000 sales was a credit sale to C Yates for £250. C Yates has died, leaving no money, and he had not paid his account. The £250 debt is, therefore, a bad debt and should be charged in the profit and loss account as an expense.

Besides that debt, a credit sale of £550 on 1 December 2000 to L Hall is unlikely to get paid. Clark cannot yet be certain about this, but he has been told by others that Hall had not paid his debts to other businesses. As Clark had given three months credit to Hall, the debt is not repayable until 28 February 2001. However, the final accounts for the year 2000 are to be drawn up in January 2001, because the bank wants to see them. Clark cannot wait until after 28 February 2001 to see if the debt of £550 owing by Hall will be a bad debt.

What, therefore, can Clark do? When he shows the bank his final accounts, he wants to achieve the following objectives:

(a) To charge as expenses in the profit and loss account for that year an amount representing sales of *that year* for which he will never be paid.

(b) To show in the balance sheet a figure that is as near as possible to the true value of debtors at the balance sheet date.

He can carry out (a) above by writing off Yates's debt of £250 and then charging it as an expense in his profit and loss account.

For (b) he cannot yet write off Hall's debt of £550 as a bad debt, because he is not yet certain that it is a bad debt. If he does nothing about it, then the debtors shown on the balance sheet will include a debt that is probably of no value. The debtors on 31 December 2000, after deducting Yates's £250 bad debt, amounted to £10,000.

The answer to this is as follows:

K Clark
Trading and Profit and Loss Account
for the year ended 31 December 2000

	£	£
Sales		50,000
Less Cost of goods sold:		36,000
Gross profit		14,000
Less Expenses:		
Other expenses	5,000	
Bad debts	250	
Provision for bad debts	550	5,800
Net profit		8,200

K Clark
Balance Sheet as at 31 December 2000 (extracts)

	£	£
Debtors	10,000	
Less Provision for bad debts	550	9,450

Exactly how we will do the double entry for this is explained in Section 11.4. What we have achieved so far is to show bad debts and **provision for bad debts** as an expense in the year when the sales were made. The debtors are also shown at probably what is their true value.

11.3   Provisions for bad debts: estimating provisions

The estimates of provisions for bad debts can be made:

- by looking into each debt, and estimating which ones will be bad debts;
- by estimating, on the basis of experience, what percentage of the debts will result in bad debts.

It is well known that the longer a debt is owed, the more likely it will become a bad debt. Some firms draw up an ageing debtors' schedule, showing how long debts have been owed. Older debtors need higher percentage estimates of bad debts than newer debtors. Exhibit 11.2 gives an example of such an ageing schedule.

Exhibit 11.2

Ageing Debtors' Schedule			
Period debt owing	*Amount*	*Estimated percentage doubtful*	*Provision for bad debts*
	£		£
Less than 1 month	5,000	1	50
1 month to 2 months	3,000	3	90
2 months to 3 months	800	5	40
3 months to 6 months	200	20	40
Over 6 months	160	50	80
	9,160		300

A provision may be a specific amount, e.g. a £5,000 provision to cover the specified debts of W Cooper £3,000 and T Smith £2,000. On the other hand it may be a general provision not linked to any specified debts, and usually calculated in a percentage fashion.

11.4 Accounting entries for provisions for bad debts

When the decision has been taken on the amount of provision to be made, the accounting entries needed for the provision are:

The year in which *provision is first made:*

> *Debit:* Profit and loss account with the amount of provision
> *Credit:* Provision for bad debts account

Exhibit 11.3 shows the entries needed for a provision for bad debts.

Exhibit 11.3

As at 31 December 2003 the debtors figure amounted to £10,000 after writing off £422 of definite bad debts. It is estimated that 2% of debts (i.e. £10,000 × 2% = £200) will prove to be bad debts, and it is decided to make a provision for these. The accounts would appear as follows:

**Profit and Loss Account
for the year ended 31 December 2003 (extracts)**

		£	£
Gross profit			xxx
Less Expenses:			
Bad debts		422	
Provision for bad debts		200	622

Dr		Provision for Bad Debts Account		Cr

2003		£	2003		£
Dec 31	Balance c/d	200	Dec 31	Profit and loss a/c	200
			2004		
			Jan 1	Balance b/d	200

In the balance sheet, the balance on the provision for bad debts will be deducted from the total of debtors:

Balance Sheet (extracts) 31 December 2003

	£	£
Current assets		
Debtors	10,000	
Less Provision for bad debts	200	9,800

11.5 Increasing the provision

Let us suppose that, for the same firm as in Exhibit 11.3, the bad debts provision at the end of the following year (31 December 2004) needed to be increased, because the provision had been kept at 2% but the debtors had risen to £12,000. Not included in the figure of £12,000 debtors is £884 in respect of debts which had already been written-off as bad debts during the year. A provision of £200 had been brought forward from the *previous* year, but we now want a total provision of £240 (i.e. 2% of £12,000). All that is needed is a provision for an extra £40. The double entry will be:

Debit: Profit and loss account
Credit: Provision for bad debts account

Profit and Loss Account for the year ended 31 December 2004

	£	£
Gross profit		xxx
Less Expenses:		
Bad debts	884	
Provision for bad debts	40	

Dr		Provision for Bad Debts Account		Cr
2004	£	*2004*		£
Dec 31 Balance c/d	240	Jan 1 Balance b/d		200
		Dec 31 Profit and loss a/c		40
	240			240
		2005		
		Jan 1 Balance b/d		240

The balance sheet as at 31 December 2004 will appear as:

Balance Sheet (extracts) 31 December 2004

	£	£
Current Assets		
Debtors	12,000	
Less Provision for bad debts	240	11,760

The provision is shown as a credit balance. To reduce it, we would need a debit entry in the provision account. The credit would be in the profit and loss account. Again, using the example above, let us assume that on 31 December 2005, the debtors figure had fallen to £10,500 but the provision remained at 2%, i.e. £210 (£10,500 × 2%). As the provision had previously been £240, it now needs a reduction of £30. Bad debts of £616 had already been written off during the year and are not included in the debtors figure of £10,500. The double entry is:

Debit: Provision for bad debts account
Credit: Profit and loss account

Profit and Loss Account for the year ended 31 December 2005

		£
Gross profit		xxx
Add Reduction in provision for bad debts		30
		xxx
Less Expenses:		
Bad debts	616	616

Dr			Provision for Bad Debts Account		Cr
2005		£	*2005*		£
Dec 31	Profit and loss a/c	30	Jan 1 Balance b/d		240
31	Balance c/d	210			
		240			240
			2006		
			Jan 1 Balance b/d		210

The balance sheet will appear:

Balance Sheet (extracts) 31 December 2005

	£	£
Current Assets		
Debtors	10,500	
Less Provision for bad debts	210	10,290

The main points to remember about provisions for bad debts are:

■ *Year 1: Provision first made*

    (a) Debit profit and loss account with full provision.
    (b) Show in balance sheet as a deduction from debtors.

■ *Later years*

    (a) Only the increase, or decrease, in the provision is shown in the profit and loss account.

       To increase: Debit the profit and loss account, credit the provision for bad debts account.
       To decrease: Credit the profit and loss account, debit the provision for bad debts account.

    (b) The balance sheet will show the amended figure of the provision as a deduction from debtors.

11.7 A worked example

Let us now look at a comprehensive example in Exhibit 11.4.

Exhibit 11.4

A business was started on 1 January 2002 and its financial year end is 31 December annually. A table of debtors – the bad debts written off and the estimated bad debts at the rate of 2% of debtors at the end of each year – is given. The double entry accounts, and the extracts from the final accounts follow.

Year to 31 December	Debtors at end of year (after bad debts written off)	Bad debts written off during year	Debts thought at end of year to be impossible to collect: 2% of debtors
	£	£	£
2002	6,000	423	120 (2% of £6,000)
2003	7,000	510	140 (2% of £7,000)
2004	7,750	604	155 (2% of £7,750)
2005	6,500	610	130 (2% of £6,500)

Dr		Provision for Bad Debts Account			Cr
2002		£	*2002*		£
Dec 31	Balance c/d	120	Dec 31	Profit and loss a/c	120
2003			*2003*		
Dec 31	Balance c/d	140	Jan 1	Balance b/d	120
			Dec 31	Profit and loss a/c	20
		140			140
2004			*2004*		
Dec 31	Balance c/d	155	Jan 1	Balance b/d	140
			Dec 31	Profit and loss a/c	15
		155			155
2005			*2005*		
Dec 31	Profit and loss a/c	25	Jan 1	Balance b/d	155
31	Balance c/d	130			
		155			155
			2006		
			Jan 1	Balance b/d	130

Dr		Bad Debts Account			Cr
2002		£	*2002*		£
Dec 31	Debtors	423	Dec 31	Profit and loss a/c	423
2003			*2003*		
Dec 31	Debtors	510	Dec 31	Profit and loss a/c	510
2004			*2004*		
Dec 31	Debtors	604	Dec 31	Profit and loss a/c	604
2005			*2005*		
Dec 31	Debtors	610	Dec 31	Profit and loss a/c	610

Exhibit 11.4 (continued)

Profit and Loss Account(s) (extracts) for the year ended

		£	£
Gross profit for 2002, 2003, 2004			xxx
2002	*Less* Expenses:		
	Bad debts	423	
	Provision for bad debts (increase)	120	543
2003	*Less* Expenses:		
	Bad debts	510	
	Provision for bad debts (increase)	20	530
2004	*Less* Expenses:		
	Bad debts	604	
	Provision for bad debts (increase)	15	619
2005	Gross profit for 2005		xxx
	Add Reduction in provision for bad debts		25
			xxx
	Less Bad debts		610
			xxx

Balance Sheet (extracts) as at 31 December

		£	£
2002	Debtors	6,000	
	Less Provision for bad debts	120	5,880
2003	Debtors	7,000	
	Less Provision for bad debts	140	6,860
2004	Debtors	7,750	
	Less Provision for bad debts	155	7,595
2005	Debtors	6,500	
	Less Provision for bad debts	130	6,370

You may see the term **provision for doubtful debts**. This means exactly the same as provision for bad debts. It is simply that some accountants prefer the other wording.

11.8 Bad debts recovered

It is not uncommon for a debt written off in previous years to be recovered in later years. When this occurs, the book keeping procedures are as follows:

First, reinstate the debt by making the following entries:

Debit: Debtor's account
Credit: Bad debts recovered account

The reason for reinstating the debt in the ledger account of the debtor is to have a detailed history of the account as a guide for granting credit in future. By the time a debt is written off as bad, it will be recorded in the debtor's ledger account. Therefore, when such a debt is recovered, it must also be shown in the debtor's ledger account.

When cash or cheque is later received from the debtor in settlement of the account, or part thereof:

Debit: Cash/Bank
Credit: Debtor's account

with the amount received.

At the end of the financial year, the credit balance on the bad debts recovered account will be transferred to either the bad debts account or direct to the credit side of the profit and loss account. The net effect of either of these entries is the same since the bad debts account will be transferred to the profit and loss account at the end of the financial year. In other words, the net profit will be the same no matter which method is used.

11.9 Step-by-step guide to dealing with bad debts and provisions for bad debts

Dealing with bad debts written off and provision for bad debts in the final accounts can cause confusion, especially when either increasing or reducing the provision. A step-by-step guide is given below to help with this topic:

1. **Bad debts written off**
   Simply write off the debt as an expense in the profit and loss account.

2. **Provision for bad debts**

   Creation
   (a) Decide on the amount of provision to be created (say 1% of debtors of £5,000 = £50), *then*:
      (i) charge the provision £50 to profit and loss account as an expense;
      (ii) in the balance sheet deduct provision £50 from debtors, i.e.

Debtors	5,000	
Less Provision for bad debts	50	4,950

   Increase in provision
   (a) Calculate the new provision (i.e. this year's).
   (b) Find out the old provision (i.e. last year's – look in trial balance, credit side).
   (c) Find the difference, *then*
      (i) charge the *difference* only to profit and loss account
      (ii) deduct the *new provision* from debtors in balance sheet.

   Reduction in provision
   (a) Calculate the new provision (i.e. this year's).
   (b) Find out the old provision (i.e. last year's – look in trial balance, credit side).
   (c) Find the difference, *then*
      (i) add back the difference as *income* in profit and loss account
      (ii) deduct the *new provision* from debtors in balance sheet.

NEW TERMS   **Bad debts**   A debt owing to a business which is unlikely to be paid.

Bad debt recovered   A debt that has previously been written off which is subsequently paid by the debtor.

Provision for bad debts   An account showing the expected amounts of debtors, who at the balance sheet date, may not be able to pay their outstanding accounts.

11.1 Data Computer Services commenced in business on 1 January 2004 but during their first year of trading the following debts were found to be bad and it was decided to write them off as bad:

2004

April 30	H Gordon	£1,110
August 31	D Bellamy Ltd	£640
October 31	J Alderton	£120

On 31 December 2004 the schedule of remaining debtors, amounting in total to £68,500, was examined, and it was decided to make a provision for bad debts of £2,200.

You are required to show:

(a) The bad debts account and the provision for bad debts accounts.

(b) The charge to the profit and loss account.

(c) The relevant extracts from the balance sheet as at 31 December 2004.

11.2 A business has always made a provision for bad debts at the rate of 5% of debtors. On 1 January 2003 the provision for this, brought forward from the previous year, amounted to £2,600.

During the year to 31 December 2003 the bad debts written off amounted to £540. On 31 December 2003 the remaining debtors totalled £62,000 and the usual provision for bad debts is to be made.

You are to show:

(a) The bad debts account for the year ended 31 December 2003.

(b) The provision for bad debts account for the year.

(c) Extract from the profit and loss account for the year.

(d) The relevant extract from the balance sheet as at 31 December 2003.

11.3 A business started trading on 1 January 2006. During the two years ended 31 December 2006 and 2007 the following debts were written off to the bad debts account on the dates stated:

31 August 2006	W Best	£85
30 September 2006	S Avon	£140
28 February 2007	L J Friend	£180
31 August 2007	N Kelly	£60
30 November 2007	A Oliver	£250

On 31 December 2006 there had been a total of debtors remaining of £40,500. It was decided to make a provision for doubtful debts of £550. On 31 December 2007 there had been a total of debtors remaining of £47,300. It was decided to make a provision for doubtful debts of £600. You are required to show:

(a) The bad debts account and the provision for bad debts account for each of the two years.

(b) The relevant extracts from the balance sheets as at 31 December 2006 and 2007.

11.4X A business, which started trading on 1 January 2005, adjusts its bad debt provisions at the end of each year on a percentage basis, but each year the percentage rate is adjusted in accordance with the current 'economic climate'. The following details are available for the three years ended 31 December 2005, 2006 and 2007.

Year	Bad debts written off to 31 December	Debtors at 31 December	Per cent provision for bad debts
	£	£	
2005	656	22,000	5
2006	1,805	40,000	7
2007	3,847	60,000	6

You are required to show:

(a) Bad debts accounts for each of the three years.

(b) Provision for bad debts accounts for each of the three years.

(c) Balance sheet extracts as at 31 December 2005, 2006 and 2007.

11.5 A business started on 1 January 2003, and its financial year end is 31 December.

Date: 31 Dec	Total Debtors	Profit and Loss	Dr/Cr	Final Figure for Balance Sheet
2003	7,000			
2004	8,000			
2005	6,000			
2006	7,000			

The table shows the figure for debtors appearing in a trader's books on 31 December of each year from 2003 to 2006. The provision for bad debts is to be 1% of debtors from 31 December 2003. Complete the table indicating the amount to be debited or credited to the profit and loss accounts for the year ended on each 31 December, and the amount for the final figure of debtors to appear in the balance sheet on each date.

11.6X A business started on 1 January 2005 and its financial year end is 31 December annually. The table shows the debtors, the bad debts written off and the estimated bad debts at the end of year.

Year to 31 December	Debtors at end of year (after bad debts written off)	Bad Debts written off during the year	Debts thought at end of year to be impossible to collect
2005	12,000	298	100
2006	15,000	386	130
2007	14,000	344	115
2008	18,000	477	150

Show the items in the double entry accounts, as well as the extracts from the profit and loss account for each year and the balance sheet extracts.

11.7 (a) On 1 January 2004 there was a balance of £2,500 in the provision for bad debts account and it was decided to maintain the provision at 5% of the debtors at the end of each year.

The debtors on 31 December each year were as follows:

	£
2004	60,000
2005	40,000
2006	40,000

You are required to show the accounting entries for the three years ended 31 December 2004, 2005 and 2006 as follows:
   (i)   the provision for bad debts account
   (ii) the profit and loss accounts
   (iii) the balance sheet extracts.

(b) Explain the difference between bad debts and a provision for bad debts.

(c) As more and more businesses are experiencing difficulty collecting debts they find it important to create a provision for bad debts to provide for such a contingency. What is the purpose of creating such a provision and which accounting concept covers this area?

11.8 E Chivers commenced business on 1 January 2007 and makes his accounts to 31 December every year. For the year ended 31 December 2007, bad debts written off amounted to £1,200. It was also found necessary to create a provision for doubtful debts of £2,000.

In 2008, debts amounting to £1,600 proved bad and were written off. Mrs P Iles, whose debt of £350 was written off as bad in 2007, settled her account in full on 30 November 2008. As at 31 December 2008 total debts outstanding were £56,000. It was decide to bring the provision up to 5% of this figure on that date.

In 2009, £2,350 debts were written off during the year, and another recovery of £150 was made in respect of debts written off in 2007. As at 31 December 2009, total debts outstanding were £42,000. The provision for doubtful debts is to be maintained at 5% of this figure.

You are required, for the years 2007, 2008, and 2009, to show the:

(a) bad debts account
(b) bad debts recovered account
(c) provision for bad debts account
(d) extract from the profit and loss account.

CHAPTER 12

Other adjustments for final accounts

AIMS

■ To be able to adjust expense accounts for accruals and prepayments.

■ To be able to adjust revenue accounts for amounts owing.

■ To ascertain the amounts of expense and revenue items to be shown in the profit and loss account.

■ To show accruals, prepayments and revenue debtors in the balance sheet.

■ To be able to enter up the necessary accounts for goods taken for own use.

■ To know how to prepare final accounts for service sector organisations.

12.1 The final accounts so far

The trading and profit and loss account that has been considered until now has taken sales for a period and deducted *all* the expenses for that period, resulting in either a net profit or a net loss.

So far, it has been assumed that the expenses incurred belonged exactly to the period of trading and profit and loss account. If, for example, the trading and profit and loss account for the year ended 31 December 2005 was being drawn up, then the rent paid, as shown in the trial balance, was exactly that due for 2005, there being no rent owing at the beginning of 2005 nor any owing at the end of 2005, nor had any rent been paid in advance. It is easier to consider a simple example at first to understand the principles of final accounts.

12.2 Adjustments needed for expenses owing or paid in advance

Not all businesses pay their rent exactly on time and, indeed, some businesses prefer to pay their rent in advance. The following examples will illustrate the adjustments necessary if expenses are either owing, or paid in advance, at the end of a financial period.

Two firms in Oxford rent their premises for £1,200 per year:

1. Firm A pays £1,000 during the year and owes £200 rent at the end of the year:

   Rent expense used up during the year = £1,200
   Rent actually paid in the year   = £1,000

2. Firm B pays £1,300 during the year, including £100 in advance for the following year:

   Rent expense used up during the year = £1,200
   Rent actually paid for in the year   = £1,300

A profit and loss account for the 12 months needs 12 months' rent as an expense (= £1,200). This means that in the above two examples the double entry accounts will have to be adjusted.

In all the examples in this chapter the trading and profit and loss accounts are for the period ended 31 December 2005.

12.3 Accrued expenses (i.e. expenses owing)

Assume that a rent of £1,000 per year was payable at the end of every three months and that the rent was not always paid on time. Details were:

Amount	Rent due	Rent paid
£250	31 March 2005	31 March 2005
£250	30 June 2005	2 July 2005
£250	30 September 2005	4 October 2005
£250	31 December 2005	5 January 2006

The rent account appeared as:

Dr		Rent Account		Cr
2005		£		
Mar 31	Cash	250		
Jul 2	Cash	250		
Oct 4	Cash	250		

The rent paid on 5 January 2006 will appear in the books of the year 2006 as part of the double entry.

The expense for 2005 is obviously £1,000, as that is the year's rent, and this is the amount needed to be transferred to the profit and loss account. But if £1,000 was put on the credit side of the rent account (the debit being in the profit and loss account) the account would not balance. We would have £1,000 on the credit side of the account and only £750 on the debit side.

To make the account balance the £250 rent owing for 2005, but paid in 2006, must be carried down to 2006 as a credit balance because it is a liability on 31 December 2005. Instead of rent owing it could be called rent accrued, or just simply **an accrual**. The completed account can now be shown:

Dr			Rent Account		Cr
2005		£	*2005*		£
Mar 31	Cash	250	Dec 31	Profit and loss	1,000
Jul 2	Cash	250			
Oct 4	Cash	250			
Dec 31	Accrued c/d	250			
		1,000			1,000
			2006		
			Jan 1	Accrued b/d	250

The balance c/d has been described as accrued c/d, rather than as a balance. This is to explain what the balance is for; it is for an **accrued expense**.

<h2>12.4   Prepaid expenses</h2>

Insurance for a firm is at the rate of £840 a year, starting from 1 January 2005. The firm has agreed to pay this at the rate of £210 every three months. However, payments were not made at the correct times. Details were:

Amount	Insurance due	Insurance paid
£210	31 March 2005	£210 28 February 2005
£210 £210	30 June 2005 30 September 2005	£420 31 August 2005
£210	31 December 2005	£420 18 November 2005

The insurance account for the year ended 31 December 2005 will be shown in the books as:

Dr			Insurance Account	Cr
2005		£		
Feb 28	Bank	210		
Aug 31	Bank	420		
Nov 18	Bank	420		

The last payment of £420, however, is not just for 2005; it can be split as £210 for the three months to 31 December 2005 and £210 for the three months ended 31 March 2006. For a period of 12 months the cost of insurance is £840 and this is, therefore, the figure that must be transferred to the profit and loss account.

If this is entered, then the amount needed to balance the account will be £210, and at 31 December 2005 this is a benefit paid for but not used up; it is an asset and needs to be carried forward as such to 2006, i.e. as a debit balance. It is a **prepaid expense**.

The account can now be completed:

Dr			Insurance Account			Cr
2005		£	2005			£
Feb 28	Bank	210	Dec 31	Profit and loss		840
Aug 31	Bank	420				
Nov 18	Bank	420	Dec 31	Prepaid c/d		210
		1,050				1,050
2006						
Jan 1	Prepaid b/d	210				

Prepayment will also happen when items other than purchases are bought for use in the business and are not fully used up in the period. For instance, packing materials are normally not entirely used up over the period in which they are bought, and there is usually a stock of packing materials in hand at the end of the period. This stock is, therefore, a form of prepayment and needs to be carried down to the following period in which it will be used. This can be seen in the following example:

Year ended 31 December 2005:
Packing materials bought in the year   £2,200.
Stock of packing materials in hand as at 31 December 2005   £400.

Looking at the example, it can be seen that in 2005 the packing materials used up will have been £2,200 – £400 = £1,800. We will still have a stock of £400 packing materials at 31 December 2005 to be carried forward to 2006. The £400 stock of packing materials will be carried forward as an asset balance (debit balance) to 2006.

Dr			Packing Materials Account			Cr
2005		£	2005			£
Dec 31	Bank	2,200	Dec 31	Profit and loss		1,800
			31	Stock c/d		400
		2,200				2,200
2006						
Jan 1	Stock b/d	400				

The stock of packing materials is not added to the stock of unsold goods in hand in the balance sheet, but is added to the other prepayments of expenses.

12.5 Revenue owing at the end of period

The **revenue** owing for sales is already shown in the books. These are the debit balances on our customers' accounts, i.e. debtors. There may be other kinds of revenue, all of which have not been received by the end of the period, e.g. rent receivable, as in the following example.

A firm's warehouse is larger than it needs. They rent part of it to another firm for £800 per annum. Details for the year ended 31 December were as follows:

Amount	Rent due	Rent received
£200	31 March 2005	4 April 2005
£200	30 June 2005	6 July 2005
£200	30 September 2005	9 October 2005
£200	31 December 2005	7 January 2006

The account for 2005 will appear as:

Dr		Rent Receivable Account		Cr
		2005		£
		Apr 4 Bank		200
		Jul 6 Bank		200
		Oct 9 Bank		200

The rent received of £200 on 7 January 2006 will be entered in the books in 2006.

Any rent paid by the firm would be charged as a debit to the profit and loss account. Any rent received, being the opposite, is transferred to the credit of the profit and loss account, as it is a revenue.

The amount to be transferred for 2006 is that earned for the 12 months, i.e. £800. The rent received account is completed by carrying down the balance owing as a debit balance to 2006. The £200 owing is an asset on 31 December 2005.

The rent receivable account can now be completed:

Dr			Rent Receivable Account			Cr
2005		£	2005			£
Dec 31 Profit and loss		800	Apr 4	Bank		200
			Jul 6	Bank		200
			Oct 9	Bank		200
		___	Dec 31	Accrued c/d		200
		800				800
2006						
Jan 1 Accrued b/d		200				

12.6 Expenses and revenue account balances and the balance sheet

In all the cases listed dealing with adjustments in the final accounts, there will still be a balance on each account after the preparation of the trading and profit and loss accounts. All such balances remaining should appear in the balance sheet. The only question left is where and how they should be shown.

The amounts owing for expenses are usually added together and shown as one figure. These could be called *expense creditors*, *expenses owing* or *accrued expenses*. The item would appear under current liabilities as they are expenses which have to be discharged in the near future.

The items prepaid are also added together and called *prepayments*, *prepaid expenses* or *payments in advance*. They are shown next under the debtors. Amounts owing for rents receivable or other revenue owing are usually added to debtors.

The balance sheet shows the accounts so far seen in this chapter.

Balance Sheet as at 31 December 2005

	£	£	£
Current assets			
Stock		xxx	
Debtors		200	
Prepayments (210 + 400)		610	
Bank		xxx	
Cash		xxx	
		x,xxx	
Less Current liabilities			
Trade creditors	xxx		
Accrued expenses	250	xxx	
Net current assets			x,xxx

12.7 Expenses and revenue accounts covering more than one period

Students are often asked to draw up an expense or revenue account for a full year, and there are amounts owing or prepaid at both the beginning and end of a year. We can now see how this is done.

Example A

The following details are available:

(A) On 31 December 2004, three months' rent of £3,000 was owing.

(B) The rent chargeable per year was £12,000.

(C) The following payments were made in the year 2005:
6 January £3,000; 4 April £3,000; 7 July £3,000; 18 October £3,000.

(D) The final three months' rent for 2005 is still owing.

Now we can look at the completed rent account. The letters (A) to (D) give reference to the details above.

Dr				Rent Account			Cr
2005			£	2005			£
Jan 6	Bank	(C)	3,000	Jan 5	Owing b/d	(A)	3,000
Apr 4	Bank	(C)	3,000	Dec 31	Profit and loss	(B)	12,000
Jul 7	Bank	(C)	3,000				
Oct 18	Bank	(C)	3,000				
Dec 31	Accrued c/d	(D)	3,000				
			15,000				15,000
				2006			
				Jan 1	Accrued b/d		3,000

Example B

The following details are available:

(A) On 31 December 2004 packing materials in hand amounted to £1,850.

(B) During the year to 31 December 2005 £27,480 was paid for packing materials.

(C) There were no stocks of packing materials on 31 December 2005.

(D) On 31 December 2005 we still owed £2,750 for packing materials already received and used.

The packing materials account is shown below. The letters (A) to (D) refer to the details above.

Dr			Packing Materials Account		Cr
2005		£	2005		£
Jan 1 Stocks b/d	(A)	1,850	Dec 31 Profit and loss		32,080
Dec 31 Bank	(B)	27,480			
Dec 31 Owing c/d	(D)	2,750			
		32,080			32,080
			2006		
			Jan 1 Owing b/d		2,750

The figure of £32,080 is the difference on the account, and is transferred to the profit and loss account. By formulating the following account, we can prove that this is correct.

	£	£
Stock at start of year		1,850
Add Bought and used:		
Paid for	27,480	
Still owed for	2,750	30,230
Cost of packing materials used in the year		32,080

Example C

Where different expenses are put together in one account, it can become even more confusing. Let us look at where rent and rates are joined together. The details for the year ended 31 December 2005 are:

(A) Rent is payable of £6,000 per annum.

(B) Rates of £4,000 per annum are payable by instalments.

(C) At 1 January 2005 rent £1,000 had been prepaid in 2004.

(D) On 1 January 2005 rates were owing of £400.

(E) During 2005 rent was paid of £4,500.

(F) During 2005 rates were paid £5,000.

(G) On 31 December 2005 rent £500 was owing.

(H) On 31 December 2005 rates of £600 had been prepaid.

A combined rent and rates account is to be drawn up for the year 2005 showing the transfer to the profit and loss account, and balances are to be carried down to 2006. The letters (A) to (H) refer to the above details.

Dr				Rent and Rates Account				Cr
2005			£	2005				£
Jan 1	Rent prepaid b/d	(C)	1,000	Jan 1	Rates owing b/d	(D)		400
Dec 31	Bank: rent	(E)	4,500	Dec 31	Profit & loss a/c (A) + (B)			10,000
31	Bank: rates	(F)	5,000					
31	Rent owing c/d	(G)	500	31	Rates prepaid c/d	(H)		600
			11,000					11,000
2006				2006				
Jan 1	Rates prepaid b/d	(H)	600	Jan 1	Rent owing b/d	(G)		500

12.8 Goods for own use

Traders will often take items out of their business stocks for their own use, without paying for them. There is nothing wrong about this, but an entry should be made to record the event. This is done by:

Credit purchases account, to reduce cost of goods available for sale.
Debit drawings account, to show that the proprietor has taken the goods for private use.

In the United Kingdom, an adjustment may be needed for value added tax. If goods supplied to a trader's customers have VAT added to their price, then any such goods taken for own use will need such an adjustment. This is because the VAT regulations state that VAT should be added to the cost of goods taken. The double entry for the VAT content would be:

Debit drawings account.
Credit VAT account.

Adjustments may also be needed for other private items. For instance, if a trader's private insurance had been incorrectly charged to the insurance account, then the correction would be:

Credit insurance account.
Debit drawings account.

12.9 Distinctions between various kinds of capital

The capital account represents the claim of the proprietor against the assets of the business at a point in time. The word **capital** is, however, often used in a specific sense. The main dealings are listed below.

Capital invested

This means the actual amount of money, or money's worth, brought into the business by the proprietor from his outside interests. The amount of capital invested is not disturbed by the amounts of profits made by the business or losses incurred.

Capital employed

This term has many meanings but basically it means the amount of money that is being used (or 'employed') in the business. If, therefore, all the assets were added up together and the liabilities of the business deducted, the answer would be that the difference is the amount of money employed in the business (i.e. the net assets).

Another way of looking at the calculation of capital employed is to take the balance of the capital account and add this to any long-term loan; the answer will be the same as the net assets, i.e. the capital employed.

Working capital (net current assets)

The difference between the current assets and current liabilities is often referred to as 'working capital' or 'net current assets'. This amount represents the money that is available to pay the running expenses of the business and ideally the current assets should exceed the current liabilities twice over, i.e. 2 : 1. In simple terms it means that for every £1 owed, the business should be able to raise £2.

12.10 Final accounts in the services sector

All the accounts considered so far have been for businesses that trade in some sort of goods. To enable the business to ascertain the amount of gross profit made on selling the goods a trading account is drawn up. There are, however, many organisations that do not deal in goods but instead supply customers with a 'service'. These will include professional firms such as accountants, solicitors, doctors, estate agents, and firms that provide such services as window cleaning, gardening, hairdressing, repairs and maintenance to washing machines, and so on. Since they do not deal in 'goods' there is no need for trading accounts to be drawn up; and a profit and loss account, together with a balance sheet, is prepared instead.

The first item in the profit and loss account will be the revenue which might be called 'fees', 'charges', 'accounts rendered', etc., depending on the nature of the organisation. Any other item of income will also be added, e.g. rent receivable. Following this, the expenses incurred in running the business will be deducted to arrive at the net profit or loss.

An example of the profit and loss account of a solicitor is illustrated in Exhibit 12.1.

Exhibit 12.1

E B Brown, Solicitor
Profit and Loss Account for the year ended 31 December 2003

	£	£
Revenue:		
Fees charged		87,500
Insurance commissions		1,300
		88,800
Less Expenses:		
Wages and salaries	29,470	
Rent and rates	11,290	
Office expenses	3,140	
Motor expenses	2,115	
General expenses	1,975	
Depreciation	2,720	50,710
Net profit		38,090

NEW TERMS

Accrued expenses   Expenses that have been incurred and the benefit received but which have not been paid for at the end of the accounting period. Also referred to as an accrual.

Capital employed   This term has many meanings but basically it means the amount of money that is being used up (or 'employed') in the business. It is the balance of the capital account plus any long-term loan or, alternatively, the total net assets of the business.

Prepaid expenses   An expense, usually a service, that has been paid for in one accounting period, the benefit of which will not be received until a subsequent period. It is an expense that has been paid for in advance.

Working capital   The amount by which the current assets exceed the current liabilities. Also known as 'net current assets'.

Student Activities

12.1   The first financial year's trading of C Homer ended on 31 December 2008. You are required to present ledger accounts showing the amount transferred to the profit and loss account in respect of the following items:

(a)   Rent: Paid in 2008 amounted to £1,600; owing at 31.12.2008 £400.

(b)   Insurance: Paid in 2008 amounted to £900. Of the amount paid £265 was in respect of insurance for 2009.

(c)   Motor expenses: Paid in 2008 £7,215; owing at 31.12.2008 £166.

(d)   Rates: Paid six months' rates on 1.1.2008 £750; on 1.7.2008 paid nine months' rates for the period 31.3.2009 £1,125.

(e)   K Whalley rented part of the buildings from C Homer for £400 per month from 1.1.2008. On 15.4.2008 he paid C Homer £2,000 and on 15.12.2008 he paid £4,400. Show these transactions in C Homer's accounts.

12.2 The financial year of H Saunders ended on 31 December 2006. Show the ledger accounts for the following items, including the balance transferred to the necessary part of the final accounts, also the balances carried down to 2007.

   (a) Motor expenses: Paid in 2006 £744; owing at 31.12.2006 £28.

   (b) Insurance: Paid in 2006 £420; prepaid as at 31.12.2006 £35.

   (c) Stationery: Paid during 2006 £1,800; owing as at 31.12.2005 £250; owing as at 31.12.2006 £490.

   (d) Rates: Paid during 2006 £950; prepaid as at 31.12.2005 £220; prepaid as at 31.12.2006 £290.

   (e) Saunders sublets part of the premises. He receives £550 during the year ended 31.12.2006. The tenant owed Saunders £180 on 31.12.2005 and £210 on 31.12.2006.

12.3X The following accounts are from T Norton's books during his first year of trading to 31 December 2005.

   (a) General expenses: Paid in 2005 £615; still owing at 31.12.2005 £56.

   (b) Telephone: Paid in 2005 £980; owing at 31.12.2005 £117.

   (c) Norton received commission from the sale of goods. In 2005 he received £3,056 and was owed a further £175 on 31.12.2005.

   (d) Carriage outwards: Paid in 2005 £666; still owing at 31.12.2005 £122.

   (e) Insurance: Paid 1.1.2005 for nine months' insurance £1,080; paid 1.10.2005 the sum of £1,080 for insurance to 30.6.2006.

Show the ledger accounts balanced off at the end of the year, showing balances carried down and the amounts transferred to the final accounts for the year 2005.

12.4X T Dale's financial year ended on 30 June 2004. Write up the ledger accounts, showing the transfer to the final accounts.

   (a) Stationery: Paid for the year to 30.6.2004 £855; stocks of stationery at 30.6.2003 £290; at 30.6.2004 £345.

   (b) General expenses: Paid for the year to 30.6.2004 £590; owing at 30.6.2003 £64; owing at 30.6.2004 £90.

   (c) Rent and rates (combined account): Paid in the year to 30.6.2004 £3,890; rent owing at 30.6.2003 £160; rent paid in advance at 30.6.2004 £250; rates owing at 30.6.2003 £205; rates owing at 30.6.2004 £360.

   (d) Motor expenses: Paid in the year to 30.6.2004 £4,750; owing as at 30.6.2003 £180; owing as at 30.6.2004 £375.

   (e) Dale earned commission from the sales of goods. Received for the year to 30.6.2004 £850; owing at 30.6.2003 £80; owing at 30.6.2004 £145.

12.5 On 1 January 2008 the following balances, among others, stood in the books of M Baldock, a sole trader:

   (a) Rates, £104 (Dr);

   (b) Packing materials, £629 (Dr).

During the year ended 31 December 2008 the information related to these two accounts is as follows:

(i) Rates of £1,500 were paid to cover the period 1 April 2008 to 31 March 2009.

(ii) £5,283 was paid for packing materials bought.

(iii) £357 was owing on 31 December 2008 in respect of packing materials bought on credit.

(iv) Old materials amounting to £172 were sold as scrap for cash.

(v) Closing stock of packing materials was valued at £598.

You are required to write up the two accounts showing the appropriate amounts transferred to the profit and loss account at 31 December 2008, the end of the financial year of the trader.

! *No separate accounts are opened for creditors for packing materials bought on credit.*

12.6X On 1 January 2006 the following balances, among others, stood in the books of T Thomas:

(a) Lighting and heating, (Dr) £277.

(b) Insurance, (Dr) £307.

During the year ended 31 December 2006 the information related to these two accounts is as follows:

(i) Fire insurance, £960, covering the year ended 30 April 2007 was paid.

(ii) General insurance, £630, covering the year ended 31 August 2007 was paid.

(iii) An insurance rebate of £55 was received on 30 June 2006.

(iv) Electricity bills of £874 were paid.

(v) An electricity bill of £83 for December 2006 was unpaid as on 31 December 2006.

(vi) Oil bills of £1,260 were paid.

(vii) Stock of oil as on 31 December 2006 was £92.

You are required to write up the accounts for lighting and heating, and for insurance, for the year to 31 December 2006. Carry forward necessary balances to 2007.

12.7 The following trial balance was extracted from the books of S Bayley at the close of business on 31 March 2007.

	Dr	Cr
	£	£
Purchases and sales	112,800	197,400
Cash at bank	11,400	
Cash in hand	2,100	
Capital account 1 April 2006		99,000
Drawings	28,500	
Office equipment	14,400	

	Dr	Cr
	£	£
Rent	10,200	
Wages and salaries	25,800	
Discounts	6,900	3,600
Debtors and creditors	49,200	24,900
Stock 1 April 2006	29,700	
Provision for bad debts 1 April 2006		2,700
Motor Vans	24,000	
Motor Expenses	4,500	
Bad debts written off	910	
Lighting and heating	1,550	
General expenses	5,640	
	327,600	327,600

Notes

(a)   Stock 31 March 2007 £35,100.

(b)   Wages and salaries accrued at 31 March 2007 £900.

(c)   Rent prepaid at 31 March 2007 £1,400.

(d)   Motor expenses owing at 31 March 2007 £600.

(e)   Increase the provision for bad debts by £600.

(f)   Provide for depreciation as follows:
Office equipment £1,800
Motor vans £4,800

Required   Draw up the trading and profit and loss account for the year ended 31 March 2007 and a balance sheet as at 31 March 2007, using vertical formats throughout.

 J Marston, a sole trader, extracted the following trial balance from his books at the close of business on 31 March 2009.

	Dr	Cr
	£	£
Purchases and sales	228,600	419,700
Stock 1 April 2008	51,600	
Capital 1 April 2008		72,000
Bank overdraft		43,500
Cash	900	
Discounts	14,400	9,300
Returns inwards	8,100	
Returns outwards		5,700
Carriage outwards	21,600	
Rent and insurance	17,400	
Provision for bad and doubtful debts		6,600
Fixtures and fittings	12,000	
Delivery vans	21,000	
Debtors and creditors	119,100	60,600
Drawings	28,800	
Bad debts written off	400	
Wages and salaries	89,000	
General office expenses	4,500	
	617,400	617,400

(a) Stock 31 March 2009 £42,900.

(b) Wages and salaries accrued at 31 March 2009 £2,100; office expenses owing £200.

(c) Rent prepaid 31 March 2009 £1,800.

(d) Increase the provision for bad debts by £1,500 to £8,100.

(e) Provide for depreciation as follows:
  Fixtures and fittings £1,200.
  Delivery van £3,000.

Required Prepare the trading and profit and loss account for the year ended 31 March 2009 together with a balance sheet as at that date, using vertical formats.

 The following trial balance has been extracted from the books of S Ross, a sole trader.

S Ross
Trial Balance as at 30 June 2006

	Dr £	Cr £
Capital		79,637
Office equipment at cost	87,000	
Accumulated depreciation		28,500
Sales		207,117
Purchases	123,525	
Carriage inwards	7,716	
Rent, rates and insurance	9,033	
Printing, stationery and advertising	5,402	
Sundry expenses	1,995	
Salaries and wages	39,630	
Bad debts	1,315	
Provision for bad debts		195
Debtors	18,180	
Creditors		9,706
Cash in hand	265	
Cash at bank	1,503	
Stock as at 1 July 2005	17,891	
Drawings	11,700	
	325,155	325,155

The following additional information as at 30 June 2006 is available:

(a) Stock at the close of business on 30 June 2006 was valued at £20,325.

(b) Rates have been prepaid by £1,320.

(c) Rent owing amounts to £315.

(d) Office equipment is to be depreciated at 15% per annum using the straight line method.

(e) The provision for bad debts is to be increased to £360.

You are required to prepare a trading and profit and loss account for the year ended 30 June 2006 and a balance sheet as at that date.

CHAPTER 13

Stock valuation

AIMS

■ To understand that there can be more than one way of valuing stock.

■ To be able to calculate the value of stock using the different methods.

■ To be able to adjust stock valuations, where necessary, by a reduction to net realisable values.

■ To understand the factors affecting the choice of method taken.

■ To be able to adjust stock valuations in respect of goods on sale or return.

■ To realise that not all stock may be valued on the balance sheet date, thus needing various adjustments.

13.1   Different valuations of stocks

Most people would assume that there can only be one figure for the valuation of stock. This is, however, untrue. This chapter will examine how the valuation of stock can be calculated using different figures.

Assume that a firm has just completed its first financial year and is about to value stock on hand at cost price. The firm has only dealt with one type of goods. A record of the transactions is shown in Exhibit 13.1.

Exhibit 13.1

Bought			Sold		
2005		£	*2005*		£
January	10 at £30 each	300	May	8 for £50 each	400
April	10 at £34 each	340	November	24 for £60 each	1,440
October	20 at £40 each	800			
	40	1,440		32	1,840

The balance of stock on hand at 31 December 2005 is 8 units. The total figure of purchases is £1,440 and that of sales is £1,840. The trading account for the first year of trading can now be completed if the closing stock is brought into the calculations.

But what value do we put on each of the 8 units left in stock at the end of the year? If all of the units bought during the year had cost £30 each, then the closing stock would be 8 × £30 = £240. However, we have bought goods at different prices. This means that the valuation depends on which goods are taken for this calculation, the units at £30 or at £34, or at £40.

Many firms do not know exactly whether they have sold all the oldest units before they sell the new units. For instance, a firm selling spanners may not know if the oldest spanners had been sold before the newest spanners.

The stock valuation will, therefore, be based on an accounting custom, and not on the facts of exactly which units were still in stock at the year end. The three main methods of doing this are now shown.

13.2 First In/First Out method (FIFO)

This method, usually known as **FIFO** – the first letters of each word – says that the first goods to be received are the first to be issued. Using the figures in Exhibit 13.1 we can now calculate the closing figure of stock.

	Received	Issued	Stock		
2005				£	£
January	10 at £30 each		10 at £30		300
April	10 at £34 each		10 at £30	300	
			10 at £34	340	640
May		8 at £30 each	2 at £30	60	
			10 at £34	340	400
October	20 at £40 each		2 at £30	60	
			10 at £34	340	
			20 at £40	800	1,200
November		2 at £30 each			
		10 at £34 each			
		12 at £40 each			
			8 at £40		320

Therefore, the closing stock at 31 December 2005 is valued at £320.

13.3 Last In/First Out method (LIFO)

This method is usually known as **LIFO**. As each issue of goods is made it is said to be from the last batch of goods received before that date. Where there is not enough left of the last batch of goods, then the balance of goods needed is said to come from the previous batch still unsold.

From the information in Exhibit 13.1, the calculation can now be shown.

	Received	Issued	Stock		
2005				£	£
January	10 at £30 each		10 at £30		300
April	10 at £34 each		10 at £30	300	
			10 at £34	340	640
May		8 at £34 each	10 at £30	300	
			2 at £34	68	368
October	20 at £40 each		10 at £30	300	
			2 at £34	68	
			20 at £40	800	1,168
November		20 at £40 each			
		2 at £34 each			
		2 at £30 each	8 at £30	240	240

Therefore, the closing stock at 31 December 2005 is valued at £240.

<h2>13.4   Average cost method (AVCO)</h2>

Using the **AVCO** method, the average cost for each item of stock is recalculated with each receipt of goods. Further issues of goods are then at that figure, until another receipt of goods means that another recalculation is needed. From the information in Exhibit 13.1 the calculation can be shown.

Received		Issued	Average cost per unit of stock held	Number of units in stock	Total value of stock
			£		£
January	10 at £30		30	10	300
April	10 at £34		32*	20	640
May		8 at £32	32	12	384
October	20 at £40		37*	32	1,184
November		24 at £37	37	8	296

* In April, this is calculated as follows: Stock 10 × £30 = £300 + stock received (10 × 34) £340 = total £640; 20 units in stock, so the average is £640 ÷ 20 = £32. In October this is calculated as follows: Stock 12 × £32 = £348 + stock received (20 × £40) £800 = £1,184; 32 units in stock, so the average is £1,184 ÷ 32 = £37.

Therefore, the closing stock at 31 December 2005 is valued at £296.

<h2>13.5   Stock valuation and the calculation of profits</h2>

Using the figures from Exhibit 13.1 with stock valuations shown by the three methods of FIFO, LIFO and AVCO, the trading accounts would appear as:

Trading Account for the year ended 31 December 2005

	FIFO		LIFO		AVCO	
	£	£	£	£	£	£
Sales		1,840		1,840		1,840
Less Cost of Sales:						
Purchases	1,440		1,440		1,440	
Less Closing stock	320	1,120	240	1,200	296	1,444
Gross profit		720		640		696

As can be seen, different methods of stock valuation will mean that different profits are shown.

13.6   Reduction to net realisable value

The **net realisable value** of stock is calculated as follows:

Saleable value less expenses needed to complete the item or get it in a condition to be sold = **Net realisable value**

Example 13.1

An item of stock was purchased at cost price £300. Unfortunately, the item was damaged in the warehouse and the cost of repair and repainting amounted to £50 after which it was estimated it could be sold for £200. The item would be valued as follows:

Saleable value £200 less cost of repair and repainting £50 = **Net realisable value of £150**.

It must be remembered that, according to SSAP 9 (Stocks and Long-term Contracts), stocks of unsold goods are valued at the lower of cost or net realisable value. Stock is valued at cost because profit is not regarded as being earned until the goods are sold. (This is known as the *prudence* concept.) Stock should not be over-valued otherwise profits shown would be too high. Therefore, if the net realisable value of stock is less than the cost of the stock, then the figure to be taken for the final accounts is that of net realisable value.

A somewhat exaggerated example will show the necessity for this action. Assume that an art dealer has bought only two paintings during the financial year ended 31 December 2008. He starts off the year without any stock, then buys a genuine masterpiece for £6,000, selling this later in the year for £11,500. The other picture is a fake, but the dealer does not realise this when he purchases it for £5,100, only to discover during the year that in fact he has made a terrible mistake and that the net realisable value is £100. The fake remains unsold at the end of the year. The trading account (Exhibit 13.2) would appear as (*a*) if stock is valued at cost, and as (*b*) if stock is given a net realisable value.

Exhibit 13.2

Trading Account for the year ended 31 December 2008

	(a) £		(b) £	
Sales		11,500		11,500
Purchases	11,100		11,100	
Closing stock	5,100	6,000	100	11,000
Gross profit		5,500		500

Method (*a*) ignores the fact that the dealer had a bad trading year owing to his skill being found wanting in 2008. If this method was used, then the loss on the fake would reveal itself in the following year's trading account. Method (*b*), however, realises that the loss really occurred at the date of purchase rather than at the date of sale. Accounting practice would apply the concept of prudence and choose method (*b*).

At one time the terminology was 'lower of cost or market value'. Changing it to 'lower of cost or net realisable value' gives a more precise definition to the terms used.

13.7 Some other bases in use

Retail businesses often estimate the cost of stock by calculating it in the first place at selling price, and then deducting the normal margin of gross profit on such stock. Adjustment is made for items which are to be sold at other than normal selling prices. Where standard costing is in use, the figure of standard cost is frequently used.

13.8 Factors affecting the stock valuation decision

Obviously the overriding consideration applicable in all circumstances when valuing stock is the need to give a 'true and fair view' of the state of the affairs of the undertaking on the balance sheet date and of the trend of the firm's trading results. There is, however, no precise definition of 'true and fair view'; it obviously rests on the judgement of the persons concerned. It would be necessary to study the behavioural sciences to understand the factors that affect judgement. However, it should be possible to state that the judgement of any two persons will not always be the same in the differing circumstances of various firms.

In fact, the only certain thing about stock valuation is that the concept of consistency should be applied, i.e. that once adopted, the same basis should be used in the annual accounts until some good reason occurs to change it. A reference should then be made in the final accounts to the effect of the change on the reported profits, if the amount involved is material.

It will perhaps be useful to look at some of the factors which cause a particular basis to be chosen. The list is intended to be indicative rather than comprehensive, and is merely intended as a first brief look at matters which will have to be studied in depth by those intending to make a career in accountancy.

1. **Ignorance**   The personalities involved may not appreciate the fact that there is more than one possible way of valuing stock.

2. **Convenience**   The basis chosen may not be the best for the purposes of profit calculation but it may be the easiest to calculate. It must always be borne in mind that the benefits which flow from possessing information should be greater than the costs of obtaining it. The only difficulty with this is actually establishing when the benefits do exceed the cost, but in some circumstances the decision not to adopt a given basis will be obvious.

3. **Custom**   It may be the particular method used in a certain trade or industry.

4. **Taxation**   The whole idea may be to defer the payment of tax for as long as possible. Because the stock figures affect the calculation of profits on which the tax is based the lowest possible stock figures may be taken to show the lowest profits up to the balance sheet date.

5. **The capacity to borrow money or to sell the business at the highest possible price**   The higher the stock value shown, then the higher will be the profits calculated to date, and therefore at first sight the business looks more attractive to a buyer or lender. Either of these considerations may be more important to the proprietors than anything else. It may be thought that those in business are not so gullible, but all business people are not necessarily well acquainted with accounting customs. In fact, many small businesses are bought, or money is lent to them, without the expert advice of someone well versed in accounting.

6. **Remuneration purposes**   Where someone managing a business is paid in whole or in part by reference to the profits earned, then one basis may suit him or her better than others. The manager may therefore strive to have that basis used to suit his or her own ends. The owner, however, may try to follow another course to minimise the remuneration that he or she will have to pay out.

7. **Lack of information**   If proper stock records have not been kept, then such bases as the average cost method or the LIFO method may not be calculable.

8. **Advice of the auditors**   Many firms use a particular basis because the auditors advised its use in the first instance. A different auditor may well advise that a different basis be used.

13.9   The conflict of aims

The list of some of the factors which affect decisions is certainly not exhaustive, but it does illustrate the fact that stock valuation is usually a compromise. There is not usually only one figure which is true and fair, there must be a variety of possibilities. Therefore the desire to borrow money, and in so doing to paint a good picture by being reasonably optimistic in valuing stock, will be tempered by the fact that this may increase the tax bill. Stock valuation is therefore a compromise between the various ends for which it is to be used.

13.10 Work in progress

The valuation of work in progress is subject to all the various criteria and methods used in valuing stock. Probably the cost element is more strongly pronounced than in stock valuation, as it is very often impossible or irrelevant to say what net realisable value or replacement price would be applicable to partly finished goods. Firms in industries such as those which have contracts covering several years have evolved their own methods.

 Long-term contract work in progress is not required at NVQ Level 3.

13.11 Goods on sale or return

Goods received on sale or return

Sometimes we may receive goods from a supplier on a **sale or return** basis. This means that we do not have to pay for the goods until we sell them. If we do not sell them we have to return them to our supplier.

This means that the goods do not belong to us. If we have some goods on sale or return at the stocktaking date, they should not be included in our stock valuation.

Goods sent to our customers on sale or return

We may send goods on a sale or return basis to our customers and the stock will belong to us until it is sold. At our stocktaking date any goods held by our customers on sale or return should be included in our stock valuation.

13.12 Stocktaking and the balance sheet date

Students often think that all the counting and valuing of stock is done on the last day of the accounting period. This might by true in a small business, but it is often impossible in larger businesses. There may be too many items of stock to do it so quickly.

This means that stocktaking may take place over a period of days. To get the figure of the stock valuation as on the last day of the accounting period, we will have to make adjustments. Exhibit 13.3 gives an example of such calculations.

Exhibit 13.3

Lee Ltd has a financial year which ends on 31 December 2007. The stocktaking is not in fact done until 8 January 2008. When the items in stock on that date are priced out, it is found that the stock value amounts to £28,850. The following information is available about transactions between 31 December 2007 and 8 January 2008:

1. Purchases since 31 December 2007 amounted to £2,370 at cost.
2. Returns inwards since 31 December 2007 were £350 at selling price.
3. Sales since 31 December 2007 amounted to £3,800 at selling price.
4. The selling price is always cost price + 25%.

Exhibit 13.3 (continued)

Lee Ltd
Computation of stock as on 31 December 2007

	£	£	£
Stock (at cost)			28,850
Add Items which were in stock on			
31 December 2007 (at cost):			
Sales		3,800	
Less Profit content (20% of selling price)*		760	3,040
			31,890
Less Items which were not in stock on			
31 December 2007 (at cost):			
Returns inwards	350		
Less Profit content (20% of selling price)*	70	280	
Purchases (at cost)		2,370	2,650
Stock in hand as on 31 December 2007			29,240

* Stock at cost (or net realisable value), and not at selling price. As this calculation has a sales figure in it which includes profit, we must deduct the profit part to get to the cost price. This is true also for returns inwards. At one time it was very rare for the auditors to attend at stocktaking time as observers. The professional accounting bodies now encourage the auditors to be present if at all possible.

13.13 Stock levels

One of the most common faults found in the running of a business is that too high a level of stock is maintained. A considerable number of firms that have problems with a shortage of finance will find that they can help matters by having a sensible look at the amounts of stock they hold. It would be a very rare firm indeed which, if they had not investigated the matter previously, could not manage to let parts of their stock run down. As this would save spending cash on items not really necessary, this cash could be better utilised elsewhere.

13.14 SSAP 9: Stocks and long-term contracts

SSAP 9 covering the requirements of the accounting standard is covered fully in Chapter 7, Section 7.7 (see page 70). It is recommended that this chapter is read in conjunction with statements made there.

NEW TERMS

AVCO   A method by which the goods used are priced out at average cost.

FIFO   A method by which the first goods to be received are said to be the first to be sold.

LIFO   A method by which the goods sold are said to have come from the last batch of goods received.

Net realisable value   The value of goods calculated as the selling price less expenses before sale.

Sale or return   Goods that do not belong to the person holding them.

13.1 From the following figures calculate the closing stock-in-trade that would be shown using (i) FIFO, (ii) LIFO and (iii) AVCO methods.

Bought		Sold	
January	10 at £30 each	April	8 for £46 each
March	10 at £34 each	December	12 for £56 each
September	20 at £40 each		

13.2 Using the figure from Question 13.1 draw up the trading account for the year ended 31 December 2001 showing the gross profits that would have been reported using (i) FIFO, (ii) LIFO and (iii) AVCO methods.

13.3X From the following figures calculate the closing stock-in-trade that would be shown using (i) FIFO, (ii) LIFO and (iii) AVCO methods on a perpetual inventory basis.

Bought		Sold	
January	24 at £10 each	June	30 at £16 each
April	16 at £12.50 each	November	34 at £18 each
October	30 at £13 each		

13.4X Draw up trading accounts using each of the three methods from the details in Question 13.3X for the year ended 31 December 2002.

13.5 D.C. Ltd, for which the financial year end was 31 December 2008, did not take a stock check until 8 January 2009 when it was shown to be £50,850 at cost.

The following were established:

(a) A calculation of 1,000 items at £1.60 was shown as £160.

(b) During the period 31.12.2008 to 8.1.2009 no purchases were made, but sales of £500 were made. The profit margin is 20%.

(c) Some goods costing £560 had a net realisable value of £425.

(d) One stock sheet has been added up to be £2,499. The total should have been £4,299.

Calculate the correct figure of stock on 31 December 2008.

13.6 (a) If the closing stock of a business had been mistakenly over-valued by £5,000, and the error had gone unnoticed, what would be the effect of the error on:

(i) this year's profit?

(ii) next year's profit?

(b) A company which sold videos and electrical goods valued its closing stock at £72,050 (cost price) at 30 June 2003. However, it was found that this figure included the following:

(i) 5 videos which had cost £300 each but which have now been replaced by an improved model. In order to sell these obsolete models it is thought that they will have to be sold at £250 each.

(ii) A music centre that cost £500 but which had been damaged and it is estimated that repairs will cost £100 before it can be sold.

Calculate the value of the closing stock after taking into the account the above adjustments.

13.7X On 30 November 2008, the last day of its financial year, The Pine Warehouse made a cash sale of some pine tables and chairs. These had originally cost £1,000 and were sold for £1,500. Although the sale was immediately recorded in the accounts of the business and the cash had been paid at the time of the sale, the customer asked for delivery to take place on 22 December 2008. The tables and chairs were therefore still in stock at the financial year end. The proprietor of the business, Pat Hall, has suggested that the tables and chairs should be included in the valuation of the closing stock at the selling price of £1,500. Pat Hall comments to you: 'This seems to be in accordance with the prudence concept since profits can be recognised once they are realised.'

You are required to write a memo to Pat Hall stating whether or not you agree with the proposed accounting treatment for the tables and chairs. Clearly explain the reasons for your answer.

(AAT Central Assessment)

13.8 (a) You are required to value the closing stock, after taking into account the necessary adjustments, in the following situations:

(i) Closing stock was valued at cost at £43,795. However, this figure includes two items, cost price £175 each, which have been damaged in storage. It has been estimated that if a total of £35 was spent on repairing them, they could be sold for £140 each.

(ii) The value of the closing stock had been valued at cost on 31 October 2007 at £107,300. However, this includes some discontinued kitchen cabinets the details of which are as follows:

Cost	£2,300
Normal selling price	£3,500
Net realisable value	£1,800

(b) Stock has always been valued by Electronics World Ltd on a FIFO basis and this includes the closing stock figure of £198,650 as at 31 May 2007. It has been suggested that the closing stock figure should now be recalculated on a LIFO basis.

(i) Assuming that the prices of electronic goods have been gradually rising throughout the year, would the change suggested increase profit for the year ended 31 May 2007, decrease profit or would profit remain the same?

(ii) Which accounting concept states that the company should not normally change its basis for valuing stock unless it has very good reasons for doing so?

(AAT Central Assessment)

13.9X (a) The following is an extract of the stock sheets from Highbury Discs as at 31 May 2005 along with comments made by the proprietor, Anthony Sedgewick.

Stocks of compact discs are valued at cost. Cost includes a share of the recording, mastering and production costs as well as any direct overheads attributable to that recording.

Stock Sheets					
Title	Number of discs in stock	Total cost £	Total price to retailers £	Total recommended retail price £	Comments
Total b/f from previous pages	4,500	18,000	27,600	39,800	No problems with any of these. We'll be able to make a profit on all of these discs.
Bambino choir of Prague	1,000	3,500	8,500	12,000	This batch of CDs arrived too late for the 2004 Christmas season. We're keeping them for the 2005 Christmas season. I think they will sell very well then.
The Joyful Singers sing Wesley	400	2,000	3,600	4,800	We just cannot get rid of these. We'll have to reduce the price to retailers to £3 a disc and recommend that retailers sell them for £5.50 a disc.
Bach at St Thomas's	2,000	7,000	14,000	20,000	This has not sold at all well. We're going to withdraw these discs and repackage them as 'The King of Instruments' and sell them to a chain store for £4 a disc. The repackaging will cost £1.50 per disc.
Total	7,900	30,500	53,700	76,600	

You are required to complete the following table to calculate the value of closing stock.

Stock Sheets	Value £
Total b/f from previous pages	
Bambino choir of Prague	
The Joyful Singers sing Wesley	
Bach at St Thomas's	
Value of stock as at 31 May 2005	

(b) You are required to write a memo to Anthony Sedgewick explaining the rules you have used to calculate the value of closing stock. He would like you to refer to any relevant SSAPs and/or FRSs.

(AAT Central Assessment)

CHAPTER 14

The journal

AIMS

■ To be able to identify the journal as a book of original entry.

■ To be able to use the journal for entering a range of different transactions.

■ To be able to post items from the journal to the ledgers.

14.1 The journal: a book of original entry

It has already been shown in Chapter 2 (Section 2.3) that a book of original entry is where a transaction is first recorded. One of the less commonly used books of original entry is the journal which tends to be used for more complicated transactions. It would be easy for a book keeper to forget details of these transactions or perhaps the book keeper may leave the company making it impossible at a later date to understand such book keeping entries.

It is, therefore, important to record such transactions in a form of diary to relate to entries being made in the double entry accounts. The book used to record these transactions is called the **journal** and contains the following details for each transaction:

■ The date.
■ The name of the account(s) to be debited and credited and the amount(s).
■ A description and explanation of the transaction (this is called a '**narrative**').
■ A reference number for the source of the documents giving proof of the transaction.

The use of the journal makes errors or fraud by book keepers more difficult. It also reduces the risk of entering the item once only instead of having the complete double entry. Despite these advantages there are many firms which do not use the journal.

14.2 Typical uses of the journal

Some of the main uses of the journal are listed below. It must not be thought that this is a fully detailed list.

1. The purchase and sale of fixed assets on credit (refer also to Chapter 10)
2. The correction of errors
3. Writing off bad debts
4. Opening entries: the entries needed to open a new set of books
5. Other items

The layout of the journal can be shown:

The Journal

Date	Details	Folio	Dr	` Cr
	The name of the account to be debited. The name of the account to be credited. The narrative.			

It can be seen that on the first line the name of the account to be **debited** is entered while the second line gives the account to be **credited**. The name of the account to be **credited** is indented slightly and *not* shown directly under the name of the account to be debited as this makes it easier to distinguish between the debit and credit items.

It should be remembered that the journal is not a double entry account; it is a form of diary, and entering an item in the journal is not the same as recording an item in an account. Once the journal entry has been made, the entry into the double entry accounts can be made.

14.3 Journal entries in examination questions

If you were to ask examiners about what types of book keeping and accounting questions are most often answered badly, they would certainly include 'Questions involving journal entries'. This is not because questions about journal entries are actually more difficult than other types, but rather because many students seem to get some sort of a mental blockage when dealing with them.

The authors believe that this difficulty arises because students often think in terms of the debits and credits in accounts. Instead, they should think of the journal simply as a form of written instruction stating which account is to be debited and which account is to be credited, with a description of the transaction involved.

To help you to avoid this sort of problem with journal entries, we will first of all show what the entries are in the accounts, and then write up the journal for those entries. We will now look at a few examples, which include folio numbers.

14.4 Purchase and sale on credit of fixed assets

Example 14.1

A computer is bought on credit from Acorn Business Products for £1,000 plus 17.5% VAT on 1 January 2002. The company is registered for VAT. From your previous knowledge of book keeping you will know that the double entry would be as follows:

Computer Equipment Account (Folio GL 1)

2002			£			£
Jan 1	Acorn Business Products	PL55	1,000			

VAT Account (Folio GL 2)

2002			£			£
Jan 1	Acorn Business Products	PL55	175			

Acorn Business Products Account (Folio PL 55)

	£	2002			£
		Jan 1	Computer equipment	GL1	1,000
		Jan 1	VAT	GL 2	175

Now we have to record these entries in the journal. Remember, the journal is simply a kind of diary, not in account form, but in ordinary written form. It says which account has been debited, which account has been credited, and then gives the narrative which simply describes the nature of the transaction. For the transaction above, the journal entry will appear as follows:

The Journal

Date	Details	Folio	Dr	Cr
2002			£	£
Jan 1	Computer	GL1	1,000	
	VAT	GL2	175	
	Acorn Business Products	PL55		1,175
	Purchase of CV 21 computer on credit from Acorn Business Products, Invoice No. 8367. Note: Capital expenditure budget Ref.: CP 98			

Example 14.2

Sale of stationery, surplus to requirements, on credit to B Kenyon for £200 plus VAT of £35 on 18 January 2002.

Here again, it is not difficult to work out the entries which are needed in the double entry accounts. They are as follows:

Exhibit 14.2 (continued)

B Kenyon Account					(Folio SL79)
2002			£		£
Jan 18	Stationery	GL51	200		
18	VAT	GL60	35		

Stationery Account				(Folio GL51)
	£	2002		£
		Jan 18 B Kenyon	SL79	200

VAT Account				(Folio GL60)
	£	2002		£
		Jan 18 B Kenyon	SL79	35

These are now shown in journal form as follows:

The Journal

Date	Details	Folio	Dr	Cr
2002			£	£
Jan 18	B Kenyon	SL79	235	
	Stationery	GL51		200
	VAT	GL60		35
	Sale of stationery surplus to requirements.			

 Journal entries of the purchase and sale of fixed assets is also covered in Chapter 10.

14.5 Correction of errors

Correction of errors not affecting trial balance agreement

It is inevitable that errors will occur when data are entered into the books of account. One of the main uses of the journal is to record such errors and show the corrective entry necessary to amend the double entry accounts. One of the ways in which errors are identified is through the trial balance. In Chapter 3 a trial balance was drawn up from a list of balances in the books of account at the end of an accounting period. Each side of the trial balance was then added up and, provided no error had occurred, the two sides should equal each other, i.e.

Total debit balances = Total credit balances

While both sides of the trial balance may agree, complete accuracy cannot be guaranteed. Certain errors can still be made which do not affect the balancing of the trial balance, i.e. the trial balance would still appear to balance even though certain errors have occurred. The errors which lead to this situation are listed below, but they have previously been explained in Chapter 3.

1. Errors of commission
2. Errors of principle
3. Errors of original entry
4. Errors of omission
5. Compensating errors
6. Complete reversal of entries

Each of the above errors will now be discussed and the corrected entries shown in the journal.

1. Errors of commission

An error of commission arises when the correct amounts are entered, but in the wrong person's account.

Example 14.3

D Long paid us by cheque £50 on 18 May 2001. It is correctly entered in the cash book, but it is entered by mistake in the account for D Lee.

This means that there had been both a debit of £50 and a credit of £50. It appeared in the personal account as follows:

D Lee Account		(Folio SL22)
	2001	£
	May 18 Cash CB7	50

The error was found on 31 May 2001. This will now have to be corrected and needs two entries:

Accounting entries	Explanation
(i) Debit D Lee's account	To cancel out the error on the credit side of that account
(ii) Credit D Long's account	To enter the amount in the correct account

The accounts will now appear:

D Lee Account (Folio SL22)

2001			£	2001			£
May 31	D Long:						
	Error corrected (i)	J12	50	May 18	Cash	CB7	50

D Long Account (Folio SL26)

2001		£	2001			£
			May 31	Cash entered in error		
				in D Lee's account		
May 1	Balance b/d	50		(ii)	J12	50

The journal

The ways by which errors have been corrected should all be entered in the journal. The correction has already been shown above in double entry. In fact the journal entries should be made before completing the double entry accounts for the transaction. For teaching purposes only in this chapter, the journal entries are shown last as previously stated.

The Journal   (Folio J12)

Date	Details	Folio	Dr	Cr
2001			£	£
May 31	D Lee	SL22	50	
	D Long	SL26		50
	Cash received . . . entered in wrong personal account, now corrected.			

2. Errors of principle

This is where a transaction is entered in the wrong type of account. For instance, the purchase of a fixed asset should be debited to a fixed asset account. If it is debited to an expense account in error, then it has been entered in the wrong type of account.

Example 14.4

The purchase of a motor lorry £5,500 by cheque on 14 May 2001 has been debited in error to a motor expenses account. In the cash book it is shown correctly, which means that there has been both a debit of £5,500 and a credit of £5,500. It will have appeared in the motor expenses account as:

Motor Expenses Account   (Folio GL27)

2001			£	
May 14	Bank	CB40	5,500	

The error is found on 31 May 2001, and two entries are needed to correct it:

Accounting entry	Explanation
(i) Debit motor lorry account	To put the amount in the correct account
(ii) Credit motor expenses account	To cancel the error previously made in the motor expenses account

The accounts will now appear as:

Motor Lorry Account   (Folio GL30)

2001			£	
May 31	Bank: Entered originally in motor expenses (i)	J52	5,500	

Motor Expenses Account   (Folio GL27)

2001			£	2001			£
May 14	Bank	CB40	5,500	May 31	Motor lorry: Error corrected (ii)	J52	5,500

The journal

The journal entries to correct the error will be shown as:

The Journal   (Folio J52)

Date	Details	Folio	Dr	Cr
2001			£	£
May 31	Motor lorry	GL30	5,500	
	Motor expenses	GL27		5,500
	Correction of error whereby purchase of motor lorry was debited to motor expenses account.			

3. Errors of original entry

This occurs when an incorrect figure is posted to the correct sides of the correct accounts.

Example 14.5

If sales of £150 to T Higgins on 31 May 2001 had been entered as both a debit and a credit of £130, the accounts would appear:

T Higgins Account   (Folio SL7)

2001			£			
May 31	Sales	SDB3	130			

Sales Account   (Folio GL52)

				2001		£
				May 31	Sales journal (part of total) SDB3	130

The error is found on 31 May 2001. The following entries are required to correct it:

Accounting entry	Explanation
(i) Debit T Higgins account £20	To correct the error made in recording sale of goods to Higgins as £130 instead of £150
(ii) Credit sales account £20	To amend the sales account by £20

T Higgins Account   (Folio SL7)

2001			£		
May 31	Sales	SDB3	130		
31	Sales: Error corrected	J33	20		

Sales Account   (Folio GL52)

			2001		£
			May 31	Sales journal SDB3	130
			31	T Higgins: Error corrected J33	20

The journal

To correct the error the journal entries will be:

The Journal (Folio J33)

Date	Details	Folio	Dr	Cr
2001			£	£
May 31	T Higgins	SL7	20	
	Sales account	GL52		20
	Correction of error. Sales of £150 had been incorrectly entered as £130.			

4. Errors of omission

This type of error occurs when the book keeper omits to record a transaction.

Example 14.6

If we purchased goods from T Hope for £250 but did not enter it in the accounts there would be nil debits and nil credits. We find the error on 31 May 2001. The entries to record it will be:

Purchases Account (Folio GL63)

2001			£
May 31	T Hope:		
	Error corrected	J22	250

T Hope Account (Folio PL44)

2001			£
May 31	Purchases:		
	Error corrected	J22	250

The journal

The journal entries to correct the error will be:

The Journal (Folio J22)

Date	Details	Folio	Dr	Cr
2001			£	£
May 31	Purchases	GL63	250	
	T Hope	PL44		250
	Correction of error. Purchases omitted from books.			

5. Compensating errors

These are where errors cancel each other out. They are known as compensating errors.

Example 14.7

Let us take a case where the sales day book is added up to be £100 too much. In the same period the purchases day book is also added up to be £100 too much.

If these were the only errors in our books the trial balance totals would equal each other. Both totals would be wrong – they would both be £100 too much, but they would be equal totals.

If in fact the *incorrect* totals had purchases £7,900 and sales £9,900, the accounts would have appeared as:

Purchases Account				(Folio GL37)
2001		£		
May 31 Purchases		7,900		

Sales Account				(Folio GL49)
		2001		£
		May 31 Sales		9,900

When corrected, the accounts will appear as:

Purchases Account				(Folio GL37)
2001	£	*2001*		£
May 31 Purchases	7,900	May 31 The journal:		
		Error corrected	J17	100

Sales Account				(Folio GL49)
2001	£	*2001*		£
May 31 The journal:		May 31 Sales		9,900
Error corrected J17	100			

The journal

The journal entries to correct these two errors will be:

	The Journal			(Folio J17)

Date	Details	Folio	Dr	Cr
2001			£	£
May 31	Sales account	GL49	100	
	Purchases account	GL37		100
	Correction of compensating errors. Totals of both purchases and sales day books incorrectly added up to £100 too much.			

6. Complete reversal of entries

This is where the correct amounts are entered in the correct accounts, but each item is shown on the wrong side of each account. There has therefore been both a debit and a credit entry of equal amounts.

Example 14.8

For instance, we pay a cheque for £200 on 28 May 2001 to D Charles. We enter it as follows in accounts with the letter (A):

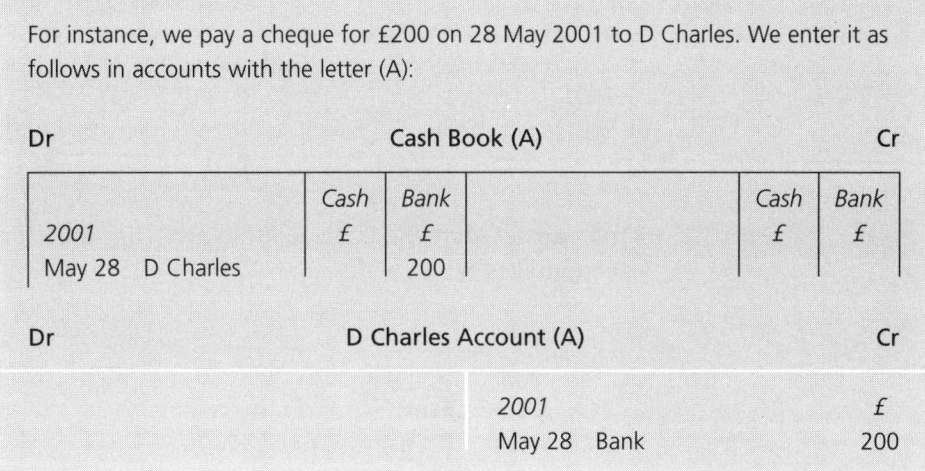

Dr			Cash Book (A)			Cr
	Cash £	Bank £			Cash £	Bank £
2001						
May 28 D Charles		200				

Dr		D Charles Account (A)		Cr
		2001		£
		May 28 Bank		200

This is incorrect. It should have been debit D Charles Account £200, credit Bank £200. Both items have been entered in the correct accounts, but each is on the wrong side of its account.

The way to correct this is more difficult to understand than with other errors. Let us look at how the items would have appeared if we had done it correctly in the first place. We will show the letter (B) after the account names:

Dr			Cash Book (B)			Cr
	Cash £	Bank £			Cash £	Bank £
			2001			200
			May 28 D Charles			

Dr		D Charles Account (B)		Cr
2001		£		
May 28 Bank		200		

We have found the error on 31 May 2001. By using double entry we have to make the amounts shown to cancel the error by twice the amount of the error because:

1. First we have to cancel the error. This would mean entering these amounts:

   Debit: D Charles   £200
   Credit: Bank   £200

2. Then we have to enter up the transaction:

   Debit: D Charles   £200
   Credit: Bank   £200

Altogether then, the entries to correct the error are twice the amounts first entered. When corrected the accounts appear as follows, marked (C):

Dr		D Charles Account (C)		Cr
2001	£	2001		£
May 31 Bank: Error corrected	400	May 28 Bank		200

Dr			Cash Book (C)			Cr
	Cash £	*Bank* £		*Cash* £	*Bank* £
2001 May 28 D Charles		200	*2001* May 31 D Charles: Error corrected		400

You can see that the (C) accounts give the same final answer as the (B) accounts:

			£	£
(B)	*Debit*:	D Charles	200	
	Credit:	Bank		200
(C)	*Debit*:	D Charles (£400 – £200)	200	
	Credit:	Bank (£400 – £200)		200

The journal

Journal entries would be shown as follows:

The Journal

Date	Details	Folio	Dr	Cr
2001 May 31	D Charles Bank Payment of £200 on 28 May 2001 to D Charles incorrectly credited to his account, and debited to bank. Error now corrected.		£ 400	£ 400

Correction of errors affecting trial balance agreement

In the previous section errors which did not affect the balancing of the trial balance were discussed. However, there are many errors which occur that do affect the balancing of the trial balance, for example:

- incorrect additions in any account;
- making an entry on only one side of the accounts, e.g. a debit but no credit; a credit and no debit;
- entering a different amount on the debit side from the amount on the credit side.

Suspense account

If a trial balance does not balance it is important that errors are located and corrected as soon as possible. When they cannot be found, then the trial balance totals should be made to agree with each other by inserting the amount of the difference between the two sides in a **suspense account**. This occurs in Exhibit 14.1 where there is a difference of £40.

Exhibit 14.1

Trial Balance as on 31 December 2001		
	Dr	Cr
	£	£
Totals after all the accounts have been listed	100,000	99,960
Suspense account		40
	100,000	100,000

To make the two totals the same, a figure of £40 for the suspense account has been shown on the credit side. A suspense account is opened and the £40 difference is also shown there on the credit side.

Suspense Account			(GL30)
Dr			Cr
	2001		£
	Dec 31	Difference per trial balance	40

Suspense account and the balance sheet

If the errors are not found before the final accounts are prepared, the suspense account balance will be included in the balance sheet. Where the balance is a credit balance, it should be included under current liabilities on the balance sheet. When the balance is a debit balance it should be shown under current assets on the balance sheet. Large errors should always be found before the final accounts are drawn up.

Correction of errors via the suspense account

When the errors are found they must be corrected, using double entry. Each correction must be described by an entry in the journal.

One error only

We will look at two examples:

Example 14.9

Assume that the error of £40 shown in Exhibit 14.1 is found in the following year on 31 March 2002, the error being the sales account which was undercast by £40. The action taken to correct this is:

Debit suspense account to close it: £40.
Credit sales account to show item where it should have been: £40.

The accounts and journal entry now appear as in Exhibit 14.2.

Exhibit 14.2

	Suspense Account		(GL30)
Dr			Cr

2002			£	2002			£
				Dec 31	Difference per		
Mar 31	Sales	J9	<u>40</u>		trial balance		<u>40</u>

	Sales Account		(GL25)
Dr			Cr

				2002			£
				Mar 31	Suspense	J9	40

	The Journal			(J9)
2002		Folio	Dr	Cr

			£	£
Mar 31	Suspense	GL30	40	
	Sales	GL25		40
	Correction of undercasting of sales by £40 in last year's accounts			

Example 14.10

The trial balance on 31 December 2001 had a difference of £168. It was a shortage on the debit side. A suspense account is opened and the difference of £168 is entered on the debit side.

On 31 May 2002 the error was found. We had made a payment of £168 to K Leek to close his account. It was correctly entered in the cash book, but it was not entered in K Leek's account. To correct the error, the account of K Leek is debited with £168, as it should have been in 2001 and the suspense account is credited with £168 so that the account can be closed.

The accounts and journal entry now appear as in Exhibit 14.3.

Exhibit 14.3

	K Leek Account		(PL17)
Dr			Cr

2002			£	2002			£
May 31	Suspense	J40	<u>168</u>	Jan 1	Balance b/d		<u>168</u>

	Suspense Account		(GL51)
Dr			Cr

2002			£	2002			£
May 31	Difference per			May 31	K Leek: Error		
	trial balance		<u>168</u>		corrected	J40	<u>168</u>

Exhibit 14.3 (continued)

The Journal				(J40)
2002		*Folio*	*Dr*	*Cr*
			£	£
May 31	K Leek	PL17	168	
	Suspense	GL51		168
	Correction of non-entry of payment last year in K Leek's account.			

More than one error

We can now look at Exhibit 14.4 where the suspense account difference was caused by more than one error.

Exhibit 14.4

The trial balance at 31 December 2001 showed a difference of £77, being a shortage on the debit side. A suspense account is opened, and the difference of £77 is entered on the debit side of the account.

On 28 February 2002 all the errors from the previous year were found.

(1)   A cheque of £150 paid to L Kent had been correctly entered in the cash book but had not been entered in Kent's account.

(2)   The purchases account had been undercast by £20.

(3)   A cheque of £93 received from K Sand had been correctly entered in the cash book but had not been entered in Sand's account.

These three errors resulted in a net error of £77, shown by a debit of £77 on the debit side of the suspense account. These are corrected by:

■ making correcting entries in the accounts for (1), (2) and (3);

■ recording the double entry for these items in the suspense account.

L Kent Account				(PL15)
Dr				*Cr*
2002			£	
Feb 28	Suspense (1)	J9	150	

Purchases Account				(GL28)
Dr				*Cr*
2002			£	
Feb 28	Suspense (2)	J9	20	

K Sand Account				(SL42)
Dr				*Cr*
			2002	£
			Feb 28 Suspense (3) J9	93

Exhibit 14.4 (continued)

Suspense Account (GL33)

Dr				Cr	
2002		£	2002		£
Jan 1	Balance b/d	77	Feb 28 L Kent (1)	J9	150
Feb 28	K Sand (3)	J9 93	Feb 28 Purchases (2)	J9	20
		170			170

The Journal (J8)

2002		Folio	Dr	Cr
			£	£
Feb 28	L Kent	PL15	150	
	Suspense	GL33		150
	Cheque paid omitted from Kent's account			
Feb 28	Purchases	GL28	20	
	Suspense	GL33		20
	Undercasting of purchases by £20 in last year's accounts			
Feb 28	Suspense	GL33	93	
	K Sand	SL42		93
	Cheque received omitted from Sand's account			

Only those errors which make the trial balance totals different from each other have to be corrected via the suspense account

14.6 Bad debts

A debt of £78 owed to the business from H Mander is written off as a bad debt on 31 August 2003.

As the debt is now of no value, it should no longer be shown as an asset. This means that we must credit H Mander's account to cancel the amount out of his account. A bad debt is an expense, and so we will debit the amount to the bad debts account. In double entry form this is shown as:

Bad Debts Account (Folio GL16)

2005			£	
Aug 31	H Mander	SL99	78	

H Mander Account (Folio SL99)

2005			£	2005			£
Aug 1	Balance b/d		78	Aug 31	Bad debts	GL16	78

The journal entry showing this is as follows:

The Journal

Date	Details	Folio	Dr	Cr
2005			£	£
Aug 31	Bad debts	GL16	78	
	H Mander	SL99		78
	Debt written off as bad. See letter in file 7/8906.			

14.7 Opening entries

J Brew, after being in business for some years without keeping proper records, now decides to keep a double entry set of books. On 1 July 2003 he establishes that his assets and liabilities are as follows:

- *Assets*:　　Motor van £840; fixtures £700; stock £390
　　　　　　Debtors – B Young £95; D Blake £45
　　　　　　Bank £80; Cash £20.
- *Liabilities*:　Creditors – M Quinn £129; C Walters £41.

The assets therefore total £840 + £700 + £390 + £95 + £45 + £80 + £20 = £2,170 and the liabilities total £129 + £41 = £170. The capital consists of:

Assets – Liabilities = £2,170 – £170 = £2,000.

To write up the books of account on 1 July 2003 the following actions are carried out:

1. Open asset accounts, one for each asset. Each opening asset is shown as a debit balance.
2. Open liability accounts, one for each liability. Each opening liability is shown as a credit balance.
3. Open an account for the capital. Show it as a credit balance.

The journal is used to record these transactions and the reason. Exhibit 14.5 shows:

- the journal;
- the opening entries in the double entry accounts.

Exhibit 14.5

The Journal					Page 5
2003			Folio	Dr	Cr
				£	£
Jul 1	Motor van		GL1	840	
	Fixtures		GL2	700	
	Stock		GL3	390	
	Debtors – B Young		SL1	95	
		D Blake	SL2	45	
	Bank		CB1	80	
	Cash		CB1	20	
		Creditors – M Quinn	PL1		129
		C Walters	PL2		41
		Capital	GL4		2,000
	Assets and liabilities at the date entered				
	to open the books			2,170	2,170

General Ledger
Motor Van Account

Dr					Page 1 Cr
2003				£	
Jul 1	Balance		J5	840	

Fixtures Account

Dr					Page 2 Cr
2003				£	
Jul 1	Balance		J5	700	

Stock Account

Dr					Page 3 Cr
2003				£	
Jul 1	Balance		J5	390	

Capital Account

Dr					Page 4 Cr
		2003			£
		Jul 1	Balance	J5	2,000

Sales Ledger
B Young Account

Dr					Page 1 Cr
2003				£	
Jul 1	Balance		J5	95	

D Blake Account

Dr					Page 2 Cr
2003				£	
Jul 1	Balance		J5	45	

Exhibit 14.5 (continued)

Purchases Ledger
M Quinn Account — Page 1

Dr						Cr
			2003			£
			Jul 1	Balance	J5	129

C Walters Account — Page 2

Dr						Cr
			2003			£
			Jul 1	Balance	J5	41

Cash Book

Page 1

Dr		Cash	Bank		Cr
2003		£	£		
Jul 1 Balances	J5	20	80		

14.8 Other items

These can be of many kinds and it is impossible to write out a complete list, but several examples are shown below.

Example 14.11

K Young, a debtor, owed £2,000 on 1 July 2003. He was unable to pay his account in cash, but offers a motor car in full settlement of the debt. The offer is accepted on 5 July 2003. This means that K Young does not now owe us the money. His account will, therefore, have to be credited. On the other hand, the firm now has an extra asset, i.e. a motor car, therefore, the motor car account needs to be debited.

The double entry records are therefore:

K Young Account (Folio SL333)

2003		£	2003			£
Jul 1	Balance b/d	2,000	Jul 5	Motor car	GL171	2,000

Motor Car Account (Folio GL171)

2003			£	
Jul 5	K Young	SL333	2,000	

This is shown in the journal as:

The Journal

Date	Details	Folio	Dr	Cr
2003			£	£
Jul 5	Motor car	GL171	2,000	
	K Young	SL333		2,000
	Accepted motor car in full settlement of debt as per letter dated 5.7.2003			

Example 14.12

T Jones is a creditor. On 10 July 2003 his business is taken over by A Lee to whom a debt of £150 is now to be paid.

Here one creditor is being exchanged for another. The action needed is to cancel the amount owing to T Jones by debiting his account, and to show it owing to Lee by opening an account for Lee and crediting it.

The double entry records are:

T Jones Account (Folio SL92)

2003			£	2003		£
Jul 10	A Lee	SL244	150	Jul 1	Balance b/d	150

A Lee Account (Folio SL244)

				2003			£
				Jul 10	T Jones	SL92	150

The journal entries are:

The Journal

Date	Details	Folio	Dr	Cr
2003			£	£
Jul 10	T Jones	SL92	150	
	A Lee	SL244		150
	Transfer of indebtedness as per letter ref. G/1335			

Example 14.13

We had previously bought office equipment for £310 which was found to be faulty. On 12 July 2003 we returned it to the supplier, RS Ltd. An allowance of £310 was agreed, so that we will not have to pay for it.

The double entry records are:

RS Ltd Account (Folio PL24)

2003			£	2003		£
Jul 12	Office equipment	J6	310	Jul 1	Balance b/d	310

Example 14.13
(continued)

Office Equipment Account					(Folio GL88)
2003		£	*2003*		£
Jul 1	Balance b/d	<u>310</u>	Jul 12 RS Ltd	J6	<u>310</u>

The journal entries are:

The Journal   (J6)

Date	Details	Folio	Dr	Cr
2003			£	£
Jul 12	RS Ltd	PL24	310	
	Office equipment	GL88		310
	Faulty office equipment returned to supplier.			
	Full allowance given. See letter 10/7/2003.			

14.9 Examination questions involving the journal and control accounts

Control accounts will be dealt with in Chapter 15 when the answering of examination questions involving journal entries and control accounts will be fully discussed.

NEW TERM   **Suspense account**   An account showing the balance equal to the difference in a trial balance.

Student Activities

14.1   Show the journal entries to record the following:

2002
Jan   1   Bought computer on credit from Data Systems Ltd for £4,000.
     5   Goods taken from the business for own use £120. The goods were not paid for by the proprietor.
     8   A debt of £220 owing to us by J Oddy is written off as a bad debt.
   15   Bought a motor vehicle from Smithy Garage paying by cheque £15,500.
   29   J Street owes us £250. He is unable to pay his debt and we agree to take some filing cabinets valued at £250 from him to cancel the debt.

Narratives are not required.

14.2X   Tom Ainsworth runs a successful stationery business. After the preparation of his month end accounts the following errors were revealed:

(a)   The sale of unwanted fixtures and fittings for £1,000 had been credited to the sales account.

(b)   Expenditure incurred repairing the motor van £420, had been debited to motor van account.

(c) A payment of £800 received from C Clark had been posted in error to the credit of C Clarkson's account.

(d) Drawings of £500 taken by Mr Ainsworth had been debited to the salaries account.

(e) A payment of £240 for office cleaning had been debited to office equipment account in error.

Required   Write up the journal entries, including narratives, to correct the above errors.

14.3   The trial balance of Philip Hogan as at 31 December 2003 did not balance. The difference of £5,400 was credited to a suspense account. The following errors were subsequently discovered:

(a) The sales day book was undercast by £3,000.

(b) Purchases received from Dawson & Co, amounting to £1,147, had been received on 31 December 2003, and included in the closing stock at that date. Unfortunately, the invoice had not been entered in the purchases day book.

(c) Motor repairs of £585 had been charged to the motor vehicles account.

(d) Credit sales of £675 made to J Greenway had been debited to the account of J Green.

(e) A payment of £425 in respect of electricity had been debited to the electricity account as £575.

(f) A cheque for £2,250 received from Teape Ltd, a debtor, had been correctly entered in the cash book but no entry had been made in Teape's account.

Required

(i) Show the journal entries, including narratives, to correct the above errors.

(ii) Write up the suspense account after the correction of the above errors.

14.4   The following is a trial balance which has been incorrectly drawn up:

Trial Balance as at 31 January 2009

	£	£
Capital 1 February 2008	5,500	
Drawings	2,800	
Stock 1 February 2008		2,597
Trade debtors		2,130
Furniture and fittings	1,750	
Cash in hand	1,020	
Trade creditors		2,735
Sales		7,430
Returns inwards		85
Discount received	46	
Business expenses	950	
Purchases	4,380	
	16,446	14,977

In addition to the mistakes evident above, the following errors were also discovered:

1. A payment of £75 made to a creditor had not been posted from the cash book into the purchases ledger.
2. A cheque for £56 received from a customer had been correctly entered in the cash book but posted to the customer's account as £50.
3. A purchase of fittings £120 had been included in the purchases account.
4. The total of the discounts allowed column in the cash book of £38 had not been posted into the general ledger.
5. A page of the sales day book was correctly totalled as £564 but carried forward as £456.

Show the trial balance as it would appear after all the errors had been corrected. You are required to show all workings.

14.5 H Logan extracted a trial balance as at 31 December 2004. He was unable to balance it, but as he urgently needed his accounts for tax purposes, he opened a suspense account and entered £705 debit balance in it.

The following year he found the errors now listed:

(a) The returns inwards journal had been undercast by £100.
(b) Drawings £80 had been debited to wages account.
(c) Carriage inwards £75 had been debited to carriage outwards.
(d) A payment of bank charges £270 had not been posted to the expense account.
(e) A sale of goods £385 to K Abbott on 30 December 2004 had not been entered in the books at all.
(f) Discounts allowed of £218 had been credited to the discounts allowed account.
(g) A rent rebate of £200 had been entered in the cash book but not posted elsewhere.
(h) The purchases journal had carried forward a figure of £24,789 when it should have been £24,897.

Required

(i) Show the journal entries needed to correct the errors. Narratives are not required.
(ii) Show the suspense account balanced off.
(iii) If the original incorrect gross profit was shown as £129,487 and the original net profit was shown as £77,220, calculate the corrected figures for gross and net profits after the above items have been corrected.

14.6X Write up journal entries to record the following transactions, narratives are not required:

(a) Paid a cheque for £485 to the insurance company. Part of it, £118, is in respect of private house insurance, the remainder being for insurance of the business premises.

(b) Received a refund by cheque of £1,970 from the landlord from whom we rent the business premises. Of this, £1,278 was in respect of rent rebate and the remainder was a refund of the cost of building repairs done by us on his behalf.

(c) A computer is shown in the equipment account, valued at £5,800. It is not compatible with some new equipment we have bought. We exchanged it in return for a motor van of the same value from one of our customers.

(d) We have charged stationery £495 to the equipment account.

(e) Extra capital of £10,000 introduced by the proprietor has been credited to the sales account.

(f) We had charged postages of £9,600 for the year. In fact, £1,200 was in respect of the proprietor's private mail, and, of the remainder, 75% was for an advertising campaign where free postage stamps were given to customers.

(g) H Owen owes us £2,700. He was declared bankrupt, and the official receiver sent us a cheque representing 20p for each £1 owed as a final payment.

(h) Discounts allowed, £88, were incorrectly credited to returns outwards.

14.7X Marie Luiz has drawn up the final accounts for her first year in business. They are as follows:

Marie Luiz
Trading and Profit and Loss Account as at 31 December 2004

	£	£
Sales		148,920
Less Cost of goods sold:		
Stock at 1.1.2004	NIL	
Add Purchases	78,400	
Add Carriage outwards	560	
	78,960	
Less Stock at 31.12.2004	6,410	72,550
		76,370
Add returns outwards		490
Gross profit		76,860
Less Expenses:		
Wages	11,490	
Rent and rates	7,870	
Carriage inwards	1,300	
General expenses	2.460	
Drawings	38,770	61,890
Net profit		14,970

Balance Sheet for the year ended 31 December 2004

	£	£
Fixed assets		
Equipment		4,000
Current assets		
Stock	6,410	
Bank	12,050	
	18,460	
Current liabilities		
Creditors	1,230	17,230
Suspense		880
		22,110
Capital		
Cash introduced	7,140	
Add Net profit	14,970	22,110
		22,110

You examine the book keeping records and find the following errors in her double entry records:

(a) Purchases have been undercast by £563.

(b) Included in rent is £1,000 in respect of a private cottage.

(c) Marie Luiz introduced £500 extra capital in cash during the year, but her book keeper recorded it as cash sales.

(d) A payment of £245 wages was shown in the cash book but not in the wages account.

(e) An item of £36 paid for carriage outwards has been credited to the carriage outwards account.

(f) Goods taken for own use of £350 have not yet been recorded in the books.

Required

(i) Write up the journal entries needed to correct the above. Narratives are not required.

(ii) Draw up the suspense account showing the adjustments needed.

(iii) Redraft the final accounts after corrections have been made. Note that besides items (a) to (f) already listed, the original final accounts also contain items displayed in the wrong manner.

CHAPTER 15

Control accounts and reconciliation of ledger accounts

AIMS

- To be able to draw up sales ledger control accounts.

- To be able to draw up purchases ledger control accounts.

- To know the sources of information for control accounts.

- To appreciate the advantages of using control accounts.

- To understand the concept of control accounts in relation to double entry.

- To be able to reconcile the purchases ledger and the sales ledger with their respective control accounts.

- To prepare creditor and debtor reconciliations.

15.1　Need for control accounts

Where a business is small the accounts may all be contained in one ledger and at the end of the accounting period a trial balance could easily be drawn up as a test of the arithmetical accuracy of the accounts. However, it must be remembered that certain errors may not be revealed by the trial balance (see Chapter 14). If the trial balance totals disagree, the books could easily and quickly be checked to find the errors.

However, as the business grows the accounting requirements also expand and the work has to be divided up into various separate ledgers and, consequently, errors are not as easily identifiable. The error or errors could be very difficult to find and it may be necessary to check every item in every ledger. Therefore, what is required is a type of trial balance for each ledger, and this requirement is met by the **control account**. Thus it is only the ledgers where the control accounts do not balance that need detailed checking to locate any errors.

Exhibit 15.1

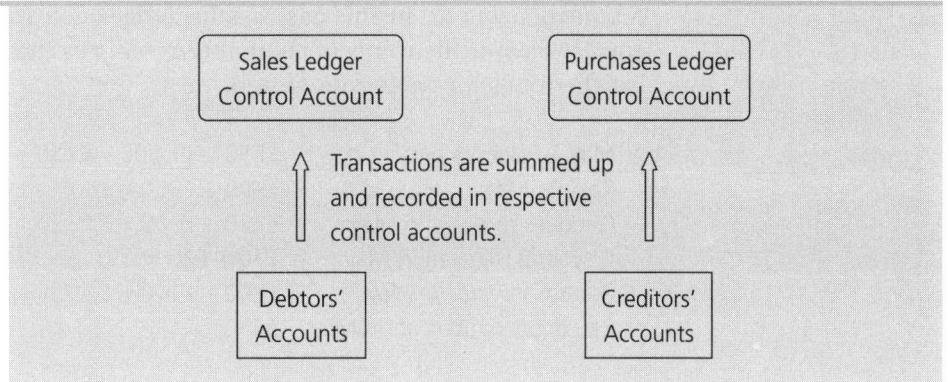

15.2 Principle of control accounts

The principle on which the control account is based is simple, and is as follows. If the opening balance of an account is known, together with the information of the additions and deductions entered in the account, the closing balance can be calculated.

This idea can be applied to a complete ledger. Suppose that there were only four accounts in the sales ledger for the month of May 2002 as follows:

Sales Ledger

Dr			T Allen Account				Cr
2002			£	*2002*			£
May	1	Balance b/d	850	May	7	Bank	820
	4	Sales	900		7	Discounts allowed	30
	30	Sales	350		31	Balance c/d	1,250
			2,100				2,100
Jun	1	Balance b/d	1,250				

Dr			P May Account				Cr
2002			£	*2002*			£
May	1	Balance b/d	1,500	May	9	Returns inwards	200
	28	Sales	400		14	Bank	900
					14	Discounts allowed	20
					31	Balance c/d	780
			1,900				1,900
Jun	1	Balance b/d	780				

Dr			K Winters Account				Cr
2002			£	*2002*			£
May	1	Balance b/d	750	May	20	Returns inwards	110
	15	Sales	600		31	Balance c/d	1,240
			1,350				1,350
Jun	1	Balance b/d	1,240				

Dr			C Young Account				Cr
2002			£	*2002*			£
May	1	Balance b/d	450	May	28	Bad debts	450

A control account, in this case a **sales ledger control account**, would consist only of the totals of each of the items in the sales ledger. Let us first list the totals for each type of item.

May 1 Balances b/d:	£850 + £1,500 + £750 + £450 = £3,550
Sales in May:	£900 + £350 + £400 + £600 = £2,250
Cheques received in May:	£820 + £900 = £1,720
Discounts allowed in May:	£30 + £20 = £50
Returns inwards in May:	£200 + £110 = £310
Bad debts written off in May:	£450

Now, looking at the totals only, it is possible to draw up a sales ledger control account. Debits are shown as usual on the left-hand side, and credits on the right-hand side.

Dr			Sales Ledger Control Account			Cr
2002		£	2002			£
May 1	Balances b/d	3,550	May 31	Bank		1,720
31	Sales for the month	2,250	31	Discounts allowed		50
			31	Returns inwards		310
			31	Bad debts		450
			31	Balances c/d	(A)	?
		5,800				5,800
Jun 1	Balances b/d	(B) ?				

From your studies so far of double entry, you should be able to see that the balance c/d (A) is the figure needed to balance the account, i.e. the difference between the two sides. It works out to be £3,270.

We can now look at the ledger and see if that is correct. The balances are £1,250 + £780 + £1,240 = £3,270. As this has now been proved to be correct, the figure of £3,270 can be shown in the sales ledger control account as the balances carried down (A) and the balances brought down (B).

In the above very simple example, there were only four ledger accounts. Suppose instead that there were 400 or 4,000 or 40,000 ledger accounts. In these cases the information concerning the totals of each type of item cannot be obtained so easily.

Remember that the main purpose of a control account is to act as a check on the accuracy of the entries in the ledgers. The total of a list of all the balances extracted from the ledger should equal the balance on the control account. If not, a mistake, or even many mistakes, may have been made and will have to be found.

15.3 Information for control accounts

The following tables show where information is obtained from to draw up control accounts:

Sales Ledger Control	Source
1. Opening debtors	List of debtors' balances drawn up at the end of the previous period.
2. Credit sales	Total from sales day book.
3. Returns inwards	Total of returns inwards day book.
4. Cheques received	Cash book: Bank column on received side. List extracted or total of a special column which has been included in the cash book.
5. Cash received	Cash book: Cash column on received side. List extracted or total of a special column which has been included in the cash book.
6. Discounts allowed	Total of discounts allowed column in the cash book.
7. Closing debtors	List of debtors' balances drawn up at the end of the period.

Purchases Ledger Control	Source
1. Opening creditors	List of creditors' balances drawn up at the end of the previous period.
2. Credit purchases	Total from purchases day book.
3. Returns outwards	Total of returns outwards day book.
4. Cheques paid	Cash book: Bank column on payments side. List extracted or total of a special column which has been included in the cash book.
5. Cash paid	Cash book: Cash column on payments side. List extracted or total of a special column which has been included in the cash book.
6. Discounts received	Total of discounts received column in the cash book.
7. Closing creditors	List of creditors' balances drawn up at the end of the period.

15.4 Form of control accounts

It is usual to find control accounts in the same form as an account with the totals of the debit entries in the sales and purchases ledgers on the left-hand side of the control account, and the totals of the various credit entries in the ledgers on the right-hand side of the control account.

This can also be shown in the form of two diagrams. Exhibit 15.2 shows how information is used to construct a sales ledger control account for the month of May 2006, whereas Exhibit 15.3 illustrates the construction of a purchases ledger control account for May 2006. The letters A, B, C and so on refer to the information used in the control accounts.

Exhibit 15.2

Sales ledger control account – source of data

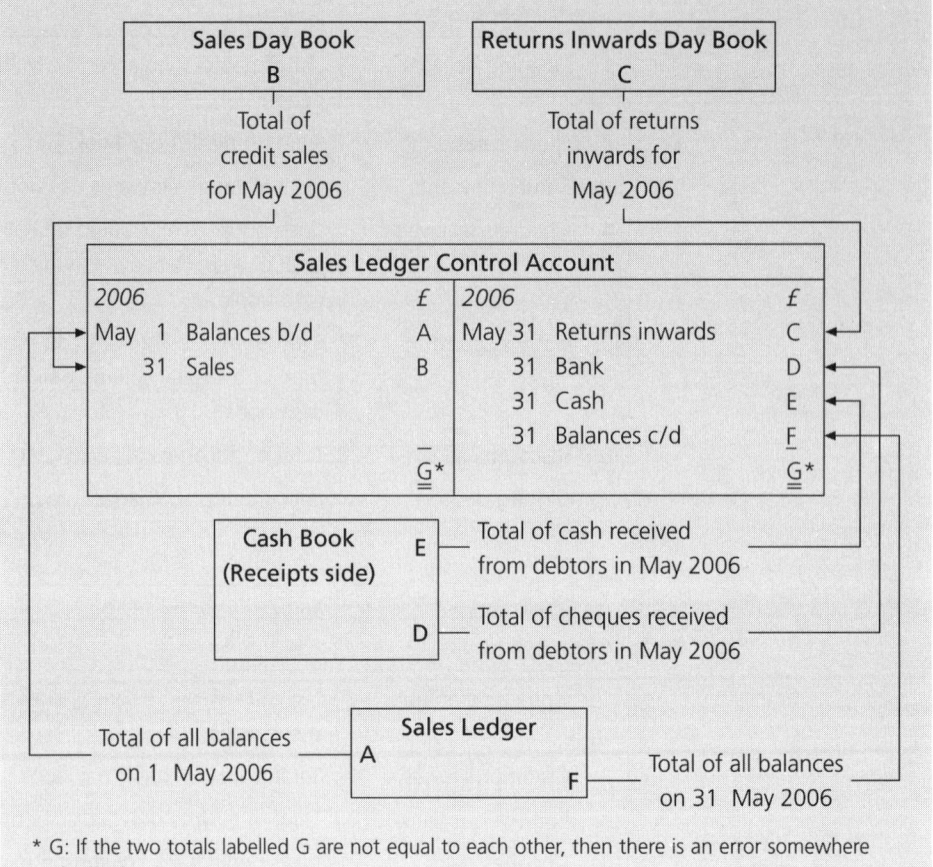

* G: If the two totals labelled G are not equal to each other, then there is an error somewhere in the books.

Exhibit 15.3

Purchases ledger control account – source of data

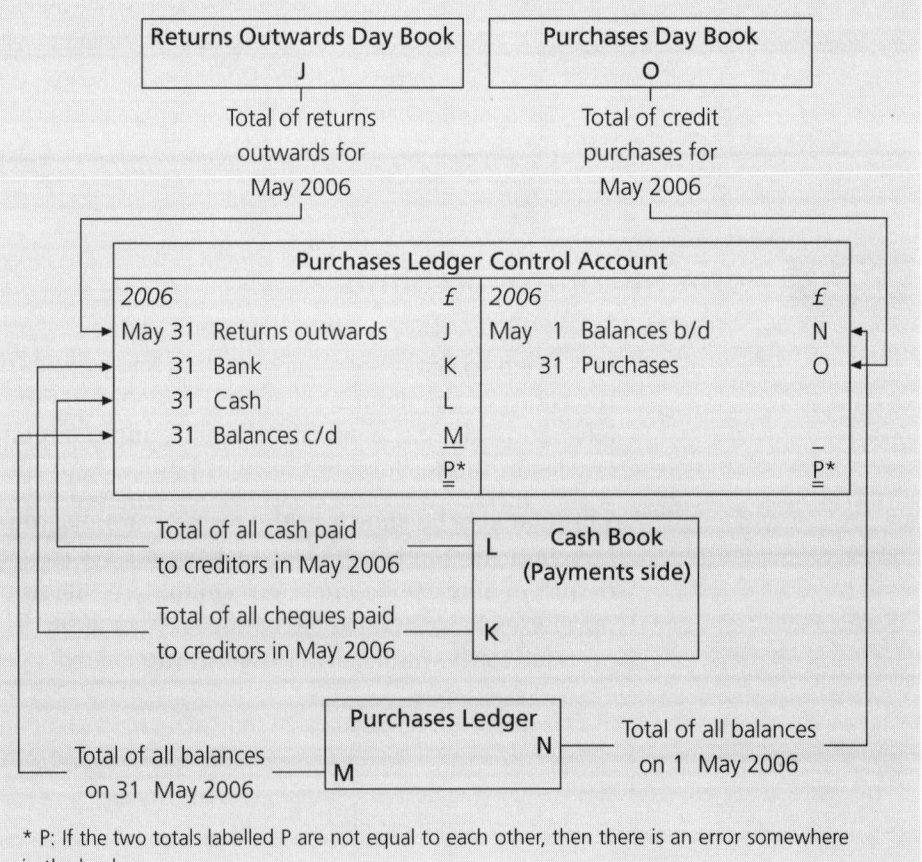

* P: If the two totals labelled P are not equal to each other, then there is an error somewhere in the books.

Exhibit 15.4 shows an example of a sales ledger control account for a sales ledger in which all the entries are arithmetically correct.

Exhibit 15.4

Sales ledger	£
Debit balances on 1 January 2006	1,894
Total credit sales for the month	10,290
Cheques received from customers in the month	7,284
Cash received from customers in the month	1,236
Returns inwards from customers during the month	296
Debit balances on 31 January as extracted from the sales ledger	3,368

Dr		Sales Ledger Control Account			Cr
2006		£	2006		£
Jan 1	Balances b/d	1,894	Jan 31	Bank	7,284
31	Sales	10,290	31	Cash	1,236
			31	Returns inwards	296
			31	Balances c/d	3,368
		12,184			12,184

We have proved the ledger to be arithmetically correct, because the totals of the control account equal each other. If the totals are not equal, then this proves that there is an error somewhere.

Exhibit 15.5 shows an example of where an error is found to exist in the purchases ledger. The ledger will have to be checked in detail, the error found, and the control account then corrected.

Exhibit 15.5

Purchases ledger	£
Credit balances on 1 January 2006	3,890
Cheques paid to suppliers during the month	3,620
Returns outwards to suppliers in the month	95
Bought from suppliers in the month	4,936
Credit balances on 31 January as extracted from the purchases ledger	5,151

Dr		Purchases Ledger Control Account			Cr
2006		£	2006		£
Jan 31	Bank	3,620	Jan 1	Balances b/d	3,890
31	Returns outwards	95	31	Purchases	4,936
31	Balances c/d	5,151			
		8,866*			8,826*

* There is a £40 error in the purchases ledger, therefore, the ledger will have to be checked in detail to find the error.

 Notice that a double line does not appear under the totals figures. We will not finalise the account until the error is traced and corrected.

15.5 Other transfers

Transfers to bad debts accounts will have to be recorded in the sales ledger control account as they involve entries in the sales ledgers.

Similarly, a contra account, whereby the same firm is both a supplier and a customer and inter-indebtedness is *set-off*, will also need entering in the control accounts. For example:

(1) The firm sold A Hall £600 goods on 1 May 2005.

(2) Hall supplied the firm with £880 goods on 12 May 2005.

(3) The £600 owing by Hall was set-off against £600 owing to him on 30 May 2005.

(4) This left £280 owing to Hall on 31 May 2005.

Sales Ledger

Dr			A Hall Account			Cr
2005			£			
May 1	Sales	(1)	600			

Purchases Ledger

Dr			A Hall Account			Cr
			2005			£
			May 12	Purchases	(2)	880

The set-off now takes place:

Sales Ledger

Dr			A Hall Account			Cr
2005			£	*2005*		£
				May 30 Set-off:		
May 1 Sales		(1)	600	Purchases ledger	(3)	600

Purchases Ledger

Dr			A Hall Account			Cr
2005			£	*2005*		£
May 30	Set-off: Sales ledger	(3)	600	May 12 Purchases	(2)	880
31	Balance c/d	(4)	280			
			880			880
				Jun 1 Balance b/d	(4)	280

The transfer of the £600 will therefore appear on the credit side of the sales ledger control account and on the debit side of the purchases ledger control account.

 *Many students become confused when making postings to control accounts and might find it useful to remember that when posting entries to control accounts the entry goes on the same side as it would in the personal account. Another useful hint can also be applied when entering 'contra' or 'set-off' items – here think of the contra or set-off as **cash** and enter the item where you would normally enter cash on the respective control account.*

15.6 A more complicated example

Exhibit 15.6 shows a worked example of a more complicated control account. You will see that there are sometimes credit balances in the sales ledger as well as debit balances. Suppose we sold £500 goods to W Young. He then paid in full for them, and returned £40 goods to us afterwards. This would leave a credit balance of £40 on the account, whereas usually the balances in the sales ledger are debit balances.

Exhibit 15.6

2006		£
Aug 1	Sales ledger – debit balances	3,816
1	Sales ledger – credit balances	22
31	*Transactions for the month:*	
	Cash received	104
	Cheques received	6,739
	Sales	7,090
	Bad debts written off	306
	Discounts allowed	298
	Returns inwards	164
	Cash refunded to a customer who had overpaid his account	37
	Dishonoured cheques	29
	Customer debited with interest charged by us on overdue debt	50
31	*At the end of the month:*	
	Sales ledger – debit balances	3,429
	Sales ledger – credit balances	40

Dr		Sales Ledger Control Account			Cr
2006		£	2006		£
Aug 1	Balances b/d	3,816	Aug 1	Balances b/d	22
31	Sales	7,090	31	Cash	104
31	Cash refunded	37	31	Bank	6,739
31	Bank: Dishonoured		31	Bad debts	306
	cheques	29	31	Discounts allowed	298
31	Interest on debt	50	31	Returns inwards	164
31	Balances c/d	40	31	Balances c/d	3,429
		11,062			11,062

15.7 Other advantages of control accounts

Control accounts have merits other than that of locating errors. Normally the control accounts are under the charge of a responsible official, and fraud is made more difficult because transfers made (in an effort) to disguise frauds will have to pass the scrutiny of this person.

For management purposes the balances on the control account can always be taken to equal debtors and creditors without waiting for an extraction of individual balances. Management control is thereby aided because the speed at which information is obtained is one of the prerequisites of efficient control.

15.8 Other sources of information for control accounts

With a large organisation there may well be more than one sales ledger or purchases ledger. The accounts in the sales ledgers may be divided up in ways such as:

- *Alphabetically* – Thus we may have three sales ledgers, split A–F, G–O and P–Z.
- *Geographically* – This could be split: Europe, Far East, Africa, Australasia, North and South America.

For each ledger we must therefore have a separate control account.

15.9 Control accounts as part of double entry

A **sales ledger control account** shows, in total form, all the individual items debited and credited in the sales ledger for a particular period. A **purchases ledger control account** does exactly the same thing but for the purchases ledger. If both the control accounts and the ledgers contain exactly the same information, one by using totals and the other containing a large number of individual entries, then the question arises as to whether it is the ledgers that are part of the double entry or the control accounts.

One way of looking at this question is to say that the sales ledger and the purchases ledger are part of the double entry, while the control accounts are not part of the double entry but are simply 'memorandum accounts' and act as a form of trial balance checking on whether the ledgers 'balance' (see Exhibit 15.7).

Another way of looking at it is to say that the sales and purchases ledger control accounts are part of the double entry, while the sales ledger and the purchases ledger are not part of double entry and contain memorandum accounts only (see Exhibit 15.8). Obviously there is a need for a sales ledger and purchases ledger otherwise the business would not know the identity of each individual debtor and creditor, nor would it know the amounts owing to or by each of them.

In Exhibit 15.8 the balance of outstanding debtors and creditors is taken from the control accounts and included in the trial balance at the end of the month or year end, as required. In this case the personal accounts of the debtors and creditors, i.e. A Account, B Account, C Account, etc., are not part of the double entry system and are referred to as **memorandum accounts**. It is, however, important to balance the memorandum accounts periodically with the sales and purchases ledger control accounts so that errors can be located and corrected.

In larger organisations it would be normal to find that control accounts are an integral part of the double entry system, the balances of the control accounts being taken for the purpose of extracting a trial balance. In this case the personal accounts are used as subsidiary records or memorandum accounts.

This view which the larger organisation takes is the one that is most favoured by the various examining bodies. In practical terms, as a student,

Exhibit 15.7

Control account as a memorandum account

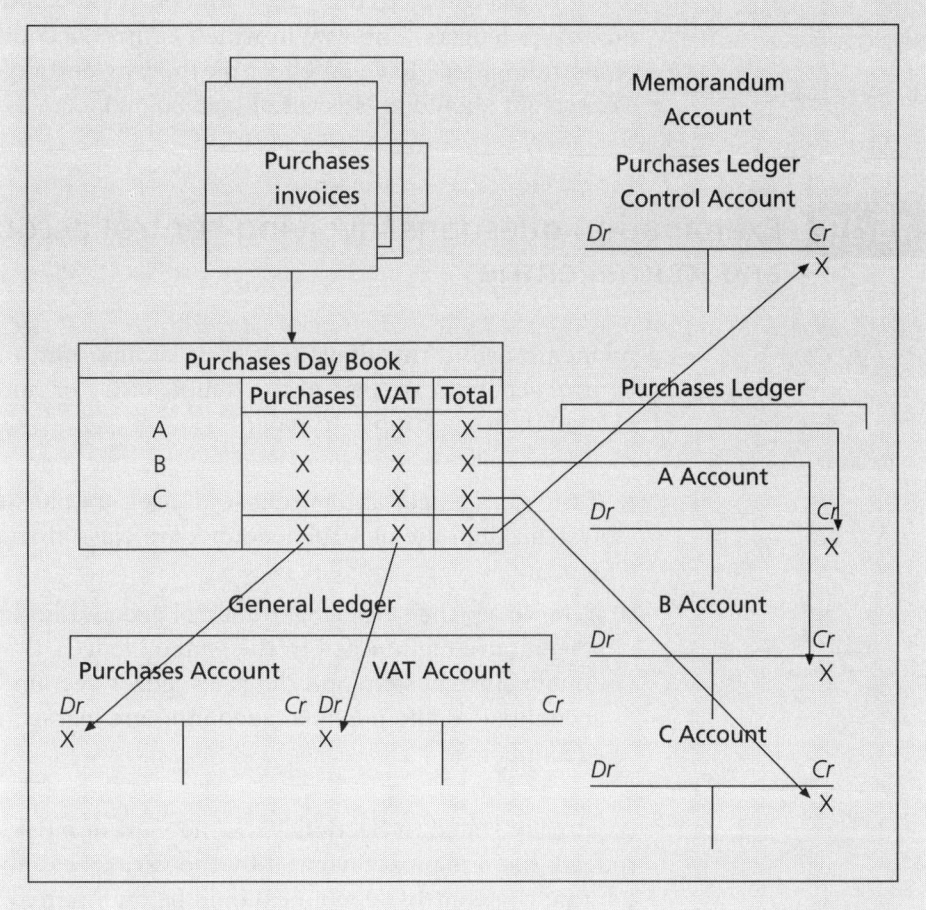

Exhibit 15.8

Control account as part of a double entry system

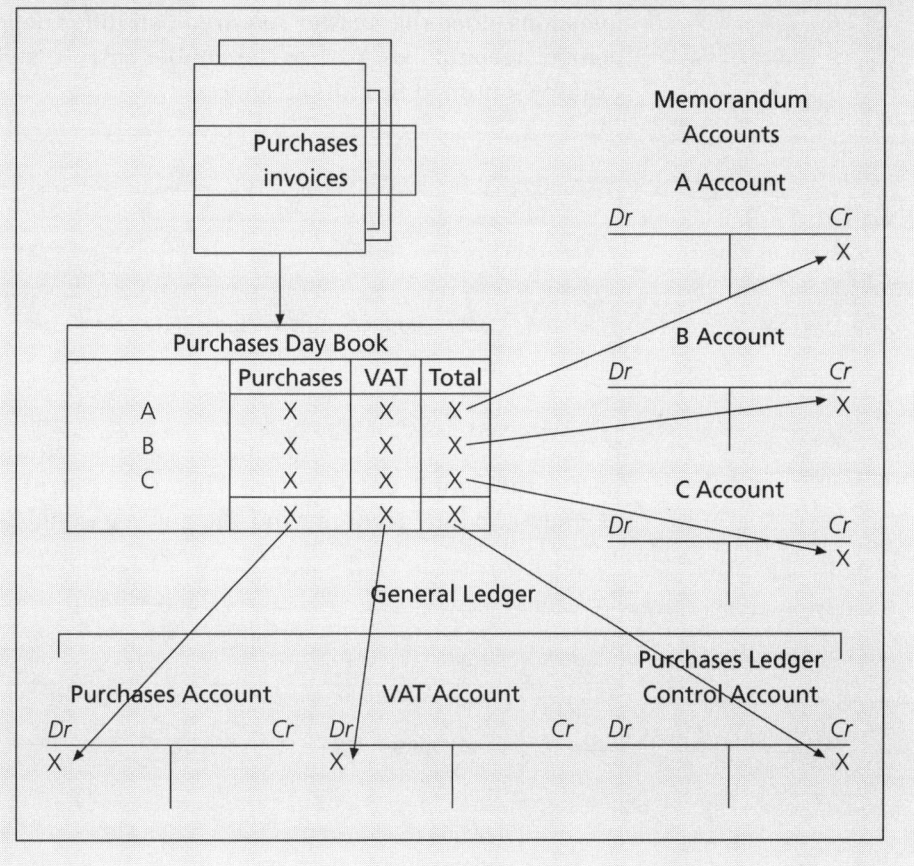

it will be necessary to draw up both control accounts and the sales and purchases ledgers. The way in which control accounts are used within an organisation does have an effect on the way certain questions in an assessment should be answered (see below).

15.10 Examination questions involving control accounts and journal entries

As mentioned in the above section it is important to ascertain whether control accounts are part of the double entry or not when answering examination questions. To recap:

- If the sales ledger and purchases ledger are part of the double entry system, then the control accounts are classed as 'memorandum accounts'.
- If, however, the sales ledger control account and purchases ledger control account are maintained in the general ledger, then they are part of the double entry system and the sales ledger accounts and purchases ledger accounts (i.e. the personal accounts) are classed as 'memorandum accounts'.

As already stated in Section 15.9, the view of most large organisations and, indeed, the one most favoured by the various examining bodies is the latter, i.e. that the control accounts should be maintained in the general ledger and are, therefore, part of the double entry system.

It is important for students to be aware of this when answering examination questions since the answer required can differ depending upon whether the control accounts are part of the double entry system or not. Consider the example outlined in Exhibit 15.9.

Exhibit 15.9

Wesley Davies & Co receive a cheque for £525 from one of their debtors, Clive Johnson Ltd. They bank the cheque on 4 April 2001. However, on 15 April 2001 the company is advised that the cheque has been dishonoured. Show the journal entries necessary to record the dishonoured cheque.

If Wesley Davies & Co maintain sales and purchases ledgers which are part of the double entry system, then the control accounts will be classed as memorandum accounts and the answer would be as follows:

The Journal

Date	Details	Folio	Dr	Cr
2001			£	£
Apr 15	Clive Johnson Ltd		525	
	Cash book			525
	Cheque received from Clive Johnson Ltd dishonoured by the bank			

Sales Ledger

Dr			Clive Johnson Ltd Account			Cr
2001		£	*2001*			£
Apr 1	Balance b/d	525	Apr 1	Bank		525
15	Bank dishonoured cheque	525				

Dr		Cash Book		Cr
		2001		£
		Apr 15	Clive Johnson Ltd	
			dishonoured cheque	525

If, however, Wesley Davies & Co maintain the sales and purchases ledger control accounts in the general ledger and they are part of the double entry system, with the sales and purchases ledger accounts being memorandum accounts, then the answer to the question would be as follows:

The Journal

Date	Details	Folio	Dr	Cr
2001			£	£
Apr 15	Sales ledger control account		525	
	Cash book			525
	Cheque received from Clive Johnson Ltd dishonoured by the bank			

General Ledger

Dr			Sales Ledger Control Account		Cr
2001		£			
Apr 15	Bank – dishonoured cheque Clive Johnson Ltd	525			

Dr		Cash Book		Cr
		2001		£
		Apr 15	Dishonoured cheque Clive Johnson Ltd	525

The student will notice that if the control accounts *are part of the double entry system* then any entry affecting an individual debtor or creditor account is posted direct to the control account for the purpose of answering examination questions. If, however, the control accounts *are not part of the double entry system* but are classed as memorandum accounts, then any entry necessary would be made to the individual debtor or creditor account.

It is very important that students familiarise themselves with this topic, and when answering questions on control accounts in an examination must ensure that they read the question carefully to ascertain whether the control accounts are part of the double entry system or not, as this will affect the answer.

15.11 Reconciliation of control accounts

Errors and omissions can occur when entering information into the accounting records, as was illustrated in the previous chapter which dealt with the correction of errors via the journal. When a ledger control account is not in balance, it indicates that something has gone wrong with the entries made to the accounting records. This leads to an investigation which (hopefully) reveals the cause(s). Then, in order to verify whether the identified item(s) caused the failure to balance the control account, a reconciliation is carried out.

Exhibit 15.10 shows an example of a **purchases ledger control account reconciliation**. It takes the original control account balance and adjusts it to arrive at an amended balance which should equal the revised total of the individual creditors' balances.

It can be seen that the general approach is similar to that adopted for bank reconciliation statements. However, as each control account may be constructed using information from a number of sources (see Section 15.3) the extent of the investigation to identify the cause of the control account imbalance may be far greater than that undertaken when performing a bank reconciliation.

Exhibit 15.10

G Owen, the sales ledger clerk for Joinery Ltd, found that the balance on the sales ledger control account on 31 January 2004 was £115,790. However, when he compared this with a list of the balances on the individual debtors' accounts in the memorandum sales ledger, he found that the total of these was £115,261.

He then checked all of the entries concerning sales and debtors for the month of January 2004. He found the following errors:

(a) A sales invoice for £179 had been correctly entered in the debtors account, but had not been entered in the sales journal.

(b) The total of the sales journal had been overcast by £400.

(c) A credit note for goods returned by a customer for £88 had been shown in the customer's account but was not entered in the returns inwards account.

(d) A debt for £220 had been written off as a bad debt, and entered in the customer's account. It was not, however, included in the sales ledger control account.

Before amending the sales ledger control account, Owen drafted a sales ledger reconciliation account as follows:

Sales Ledger Reconciliation Statement as at 31 January 2004

			£	£
Original sales ledger control account balance				115,790
Add	(a)	sales invoice omitted		179
				115,969
Less	(b)	Sales journal total overcast	400	
	(c)	Returns inwards omitted	88	
	(d)	Bad debt omitted	220	708
Corrected figure of sales ledger control account balance				115,261

He therefore established he had found all the errors, and consequently amended the control account figures.

15.12 Reconciliation of ledger accounts

In addition to reconciling the control accounts with lists of outstanding creditors and debtors, it is important that individual ledger accounts are reconciled.

Reconciling ledger accounts with the supplier's statement of account

A supplier's statement of account should be checked against his or her ledger account in the firm's own books and the balance reconciled before making a payment. Sometimes, because of the differences in timing, the balance on a supplier's statement on a certain date can differ from the balance on that supplier's account in the firm's purchases ledger. This is similar to a bank statement whose balance may differ from that in the cash book and require the preparation of a 'bank reconciliation statement' to reconcile the two balances. If the balance on the statement of account does differ from the supplier's account in the purchases ledger, then it will be necessary to check the statement against the ledger account and reconcile the difference by preparing a 'supplier's reconciliation statement'.

The reasons for the differences in balances may be due to:

- Goods returned by the customer but not recorded by the supplier until after the statement of account has been issued.
- A supplier sending goods to a customer, together with an invoice, but neither being received by the customer until a later date. The customer is, therefore, unable to enter the invoice in their books of the account until receipt.
- Payments in transit.
- Other errors which may be made by either the supplier or buyer when entering data, i.e. transposing figures, or an error in the calculation of a balance where manual accounts are maintained.

Reconciling remittance advices with ledger accounts

In the same way that it is important to reconcile suppliers' statements of accounts with a firm's own records prior to making a payment, it is equally important to check that all outstanding invoices have been paid by the firm's debtors.

Most businesses send a remittance advice when making payment either by cheque or by BACS. On receipt of the remittance advice the details of the payment should be checked against the debtor's ledger account in the firm's own records to ensure that all outstanding invoices have been paid. Again, there may be a difference in the balance on the ledger account with the amount of payment made by the debtor. This difference may be due to any of the above-mentioned reasons, or it may be that there is a query on an invoice which has not yet been resolved. This should be taken up with the customer as soon as possible to enable prompt settlement of the outstanding invoice.

It is important that regular reconciliation is carried out with all suppliers' and customers' accounts to maintain the accuracy of the purchase and sales ledgers outstanding balances.

 This topic is covered more fully in Transaction Accounting . . . (Chapter 26).

NEW TERMS

Control account   An account which contains the total of the various individual personal account balances which are held in subsidiary ledgers such as the 'sales ledger' or 'purchases ledger'. By comparing the balance on the control account with the total outstanding balances in a subsidiary ledger the arithmetical accuracy can be checked. Errors can more easily be located and rectified.

Memorandum accounts   Accounts which are not part of the double entry system. These may be the personal accounts of debtors or creditors where the control account is part of the double entry system and the personal accounts are classified as 'memorandum accounts'. Alternatively, the sales and purchases ledgers may be part of the double entry and the control accounts classified as 'memorandum accounts'.

Reconciling a supplier's statement   Checking a supplier's statements of account with a firm's own ledger account for the individual creditor and preparing a 'reconciliation statement' to identify the differences.

Remittance advice   A document which accompanies payment by cheque or via BACS and gives details of the payment.

Set-offs (Contra entries)   A set-off or contra item occurs where a balance in the purchases ledger is set-off against a balance in the sales ledger and vice versa.

Statement of account   This is normally sent to debtors at the end of each month. It states the amount owing by them at the end of that particular month.

Student Activities

15.1   You are required to prepare a sales ledger control account from the following for the month of May.

2006		£
May 1	Sales ledger balances	4,936
	Totals for May:	
	Sales day book	49,916
	Returns inwards day book	1,139
	Cheques and cash received from customers	46,490
	Discounts allowed	1,455
31	Sales ledger balances	5,768

15.2X You are required to prepare a purchases ledger control account from the following for the month of June. The balance of the account is to be taken as the amount of creditors as on 30 June.

2006		£
Jun 1	Purchases ledger balances	3,676
	Totals for June:	
	Purchases day book	42,257
	Returns outwards day book	1,098
	Cheques paid to suppliers	38,765
	Discounts received from suppliers	887
30	Purchases ledger balances	?

15.3 Prepare a sales ledger control account from the following:

2005		£
May 1	Debit balances	6,420
	Totals for May:	
	Sales day book	12,800
	Cash and cheques received from debtors	10,370
	Discounts allowed	395
	Debit balances in the sales ledger set-off against credit balances in the purchases ledger	145
31	Debit balances	?
	Credit balances	50

15.4X Prepare a sales ledger control account from the following information for July 2009 carrying down the balance at 31 July:

2009		£
Jul 1	Sales ledger balances	9,700
31	Sales day book	99,280
	Bad debts written off	279
	Cheques received from debtors	95,120
	Discounts allowed	1,285
	Cheques dishonoured	226
	Returns inwards day book	3,170
	Set-offs against balances in purchases ledger	400

15.5 The trial balance of Queen & Square Ltd revealed a difference in the books. In order that the error(s) could be located it was decided to prepare purchases and sales ledger control accounts.

From the following prepare the control accounts and show where an error may have been made:

		£
2006		
Jan 1	Purchases ledger balances	11,874
	Sales ledger balances	19,744
	Totals for the year 2006:	
	Purchases day book	154,562
	Sales day book	199,662
	Returns outwards day book	2,648
	Returns inwards day book	4,556
	Cheques paid to suppliers	146,100
	Petty cash paid to suppliers	78
	Cheques and cash received from customers	185,960
	Discounts allowed	5,830
	Discounts received	2,134
	Balances on the sales ledger set-off against balances in the purchases ledger	1,036
Dec 31	The list of balances from the purchases ledger shows a total of £14,530 and that from the sales ledger a total of £22,024	

15.6X A company controls its debtors collection period by maintaining a 'sales ledger control account' which it regularly reconciles with the total of debtors outstanding in the sales ledger. When preparing the final accounts for the year ended 30 June 2004 the total of the individual debtors' accounts outstanding amounted to £38,406, whereas the balance on the sales ledger control account amounted to £37,650.

The accountant carried out an investigation and the following errors were identified.

(a) One of the debtor's personal account balances had been shown as £800 instead of the correct amount of £1,400.

(b) A set-off of £1,200 with the customer's account in the purchases ledger had been entered in the personal account but not in the control account.

(c) Cash received from a debtor of £750 had been debited to the personal account in error.

(d) Bad debts written off amounting to £2,100 had been omitted from the control account.

(e) Sales of £2,550 had not been entered in the control account.

(f) Cash received of £1,540 had been posted to the debtors' account as £1,000.

(g) A Adams, whose balance outstanding amounted to £750, had not been included in the list of outstanding debtors.

(h) A cheque received from a debtor for £900 has been dishonoured by the bank. No entry has been made in the control account in respect of this transaction.

(i) Cash received from a debtor amounting to £240 had been credited as £24 in the personal account.

(j) Discounts allowed to the customers amounting to £300 had not been entered in the control account.

Required

1. Make the necessary corrections to the sales ledger control account and bring down the corrected balance on 1 July 2004.

2. List the corrections required to the list of outstanding debtors so that the total balance outstanding agrees with the balance on the sales ledger control account.

 On checking the books of Deacon's Suppliers Ltd you discover that the balances brought down on 1 January 2005 in the purchases ledger control account were as follows:

Debit: £945
Credit: £56,115

For the year ended 31 December 2005 the following information was extracted from the ledgers:

	£
Purchases	359,766
Amount paid to creditors by cheque	335,763
Returns outwards	4,815
Discounts received	13,275
Cheques received in respect of the debit balances in the purchases ledger	945
Balance on the sales ledger set off against a balance on the purchases ledger	3,906

Required

1. Write up the purchases ledger control account.
2. Discuss the advantages of a business using control accounts.

CHAPTER 16

The extended trial balance

AIMS

■ To be able to enter balances from the general ledger and other records on the extended trial balance (ETB).

■ To be able to deal with adjustments, including accruals and prepayments, and enter them correctly on the ETB.

■ To be able to enter the closing stock valuation on the ETB.

■ To deal with other adjustments such as depreciation and provision for bad debts and enter them on the ETB.

■ To deal with any errors and discrepancies and enter them on the ETB.

■ To be able to extend the ETB entries into appropriate columns of adjustments, profit and loss account and balance sheet and total them correctly.

16.1 Introduction

As already mentioned in Chapters 2 and 3, a **trial balance** is a list of all balances on the double entry (the ledgers) accounts and the cash book at a particular point in time. The main purpose of the trial balance is to ensure that the books 'balance' and, if any errors are identified, to make the necessary corrections. Another important function of the trial balance is to provide the balances to be used in preparation of the financial statements of the business, the trading and profit and loss account and the balance sheet.

16.2 The extended trial balance

The extended trial balance is often referred to as a 'worksheet' which provides a useful aid where a large number of adjustments are needed prior to the preparation of the financial statements. The extended trial balance is drawn up on specially preprinted stationery on which suitable columns are printed. Exhibit 16.1 shows an example of an extended trial balance. You may wish to photo-copy this format and use it when carrying out some of the student activities at the end of the chapter.

Exhibit 16.1 Format for an extended trial balance

Description	Ledger Balances		Adjustments		Profit and Loss		Balance Sheet	
	Dr £	Cr £	Dr £	Cr £	Dr £	Cr £	Dr £	Cr £

It should be noted, however, that some examining bodies may require a slightly different format which needs more columns. It is advisable to find out in which format the examining body, whose syllabus you are studying, require the extended trial balance to be shown.

16.3 Preparing the extended trial balance

Once the trial balance has been drawn up and balanced off correctly, the next task is to implement the following adjustments:

- accruals and prepayments
- include the closing stock valuation
- make provision for depreciation and provision for bad debts
- correct any errors.

16.4 A worked example

In Exhibit 16.2 you will find the trial balance which was extracted from the books of D Simpson, a retailer, at 31 December 2002.

Exhibit 16.2

Trial Balance of D Simpson as at 31 December 2002

	£	£
Purchases	138,872	
Sales		202,460
Carriage inwards	490	
Carriage outwards	1,406	
Returns inwards and outwards	424	2,280
Stock 1 January 2002	9,820	
Wages and salaries	29,950	
Rent	11,000	
Rates and insurance	3,900	
Heating and lighting	1,254	
Motor vehicle	9,000	
Motor expenses	2,500	
Capital 1 January 2002		37,896
Bank overdraft		5,638
Fixtures and fittings	6,400	
Drawings	27,900	
Debtors	23,200	
Creditors		17,842
	266,116	266,116

Notes

(a) Rent owing amounted to £1,000 as at 31 December 2002.

(b) Rates paid in advance amounted to £500.

(c) Closing stock was valued at £12,042 as at 31 December 2002.

(d) Depreciate the motor vehicle at 20% using the straight line method.
[*Note: Fixtures and fittings are not to be depreciated in this example.*]

(e) Provide for the creation of a provision for bad debts amounting to 2% of the debtors.

You are required to:

1. Prepare an extended trial balance at 31 December 2002.
2. Prepare a trading and profit and loss account for the year ended 31 December 2002 and a balance sheet as at that date.

Since many students have difficulty in preparing extended trial balances the above example will be carried out using the 'Step-by-step Guide' shown below.

Step-by-step-guide

Step 1 First of all draw up a trial balance in the usual way (refer to Chapter 3, Exhibit 3.1). Remember:

> Debit Balances are Assets or Expenses
> *and*
> Credit Balances are Liabilities, Capital or Income

If there have been no errors then the two sides should agree. Refer to Exhibit 16.3 and note that the balances have now been entered on the ETB under the heading 'ledger balances'.

Step 2 Deal with the **adjustments** at the bottom of the trial balance.
*[Note: Each item must be dealt with **twice** to comply with the double entry rules.]*

Adjustments fall into four categories

1. Accruals
2. Prepayments
3. Closing stock valuation
4. Other adjustments:
   depreciation provision
   provision for bad debts
   correction of errors

When dealing with **adjustments** think **double entry**, i.e.

> which account should be **debited**
> *and*
> which account should be **credited**

When entering the adjustment on the ETB first of all look to see if there is already an 'Account' for the transaction and, if so, use it. If not, then open an account at the foot of the ETB. (This is illustrated in the following examples.)

Step 3 Deal with accruals and prepayments.

1. Accruals (amounts owing)

For example, referring to Exhibit 16.2(a) rent owing amounts to £1,000, which is entered as follows:

> **Debit** Rent Account £1,000
> **Credit** Accruals – Rent £1,000 (as this item is a liability).

This transaction is now shown in Exhibit 16.3 below as '(a)' under the 'Adjustments' column – see the debit entry of £1,000 next to the 'Rent Account' and the credit entry of £1,000 entered below the totals of the trial balance under the heading 'Accruals – Rent'.

2. Prepayments (amounts paid in advance)

Exhibit 16.2(b) shows a rates prepayment of £500, which is entered as follows:

> **Debit** Prepayments – rates £500
> **Credit** Rates account £500

This again is shown in Exhibit 16.3(b) under the Adjustments column – see the debit entry of £500 entered below the totals of the trial balance under the heading 'Prepayment – rates £500' and the corresponding credit entry shown next to the 'rates account'.

3. Dealing with the closing stock valuation

At the end of the financial year a business usually undertakes a valuation of the stock. Exhibit 16.2(c) shows a closing stock of £12,042, which is entered as follows:

> **Debit** Stock account (to be shown in the balance sheet as an asset)
> **Credit** Stock account (shown in the profit and loss account as a deduction from the cost of goods sold calculation).

This is shown in Exhibit 16.3(c) under the trial balance totals in the Adjustments column.

4. Dealing with other adjustments

Depreciation provision Exhibit 16.2(d) requires provision for depreciation of 20% on motor vehicles using the straight line method. Motor vehicles cost £9,000, therefore, 20% of cost equals £1,800 depreciation to be charged against the profit and loss account. This transaction is entered on the ETB under the Adjustments column, see note (d) as follows:

> **Debit** Depreciation of motor vehicle £1,800 (amount to be charged to profit and loss account)
> **Credit** Depreciation provision of motor vehicle £1,800 (amount to be shown as a deduction from the value of the asset in the balance sheet).

Provision for bad debts Exhibit 16.3(e) requires the creation of a provision for bad debts amounting to 2% of the debtors figure of £23,200

Exhibit 16.3   D Simpson – Extended Trial Balance at 31 December 2002

	Description	Ledger Balances Dr £	Ledger Balances Cr £	Adjustments Dr £	Adjustments Cr £	Profit and Loss Dr £	Profit and Loss Cr £	Balance Sheet Dr £	Balance Sheet Cr £
PL	Purchases	138,872				138,872			
PL	Sales		202,460				202,460		
PL	Carriage inwards	490				490			
PL	Carriage outwards	1,406				1,406			
PL	Returns inwards and outwards	424	2,280			424	2,280		
PL	Stock 1 January 2002	9,820				9,820			
PL	Wages and salaries	29,950				29,950			
PL	Rent	11,000		(a) 1,000		12,000			
PL	Rates and insurance	3,900			(b) 500	3,400			
PL	Heating and lighting	1,254				1,254			
BS	Motor vehicle	9,000						9,000	
PL	Motor expenses	2,500				2,500			
BS	Capital 1 January 2002		37,896						37,896
BS	Bank overdraft		5,638						5,638
BS	Fixtures and fittings	6,400						6,400	
BS	Drawings	27,900						27,900	
BS	Debtors	23,200						23,200	
BS	Creditors		17,842						17,842
		266,116	266,116						
BS	Accrual – Rent				(a) 1,000				1,000
BS	Prepayment – Rates			(b) 500				500	
BS	Stock 31 December 2002			(c) 12,042				12,042	
PL	Stock 31 December 2002				(c) 12,042		12,042		
PL	Depreciation – Motor vehicle			(d) 1,800		1,800			
BS	Depreciation – Provision for motor vehicle				(d) 1,800				1,800
PL	Provision for bad debts			(e) 464		464			
BS	Provision for bad debts				(e) 464				464
				15,806	15,806				
				(Step 4)					
	Net profit (Step 6)					14,402			14,402
						216,782	216,782	79,042	79,042
								(Step 7)	

which amounts to £464. The entry in the ETB will appear in the Adjustments column – note (e) as follows:

Debit Creation of provision for bad debts £464 (this amount to be charged in the profit and loss account)

Credit Provision for bad debts £464 (this amount to be shown as deduction from the debtors in the balance sheet).

Correction of errors   To keep the worked example as straightforward as possible, no errors require correcting in Exhibit 16.2. This topic will be covered later in this chapter.

Step 4   The next step is to add up both parts of the Adjustments column. Providing the adjustments have been carried out correctly, the two columns should agree – in other words, the Adjustments column acts rather like a mini trial balance.

Step 5   It is now necessary to add/subtract the figures **across** the ETB and enter the **total** in either the Profit and Loss Account or Balance Sheet column. This step requires a certain amount of skill from the students since they must be fully conversant with the position of each balance figure in the financial statements. A useful hint is to carry out this identification *before* starting the analysis by entering either of the following immediately before the Description column (see Exhibit 16.3) viz.:

PL   Profit and Loss Account
BS   Balance Sheet

to indicate which analysis column to use.

It is important to note when carrying out the analysis that if the balance is shown as a **debit balance** in the Ledger Balance column then it will appear as a **debit balance** in either the Profit and Loss Account column or the Balance Sheet column. The same thing applies to the **credit balances**, which will appear in either the Profit and Loss Account column or Balance Sheet column as a **credit balance**. While carrying out the analysis, any figures appearing in the Adjustments column must be taken into consideration; for example, referring to Exhibit 16.3(a), the balance of rent will be analysed as:

Rent £11,000 plus £1,000 (owing) = £12,000

This will be analysed into the 'Profit and Loss Account' column as a **debit balance** of £12,000.

Refer to Exhibit 16.3 where this task has been carried out.

A further example can also be seen in Exhibit 16.3(b) where the prepayment of rates £500 will be analysed as follows:

Rates and Insurance	£3,900
Less amount paid in advance	500
	£3,400

The amount to be shown in the Profit and Loss Account column will be £3,400 **debit balance**.

Step 6 Add up the Profit and Loss Account columns. The difference between the two figures will represent a **Profit** or **Loss** for the period. In our example of D Simpson the difference between these two columns is £14,402, representing a **Net Profit**. This figure will now be entered on the ETB as **Net Profit £14,402**, a *debit entry* in the Profit and Loss Account column.

The corresponding *credit entry* will appear as under the Balance Sheet columns.

Step 7 The only remaining task to carry out is to add up the Balance Sheet column totals and, provided all transactions have been carried out correctly, the totals should agree.

❗ *Refer to Exhibit 16.3 where you can see that the ETB balances with a total of £79,042.*

The trading and profit and loss account and balance sheet of D Simpson for the year ended 31 December 2002 is shown in Exhibit 16.4.

Exhibits 16.4

D Simpson
Trading and Profit and Loss Account
for the year ended 31 December 2002

	£	£	£
Sales		202,460	
Less Returns inwards		424	202,036
Less Cost of goods sold:			
Opening stock		9,820	
Purchases		138,872	
Carriage inwards		490	
		149,182	
Less Returns outwards	2,280		
Closing stock	12,042	14,322	134,860
Gross profit			67,176
Less Expenses:			
Carriage outwards		1,406	
Wages and salaries		29,950	
Rent (11,000 + 1,000)		12,000	
Rates and insurance (3,900 – 500)		3,400	
Heating and lighting		1,254	
Motor expenses		2,500	
Depreciation – Motor vehicle		1,800	
Creation of provision for bad debts		464	52,774
Net profit			14,402

Exhibit 16.4 (continued)

D Simpson
Balance Sheet as at 31 December 2002

	Cost	Total Dep'n	Net Book Value
	£	£	£
Fixed assets:			
Fixtures and fittings	6,400	–	6,400
Motor vehicles	9,000	1,800	7,200
	15,400	1,800	13,600
Current assets:			
Stock	12,042		
Debtors	23,200		
Less Provision for bad debts	464	22,736	
Prepayments	500	35,278	
Less Current liabilities:			
Bank overdraft	5,638		
Creditors	17,842		
Accruals	1,000	24,480	
Net current assets			10,798
			24,398
Financed by:			
Capital: Balance 1 January 2002			37,896
Add Net profit for the year			14,402
			52,298
Less Drawings			27,900
			24,398

16.5 Other considerations

In the above example of D Simpson the transactions involving depreciation and provision for bad debts was kept as straight forward as possible to avoid complications. However, assuming it is the next accounting period of D Simpson, the following adjustments will now be shown:

1. Depreciate the motor vehicle by 20% using the straight line method (for the second year).
2. Increase the provision for bad debts to £550.
3. Write off a bad debt amounting to £100.

1. Depreciate the motor vehicle by 20% using the straight line method

First of all the amount of depreciation to be charged against the profit and loss account needs to be calculated. As the method of depreciation to be used is the straight line method, the amount of depreciation will be the same each year, namely, 20% of £9,000 = £1,800. This amount is then entered on the ETB as follows:

D Simpson
Extended Trial Balance (extract) as at 31 December 2003

Description	Ledger balances		Adjustments		Profit and loss		Balance sheet	
	Dr	Cr	Dr	Cr	Dr	Cr	Dr	Cr
	£	£	£	£	£	£	£	£
Motor vehicle	9,000						9,000	
Provision for Dep'n Motor vehicle*		1,800		1,800				3,600
Depreciation of Motor vehicle			1,800		1,800			

The above example shows that the motor vehicle remains a debit balance of £9,000 which appears in the Balance Sheet column as a debit (an asset). The provision for depreciation of motor vehicle* appears under the Ledger Balances column as £1,800, representing the amount of depreciation charged for the first year. To this figure another £1,800 is added representing the depreciation for this year showing a total of depreciation to date of £3,600. This is shown as a **credit balance** in the Balance Sheet column of the ETB.

When the balance sheet is prepared it will appear as follows:

D Simpson
Balance Sheet (extract) as at 31 December 2003

	Cost	Total dep'n	Net book value
Fixed assets	£	£	£
Motor vehicle	9,000	3,600	5,400

The remaining **debit balance** of depreciation of motor vehicle £1,800 will be charged in the profit and loss account. This is shown in the ETB under the Profit and Loss Account column as a **debit balance** (see above in the ETB extract).

2. Increase the provision for bad debts to £550

In the accounts for the year ended 31 December 2002, D Simpson created a provision for bad debts equal to 2% of the debtors which amounted to £464 (this is illustrated in the extract from ETB below).

In the year to 31 December 2003 it was decided to increase the provision to £550, representing an increase of £86 (£550 *less* £464). To record this increase the following entries need to be made:

- Show the increase of provision for bad debts of £86 as a **debit entry** in the Adjustments column to be charged in the profit and loss account.
- Increase the existing 'provision for bad debts account' by £86 to £550; this will be shown as a **credit entry** in the Adjustments column of the ETB. This figure is then extended to the Balance Sheet column as £550 (**credit entry**).

This can now be seen in the following extract from the extended trial balance.

D Simpson
Extended Trial Balance (extract) as at 31 December 2003

Description	Ledger balances		Adjustments		Profit and loss		Balance sheet	
	Dr	Cr	Dr	Cr	Dr	Cr	Dr	Cr
	£	£	£	£	£	£	£	£
Provision for Bad Debts		464		86				550
Increase in Provision for Bad Debts			86		86			

3. Write off a bad debt amounting to £100

After the preparation of the draft accounts one of the firm's debtors was reported to have been declared bankrupt. The balance on the debtor's account was £100 and it was decided to write the debt off as bad.

This would be entered on the extended trial balance as follows:

D Simpson
Extended Trial Balance (extract) as at 31 December 2003

Description	Ledger balances		Adjustments		Profit and loss		Balance sheet	
	Dr	Cr	Dr	Cr	Dr	Cr	Dr	Cr
	£	£	£	£	£	£	£	£
Debtors (say)	26,000			100			25,900	
Bad Debts			100		100			

The above entries show that the debtors, which we have assumed are £26,000 for this year ended 2003, have been reduced by £100 and will appear in the balance sheet as £25,900. The bad debt will also be charged to the profit and loss account. This is shown as a **debit entry** in both the Adjustments column and the Profit and Loss Account column.

16.6 A more complicated example

Exhibit 16.5 shows a worked example of a more complicated extended trial balance.

Exhibit 16.5

J Blake is a sole trader. He extracted the following list of balances from the books of his business on 31 March 2003:

	Dr £	Cr £
Sales		80,650
Purchases	45,380	
Returns inwards	510	
Returns outwards		930
Discounts allowed	1,120	
Discounts received		390
Stock at 1 April 2002	12,460	
Motor van, at cost	12,500	
Office equipment	9,600	
Provision for depreciation of motor van 1 April 2002		3,800
Provision for depreciation of office equipment 1 April 2002		2,150
Salaries and wages	17,620	
Motor van running expenses	3,910	
Sundry expenses	1,140	
Rent and rates	3,200	
Bad debts	375	
Provision for bad debts 1 April 2002		320
Debtors	12,870	
Creditors		9,100
Bank	8,040	
Cash	60	
Drawings	7,000	
Capital		38,445
	135,785	135,785

This additional information is available at 31 March 2003:

(a) Stock was valued at £20,100.

(b) Salaries and wages of £490 are to be accrued.

(c) The following have been prepaid: rent and rates £790.

(d) An additional £270 is to be written off as bad debts, and the provision for bad debts is to be adjusted to 2% of debtors.

(e) Goods taken by Blake for his private use during the year amounted at cost to £370. No record of this has yet been made in the books.

(f) Depreciation is to be written off as follows: motor van £2,000; office equipment at 15% using the straight line method.

You are required to:

1. Prepare an extended trial balance as at 31 March 2003.

2. Prepare a trading and profit and loss account for the year ended 31 March 2003 and a balance sheet as at that date.

Remember to follow the 'Step-by-step guide' to assist you in following the workings of Exhibit 16.5 and note the order of dealing with the 'Adjustments':

Exhibit 16.6   J Blake – Extended Trial Balance at 31 March 2003

	Description	Ledger Balances Dr £	Ledger Balances Cr £	Adjustments Dr £	Adjustments Cr £	Profit and Loss Dr £	Profit and Loss Cr £	Balance Sheet Dr £	Balance Sheet Cr £
PL	Sales		80,650				80,650		
PL	Purchases	45,380			370	45,010			
PL	Returns inwards/Returns outwards	510	930			510	930		
PL	Discounts	1,120	390			1,120	390		
PL	Stock at 1 April 2002	12,460				12,460			
BS	Motor van, at cost	12,500						12,500	
BS	Office equipment, at cost	9,600						9,600	
BS	Provision for dep'n – Motor van 1.4.2002		3,800		2,000				5,800
BS	Provision for dep'n – Office equip. 1.4.2002		2,150		1,440				3,590
PL	Salaries and wages	17,620		490		18,110			
PL	Motor van running expenses	3,910				3,910			
PL	Sundry expenses	1,140				1,140			
PL	Rent and rates	3,200			790	2,410			
PL	Bad debts	375		270		645			
BS	Provision for bad debts 1.4.2002		320	68					252
BS	Debtors	12,870			270			12,600	
BS	Creditors		9,100						9,100
BS	Bank	8,040						8,040	
BS	Cash	60						60	
BS	Drawings	7,000		370				7,370	
BS	Capital		38,445						38,445
		135,785	135,785						
BS	Accrual – Salaries and wages				490				490
BS	Prepayment – Rent and rates			790				790	
BS	Stock – 31 March 2003			20,100				20,100	
PL	Stock – 31 March 2003				20,100		20,100		
PL	Depreciation – Motor van			2,000		2,000			
PL	Depreciation – Office equipment			1,440		1,440			
PL	Reduction in provision for bad debts				68		68		
				25,528	25,528				
BS	Net profit (balancing figure)					13,383			13,383
						102,138	102,138	71,060	71,060

- accruals and prepayments
- deal with the closing stock valuation
- make provision for depreciation and provision for bad debts
- other adjustments
  - writing off the bad debt (refer back to Section 16.5(3) and Chapter 11)
  - goods taken for own use (see the worked example, Exhibit 16.6)

The extended trial balance of J Blake is now shown in Exhibit 16.6 and the trading and profit and loss account and balance sheet is shown in Exhibit 16.7 as follows:

Exhibit 16.7

J Blake
Trading and Profit and Loss Account for the year ended 31 March 2003

	£	£	£
Sales		80,650	
Less Returns inwards		510	80,140
Less Cost of goods sold:			
Opening stock		12,460	
Add Purchases (45,380 − 370 own use)	45,010		
Less Returns outwards	930	44,080	
		56,540	
Less Closing stock		20,100	36,440
Gross profit			43,700
Add Income:			
Discount received		390	
Reduction in provision for bad debts			
(320 − 2% of (12,870 − 270))		68	458
			44,158
Less Expenses:			
Discounts allowed		1,120	
Salaries and wages (17,620 + 490)		18,110	
Motor van running expenses		3,910	
Rent and rates (3,200 − 790)		2,410	
Sundry expenses		1,140	
Bad debts (375 + 270)		645	
Depreciation: Motor van		2,000	
Office equipment		1,440	30,775
Net profit			13,383

Exhibit 16.7 (continued)

J Blake
Balance Sheet as at 31 March 2003

		Cost	Total dep'n	Net book value
		£	£	£
Fixed assets				
Office equipment		9,600	3,590	6,010
Motor van		12,500	5,800	6,700
		22,100	9,390	12,710
Current assets:				
Stock		20,100		
Debtors (12,870 − 270)	12,600			
Less Provision for bad debts	252	12,348		
Prepayments		790		
Cash at bank		8,040		
Cash in hand		60	41,338	
Less Current liabilities				
Creditors		9,100		
Accruals		490	9,590	
Net current assets				31,748
				44,458
Financed by:				
Capital				38,445
Add Net profit				13,383
				51,828
Less Drawings (7,000 + 370 goods for own use)				7,370
				44,458

16.7   Skeleton trial balance

Some examining bodies provide a list of balances from which a trial balance must be drawn up, while other questions involve correction of a trial balance. It is essential to understand the basic principles of double entry to carry out this task, i.e. a **debit balance** is always an asset, expense or loss and a **credit balance** is capital, a liability or income.

A skeleton trial balance is shown below which will act as a guide, enabling you to answer such questions. Note that some of the items included on the trial balance will be found in later chapters.

Skeleton Trial Balance as at 31 May 2003

	Dr	Cr
All **debit** *balances will include:*		
	Stock (opening)	
	Cash	
	Bank	
Assets	Machinery	
	Motor vehicles	
	Furniture and fittings	
	Debtors	

Skeleton Trial Balance as at 31 May 2003

		Dr	Cr
Expenses and losses	Purchases		
	Carriage inwards		
	Carriage outwards		
	Wages and salaries		
	Advertising		
	Rent and rates		
	Stationery		
	Discounts allowed		
	Bad debts written off		
	Light and heat		
	Depreciation		
Others	Drawings		
	Stock taken for own use		
	Sales returns (returns inwards)		

*All **credit** balances will include:*

		Dr	Cr
Capital and liabilities	Capital		
	Creditors		
	Loans *from* others		
	Bank overdraft		
Income, profits and gains	Sales		
	Commissions received		
	Rent received		
	Interest received		
	Discounts received		
	Bad debts recovered		
Others	Balance of provision for depreciation account		
	Provision for bad debts		
	Purchase returns (returns out)		

 *The value added tax account can be either a debit or a credit balance depending on whether VAT is due to be paid to HM Customs and Excise in which case it is a **credit balance** (a liability) or if VAT is due to be paid to the business it is a **debit balance** (an asset).*

NEW TERM   **Extended trial balance**   A trial balance with additional columns added to enable adjustments to be made prior to the preparation of the financial statements. The extended trial balance is often referred to as a 'worksheet'.

Student Activities

16.1   The trial balance shown below has been drawn up by a new employee but unfortunately they have not been able to balance it. Redraft the trial balance correcting any errors.

D Ford
Trial Balance as at 31 December 2003

	Dr £	Cr £
Sales	26,950	
Purchases		20,300
Rent	1,680	
Electricity		1,050
Office equipment		3,500
Debtors		4,760
Creditors	6,300	
Balance at bank	10,570	
Cash in hand		140
Drawings	4,900	
Capital		14,000
Sundry expenses		350
	50,400	44,100

16.2X Reconstruct the trial balance after making the necessary corrections.

S Dickinson
Trial Balance as at 30 September 2004

	Dr £	Cr £
Capital	59,868	
Motor vehicles	22,500	
Computer equipment	18,000	
Debtors	31,059	
Creditors		30,690
Purchases	245,259	
Sales		358,317
Wages and salaries		38,476
Motor expenses		3,428
Printing and stationery	3,600	
General expenses	8,235	
Cash at bank	5,850	
Stock 1 October 2003	23,004	
Rent and rates	31,500	
Heating and lighting		6,624
Interest received	6,417	
Insurance		10,332
Rent received	5,175	
Drawings		12,600
	460,467	460,467

16.3 From the following list of balances taken from the books of G Brammer you are required to draw up a trial balance as at 31 December 2002.

	£
Capital	100,000
Premises	66,250
Motor vehicle	17,000
Office equipment	2,438
Wages	19,637
Purchases	37,455
Sales	56,170
Commission received	1,050
Electricity	925
Telephone	1,125
Motor expenses	1,500
Printing, stationery and advertising	2,050
Creditors	8,500
Debtors	12,012
General expenses	2,371
Bank overdraft	3,505
Drawings	6,462

16.4X From the list of balances from the accounts of Fraser & Co., you are required to prepare a trial balance as at 31 December 2003.

Fraser & Co.
List of Outstanding Balances as at 31 December 2003

	£
Purchases	334,500
Sales	511,050
Returns inwards	10,050
Returns outwards	8,400
Stock 1 January 2003	33,000
Discount allowed	6,900
Discount received	8,250
Wages and salaries	55,750
Carriage inwards	2,100
Carriage outwards	3,300
Printing and stationery	4,200
Electricity	7,300
Motor expenses	18,250
Telephone	3,100
General expenses	2,900
Debtors	51,000
Creditors	32,400
Bad debts written off	1,650
Provision for bad debts at 1.1.2003	675
Cash in hand	1,200
Bank overdraft	35,100
Capital	57,825
Property	75,000
Plant and equipment	96,000
Provision for depreciation at 1.1.2003:	
Property	15,000
Plant and equipment	37,500

16.5 The following is a list of balances extracted from the books of J Steadman, a sole trader, as at 31 January 2003.

J Steadman
List of Balances as at 31 January 2003

	£
Capital	58,260
Equipment	11,250
Furniture and fittings	6,000
Motor vehicles	17,370
Sales	96,030
Purchases	59,220
Cash at bank	750
General expenses	1,800
Wages	17,820
Rent, rates and insurance	7,650
Heating and lighting	2,100
Debtors	24,000
Creditors	10,800
Stock 1 February 2002	17,130

The following additional information is available as at 31 January 2003:

(a) Wages amounted to £351.

(b) Insurance paid in advance £600.

(c) Closing stock was valued at £14,730.

You are required to take the above adjustments into account and prepare the figures for the final accounts for J Steadman for the year ended 31 January 2003, using the extended trial balance.

16.6 The following is a list of balances taken from the ledgers of Rigby & Co. as at 31 July 2006, the end of the financial year.

Rigby & Co.
List of Balances as at 31 July 2006

	£
Stock at 1 August 2005	29,150
Purchases	243,800
Sales	509,450
Returns inwards	3,805
Returns outwards	2,655
Discounts allowed	6,620
Discounts received	5,750
Wages and salaries	76,500
Lighting and heating	9,250
Telephone, stationery and advertising	13,600
Motor expenses	10,500
General expenses	3,005
Rates and insurance	15,000
Motor vehicles:	
At cost	20,000
Accumulated depreciation	5,000

Rigby & Co.
List of Balances as at 31 July 2006

	£
Fixtures and fittings:	
At cost	22,100
Accumulated depreciation	9,945
Creditors	21,900
Debtors	31,700
Drawings	22,325
Cash in hand	995
Cash at bank	10,985
Capital	114,635
Land and buildings	150,000

The following additional information is available as at 31 July 2006:

(a) Motor expenses owing £200.

(b) Insurance paid in advance £3,500.

(c) Closing stock was valued at £30,700.

(d) Depreciate motor vehicles at 25% and fixtures and fittings at 15% per annum using the straight line method.

You are required to take the above adjustments into account and prepare the figures for the final accounts of Rigby & Co. for the year ended 31 July 2006, using the extended trial balance.

16.7 Amanda Carver is the proprietor of Automania, a business which supplies car parts to garages to use in servicing and repair work.

At the end of the financial year, on 30 April 2009, the balances were extracted from the general ledger and have been entered onto a trial balance, as shown on page 216.

The following adjustments need to be taken into account as at 30 April 2009:

(a) Rent payable by the business is as follows:

    For the period to 31 July 2008 – £1,500 per month
    From 1 August 2008   – £1,600 per month

(b) The insurance balance includes £100 paid for the period 1 May 2009 to 31 May 2009.

(c) Depreciation is to be calculated as follows:

    Motor vehicles   – 20% per annum straight line method
    Fixtures and fittings – 10% per annum reducing balance method

(d) The provision for bad debts is to be adjusted to a figure representing 2% of debtors.

(e) Stock has been valued at cost on 30 April 2009 at £119,360. However, this figure includes old stock, the details of which are as follows:

    Cost price of old stock   – £3,660
    Net realisable value of old stock – £2,060

Also included is a badly damaged car door which was to have been sold for £80 but will now have to be scrapped. The cost price of the door was £60.

(f) A credit note received from a supplier on 5 April 2009 for goods returned was filed away with no entries having been made. The credit note has now been discovered and is for £200 net plus £35 VAT.

Required

(i) Make appropriate entries in the adjustments columns of the extended trial balance taking account of the above information. Show all workings.

(ii) Complete the extended trial balance showing clearly the profit or loss made by Automania for the year ended 30 April 2009.

 NB: Use a photocopy of the blank extended trial balance form shown on page 197 for your answer.

(Association of Accounting Technicians – *Amended*)

Automania
Trial Balance as at 30 April 2009

Description	Ledger balances	
	Dr	Cr
	£	£
Capital		135,000
Drawings	42,150	
Rent	17,300	
Purchases	606,600	
Sales		857,300
Sales returns	2,400	
Purchases returns		1,260
Salaries and wages	136,970	
Motor vehicles (M.V.) at cost	60,800	
Provision for depreciation (M.V.)		16,740
Fixtures and fittings (F&F) at cost	40,380	
Provision for depreciation (F&F)		21,600
Bank		3,170
Cash	2,100	
Lighting and heating	4,700	
VAT		9,200
Stock at 1 May 2008	116,100	
Bad debts	1,410	
Provision for bad debts		1,050
Debtors control account	56,850	
Creditors control account		50,550
Sundry expenses	6,810	
Insurance	1,300	
Accruals		
Prepayments		
Depreciation		
Provision for bad debts – Adjustment		
Closing stock – Profit and loss		
Closing stock – Balance sheet		
	1,095,870	1,095,870

Bank reconciliation statements

AIMS

- To be able to reconcile cash book balances with bank statement balances.

- To understand how bank overdrafts effect the reconciliation process.

- To be able to make necessary entries for dishonoured cheques.

- To be able to reconcile opening balances.

17.1 Completing entries in the cash book

In our own books we will enter up the bank columns of our cash book, showing monies banked and paid out. Our bank will also record items paid into and out of our bank account.

If all the items entered in our cash book were the same as those entered by the bank in our bank account, then obviously the bank balance by our books and the bank balance by the bank's books would equal each other.

On the other hand, there may be items paid into and out of our account at the bank which have not been recorded by us in our cash book. To see what these are, if any, we will need a copy of our account as kept at the bank. They will give us such a copy, known as a **bank statement**. Let us look at an example of a cash book and a bank statement in Exhibit 17.1. We will tick off the items that are the same in both sets of records.

Exhibit 17.1

Cash Book							
Dr		(Bank columns only: *before* balancing on 31.12.2008)					Cr
2008				£	2008		£
Dec 1	Balance b/d	✓	250		Dec 5	J Gordon	✓	65
20	P Thomas	✓	100		27	K Hughes	✓	175
28	D Jones	✓	190				

Exhibit 17.1 (continued)

Bank Statement				
		Withdrawals	*Deposits*	*Balance*
2008		*£*	*£*	*£*
Dec 1	Balance b/d	✓		250
8	10625*	✓ 65		185
21	Deposit	✓	100	285
28	Deposit	✓	190	475
29	10626*	✓ 175		300
30	Bank Giro credit: P Smith		70	370
31	Bank charges	50		320

* 10625 and 10626 refer to the serial numbers on the cheques paid out.

It is now possible to see that the two items not shown in our cash book are:

Bank Giro credit: P Smith   £70
Bank charges   £50

P Smith had paid us £70, but instead of sending us a cheque he had paid the money by **credit transfer** direct into our bank account, using the bank's services. We did not know of this until we received the bank statement.

The other item was in respect of bank charges. The bank had charged us £50 for keeping our bank account and all the work connected with it. Instead of sending us an invoice they have simply taken the money out of our bank account.

Since we have now identified the items missing from our cash book, we can complete writing it up, as follows:

Cash Book

Dr	(Bank columns only: *after* balancing on 31.12.2008)				Cr
2008		£	*2008*		£
Dec 1	Balance b/d	250	Dec 5	J Gordon	65
20	P Thomas	100	27	K Hughes	175
28	D Jones	190	31	Bank charges	50
30	P Smith	70	31	Balance c/d	320
		610			610
2009					
Jan 1	Balance b/d	320			

Both closing balances are now shown as being £320.

17.2 Where closing balances differ

Although a cash book may be written up to date by us, we obviously cannot alter the bank's own records. Even after writing up entries in our cash book there may still be a difference between our cash book balance and the bank statement balance. Exhibit 17.2 shows such a case.

Exhibit 17.2

Dr	Cash Book (after being completed to date)				Cr
2009		£	*2009*		£
Jan 1	Balance b/d	320	Jan 10	C Morgan	110
16	R Lomas	160	20	M McCarthy	90
24	V Verity	140	28	Cheshire CC rates	180
31	J Soames (B)	470	30	M Peck (A)	200
31	R Johnson	90	31	Balance c/d	600
		1,180			1,180
Feb 1	Balance b/d	600			

Bank Statement

		Withdrawals £	Deposits £	Balance £
2009				
Jan 1	Balance b/d			320
12	10627	110		210
16	Deposit		160	370
23	10628	90		280
24	Deposit		140	420
28	Direct debit: Cheshire CC	180		240
31	Bank Giro credit: R Johnson		90	330

You can see that two items in the cash book are not shown on the bank statement. These are:

(A) A cheque had been paid to M Peck on January 30. He banked it at his bank on January 31 but it was not presented to our bank until February 2. This is known as an **unpresented cheque**.

(B) Although we had received a cheque for £470 from J Soames on January 31, we did not bank it until February 1. This will be known as a '**bank lodgement** not yet credited' to our bank's account.

The balance per our cash book on January 31 was £600, whereas our bank statement shows a balance of £330. To prove that although the balances are different they can be 'reconciled' with each other, a **bank reconciliation statement** will be drawn up. It will either start with the bank statement balance and then reconcile it to the cash book balance, or it will start with the cash book balance and then reconcile it to the bank statement balance. If the second approach is adopted, it would appear as:

Bank Reconciliation Statement as at 31 December 2008

		£
Balance as per cash book		600
Add Unpresented cheque	(A)	200
		800
Less Bank lodgement not credited	(B)	470
Balance per bank statement		330

If the two balances cannot be reconciled then there will be an error somewhere. This will have to be located and then corrected.

This reconciliation technique is also used when dealing with other statements drawn up outside the firm; for example, when reconciling ledger accounts to suppliers' statements, see Chapter 15 (Section 15.12).

17.3 The bank balance in the balance sheet

The balance to be shown in the balance sheet is that per the cash book after it has been written up to date. In Exhibit 17.2 the balance sheet figure would be £600.

17.4 Other terms used in banking

Standing orders   A firm can instruct its bank to pay regular amounts of money at stated dates to persons or firms. For instance, you may ask your bank to pay £200 a month to a building society to repay a mortgage.

Direct debits   These are payments which have to be made, such as rates, insurance premiums and similar items. Instead of asking the bank to pay the money, as with standing orders, you give permission to the creditor to obtain the money directly from your bank account. This is particularly useful if the amounts payable may vary from time to time, since it is the creditor who changes the payments, not you. With standing orders, if the amount is ever to be changed then you have to inform the bank. With direct debits it is the creditor who arranges that, not you.

Both of these items will be written up in your cash book before attempting a reconciliation.

17.5 Bank overdrafts

Where there is a **bank overdraft** (shown by a credit balance in the cash book), the adjustments needed for reconciliation work are opposite to those needed for a debit balance.

Exhibit 17.3 shows a cash book and a bank statement, showing an overdraft. Only the cheque from G Cumberbatch **(A)** for £106 and the cheque paid to J Kelly **(B)** for £63 need to be adjusted. Work through the reconciliation statement then see the note after it.

Exhibit 17.3

Dr			Cash Book				Cr
2004			£	2004			£
Dec 5	I Howe		308	Dec 1	Balance b/d		709
24	L Mason		120	9	P Davies		140
29	K King		124	27	J Kelly	**(B)**	63
31	G Cumberbatch	**(A)**	106	29	United Trust		77
31	Balance c/d		380	31	Bank charges		49
			1,038				1,038

Exhibit 17.3 (continued)

Bank Statement

2004		Dr £	Cr £	Balance £
Dec 1	Balance b/f			709 O/D
5	Cheque		308	401 O/D
14	P Davies	140		541 O/D
24	Cheque		120	421 O/D
29	K King: Credit transfer		124	297 O/D
29	United Trust: Standing order	77		374 O/D
31	Bank charges	49		423 O/D

Bank Reconciliation Statement as at 31 December 2004

	£
Overdraft as per cash book	380
Add Bank lodgements not on bank statement	106
	486
Less Unpresented cheque	63
Overdraft as per bank statement	423

❗ *An overdraft is often shown with the letters O/D following the amount.*

Now compare the reconciliation statements in Exhibits 17.2 and 17.3. This shows:

	Exhibit 17.2 Balances	Exhibit 17.3 Overdrafts
Balance/Overdraft as per cash book	xxxx	xxxx
Adjustments:		
Unpresented cheque	plus	less
Banking not entered	less	plus
Balance/Overdraft as per bank statement	xxxx	xxxx

Adjustments are, therefore, made in the opposite way when there is an overdraft.

17.6 Dishonoured cheques

When a cheque is received from a customer and paid into the bank, it is recorded on the debit side of the cash book. It is also shown on the bank statement as a banking by the bank. However, at a later date it may be found that the bank will not pay us the amount due on the cheque. The bank has failed to honour the cheque. It is known as a **dishonoured cheque**.

There are several possible reasons for this. Let us suppose that K King gave us a cheque for £5,000 on 20 May 2003. We bank it, but a few days later our bank returns the cheque to us. Typical reasons are:

1. King had put £5,000 in figures on the cheque, but had written it in words as five thousand five hundred pounds. You will have to give the cheque back to King for amendment.

2. Normally cheques are considered *stale* six months after the date on the cheque; in other words, the banks will not pay cheques over six months old. If King had put the year 2002 on the cheque instead of 2003, then the cheque would be returned to us by our bank.

3. King simply did not have sufficient funds in his bank account. Suppose he had previously a balance of only £2,000 and yet he has given us a cheque for £5,000. His bank has not allowed him to have an overdraft. In such a case the cheque would be dishonoured. The bank would write on the cheque '*refer to drawer*', and we would have to contact King and ask what he was going to do about it.

In all of these cases the bank would show the original banking as being cancelled by showing the cheque paid out of our bank account. As soon as this happens they will notify us. We will then also show the cheque as being cancelled by a credit in the cash book. We will then debit that amount to King's account.

When King originally paid his account our records would have appeared as:

Dr			K King		Cr
2003		£	*2003*		£
May 1	Balance b/d	5,000	May 20	Bank	5,000

Dr			Bank Account		Cr
2003		£			
May 20	K King	5,000			

After our recording the dishonour, the records will appear as:

Dr			K King		Cr
2003		£	*2003*		£
May 1	Balance b/d	5,000	May 20	Bank	5,000
25	Bank: cheque dishonoured	5,000			

Dr			Bank Account		Cr
2003		£	*2003*		£
May 20	K King	5,000	May 25	K King: cheque dishonoured	5,000

In other words, King is once again shown as owing us £5,000.

17.7 Bank reconciliation statements: Business practice and examination questions

In a real business a bank reconciliation statement will be drawn up regularly, usually at least at the end of each month. The book keeper will have compared the bank statement with the cash book, and then entered the cash book up to date, before drawing up the bank reconciliation statement.

However, examiners sometimes want to set questions that do not conform to normal practice, to test a student's ability to have to adapt to something different. Exhibit 17.4 shows how a question can be set, apparently differing from normal accounting practice.

Exhibit 17.4

At 31 January 2004 the cash book of K Rushton appeared as follows:

K Rushton
Cash Book (bank columns only)

2004			£	2004		Cheque No.		£
Jan 1	Balance b/d		1,398	Jan 1	T Jones	769	✓	84
4	Cash sales	✓	1,200	3	K Stewart	770	✓	12
5	P Shilton	✓	525	5	Petty cash	771	✓	120
5	D Swift	✓	150	6	Smithy Garage	772	–	350
7	Brownson Co.	✓	70	7	Skinners	773	–	50
12	Cash sales	✓	1,500	14	Wages	774	✓	1,025
12	D L Electric	✓	424	18	T Jones	775	–	726
20	Cash sales	✓	2,100	20	Reeves Co.	776	✓	2,525
27	Cash sales	✓	2,426	27	Post Office	777	–	150
30	P Shilton	–	190	30	Wages	778	✓	1,120
				31	Balance c/d			3,821
			9,983					9,983

The following bank statement was received by K Rushton from their bankers at the end of January 2004.

Oak Bank PLC
Bank Statement

Date	Details	Debit		Credit		Balance
		£		£		£
2004						
Jan 1	Balance					873
1	Credit			– 600		1,473
4	Credit			✓ 1,200		2,673
5	Cheque 770	✓	12			2,661
5	Cheque 769	✓	84			2,577
6	Credit			✓	675	3,252
6	Cheque 771	✓	120			3,132
8	Cheque 763	–	75			3,057
8	Credit			✓	70	3,127
13	Credit			✓ 1,924		5,051
15	Cheque 774	✓	1,025			4,026
22	Credit			✓ 2,100		6,126
25	Cheque 776	✓	2,525			3,601
28	Direct Debit: Ash Ins.	–	100			3,501
28	Credit			✓ 2,426		5,927
31	Bank Charges	–	65			5,862
31	Cheque 778	✓	1,120			4,742

You are required to:

(a) Reconcile the opening balances on 1 January 2004 on the cash book with that on the bank statement on that date.
(b) Reconcile the closing balance of £3,821 in the cash book on 31 January 2004 with the closing balance of £4,742 on the bank statement as on that date.

Before starting to look at the answers, let us remind ourselves that:

■ In a real business we would have already drawn up a bank reconciliation statement on 1 January 2004, and we wouldn't therefore need to do it again, as in (a) above.

■ Again, in a real business we would always write the cash book up to date before drafting a bank reconciliation statement. In our answer we will therefore write up the cash book first, and then prepare the bank reconciliation statement.

■ Again, the examiner may tell you to start the reconciliation statement with the balance on the cash book, or could alternatively ask for you to start with the bank statement balance. You should therefore be able to use both approaches.

The answers are now shown, plus some extra guidance.

An examination of the cash book and bank statement has revealed that cheque number 763 for £75 was presented for payment on 8 January 2004. By looking at the cheque numbers in the cash book and the bank statement it is apparent that this is an old cheque which has only just been presented for payment. It has, however, already been entered in the cash book in 2003. It is important to take this into account when reconciling the opening balances. Another difference is the £600 credit appearing on the bank statement on 1 January. This deposit will have been paid into the bank and entered in the cash book at the end of December, but does not appear on the bank statement until a couple of days later, in January.

Having identified these differences it is now possible to prepare a reconciliation of the opening balances as follows:

Answer: Part (a)

Reconciliation of the opening balances of K Rushton

	£
Balance per cash book	1,398
Add Unpresented cheque No. 763	75
	1,473
Less Banking already entered in cash book	600
Balance per bank statement 1.1.2004	873

Answer: Part (b)

The next task is to bring the cash book up to date at the end of January 2004 in the following manner:

Dr	Cash Book (bank columns only)			Cr
2004		£	*2004*		£
Jan 31	Balance b/d	3,821	Jan 28	Direct debit – Ash Ins.	100
			31	Bank charges	65
			31	Balance c/d	3,656
		3,821			3,821
Feb 1	Balance b/d	3,656			

The last task is to prepare the bank reconciliation statement as at 31 January 2004, first of all starting with the balance shown in the cash book.

K Rushton
Bank Reconciliation Statement as at 31 January 2004

		£
Balance in hand as per the cash book		3,656
Add Unpresented cheques:		
Cheque No. 772	350	
Cheque No. 773	50	
Cheque No. 775	726	
Cheque No. 777	150	1,276
		4,932
Less Cheque banked not yet entered on bank statement		190
Balance in hand as per bank statement		4,742

The following is a bank reconciliation statement, starting with the balance shown in the bank statement:

K Rushton
Bank Reconciliation Statement as at 31 January 2004

		£
Balance in hand as per the bank statement		4,742
Add Cheque banked not yet entered on bank statement		190
		4,932
Less Unpresented cheques:		
Cheque No. 772	350	
Cheque No. 773	50	
Cheque No. 775	726	
Cheque No. 777	150	1,276
Balance as per cash book		3,656

Obviously you would not show both the above reconciliation statements in your answer. You would only show one of them, using the method asked for by the examiner.

NEW TERMS

Bank lodgement Money deposited by a business into their account at the bank.
[*Note: An outstanding lodgement is when the amount has been paid into the bank by the firm but it has not been recorded on the firm's bank statement.*]

Bank overdraft An overdraft is a facility provided by the bank where they will continue to make payments from a current account even though there are insufficient funds to cover the payment. This is a short-term loan, on which the bank charges interest on a day-to-day basis.

Bank reconciliation statement   A calculation comparing the cash book balance with the bank statement balance.

Credit transfer   Also referred to as **bank giro credits** – a method used by businesses to pay creditors, wages and/or salaries direct into a bank account.

Direct debit   Where the business gives permission for an organisation to collect amounts owing direct from their bank account. This method is often used to pay mortgages, insurance premiums, etc.

Dishonoured cheque   When a bank dishonours a cheque it will not pay up on the cheque because there are insufficient funds in the *drawer's* account.

Standing order   Instructions given by a business to a bank to pay specified amounts at given dates.

Unpresented cheque   A cheque which has been sent but has not yet gone through the receiver's bank account.

Student Activities

17.1   Draw up a bank reconciliation statement, after writing the cash book up to date, ascertaining the balance on the bank statement, from the following as on 31 March 2009.

	£
Cash at bank as per bank column of the cash book (Dr)	9,740
Bankings made but not yet entered on bank statement	1,515
Bank charges on bank statement but not yet in cash book	70
Unpresented cheques: J Mason 92	
T Black 200	292
Direct debit to Rent-Equip entered on bank statement, but not in cash book	138
Credit transfer from E Mayall entered on bank statement, but not in cash book	473

17.2   The following are extracts from the cash book and bank statement of Preston & Co.

Dr		Cash Book		Cr
2009	£	2009		£
Dec 1 Balance b/d	8,700	Dec 6 S Little		1,745
7 T J Blake	440	14 L Jones		165
20 P Dyson	365	21 E Fraser		575
30 A Veale	945	31 Balance c/d		9,155
31 K Woodburn	300			
31 N May	890			
	11,640			11,640

Bank Statement

	Dr	Cr	Balance
2009	£	£	£
Dec 1 Balance b/d			8,700
9 Cheque		440	9,140
10 S Little	1,745		7,395
19 L Jones	165		7,230
20 Cheque		365	7,595
26 Credit transfer: P Todd		270	7,865
31 Bank charges	110		7,755

Required

(a) Write up the cash book and state the new balance on 31 December 2009.

(b) Prepare a bank reconciliation statement as on 31 December 2009.

17.3X The bank columns in the cash book for June 2007 and the bank statement for that month for C Grant are as follows:

Dr		Cash Book			Cr
2007		£	*2007*		£
Jun 1	Balance b/d	2,379	Jun 5	D Blake	150
7	B Green	158	12	J Gray	433
16	A Silver	93	16	B Stephens	88
28	M Brown	307	29	Orange Club	57
30	K Black	624	30	Balance c/d	2,833
		3,561			3,561

Bank Statement

	Dr	Cr	Balance
2007	£	£	£
Jun 1 Balance b/d			2,379
7 Cheque		158	2,537
8 D Blackness	150		2,387
16 Cheque		93	2,480
17 J Gray	433		2,047
18 B Stephens	88		1,959
28 Cheque		307	2,266
29 UDT standing order	44		2,222
30 Johnson: Trader's credit		90	2,312
30 Bank charges	70		2,242

Required

(a) Write the cash book up to date to take the above into account, and then

(b) Draw up a bank reconciliation statement as on 30 June 2007.

17.4 The bank statement for G Greene for the month of March 2006 is:

2006		Dr £	Cr £	Balance £
Mar 1	Balance			5,197 O/D
8	L Tulloch	122		5,319 O/D
16	Cheque		244	5,075 O/D
20	A Bennett	208		5,283 O/D
21	Cheque		333	4,950 O/D
31	M Turnbull: Trader's credit		57	4,893 O/D
31	BKS: Standing order	49		4,942 O/D
31	Bank charges	28		4,970 O/D

The cash book for March 2006 is:

Dr			Cash Book			Cr
2006		£	2006			£
Mar 16	N Marsh	244	Mar 1	Balance b/d		5,197
21	K Alexander	333	6	L Tulloch		122
31	U Sinclair	160	30	A Bennett		208
31	Balance c/d	5,280	30	J Shaw		490
		6,017				6,017

Required

(a) Write the cash book up to date.

(b) Draw up a bank reconciliation statement as on 31 March 2006.

17.5X Following is the cash book (bank columns) of E Flynn for December 2007:

Dr			Cash Book			Cr
2007		£	2007			£
Dec 6	J Hall	155	Dec 1	Balance b/d		3,872
20	C Walters	189	10	P Wood		206
31	P Miller	211	19	M Roberts		315
31	Balance c/d	3,922	29	P Phillips		84
		4,477				4,477

The bank statement for the month is:

2007		Dr £	Cr £	Balance £
Dec 1	Balance			3,872 O/D
6	Cheque		155	3,717 O/D
13	P Wood	206		3,923 O/D
20	Cheque		189	3,734 O/D
22	M Roberts	315		4,049 O/D
30	Mercantile: Standing order	200		4,249 O/D
31	K Saunders: Trader's credit		180	4,069 O/D
31	Bank charges	65		4,134 O/D

Required

(a) Write the cash book up to date to take the necessary items into account.

(b) Draw up a bank reconciliation statement as on 31 December 2007.

17.6 The following is an extract of the cash book, bank columns only, of Richard Woolley & Co., for the month of November 2005.

Dr   Cash Book (bank columns only)   Cr

2005		£	2005		Cheque No.	£
Nov 1	Balance b/d	1,620	Nov 2	D Todd	421	1,092
4	K Lamb	5,532	3	Post Office	422	150
7	J Jacobs	2,685	5	J Shaw	423	501
7	P Ash	57	5	K Marsh	424	594
7	Cash sales	2,823	7	M Lawrie	425	117
9	T Clowes	3,291	11	Smithy Garage	426	718
9	Cash sales	1,917	12	Amber & Co.	427	758
16	G Street	576	19	Ace Computer	428	18,080
16	Cash sales	2,352	23	F Worral	429	252
28	C Hall	1,098	30	Salaries	430	4,170
28	Cash sales	951	30	Petty cash	431	137
30	M Burns	864	30	D Todd	432	874
30	Cash sales	1,260	30	J Shaw	433	1,947
30	Balance c/d	4,364				
		29,390				29,390

The following bank statement was received by Richard Woolley & Co. on 1 December 2005:

	Tudor Bank PLC Bank Statement			
Richard Woolley & Co.				Account No. 01795678

Date 2005	Details	Debit £	Credit £	Balance £
Nov 1	Balance b/d			2,583 o/d
4	Credit		4,482	1,899
5	Cheque 422	150		1,749
5	Cheque 351	279		1,470
5	Credit		5,532	7,002
7	Cheque 424	594		6,408
8	Credit		5,565	11,973
8	BACS credit: Atlas Co.		270	12,243
10	Credit		5,208	17,451
10	Cheque 423	501		16,950
13	Cheque 426	718		16,232
17	Credit		2,928	19,160
21	Cheque 428	18,080		1,080
24	Standing order – Grove Insurance	108		972
29	Credit		2,049	3,021
29	Cheque referred to drawer (P Ash)	57		2,964
30	Bank charges	143		2,821
30	Cheque 429	252		2,569

Required

(a) Prepare a statement reconciling the £1,620 opening balance of the cash book with the £2,583 overdraft shown on the bank statement. Show clearly all your workings.

(b) Write up the cash book to show the correct balance as at 30 November 2005.

(c) Prepare a bank reconciliation statement as at 30 November 2005 starting with the balance as per the cash book. A postal strike had held up delivery of quite a few cheques paid out.

17.7X The bank statement below was received by Automania on 1 June 2004:

Commercial Bank PLC				
Bank Statement				
Automania				Account No. 80261995
Date 2004	Details	Debit £	Credit £	Balance £
May 17	Balance			8,700
17	Cheque 704182	290		8,410
18	Credit		360	8,770
19	Cheque 704184	310		8,460
20	Cheque 704183	200		8,260
20	Credit		1,080	9,340
21	Cheque 704185	1,360		7,980
21	Cheque 704186	2,750		5,230
24	Credit		1,400	6,630
24	Bank charges	140		6,490
25	Standing order: Anzac property	1,600		4,890
26	BACS credit: Pearson		125	5,015
26	Cheque 704188	475		4,540
27	Cash withdrawal	200		4,340
28	Cheque 704187	2,970		1,370

The following is an extract from the cash book for the same period:

Dr			Bank Account			Cr
2004		£	2004		Cheque No.	£
May 17	Balance b/d	7,900	May 17	Auto Parts	185	1,360
17	L White	360	18	Slick Oils	186	2,750
18	Field Garages	750	21	Stealth Wheels	187	2,970
19	H Smith	330	21	K Mason	188	475
20	L Sprig	190	24	P Curtis	189	395
21	Kay Cars	1,210	27	K Fabrications	190	1,880
27	Halliwells	685	28	Auto Parts	191	4,200
28	Reece Motors	470				
28	Balance c/d	2,135				
		14,030				14,030

Required

(a) Prepare a statement reconciling the opening balance of £7,900 in the cash book with the opening balance of £8,700 shown on the bank statement.

(b) Write up the cash book to show the correct balance as at 31 May 2004.

(c) Prepare a bank reconciliation statement as at 31 May 2004.

(AAT)

17.8X The bank column of Fisher Products Ltd's cash book showed a credit balance of £12,879 on 31 March 2007 which did not agree with the balance shown on the bank statement.

The following is an extract from the company's cash book (bank columns only) for the month of March 2007:

Dr				Cash Book (bank columns only)		Cr
2007		£	2007		Cheque No.	£
Mar 1	Balance b/d	10,502	Mar 2	B Wilson	731	3,585
3	B Rogers Co.	3,513	4	Quicksilver	732	20,700
5	Wood Ltd	1,740	10	Purchases	733	1,880
15	Clark & Son	6,430	21	Atlas Ltd	734	12,550
18	Sales	585	22	Ashford & Co.	735	53
31	Hamilton & Co.	15,000	25	Stationery	736	300
31	Balance c/d	12,879	25	T Moor	737	8,377
			25	Petty cash	738	1,404
			25	L Knott	739	1,800
		50,649				50,649

The bank statement for the same month was as follows:

	Oak Bank PLC Bank Statement			
Fisher Products Ltd				Account No. 582604

Date 2007	Details	Debit £	Credit £	Balance £
Mar 1	Balance b/d			11,227
2	Cheque 729	300		10,927
3	Credit		3,513	14,440
5	Credit		1,740	16,180
5	Cheque 731	3,585		12,595
12	Cheque 733	1,880		10,715
14	Cheque 732	20,700		9,985 o/d
16	Credit		6,430	3,555 o/d
17	Cheque dishonoured – Clark & Son	6,430		9,985 o/d
19	Credit		585	9,400 o/d
25	Cheque 734	12,550		21,950 o/d
26	Cheque 738	1,404		23,354 o/d
28	BACS – Premier PLC		4,250	19,104 o/d
28	Cheque 736	300		19,404 o/d
28	Cheque 739	1,800		21,204 o/d
28	Standing order – Electric Co.	1,382		22,586 o/d
28	Direct debit – Star Insurance	900		23,486 o/d
30	Bank charges	342		23,828 o/d

The following additional information is available:

The balances on 1 March 2007 were reconciled and the difference was due to the following cheques which were unpresented on that date:

Cheque No. 704 £425
729 £300

Required

(a) Calculate the correct cash book balance of Fisher Products Ltd as at 31 March 2007.
(b) Using the corrected cash book balance calculated in (a) above, prepare a bank reconciliation statement for Fisher Products as at 31 March 2007.

CHAPTER 18

Single entry and incomplete records

AIMS

- To be able to use accounting ratios to calculate missing or forecasted figures.

- To be able to deduce the figure of profits where only the increase in capital and details of drawings are known.

- To draw up a trading and profit and loss account and balance sheet from records not kept on a double entry system.

- To deduce the figures of sales and purchases from incomplete records.

- To be able to calculate the value of goods stolen or lost by fire, etc.

18.1 Accounting ratios covered in this unit

The accounting standards covered by this unit refer only to mark-up and margin, the use of other accounting ratios are outside the scope of this unit.

18.2 Mark-up and margin

The purchase and sale of goods may be shown as:

Cost Price + Profit = Selling Price

The profit when shown as a fraction, or percentage, of the cost price is known as the **mark-up**. The profit when shown as a fraction, or percentage, of the selling price is known as the **margin**.

We can now calculate these using this example:

Cost price + Profit = Selling price
£4   + £1   = £5

$$\text{Mark-up} = \frac{\text{Profit}}{\text{Cost price}} = \tfrac{1}{4} \text{ as a fraction}$$

if required as a percentage, multiply by 100: $\tfrac{1}{4} \times 100 = 25\%$

$$\text{Margin} = \frac{\text{Profit}}{\text{Selling price}} = \tfrac{1}{5} \text{ as a fraction}$$

if required as a percentage, multiply by 100: $\tfrac{1}{5} \times 100 = 20\%$

18.3 Calculating missing figures

Now we can use these ratios to complete trading accounts where some of the figures are missing. All examples in this chapter:

- assume that all the goods in a firm have the same rate of mark-up
- ignore wastages and theft of goods.

Example 18.1

The following figures are for the year 2005:

	£
Stock 1.1.2005	400
Stock 31.12.2005	600
Purchases	5,200

A uniform rate of mark-up of 20% is applied.

Find the gross profit and the sales figure:

Trading Account for the year ended 31 December 2005

	£	£
Sales		?
Less Cost of goods sold:		
Stock 1.1.2005	400	
Add Purchases	5,200	
	5,600	
Less Stock 31.12.2005	600	5,000
Gross profit		?

Answer

It is known that:	Cost of goods sold + Profit = Sales
and also that:	Cost of goods sold + Percentage Mark-up = Sales

The following figures are also known:	£5,000 + 20% = Sales
After doing arithmetic:	£5,000 + £1,000 = £6,000

The trading account can be completed by inserting the gross profit £1,000 and £6,000 for sales.

Example 18.2

Another firm has the following figures for 2006:

	£
Stock 1.1.2006	500
Stock 31.12.2006	800
Sales	6,400

A uniform rate of margin of 25% is in use.

Find the gross profit and the figure of purchases:

Trading Account for the year ended 31 December 2006

	£	£
Sales		6,400
Less Cost of goods sold:		
Stock 1.1.2006	500	
Add Purchases	?	
	?	
Less Stock 31.12.2006	800	?
Gross profit		?

Answer

Cost of goods sold + Gross profit = Sales

therefore

Sales − Gross profit = Cost of goods sold
Sales − 25% margin = Cost of goods sold
£6,400 − £1,600   = £4,800

Now the following figures are known:

		£	£
Cost of goods sold:			
Stock 1.1.2006		500	
Add Purchases	(1)	?	
	(2)	?	
Less Stock 31.12.2006		800	4,800

The two missing figures are found by normal arithmetical deduction:

No. (2) less £800 = £4,800
Therefore No. (2) = £5,600

So that: £500 opening stock + No. (1) = 5,600

Therefore No. (1) = £5,100

The completed trading account can now be shown:

	£	£
Sales		6,400
Less Cost of goods sold:		
Stock 1.1.2006	500	
Add Purchases	5,100	
	5,600	
Less Stock 31.12.2006	800	4,800
Gross profit		1,600

This technique is found to be very useful by retail stores when estimating the amount to be bought if a certain sales target is to be achieved. Alternatively, stock levels or sales figures can be estimated given information on purchases and opening stock figures.

As we will see later, we may also use this technique where the full information needed for preparing final accounts is missing. This could simply be due to the incompetence of the owner or of the loss of some of the records, by fire, in a burglary, and so on. The technique may be able at least to estimate fairly closely what the missing figures should be.

18.4 The relationship between mark-up and margin

As both of these figures refer to the same profit, but are expressed as a fraction or a percentage of different figures, there is bound to be a relationship. If one is known in fraction form, the other can soon be found.

To find the margin when the mark-up is known, take the same numerator to be the numerator of the margin; then, for the denominator of the margin, take the total of the mark-up's denominator plus the numerator:

Mark-up	*Margin*
$\dfrac{1}{4}$	$\dfrac{1}{4+1} = \dfrac{1}{5}$
$\dfrac{2}{11}$	$\dfrac{2}{11+2} = \dfrac{2}{13}$

To find the mark-up when the margin is known, take the same numerator to be the numerator of the mark-up; then, for the denominator of the mark-up, take the figure of the margin's denominator less the numerator:

Mark-up	*Margin*
$\dfrac{1}{6}$	$\dfrac{1}{6-1} = \dfrac{1}{5}$
$\dfrac{3}{13}$	$\dfrac{3}{13-3} = \dfrac{3}{10}$

18.5　Why double entry is not used

It would be ridiculous to expect every small shopkeeper, market stall or other small business to record its finances using a full double entry system. First of all, a large number of the owners of such firms would not know how to write up double entry records, even if they wanted to. It is more likely that they would enter details of a transaction once only, using a single entry system. Also, many of them would fail to record every transaction, resulting in incomplete records.

It is, perhaps, only fair to remember that accounting is after all supposed to be an aid to management; it is not something to be done as an end in itself. Therefore, many small firms, especially retail shops, can have all the information they want by merely keeping a cash book and having some form of record, not necessarily in double entry form, of their debtors and creditors.

The profits, however, will still need to be calculated in some way. This could be for the purpose of calculating income tax payable. How can profits be calculated if the book keeping records are inadequate or incomplete?

18.6　Profit as an increase in capital

Probably the way to start is to recall that, unless these has been an introduction of extra cash or resources into the firm, the only way that capital can be increased is by making profits. Therefore, profits can be found by comparing capital at the end of one period with that at the end of the next period.

Let us look at a firm where capital at the end of 2004 was £2,000. During 2005 there have been no drawings and no extra capital has been brought in by the owner. At the end of 2005 the capital was £3,000.

	This year's capital		Last year's capital	
Net profit =	£3,000	–	£2,000	= £1,000

If, on the other hand, the drawings had been £700, the profits must have been £1,700, calculated thus:

Last year's capital + Profits – Drawings = This year's capital
　£2,000　　　+　?　–　£700　=　　£3,000

We can see that £1,700 profits was the figure needed to complete the formula, filling in the missing figure by normal arithmetical deduction:

£2,000 + £1,700 – 700 = £3,000

Exhibit 18.1 shows the calculation of profit where insufficient information is available to draft a trading and profit and loss account, only information of assets and liabilities being known.

Exhibit 18.1

H Taylor has not kept proper book keeping records, but he has kept notes in diary form of the transactions of his business. He is able to give you details of his assets and liabilities as at 31 December 2005 and at 31 December 2006 as follows:

At 31 December 2005	Assets:	Motor van	£1,000
		Fixtures	£700
		Stock	£850
		Debtors	£950
		Bank	£1,100
		Cash	£100
	Liabilities:	Creditors	£200
		Loan from J Ogden	£600
At 31 December 2006	Assets:	Motor van (after depreciation)	£800
		Fixtures (after depreciation)	£630
		Stock	£990
		Debtors	£1,240
		Bank	£1,700
		Cash	£200
	Liabilities:	Creditors	£300
		Loan from J Ogden	£400
	Drawings were £900		

First of all a **statement of affairs** is drawn up as at 31 December 2005. This is the name given to what would have been called a balance sheet if it had been drawn up from a set of records. The capital is the difference between the assets and liabilities.

H Taylor
Statement of Affairs as at 31 December 2005

	£	£
Fixed assets		
Motor van		1,000
Fixtures		700
		1,700
Current assets		
Stock	850	
Debtors	950	
Bank	1,100	
Cash	100	
	3,000	
Less Current liabilities		
Creditors	200	
Net current assets		2,800
		4,500
Less Long-term liability		
Loan from J Ogden		600
		3,900
Financed by		
Capital (difference)		3,900

A statement of affairs is now drafted up as at the end of 2006. The formula of opening capital + profit − drawings = closing capital is then used to deduce the figure of profit.

H Taylor
Statement of Affairs as at 31 December 2006

	£	£
Fixed assets		
Motor van		800
Fixtures		630
		1,430
Current assets		
Stock	990	
Debtors	1,240	
Bank	1,700	
Cash	200	
	4,130	
Less Current liabilities		
Creditors	300	
Net current assets		3,830
		5,260
Less Long-term liability		
Loan from J Ogden		400
		4,860
Financed by		
Capital balance at 1.1.2006		3,900
Add Net profit	(C)	?
	(B)	?
Less Drawings		900
	(A)	?

Deduction of net profit Opening Capital + Net Profit − Drawings = Closing capital. Find the missing figures (A), (B) and (C) by deduction:

(A) is the figure needed to make the balance sheet totals equal, i.e. £4,860;

(B) is therefore £4,860 + £900 = £5,760;

(C) is therefore £5,760 − £3,900 = £1,860.

To check:

Capital		3,900
Add Net profit	(C)	1,860
	(B)	5,760
Less Drawings		900
	(A)	4,860

Obviously, this method of calculating profit is very unsatisfactory as it is much more informative when a trading and profit and loss account can be drawn up. Therefore, whenever possible, the comparisons of capital method of ascertaining profit should be avoided and a full set of final accounts drawn up from the available records.

It is important to realise that a business would have exactly the same trading and profit and loss account and balance sheet whether the books were kept by single entry or double entry. As shown previously, the double entry system uses the trial balance in preparing the final accounts, whereas the single entry system will have to arrive at the same answer by different means.

18.7 Drawing up the final accounts

The following example shows the various stages of drawing up final accounts from a single entry set of records.

The accountant discerns the following details of transactions for J Frank's retail store for the year ended 31 December 2005:

(a) The sales are mostly on a credit basis. No record of sales has been made, but £10,000 has been received, £9,500 by cheque and £500 by cash, from persons to whom goods have been sold.

(b) Amount paid by cheque to suppliers during the year = £7,200.

(c) Expenses paid during the year: by cheque, Rent £200, General expenses £180; by cash, Rent £50.

(d) J Frank took £10 cash per week (for 52 weeks) as drawings.

(e) Other information is available:

	At 31.12.2004 £	At 31.12.2005 £
Debtors	1,100	1,320
Creditors for goods	400	650
Rent owing	–	50
Bank balance	1,130	3,050
Cash balance	80	10
Stock	1,590	1,700

(f) The only fixed asset consists of fixtures which were valued at 31 December 2004 at £800. These are to be depreciated at 10% per annum.

Step 1 Draw up a statement of affairs on the closing day of the last accounting period:

J Frank
Statement of Affairs as at 31 December 2004

	£	£
Fixed assets		
Fixtures		800
Current assets		
Stock	1,590	
Debtors	1,100	
Bank	1,130	
Cash	80	
	3,900	
Less Current liabilities		
Creditors	400	
Net current assets		3,500
		4,300
Financed by		
Capital (difference)		4,300
		4,300

All of these opening figures are then taken into account when drawing up the final accounts for 2005:

Step 2 Next a cash and bank summary, showing the totals of each separate item, plus opening and closing balances, is drawn up.

	Cash	Bank		Cash	Bank
	£	£		£	£
Balances 31.12.2004	80	1,130	Suppliers		7,200
Receipts from debtors	500	9,500	Rent	50	200
			General expenses		180
			Drawings	520	
			Balances 31.12.2005	10	3,050
	580	10,630		580	10,630

Step 3 Calculate the figures for purchases and sales to be shown in the trading account. Remember that the figures needed are the same as those which would have been found if double entry records had been kept.

Purchases

In double entry, purchases means the goods that have been bought in the period irrespective of whether they have been paid for or not during that period. The figure of payments to suppliers must therefore be adjusted to find the figure for purchases.

	£
Paid during the year	7,200
Less Payments made, but which were for goods which	
were purchased in a previous year (creditors 31.12.2004)	400
	6,800
Add Purchases made in this year, but for which payment has	
not yet been made (creditors 31.12.2005)	650
Goods bought in this year, i.e. purchases	7,450

The same answer could have been obtained if the information had been shown in the form of a total creditors account, the figure for purchases being the amount required to make the account totals agree.

Dr		Total Creditors		Cr
	£			£
Cash paid to suppliers	7,200	Balances b/d		400
Balances c/d	650	Purchases (missing figure)		7,450
	7,850			7,850

Sales

The sales figure will only equal receipts where all the sales are for cash. Therefore, the receipts figures need adjusting to find sales. This can only be done by constructing a total debtors account, the sales figure being the one needed to make the totals agree.

Dr		Total Debtors			Cr
		£			£
Balances b/d		1,100	Receipts: Cash		500
			Cheque		9,500
Sales (missing figure)		10,220	Balances c/d		1,320
		11,320			11,320

 The above accounts are exactly the same as the creditors and debtors control accounts (refer to Chapter 15).

Step 4 Expenses

Where there are no accruals or prepayments either at the beginning or end of the accounting period, then expenses paid will equal expenses used up during the period. These figures will be charged to the trading and profit and loss account.

On the other hand, where such prepayments or accruals exist, then an expense account should be drawn up for that particular item. When all known items are entered, the missing figure will be the expenses to be charged for the accounting period. In this case only the rent account needs to be drawn up.

Dr	Rent Account		Cr
	£		£
Cheques	200	Rent (missing figure)	300
Cash	50		
Accrued c/d	50		
	300		300

Step 5 Now draw up the final accounts.

J Frank
Trading and Profit and Loss Account
for the year ended 31 December 2005

	£	£
Sales (step 3)		10,220
Less Cost of goods sold:		
Stock at 1.1.2005	1,590	
Add Purchases (step 3)	7,450	
	9,040	
Less Stock at 31.12.2005	1,700	7,340
Gross profit		2,880
Less Expenses:		
Rent (step 4)	300	
General expenses	180	
Depreciation: Fixtures	80	560
Net profit		2,320

J Frank
Balance Sheet as at 31 December 2005

	£	£	£
Fixed assets			
Fixtures at 1.1.2005		800	
Less Depreciation		80	720
Current assets			
Stock		1,700	
Debtors		1,320	
Bank		3,050	
Cash		10	
		6,080	
Less Current liabilities			
Creditors	650		
Rent owing	50	700	
Net current assets			5,380
			6,100
Financed by			
Capital			
Balance 1.1.2005 (per Opening Statement of Affairs)			4,300
Add Net profit			2,320
			6,620
Less Drawings			520
			6,100

18.8 Incomplete records and missing figures

In practice, part of the information relating to cash receipts or payments is often missing. If the missing information is in respect of one type of payment, then it is normal to assume that the missing figure is the amount required to make both totals agree in the cash column of the cash and bank summary. This does not happen with bank items since another copy of the bank statement can always be obtained. Exhibit 18.2 shows an example when the drawings figure is unknown; Exhibit 18.3 is an example where the receipts from debtors had not been recorded.

Exhibit 18.2

The following information on cash and bank receipts and payments is available:

	Cash	Bank
	£	£
Cash paid into the bank during the year	5,500	
Receipts from debtors	7,250	800
Paid to suppliers	320	4,930
Drawings during the year	?	–
Expenses paid	150	900
Balances at 1.1.2005	35	1,200
Balances at 31.12.2005	50	1,670

Exhibit 18.2 (continued)

	Cash	Bank			Cash	Bank
	£	£			£	£
Balances 1.1.2005	35	1,200	Bankings ¢		5,500	
Received from debtors	7,250	800	Suppliers		320	4,930
Bankings ¢*		5,500	Expenses		150	900
			Drawings		?	
			Balances 31.12.2005		50	1,670
	7,285	7,500			7,285	7,500

* ¢ means *contra*. A *contra*, for cash book terms, is where both the debit and the credit entries are shown in the cash book.

The amount needed to make the two sides of the cash columns agree is £1,265. Therefore, this is taken as the figure of drawings.

Exhibit 18.3

Information of cash and bank transactions is available as follows:

	Cash	Bank
	£	£
Receipts from debtors	?	6,080
Cash withdrawn from the bank for business use (this is the amount which is used besides cash receipts from debtors to pay drawings and expenses)		920
Paid to suppliers		5,800
Expenses paid	640	230
Drawings	1,180	315
Balances at 1.1.2005	40	1,560
Balances at 31.12.2005	70	375

	Cash	Bank			Cash	Bank
	£	£			£	£
Balances 1.1.2005	40	1,560	Suppliers			5,800
Receipts from debtors	?	6,080	Expenses		640	230
Withdrawn from			Withdrawn from Bank ¢			920
Bank ¢	920		Drawings		1,180	315
			Balances 31.12.2005		70	375
	1,890	7,640			1,890	7,640

Therefore, the amount needed to make each side of the cash column agree is £930, receipts from debtors.

It must be emphasised that balancing figures are acceptable only when all the other figures have been verified. Should, for instance, a cash expense be omitted when cash received from debtors is being calculated, then this would result in an understatement not only of expenses but also ultimately of sales.

18.9 Where there are two missing pieces of information

If both cash drawings and cash receipts from debtors were not known, it would not be possible to deduce both of these figures. The only course available would be to estimate whichever figure was more capable of being accurately assessed, use this as a known figure, and deduce the other figure. However, this is a most unsatisfactory position as both of the figures are no more than pure estimates, the accuracy of one relying entirely upon the accuracy of the other.

18.10 Cash sales and purchases for cash

Where there are cash sales as well as sales on credit terms, then the cash sales must be added to sales on credit to give the total sales for the year. This total figure of sales will be the one shown in the trading account.

Similarly, purchases for cash will need adding to credit purchases to give the figure of total purchases for the trading account.

18.11 Goods stolen or lost by fire, etc.

When goods are stolen, destroyed by fire, or lost in some other way, then their value will have to be calculated. This could be needed to substantiate an insurance claim or to settle problems concerning taxation, etc.

If the stock had been properly valued immediately before the fire, burglary, etc., then the stock loss would obviously be known. Also, if a full and detailed system of stock records were kept, then the value would also be known. However, as the occurrence of fires or burglaries cannot be foreseen, and not many businesses keep full and proper stock records, the stock loss will have to be calculated in some other way.

The methods described in this chapter are used instead. The only difference is that instead of computing closing stock at a year end, for example, the closing stock will be that as at immediately before the fire consumed it or it was stolen.

Exhibits 18.4 and 18.5 will now be considered. The first exhibit will be a very simple case, where figures of purchases and sales are known and all goods are sold at a uniform profit ratio. The second exhibit is rather complicated.

Exhibit 18.4

J Collins lost the whole of his stock by fire on 17 March 2009. The last time that a stocktaking had been carried out was on 31 December 2008, the last balance sheet date, when it was valued at £1,950 at cost. Purchases from then to 17 March 2009 amounted to £6,870 and sales for the period were £9,600. All sales were made at a uniform profit margin of 20%.

First, the trading account can be drawn up with the known figures included, and the missing figures can be deduced afterwards.

Exhibit 18.4 (continued)

J Collins
Trading Account for the period 1 January 2009 to 17 March 2009

		£	£
Sales			9,600
Less Cost of goods sold:			
Opening stock		1,950	
Add Purchases		6,870	
		8,820	
Less Closing stock	(C)	?	
	(B)		?
Gross profit	(A)		?

Now the missing figures can be deduced.

It is known that the gross profit margin is 20% therefore gross profit (A) is 20% of £9,600 = £1,920. Now (B) ? + (A) £1,920 = £9,600, so that (B) is the difference, i.e. £7,680.

Now that (B) is known, (C) can be deduced:

£8,820 − (C) ? = £7,680, so (C) is the difference, i.e. £1,140. The figure for goods destroyed by fire, at cost, is therefore £1,140.

Exhibit 18.5

T Scott had the whole of his stock stolen from his warehouse on the night of 20 August 2006. Also destroyed were his sales and purchases journals, but the sales and purchases ledgers were salvaged. The following facts are known:

(a) Stock was known at the last balance sheet date, 31 March 2006, to be £12,480 at cost.

(b) Receipts from debtors during the period 1 April to 20 August 2006 amounted to £31,745. Debtors were: At 31 March 2006 £14,278, at 20 August 2006 £12,333.

(c) Payments to creditors during the period 1 April to 20 August 2006 amounted to £17,270. Creditors were: At 31 March 2006 £7,633, at 20 August 2006 £6,289.

(d) The margin on sales has been constant at 25%.

Before we can start to construct a trading account for the period, we need to find out the figure of sales and of purchases. These can be found by drawing up total debtors and total creditors accounts, sales and purchases figures being the difference on the accounts.

Dr		Total Creditors		Cr
	£			£
Cash and bank	17,270	Balances b/d		7,633
Balances c/d	6,289	Purchases (difference)		15,926
	23,559			23,559

Exhibit 18.5 (continued)

Dr	Total Debtors		Cr
	£		£
Balances b/d	14,278	Cash and bank	31,745
Sales (difference)	29,800	Balances c/d	12,333
	44,078		44,078

The trading account can now show the figures already known.

Trading Account for the period 1 April to 20 August 2006

		£		£
Sales				29,800
Less Cost of goods sold:				
Opening stock		12,480		
Add Purchases		15,926		
		28,406		
Less Closing stock	(C)	?		
			(B)	?
Gross profit			(A)	?

Gross profit can be found, as the margin on sales is known to be 25%, therefore (A) = 25% of £29,800 = £7,450.

Cost of goods sold (B) ? + Gross profit £7,450 = £29,800, therefore (B) is £22,350. £28,406 – (C) ? = (B) £22,350, therefore (C) is £6,056.

The figure for cost of goods stolen is therefore £6,056.

18.12 Step-by-step guide to incomplete records

Questions on incomplete records are often complicated and presented in many different ways To help students tackle such questions a step-by-step guide is given below:

Step 1 Prepare a statement of affairs on the closing day of the last accounting period to ascertain the *initial capital*; remember to include the cash and bank balances.

Step 2 *Either* draw up and balance a cash and bank summary *or* if a cash and bank summary is shown in the question it may only be necessary to balance the account off.

❗ *Remember to include the final cash and bank balances in the final balance sheet.*

Step 3 Calculate the figures for *purchases* and *sales* to be shown in the trading account. There are two ways this may be achieved either as a 'calculation' or by using double entry in a 'T Account' (refer to Section 18.7).

Step 4 Calculate the figures for *expenses*. If there were no accruals or prepayments either at the beginning or end of the accounting period, then the expenses paid will equal the expenses used up during the period. If, however, there are accruals and prepayments then it will be necessary to make adjustments; and again this may carried out as a 'calculation' or by using 'T Accounts'. An example of using the calculation method is shown below and the 'T Account' method is shown in Section 18.7 (Rent account).

Accrual – Rent	£	Prepayment – Rates	£
Paid–Bank	1,650	Paid–Bank	890
Less Owing 1.1.2006	150	*Add* Prepaid 1.1.2006	210
	1,500		1,100
Add Owing 31.12.2006	Nil	*Less* Prepaid 31.12.2006	225
Rent for the year	1,500	Rates for the year	875

The above figures are taken from Student Activity 18.7 (P Kelly). All expenses for the year must be charged to the trading and profit and loss account.

Step 5 Take account of any *depreciation* before preparing the final accounts. The question may indicate the amount of depreciation to be allowed for, or alternatively, you may have to compare the value of the asset at the beginning of the period with that at the end of the period – the difference is *depreciation*. Remember to check to see if there are any additions to assets and, if so, ensure that you include them on the balance sheet and depreciate them as indicated above.

Finally, prepare the final accounts:

> Trading and profit and loss account
> *and*
> Balance sheet

NEW TERMS **Incomplete records** A system of keeping accounting records which does not involve double entry book keeping, often only one entry is made of a transaction which is why it is also referred to as a 'single entry' system.

Mark-up The profit shown as a percentage or fraction of the cost price.

Margin The profit shown as a percentage or fraction of the selling price.

Single entry Where a transaction is only recorded once in the accounting records.

Statement of Affairs A statement from which the capital of the owner is deduced by estimating assets and liabilities. Then
> Capital = Assets – Liabilities.

Student Activities

18.1 R Stubbs is a trader who sells all of his goods at 25% above cost. His books give the following information at 31 December 2009:

	£
Stock 1 January 2009	9,872
Stock 31 December 2009	12,620
Sales for year	60,000

Required

(a) Ascertain cost of goods sold.

(b) Show the value of purchases during the year.

(c) Calculate the profit made by Stubbs.

Show your answer in the form of a trading account.

18.2X   C White gives you the following information as at 30 June 2007:

	£
Stock 1 July 2006	6,000
Purchases	54,000

White's mark-up is 50% on 'cost of goods sold'. His average stock during the year was £12,000. Draw up a trading and profit and loss account for the year ended 30 June 2007.

(a) Calculate the closing stock as at 30 June 2007.

(b) State the total amount of profit and loss expenditure that White must not exceed if he is to maintain a *net* profit on sales of 10%.

18.3   B Arkwright started in business on 1 January 2005 with £10,000 in a bank account. Unfortunately he did not keep proper books of account.

He is forced to submit a calculation of profit for the year ended 31 December 2005 to the Inspector of Taxes. He ascertains that at 31 December 2005 he had stock valued at cost £3,950; a motor van which had cost £2,800 during the year and which had depreciated by £550; debtors of £4,970; expenses prepaid of £170; bank balance £2,564; cash balance £55; trade creditors £1,030; and expenses owing £470.

His drawings were: Cash £100 per week for 50 weeks; Cheque payments £673.

Draw up statements to show the profit or loss for the year.

18.4X   J Kirkwood is a dealer who has not kept proper books of account. At 31 August 2006 his state of affairs was as follows:

	£
Cash	115
Bank balance	2,209
Fixtures	4,000
Stock	16,740
Debtors	11,890
Creditors	9,052
Motor van (at valuation)	3,000

During the year to 31 August 2007 his drawings amounted to £7,560. Winnings from a football pool £2,800 were put into the business. Extra fixtures were bought for £2,000.

At 31 August 2007 his assets and liabilities were: cash £84; bank overdraft £165; stock £21,491; creditors for goods £6,002; creditors for expenses

£236; fixtures to be depreciated £600; motor van to be valued at £2,500; debtors £15,821; prepaid expenses £72.

Draw up a statement showing the profit and loss made by Kirkwood for the year ended 31 August 2007.

18.5 A Hanson is a sole trader who, although keeping very good records, does not operate a full double entry system. The following figures have been taken from his records:

	31 March 2008	31 March 2009
	£	£
Cash at bank	1,460	1,740
Office furniture	600	500
Stock	2,320	2,620
Cash in hand	60	80

Debtors on 31 March 2008 amounted to £2,980 and sales for the year ended 31 March 2009 to £11,520. During the year ended 31 March 2009, cash received from debtors amounted to £10,820.

Creditors on 31 March 2008 amounted to £1,880 and purchases for the year ended 31 March 2009 to £8,120. During the year ended 31 March 2009, cash paid to creditors amounted to £7,780.

During the year to 31 March 2009 no bad debts were incurred. Also during the same period, there were neither discounts allowed nor discounts received.

Required

(a) Calculate debtors and creditors as at 31 March 2009.
(b) Calculate his capital as at 31 March 2008 and 31 March 2009.
(c) Calculate his net profit for the year ended 31 March 2009, allowing for the fact that during that year his drawings amounted to £2,540.

Calculations must be shown.

18.6X L Lee does not keep proper double entry accounts. He does, however, have the following information available:

	30 June 2007	30 June 2008
	£	£
Fixtures at valuation	2,500	2,200
Stock of goods	8,690	9,245
Cash at bank	5,211	8,116
Cash in hand	210	97
Debtors	6,277	7,040
Creditors	5,322	3,798

During the year to 30 June 2008, Lee's drawings were cash £4,927 and goods taken for own use £371. He had paid in £1,000 cash as additional capital.

The reduction in the value of fixtures is due to depreciation.

Required

(a) Calculate Lee's capital as at 30 June 2007 and 30 June 2008.

(b) Calculate Lee's net profit for the year to 30 June 2008.

(c) Show how his capital account would have appeared in a double entry set of records.

18.7 Following is a summary of P Kelly's bank account for the year ended 31 December 2007:

	£		£
Balance 1.1.2007	405	Payments to creditors	
Receipts from debtors	37,936	for goods	29,487
Balance 31.12.2007	602	Rent	1,650
		Rates	890
		Sundry expenses	375
		Drawings	6,541
	38,943		38,943

All of the business takings have been paid into the bank with the exception of £9,630. Out of this, Kelly has paid wages of £5,472, made drawings of £1,164 and purchased goods for £2,994.

The following additional information is available:

	31.12.2006	31.12.2007
	£	£
Stock	13,862	15,144
Creditors for goods	5,624	7,389
Debtors for goods	9,031	8,624
Rates prepaid	210	225
Rent owing	150	–
Fixtures at valuation	2,500	2,250

You are to draw up a set of final accounts for the year ended 31 December 2007. *Show all of your workings.*

18.8X J Evans has kept records of his business transactions in a single entry form, but he did not realise that he had to record cash drawings. His bank account for the year 2008 is as follows:

	£		£
Balance 1.1.2008	1,890	Cash withdrawn from bank	5,400
Receipts from debtors	44,656	Trade creditors	31,695
Loan from T Hughes	2,000	Rent	2,750
		Rates	1,316
		Drawings	3,095
		Sundry expenses	1,642
		Balance 31.12.2008	2,648
	48,546		48,546

Records of cash paid were: Sundry expenses £122; trade creditors £642. Cash sales amounted to £698.

The following information is also available:

	31.12.2007	31.12.2008
	£	£
Cash in hand	48	93
Trade creditors	4,896	5,091
Debtors	6,013	7,132
Rent owing	–	250
Rates in advance	282	312
Motor van (at valuation)	2,800	2,400
Stock	11,163	13,021

You are to draw up a trading and profit and loss account for the year ended 31 December 2008, and a balance sheet as at that date. *Show all of your workings.*

18.9 Shelly Hamilton opened a fashion boutique in Cambridge on 1 January 2001. She started the business with savings of £30,000 which she deposited in a business bank account. Unfortunately she did not keep a full set of accounting records and asks you to assist her in preparing her accounts at the end of the first year's trading. Shelly is able to provide the following information:

**Summary of Cheque Payments
for the year ended 31 December 2001**

	£
Payment to trade creditors	32,250
Shop fixtures and fittings	10,500
Rent – 11 months to 30 November 2001	5,500
Salaries	12,900
Electricity – 11 months to 30 November 2001	1,823
Insurance premium (for period 1 Jan 2001 to 30 June 2002)	1,800
General expenses	936
Travel agents' bill for Shelly's holiday to USA	1,140
Drawings	12,000

The following additional information is also available:

1. All sales are for cash. The total receipts from sales amounted to £72,240. Out of the cash received, Shelly paid a telephone bill for the business amounting to £84 and cleaning charges of £150, she then banked the remaining cash takings after making these payments.

2. The electricity bill for December amounted to £234 and had not been paid. In addition, on 31 December 2001, Shelly still owed £1,575 for the purchase of goods.

3. Stock as at 31 December 2001 was valued at £7,855.

4. It is estimated that the shop fixtures and fittings have a useful life of 10 years and no residual value.

Required

(a) Prepare a cash and bank summary for the year ended 31 December 2001.

(b) Prepare a trading and profit and loss account for the year ended 31 December 2001 and a balance sheet as at that date.

18.10X Paul Moores had worked for many years as an electrical engineer for a company manufacturing washing machines but in July 2003 he decided to start his own business repairing washing machines and other electrical goods. He opened a business bank account into which he deposited his savings amounting to £20,000. His first purchase was a van costing £8,000 which he paid for by cheque. He also bought some machinery and tools for use in the business amounting to £4,000, again he paid for them by cheque.

Paul has had difficulty with his accounting records over the first year of trading and asks you if you can assist him in preparing his accounts. He has however, provided the following summary of his bank account for the year ended 30 June 2004:

Bank Summary for the year 1 July 2003 to 30 June 2004

	£		£
Capital	20,000	Motor van	8,000
Cash banked	36,000	Machinery/tools	4,000
		Purchase of machine parts, motors etc.	21,273
		Van running costs	2,150
		Telephone	350
		Electricity	930
		Drawings	4,400
		Balance c/d	14,897
	56,000		56,000

Other information available:

1. All repairs are carried out on a cash only basis. The cash is paid into the bank with the exception of the payment of some cash expenses. Unfortunately Paul does not know what his sales are for the year, but he has kept a note of his cash expenses which were as follows:

   General expenses £516
   Parts, etc.   £1,767

   He also took £6,588 cash for his own personal use during the year. Paul also keeps a cash float of £125.

2. Paul decides to depreciate his machinery and tools at 20% per annum using the reducing balance method. He doesn't think there will be any residual value. His motor van, which cost £8,000, is estimated to last 4 years and the residual value is estimated to be £2,000.

3. At the end of the financial year, 30 June 2004, Paul owes his creditors for parts £758 and a motor repair bill amounting to £93.

4. His stock of parts at 30 June 2004 was valued at £1,300.

5. The gross profit margin on all sales is 50%.

Required

(a) Calculate the total cost of materials and parts, etc., for the year ended 30 June 2004.

(b) Calculate the total cost of sales for the year ended 30 June 2004.

(c) Draw up the cash and bank summary for the year ended 30 June 2004.

(d) Calculate the total drawings for the year.

(e) Draw up a trading and profit and loss account for the year and a balance sheet as at 30 June 2004.

18.11 For the last two years Jack Costagliola had been running a hardware store which he started with an initial loan from his father of £20,000 who agreed to accept interest at a rate of 6% per annum. The repayment of the loan had been deferred until some later date when the business was more established.

Unfortunately, Jack had not kept proper records, and asks you to help him prepare his second year's final accounts. However, Jack was able to supply the following information:

1. Below is a summary of all his payments made during the year ended 30 September 2005 from his bank statements:

	£
Telephone	400
Rent of shop premises	9,600
Electricity	1,250
Purchase of computer equipment	4,000
Sundry expenses	720
Wages	17,600
Motor expenses	1,340
Decorating bedroom at home	300
Loan interest	1,100
Rates and insurance	3,860
Payments to suppliers (including £6,700 paid to creditors for previous year)	50,500
Drawings	16,000

2. At the start of the year, 1 October 2004, Jack had cash at bank of £8,200.

3. During the year Jack's sales amounted to £112,000, he did not allow credit to his customers. All receipts from sales were banked daily and all payments were made by cheque. Jack had always kept a cash float of £100 which he maintained throughout the year.

4. Sales of all stock had been arrived at by allowing a 60% profit margin on Jack's selling prices.

5. The display equipment is subject to depreciation at 15% per annum and the motor car at 20% per annum using the straight line basis. Jack calculated that if he had drawn up a balance sheet at 30 September 2004 then it would have included the following:

	Cost	Total depreciation	Net book value
	£	£	£
Display equipment	10,600	1,590	9,010
Motor car	12,000	2,400	9,600

The computer equipment bought during his second year's trading is to be depreciated at 25% on cost.

6. At the end of September 2005 Jack still had to pay an electricity bill of £96 and a telephone account of £146. Creditors for goods at 30 September amounted to £1,000.

7. Jack has always maintained a uniform stock of goods amounting to £10,000.

Required

(a) Calculate Jack's opening capital as at 1 October 2004.

(b) Calculate Jack's bank balance on 30 September 2005.

(c) Calculate the cost of sales for the year ended 30 September 2005.

(d) Draw up a trading and profit and loss account for the year ended 30 September 2005 and a balance sheet as at that date.

18.12 F Thomas is a sole trader. His warehouse, plus all his stock, was completely destroyed by fire on 17 March 2002. His trading account for the last year of business was as follows:

F Thomas
Trading Account for the year ended 31 December 2001

	£	£
Sales		27,000
Less Cost of goods sold:		
Stock 1 January 2001	6,510	
Add Purchases	24,630	
	31,140	
Less Stock 31 December 2001	8,640	22,500
Gross profit		4,500

According to his records, the purchases from 1 January 2002 to the date of the fire amounted to £4,530 and the sales during that period were £7,740. The warehouse did not contain any goods sold at the time of the fire. However, included in the figure for purchases of £4,530 were goods which were still in transit. The cost of these goods was £360.

The percentage of gross profit to sales was exactly the same during 2002 as it was in 2001.

Required Calculate, at cost price, the stock lost in the fire. Show your calculations, but these should be in the form of a trading account for the period 1 January 2002 to 17 March 2002.

**18.13X** D Bennett's trading account for the year ended 31 December 2001 was as follows:

D Bennett
Trading Account for the year ended 31 December 2001

	£	£
Sales		96,000
Less Cost of goods sold:		
Stock 1 January 2001	12,800	
Add Purchases	70,800	
	83,600	
Less Stock 31 December 2001	11,600	72,000
Gross profit		24,000

During the weekend of 5 May 2002, Bennett's warehouse was broken into and the entire stock, except for a small quantity of goods, was stolen. The value, at cost price of the stock left behind, was £760.

Bennett's records also show the following:

1. Sales 1 January 2002 to 5 May 2002 amounted to £33,120.
2. Purchases 1 January 2002 to 5 May 2002 were £25,600. Of this amount, goods costing £960 had not been received from the suppliers before the burglary.

Required Calculate the value (at cost price) of the goods stolen. Show your calculations. Assume that the gross profit percentage for sales is the same as that for the year ended 31 December 2001.

CHAPTER 19

Club and society accounts

AIMS

- To be able to draw up income and expenditure accounts and balance sheets for non-trading organisations.

- To be able to calculate profits and losses from special activities and incorporate them into the final accounts.

- To understand that various forms of revenue may need special treatment.

19.1 Non-trading organisations

Clubs, associations and other non-profit making organisations do not have trading and profit and loss accounts drawn up for them, as their purpose is not trading or profit making. They are operated so that their members can do things such as play football or chess. The kind of final accounts prepared by these organisations are either **receipts and payments accounts** or **income and expenditure accounts**.

19.2 Receipts and payments accounts

Receipts and payments accounts are a summary of the cash book for the period. Exhibit 19.1 is an example

Exhibit 19.1

The Homers Running Club
Receipts and Payments Account

Dr			for the year ended 31 December 2005		Cr
Receipts		£	Payments		£
Bank balance 1.1.2005		236	Groundsman's wages		728
Subscriptions received in 2005		1,148	Sports stadium expenses		296
Rent received		116	Committee expenses		58
			Printing and stationery		33
			Bank balance 31.12.2005		385
		1,500			1,500

19.3 Income and expenditure accounts

When assets are owned, and there are liabilities, the receipts and payments account is not a good way of drawing up final accounts. Other than the cash received and paid out, it shows only the cash balances. The other assets and liabilities are not shown at all. What is required is:

(1) a balance sheet, and

(2) an account showing whether the association's capital has increased.

In a profit-making firm, (2) would be a trading and profit and loss account.

In a non-profit organisation, (2) would be an **income and expenditure account**.

An income and expenditure account follows the same rules as trading and profit and loss accounts, the only differences being the terms used, as shown by the following comparison:

Profit-making firm	Non-profit organisation
1 Trading and profit and loss account	1 Income and expenditure account
2 Net profit	2 Surplus of income over expenditure
3 Net loss	3 Excess of expenditure over income

19.4 Profit or loss for a special purpose

Sometimes there are reasons why a non-profit-making organisation would want a profit and loss account. This is where something is done to make a profit. The profit is not to be kept, but used to pay for the main purpose of the organisation.

For instance, a football club may have discos or dances which people pay to attend. Any profit from these events helps to pay football expenses. For these discos and dances a trading and profit and loss account would be drawn up. Any profit (or loss) would be transferred to the income and expenditure account.

19.5 Accumulated fund

A sole trader or a partnership would have capital accounts. A non-profit-making organisation would instead have an **accumulated fund**. It is in effect the same as a capital account, as it is the difference between assets and liabilities.

In a sole trader or partnership:

Capital + Liabilities = Assets

In a non-profit-making organisation:

Accumulated Fund + Liabilities = Assets

19.6 Drawing up income and expenditure accounts

We can now look at the preparation of an income and expenditure account and a balance sheet of a club. A separate trading account is to be prepared for a bar, where beer and alcohol are sold to make a profit.

Long Lane Football Club
Trial Balance as at 31 December 2008

	Dr £	Cr £
Sports equipment	8,500	
Club premises	29,600	
Subscriptions received		6,490
Wages of staff	4,750	
Furniture and fittings	5,260	
Rates and insurance	1,910	
General expenses	605	
Accumulated fund 1 January 2008		42,016
Donations received		360
Telephone and postage	448	
Bank	2,040	
Bar purchases	9,572	
Creditors for bar supplies		1,040
Bar sales		14,825
Bar stocks 1 January 2008	2,046	
	64,731	64,731

The following information is also available:

(a) Bar stocks at 31 December 2008 £2,362.

(b) Provision for depreciation: Sports equipment £1,700; furniture and fittings £1,315.

Long Lane Football Club Bar
Trading Account for the year ended 31 December 2008

	£	£
Sales		14,825
Less Cost of goods sold:		
Opening stock	2,046	
Add Purchases	9,572	
	11,618	
Less Closing stock	2,362	
		9,256
Gross profit to income and expenditure account		5,569

 The result of the club bar operation is calculated separately.
The gross profit/loss will then be incorporated into the club's income and expenditure account for calculation of the overall result.

Long Lane Football Club
Income and Expenditure Account for the year ended 31 December 2008

	£	£
Income		
Gross profit from bar		5,569
Subscriptions		6,490
Donations received		360
		12,419
Less Expenditure		
Wages to staff	4,750	
Rates and insurance	1,910	
Telephone and postage	448	
General expenses	605	
Depreciation: Furniture and fittings	1,315	
Sports equipment	1,700	
		10,728
Surplus of income over expenditure		1,691

Long Lane Football Club
Balance Sheet as at 31 December 2008

	£	£	£
Fixed assets	Cost	Depreciation	Net book value
Club premises	29,600	–	29,600
Furniture and fittings	5,260	1,315	3,945
Sports equipment	8,500	1,700	6,800
	43,360	3,015	40,345
Current assets			
Bar stocks		2,362	
Cash at bank		2,040	
		4,402	
Current liabilities			
Creditors for bar supplies		1,040	
Net current assets			3,362
Net assets			43,707
Financed by			
Accumulated fund			
Balance at 1 January 2008			42,016
Add Surplus of income over expenditure			1,691
			43,707

19.7 Subscriptions

1. Where there are no subscriptions owing, or paid in advance, at the beginning and the end of a financial year, then the amount shown on the credit side of the subscriptions account can be transferred to the credit side of the income and expenditure account, as follows:

Dr		Subscriptions		Cr
2003	£	*2003*		£
Dec 31 Income & expenditure a/c	3,598	Dec 31 Bank (total received)		3,598

Income and Expenditure Account
for the year ended 31 December 2003 (extract)

Income:	£
Subscriptions	3,598

2. On the other hand, there may be subscriptions owing at both the start and the end of the financial year. In a case where £325 was owing at the start of the year, a total of £5,668 was received during the year, and £554 was owing at the end of the year, then this would appear as:

Dr		Subscriptions			Cr
2005		£	*2005*		£
Jan 1	Owing b/d	325	Dec 31	Bank (total received)	5,668
Dec 31	Income & expenditure a/c (difference)	5,897	Dec 31	Balance c/d	554
		6,222			6,222

Income and Expenditure Account
for the year ended 31 December 2005 (extract)

Income:	£
Subscriptions	5,897

In the balance sheet the subscription owing at the end of December 2005 would be shown under the heading of 'Current assets' as a debtor, as shown below:

Balance Sheet (extract) as at 31 December 2005

Current assets	£
Stock	x,xxx
Debtors (xxx + 554)	xxx

3. In the third case, at the start of the year there are both subscriptions owing from the previous year and also subscriptions paid in advance. In addition, there are also subscriptions paid in the current year for the next year (in advance) and also subscriptions unpaid (owing) at the end of the current year. This example concerns an amateur theatre organisation.

Example 19.1

An amateur theatre organisation charges its members an annual subscription of £20 per member. It accrues for subscriptions owing at the end of each year and also adjusts for subscriptions received in advance.

(A) On 1 January 2002, 18 members owed £360 for the year 2001.

(B) In December 2001, 4 members paid £80 for the year 2002.

(C) During the year 2002 the organisation received cash subscriptions £7,420.

For 2001	£360	
For 2002	£6,920	
For 2003	£140	£7,420

(D) At close of 31 December 2002, 11 members had not paid their 2002 subscriptions.

Exhibit 19.1 (continued)

Dr				Subscriptions				Cr
2002			£	*2002*				£
Jan 1	Owing b/d	(A)	360	Jan 1	Prepaid b/d	(B)		80
Dec 31	Income and			Dec 31	Bank	(C)		7,420
	expenditure a/c		*7,220	Dec 31	Owing c/d	(D)		220
Dec 31	Prepaid c/d	(C)	140					
			7,720					7,720
2003				*2003*				
Jan 1	Owing b/d	(D)	220	Jan 1	Prepaid b/d	(C)		140

* Difference between two sides of the account.

Income and Expenditure Account
for the year ended 31 December 2002 (extract)

Income:	£
Subscriptions	7,220

In this last case, in the balance sheet as at 31 December 2002, the amounts owing for subscriptions (D) £220 will be shown under current assets as a debtor. The subscriptions (C) paid in advance for 2003 will appear as an item under current liabilities as subscriptions received in advance £140.

19.8 Outstanding subscriptions and the prudence concept

So far we have treated subscriptions owing as being an asset. However, as any treasurer of a club would tell you, most subscriptions that have been owing for a long time are never paid. Many clubs do not, therefore, bring in unpaid subscriptions as an asset in the balance sheet. This is obviously keeping to the prudence concept which states that assets should not be over-valued. They are, therefore, ignored by these clubs for final accounts purposes.

 In an examination a student should assume that subscriptions owing are to be brought into the final accounts unless instructions to the contrary are given.

19.9 Donations

Any **donations** received are shown as income in the year that they are received.

19.10 Entrance fees

New members often have to pay an entrance fee in the year that they join, in addition to the membership fee for that year. Entrance fees are normally included as income in the year that they are received.

19.11 Life membership

Sometimes members can pay one amount for membership, and they will never have to pay any more money. This membership will last for their lifetime.

In this case, all of the money received from life membership should not be credited to the income and expenditure account of that year. In a club where members joined at age 20 and would probably be members for 40 years, then one-fortieth (2½%) of the life membership fee would be credited in the income and expenditure account each year. The balance not transferred to the income and expenditure account would appear in the balance sheet as a long-term liability. This is because it is the liability of the club to allow the members to use the club for the rest of their lives without paying any further membership fees.

On the other hand, a club that was especially for men over the age of 60 would transfer a much bigger share of the life membership fee paid to the income and expenditure account, since the number of years of future use of the club will be far less because people are already old when they join. Let us say that 10% of the life membership fee per year would be transferred to the credit of the income and expenditure account.

19.12 Treasurers' responsibilities

Treasurers of clubs or societies have a responsibility for maintaining proper accounting records in the same way as an accountant looking after the financial affairs of a business. It is important to ensure that any monies paid out by the treasurer have been properly authorised, especially when purchasing an item of capital expenditure such as new sound equipment for a dramatic society. In such cases the authorisation for purchase will more than likely have been approved at a committee meeting and noted in the minutes of the meeting. For smaller items of expenditure such as postages, telephone calls, etc., the club or society's rules will provide the treasurer with the authority to make payments against receipted bills.

It is also important for the treasurer to keep all invoices, receipted accounts and any other documents as evidence against payments. They should also provide receipts for any monies received. All documents should be filed and available at the year end for the club's auditor to carry out an audit and preparation of the club's year end financial statements.

NEW TERMS

Accumulated fund   A form of capital account for a non-profit making organisation.

Donations   A monetary gift donated to the club or society. Monies received should be shown as income in the year that they are received.

Income and expenditure account   An account for a non-profit making organisation to find the surplus or loss made during a period.

Life membership   Where members pay one amount for membership to last them their lifetime.

Non-profit-making organisations   Clubs, associations and societies operated to provide a service or activity for members since their main purpose is not trading or profit making.

Receipts and payments account A summary of the cash book of a non-profit-making organisation.

Subscriptions Amounts paid by members of a club or society, usually on an annual basis, to enable them to participate in the activities of the organisation.

Student Activities

19.1 A summary of the Uppertown Football Club, together with additional information, is shown below.

Cash Book Summary

	£		£
Balance 1.1.2004	180	Purchase of equipment	125
Collections at matches	1,650	Rent for football pitch	300
Profit on sale of refreshments	315	Printing and stationery	65
		Secretary's expenses	144
		Repairs to equipment	46
		Groundsman's wages	520
		Miscellaneous expenses	66
		Balance 31.12.2004	879
	2,145		2,145

Further information:

(i) At 1.1.2004 equipment was valued at £500.

(ii) Depreciate all equipment 20% for the year 2004.

(iii) At 31.12.2004 rent paid in advance was £60.

(iv) At 31.12.2004 there was £33 owing for printing.

Required

(a) Calculate the accumulated fund as at 1 January 2004.

(b) Draw up an income and expenditure account for the year ended 31 December 2004.

(c) Draw up a balance sheet as at 31 December 2004.

19.2X On 1 June 2002 the assets and liabilities of the Hartdale Social Club which meets during the evenings in the village hall were as follows:

	£
Cash at bank	1,640
Snack bar stocks	360
Equipment (cost £1,800)	1,440

During the year to 31 May 2003 the club received and paid the following amounts which are shown in the cash book summary shown below:

Cash Book Summary

Receipts	£	Payments	£
Subscriptions	4,230	Rent and rates	1,600
Snack bar income	4,500	Snack bar purchases	2,500
Jumble sale proceeds	823	Postage and stationery	115
Donation	50	Prizes for competitions	225
		Secretarial expenses	128
		Hi-fi equipment	2,230
		Snack bar expenses	570

Notes

(i) The snack bar stock at 31 May 2003 was valued at £420.

(ii) The equipment should be depreciated at 20% per annum using the straight-line method.

(iii) Subscriptions owing at 31 May 2003 amounted to £45.

Required

(a) Calculate the accumulated fund on 1 June 2002.

(b) Calculate the amount of cash at bank on 31 May 2003.

(c) Prepare a trading account to ascertain the amount of profit made on the snack bar.

(d) Prepare an income and expenditure account for the year ended 31 May 2003 and a balance sheet as at that date.

19.3 The treasurer of a local amateur drama society is trying to ascertain the amount of subscriptions to transfer to the society's income and expenditure account for the year ended 31 December 2002 and asks for your help.

The following information is made available to you:

	2001 £	2002 £
Subscriptions in arrears	235	185
Subscriptions in advance	220	140

Amount received from members during the year 2002 amounted to £2,600, all of which was banked immediately.

Required Draw up the society's subscription account for the year ended 31 December 2002 showing clearly the amount of subscriptions to be transferred to the income and expenditure account.

19.4 Pat Hall is the treasurer of a local tennis club which has 420 members. The subscription details for the club are as follows:

Subscriptions for year to 31 December 2007	£220 per member
Subscriptions for year to 31 December 2008	£240 per member
Subscriptions for year to 31 December 2009	£250 per member

On 31 December 2007, 6 members had prepaid their subscriptions for 2008. By 31 December 2008, 8 members will have prepaid their

subscriptions for 2009. All other members have paid, and will continue to pay their subscriptions during the relevant year.

Required

(a) Calculate the subscriptions figure to be entered in the income and expenditure account for the year ended 31 December 2008.

(b) Calculate the total amount of money received for subscriptions during the year ended 31 December 2008.

Show all workings.

AAT (Central Assessment)

19.5 The following trial balance of Bradnop Golf Club was extracted from the books as on 31 December 2008:

	Dr £	Cr £
Clubhouse	21,000	
Equipment	6,809	
Profits from raffles		4,980
Subscriptions received		18,760
Wages of bar staff	2,809	
Bar stocks 1 January 2008	1,764	
Bar purchases and sales	11,658	17,973
Greenkeepers' wages	7,698	
Golf professional's salary	6,000	
General expenses	580	
Cash at bank	1,570	
Accumulated fund at 1 January 2008		18,175
	59,888	59,888

Notes

(i) Bar purchases and sales were on a cash basis. Bar stocks at 31 December 2008 were valued at £989.

(ii) Subscriptions paid in advance by members at 31 December 2008 amounted to £180.

(iii) Provide for depreciation of equipment £760.

Required

(a) Draw up the bar trading account for the year ended 31 December 2008.

(b) Draw up the income and expenditure account for the year ended 31 December 2008, and a balance sheet as at 31 December 2008.

19.6X The following trial balance was extracted from the books of the Upper Harbour Sports Club at the close of business on 31 March 2008.

| | Dr | Cr |
	£	£
Club premises	13,500	
Sports equipment	5,100	
Bar purchases and sales	9,540	15,270
Bar stocks 1 April 2007	2,190	
Balance at bank	2,790	
Subscriptions received		8,640
Accumulated fund 1 April 2007		22,290
Salary of secretary	3,600	
Wages of staff	5,280	
Postage and telephone	870	
Office equipment	1,200	
Rates and insurance	1,230	
Cash in hand	60	
Sundry expenses	840	
	46,200	46,200

Notes

(i) All bar purchases and sales were on a cash basis. Bar stocks 31 March 2008 were £2,460.

(ii) No subscriptions have been paid in advance but subscriptions in arrears at 31 March 2008 amounted to £90.

(iii) Rates prepaid at 31 March 2008: £60.

(iv) Provide for depreciation as follows: Sports equipment £600; office equipment £120.

Required Prepare the bar trading account and the income and expenditure account of the Club for the year ended 31 March 2008 together with a balance sheet as on that date. For this purpose, the wages of staff £5,280 should be shown in the income and expenditure account and not the bar trading account.

19.7 The treasurer of the City Sports Club has produced the following receipts and payments account for the year ended 31 December 2007:

Receipts	£	Payments	£
Balance at bank 1.1.2007	1,298	Coffee supplies bought	1,456
Subscriptions received	3,790	Wages of attendants and	
Profits and dances	186	cleaners	1,776
Profit on exhibition	112	Rent of rooms	887
Coffee bar takings	2,798	New equipment bought	565
Sale of equipment	66	Travelling expenses of teams	673
		Balance at bank 31.12.2007	2,893
	8,250		8,250

Notes

(i) Coffee bar stocks were valued: 31 December 2006 £59, 31 December 2007 £103. There was nothing owing for coffee bar stocks on either of these dates.

(ii) On 1 January 2007 the club's equipment was valued at £2,788. Included in this figure, valued at £77, was the equipment sold during the year for £66.

(iii) The amount to be charged for depreciation of equipment for the year is £279. This is in addition to the loss on equipment sold during the year.

(iv) Subscriptions owing by members 31 December 2006 nil, at 31 December 2007 £29.

Required

(a) Draw up the coffee bar trading account for the year ended 31 December 2007. For this purpose £650 of the wages is to be charged to this account; the remainder will be charged in the income and expenditure account.

(b) Calculate the accumulated fund as at 1 January 2007.

(c) Draw up the income and expenditure account for the year ended 31 December 2007, and a balance sheet as at 31 December 2007.

 19.8X The following is a summary of the receipts and payments of the Moorside Arts Club during the year ended 30 September 2005:

Moorside Arts Club
Receipts and Payments Account

Dr		for the year ended 30 September 2005		Cr
	£			£
Cash and bank balances b/f	525	Rent of hall		3,505
Members' subscriptions	4,970	Speakers' expenses		1,190
Donations	440	Secretarial expenses		410
Sale of competition tickets	892	Donations to charity		590
Spring fair proceeds	700	Competition prizes		425
		Postages, stationery, etc.		447
		Balance c/d		960
	7,527			7,527

The following valuations are also available as at 30 September:

	2004	2005
	£	£
Equipment (cost £4,260)	2,925	2,340
Subscriptions in arrears	195	255
Subscriptions in advance	30	120
Creditors for competition prizes	174	204
Stocks of competition prizes	120	148

Required

(a) Calculate the accumulated fund as at 1 October 2004.

(b) Draw up the subscription account for the year ended 30 September 2005.

(c) Prepare a competition trading account for the year ended 30 September 2005.

(d) Prepare an income and expenditure account for the Moorside Arts Club for the year ended 30 September 2005 and a balance sheet as at that date.

19.9 The Carron Social Club has 600 members, each paying an annual subscription of £50. Rent is payable at £500 per month. All money received is banked immediately and all payments are made by cheque.

On the 31 December 2004, the financial position of the club was as follows:

	£
Balance at bank (overdraft)	1,650
Equipment (cost £20,000)	16,000
Fixtures (cost £3,000)	2,400
Refreshment bar stocks	550

Twenty-four members did not pay their 2004 subscriptions until 2005.

During the year to 31 December 2005, the following transactions occurred:

	£
Refreshment bar purchases	6,150
Refreshment bar takings	8,960
Subscriptions received	30,100
Rent paid	5,000
Wages of refreshment bar staff	1,880
Purchase of new equipment	9,000
Insurance paid	1,570
Affiliation fees paid	360
Donations received	4,240
Transport expenses	7,140
Wages of ground staff	9,370

Notes

(i) Refreshment bar stocks at 31 December 2005 were valued at £940.

(ii) Some subscriptions were owed by members at 31 December 2005.

(iii) Equipment and fixtures are to be depreciated at 20% of cost.

(iv) Rent owing amounted to £1,000 at 31 December 2005.

(v) Insurance paid in advance amounted to £210 at 31 December 2005.

(vi) No one had resigned during the year.

Required

(a) Calculate the accumulated fund at 1 January 2005.

(b) Draw up a receipts and payments account for the year ended 31 December 2005.

(c) Prepare a subscriptions account for the year ended 31 December 2005.

(d) Draw up a refreshment bar trading account for the year ended 31 December 2005.

(e) Prepare an income and expenditure account for the club for the year ended 31 December 2005 and a balance sheet as at that date.

19.10X Andrew Carver is the treasurer of the City Fields Tennis Club. As treasurer he needs to prepare some financial statements and asks you to provide assistance. The following information is available at the year end on 31 December 2008:

Dr		Bank Account Summary		Cr
	£			£
Balance b/d (1.1.2008)	1,200	Purchase of refreshments		10,600
Subscriptions	30,000	Club staff wages		28,000
Sale of refreshments	15,260	Electricity		1,780
Donations	500	Sundry expenses		1,820
Loan	6,000	Repairs to tennis courts		800
		Clubhouse improvements		6,400
		Rent of land		3,400
		Balance c/d (31.12.2008)		160
	52,960			52,960

Balances at 1 January 2008:	£
Stocks of refreshments	120
Creditors for refreshments	860
Clubhouse at cost	24,000
Provision for depreciation – clubhouse	7,200
Subscriptions in advance	400

Balances at 31 December 2008:	£
Stocks of refreshments	230
Creditors for refreshments	780
Subscriptions in advance	550

Notes

   (i) Depreciation on the clubhouse is calculated at the rate of 5% of cost at the end of the financial year.

   (ii) 15% of wages relate to refreshments, 85% to other activities.

  (iii) 20% of electricity relates to refreshments, 80% to other activities.

  (iv) The loan was taken out on 30 June 2008 at a rate of interest of 10% per annum.

   (v) Club rules state that donations over £1,000 should be capitalised.

Required

  (a) List separately the opening assets and liabilities of the club at 1 January 2008 and calculate the accumulated fund at that date.

  (b) Prepare a subscriptions account to ascertain the amount to be transferred to the income and expenditure account.

  (c) Calculate the purchase of refreshments for the year ended 31 December 2008.

  (d) Prepare a trading account to show the profit or loss on refreshments for the year ended 31 December 2008.

  (e) Prepare an income and expenditure account for the club for the year ended 31 December 2008 and a balance sheet as at that date.

AAT (Central Assessment)

19.11X The Offerton Entertainment Society was formed on 1 April 2008. At a recent committee meeting the Treasurer had presented his report for the year ended 31 March 2009. This is reproduced below:

	£
Receipts:	
Membership subscriptions:	
Year ended 31 March 2009	23,000
Year ended 3 March 2010	11,000
Ticket sales	25,650
Sale of refreshments	13,250
Proceeds of social events (before expenses)	9,575
Total receipts	82,475
Payments:	
Expenses for social events	5,894
Purchase of costumes	12,375
Rental of premises	16,250
Purchase of equipment	21,322
Printing and advertising	4,505
Purchase of refreshments	9,257
Secretarial expenses	2,141
Hire costs	10,371
Total payments	82,115
Expenses not paid at 31 March 2009:	
Refreshments	1,332
Printing costs	358
Expenses paid in advance at 31 March 2009:	
Rental of premises	2,264

One of the members questioned whether this was an appropriate format for the report. In particular she noted that some of the subscriptions for the year to 31 March 2010 had been included, as well as the costs of items which the society would be able to use in future years. She estimated that equipment could realistically be expected to last for seven years, while costumes normally have a useful life of five years.

A number of the committee members agreed that they would like the Treasurer's report to be redrafted in a more suitable format.

Required Prepare:

(i) The income and expenditure account for the year to 31 March 2009.

(ii) The balance sheet as at 31 March 2009.

ACCA (Accounting Technicians)

CHAPTER 20

Partnerships

AIMS

- To understand exactly what a partnership is.

- To be able to distinguish between limited partners and those with unlimited liability.

- To know what the main features of a partnership agreement should be.

- To realise what will happen if no agreement has been made to share profits or losses.

- To be able to draw up capital and current accounts for the partnership.

- To be able to draw up the final accounts of a partnership.

Note

The new accounting standards for Unit 5 now include methods of recording and understanding the structure of organisational accounts, including partnerships and partners' capital and current accounts. It must be noted that the new standards exclude 'Appropriation' and adjustments relating to appropriation such as interest on capital and interest on drawings. However, the authors consider it appropriate to include these topics in this chapter since it gives the student a full appreciation of partnership accounts. At the end of the chapter, a fully worked example is also shown which includes almost all the items mentioned in the text.

20.1 The need for partnerships

So far we have mainly considered businesses owned by only one person. Businesses set up to make a profit can often have more than one owner, and there are various reasons for multiple ownership.

1. The capital required is more than one person can provide.
2. The experience or ability required to manage the business cannot be found in one person alone.
3. Many people want to share management instead of doing everything on their own.
4. Very often the partners will be members of the same family.

There are two types of multiple ownership: **partnerships** and **limited companies**. This chapter deals only with partnerships; limited companies are dealt with at NVQ Level 4.

20.2 Nature of a partnership

A partnership has the following characteristics:

1. It is formed to make profits.
2. It must obey the law as given in the Partnership Act 1890. If there is a limited partner, as described in Section 20.3, the Limited Partnership Act of 1907 must also be complied with.
3. Normally there can be a minimum of two partners and a maximum of 20 partners. There is no maximum limit for firms of accountants, solicitors, stock exchange members or other professional bodies receiving the approval of the relevant government body for this purpose. Banks can have no more than ten partners.
4. Each partner (except for limited partners described below) must pay their share of any debts that the partnership could not pay. If necessary, they could be forced to sell all their private possessions to pay their share of the debts. This can be said to be unlimited liability.

20.3 Limited partners

Limited partners are not liable for the debts as in Section 20.2 (4) above. They have the following characteristics:

1. Their liability for the debts of the partnership is limited to the capital they have put in. They can lose that capital, but they cannot be asked for any more money to pay the debts.
2. They are not allowed to take part in the management of the partnership business.
3. All the partners cannot be limited partners; there must be at least one partner with unlimited liability.

20.4 Partnership agreements

Agreements in writing are not necessary. However, it is better if a proper written agreement is drawn up by a lawyer or accountant. Where there is a proper written agreement there will be fewer problems between partners. A written agreement means less confusion about what has been agreed.

The written agreement can contain as much, or as little, as the partners want. The law does not say what it must contain. The usual accounting contents are:

1. The capital to be contributed by each partner.
2. The ratio in which profits (or losses) are to be shared.
3. The rate of interest, if any, to be paid on capital before the profits are shared.
4. The rate of interest, if any, to be charged on partners' drawings.
5. Salaries paid to partners.
6. Performance-related payment to partners.

These points will now be examined in detail.

Capital contributions

Partners need *not* contribute equal amounts of capital. What matters is how much capital each partner *agrees* to contribute.

Profit (or loss) sharing ratios

Partners can agree to share profits/losses in any ratio or in any way they may wish. However, it is often thought by students that profits should be shared in the same ratio as that in which capital is contributed. For example, suppose the capitals were Allen £2,000 and Beet £1,000. Many people would share the profits in the ratio of two-thirds to one-third, even though the work to be done by each partner is similar. A look at the division of the first few years' profits on such a basis would be:

Years	1	2	3	4	5	Total
	£	£	£	£	£	£
Net profits	1,800	2,400	3,000	3,000	3,600	
Shared:						
Allen 2/3rds	1,200	1,600	2,000	2,000	2,400	9,200
Beet 1/3rd	600	800	1,000	1,000	1,200	4,600

It can now be seen that Allen would receive £9,200, or £4,600 more than Beet. To treat each partner fairly, the difference between the two shares of profit in this case, as the duties of the partners are the same, should be adequate to compensate Allen for putting extra capital into the firm. It is obvious that £4,600 extra profits is far more than adequate for this purpose, as Allen only put in an extra £1,000 as capital.

Consider too the position of capital ratio sharing of profits if one partner put in £99,000 and the other put in £1,000 as capital.

To overcome the difficulty of compensating for the investment of extra capital, the concept of interest on capital was devised.

Interest on capitals

If the work to be done by each partner is of equal value but the capital contributed is unequal, it is reasonable to grant interest on the partners' capitals. This interest is treated as a deduction prior to the calculation of profits and their distribution according to the profit-sharing ratio.

The rate of interest is a matter of agreement between the partners, but it should equal the return which they would have received if they had invested the capital elsewhere.

Taking Allen and Beet's firm again, but sharing the profits equally after charging 5% per annum interest on capital, the division of profits would become:

Years	1	2	3	4	5		Total
	£	£	£	£	£		£
Net profits	1,800	2,400	3,000	3,000	3,600		
Interest on capitals							
Allen	100	100	100	100	100	=	500
Beet	50	50	50	50	50	=	250
Remainder shared:							
Allen 1/2	825	1,125	1,425	1,425	1,725	=	6,525
Beet 1/2	825	1,125	1,425	1,425	1,725	=	6,525

Summary	Allen	Beet
	£	£
Interest on capital	500	250
Balance of profits	6,525	6,525
	7,025	6,775

Interest on drawings

It is obviously in the best interests of the firm if cash is withdrawn from the firm by the partners in accordance with the two basic principles of: (a) as little as possible, and (b) as late as possible. The more cash that is left in the firm the more expansion can be financed, the greater the economies of having ample cash to take advantage of bargains and of not missing cash discounts because cash is not available and so on.

To deter the partners from taking out cash unnecessarily the concept can be used of charging the partners interest on each withdrawal, calculated from the date of withdrawal to the end of the financial year. The amount charged to them helps to swell the profits divisible between the partners. The rate of interest should be sufficient to achieve this without being too harsh.

Suppose that Allen and Beet have decided to charge interest on drawings at 5% per annum, and that their year end was 31 December. The following drawings are made:

Allen

Drawings		Interest		£
1 January	£100	£100 × 5% × 12 months	=	5
1 March	£240	£240 × 5% × 10 months	=	10
1 May	£120	£120 × 5% × 8 months	=	4
1 July	£240	£240 × 5% × 6 months	=	6
1 October	£ 80	£ 80 × 5% × 3 months	=	1
		Interest charged to Allen	=	26

Beet

Drawings		Interest		£
1 January	£ 60	£ 60 × 5% × 12 months	=	3
1 August	£480	£480 × 5% × 5 months	=	10
1 December	£240	£240 × 5% × 1 month	=	1
		Interest charged to Beet	=	14

Salaries to partners

One partner may have more responsibility or tasks than the others. As a reward for this, rather than change the profit and loss sharing ratio, he may have a salary which is deducted before sharing the balance of profits.

Performance-related payments to partners

Partners may agree that commission or performance-related bonuses be payable to some or all the partners which are linked to their individual performance. As with salaries, these would be deducted before sharing the balance of profits.

20.6 An example of the distribution of profits

Taylor and Clarke have been in partnership for one year sharing profits and losses in the ratio of Taylor three-fifths, Clarke two-fifths. They are entitled to 5% per annum interest on capitals, Taylor having £2,000 capital and Clarke £6,000. Clarke is to have a salary of £500. They charge interest on drawings, Taylor being charged £50 and Clarke £100. The net profit, before any distributions to the partners, amounted to £5,000 for the year ended 31 December 2001.

	£	£	£
Net profit			5,000
Add Charged for interest on drawings:			
Taylor		50	
Clarke		100	
			150
			5,150
Less Salary: Clarke		500	
Interest on capital:			
Taylor	100		
Clarke	300		
		400	
			900
			4,250
Balance of profits shared:			
Taylor 3/5ths		2,550	
Clarke 2/5ths		1,700	
			4,250

The £5,000 net profits have therefore been shared as follows:

	Taylor	Clarke
	£	£
Balance of profits	2,550	1,700
Interest on capital	100	300
Salary	–	500
	2,650	2,500
Less Interest on drawings	50	100
	2,600	2,400
		£5,000

20.7 The final accounts

If the sales, stock and expenses of partnership were exactly the same as that of a sole trader, then the trading and profit and loss account would be identical with that as prepared for the sole trader. However, a partnership would have an extra section shown under the profit and loss account. This section is called the **profit and loss appropriation account**, and it is in this account that the distribution of profits is shown. The heading to the trading and profit and loss account does not include the words 'appropriation account'. It is purely an accounting custom not to include it in the heading.

The trading and profit and loss account of Taylor and Clarke from the details given would appear as:

Taylor and Clarke
Trading and Profit and Loss Account
for the year ended 31 December 2001

(Trading Account – same as for sole trader)
(Profit and Loss Account – same as for sole trader)

	£	£	£
Net profit			5,000
Interest on drawings:			
Taylor		50	
Clarke		100	150
			5,150
Less Interest on capitals:			
Taylor	100		
Clarke	300	400	
Salary		500	900
			4,250
Balance of profits shared:			
Taylor 3/5ths		2,550	
Clarke 2/5ths		1,700	4,250

20.8 Fixed and fluctuating capital accounts

A choice is available in partnership accounts, as detailed below.

Fixed capital accounts plus current accounts

The capital account for each partner remains year by year at the figure of capital put into the firm by the partners. The profits, interest on capital and the salaries to which the partner may be entitled are then credited to a separate current account for the partner, and the drawings and the interest on drawings are debited to it. The balance of the current account at the end of each financial year will then represent the amount of undrawn (or withdrawn) profits. A credit balance will be undrawn profits, while a debit balance will be drawings in excess of the profits to which the partner was entitled.

For Taylor and Clarke, capital and current accounts, assuming drawings of £2,000 each, will appear as:

	Taylor	
Dr	Capital Account	Cr
	2001	£
	Jan 1 Bank	2,000

	Clarke	
Dr	Capital Account	Cr
	2001	£
	Jan 1 Bank	6,000

Taylor

Dr			Current Account			Cr
2001		£	*2001*			£
Dec 31	Cash: Drawings	2,000	Dec 31	Profit and loss appropriation account:		
31	Profit and loss appropriation account:			Interest on capital		100
	Interest on drawings	50		Share of profits		2,550
31	Balance c/d	600				
		2,650				2,650
			2002			
			Jan 1	Balance b/d		600

Clarke

Dr			Current Account			Cr
2001		£	*2001*			£
Dec 31	Cash: Drawings	2,000	Dec 31	Profit and loss appropriation account:		
31	Profit and loss appropriation account:			Interest on capital		300
	Interest on drawings	100		Share of profits		1,700
31	Balance c/d	400		Salary		500
		2,500				2,500
			2002			
			Jan 1	Balance b/d		400

! *Notice that the salary of Clarke was not paid to him, it was merely credited to his account. If in fact it was paid in addition to his drawing, the £500 cash paid would have been debited to the current account, changing the £400 credit balance into a £100 debit balance.*

Examiners often ask for the capital accounts and current accounts to be shown in columnar form. For the previous accounts of Taylor and Clarke these would appear as follows:

Capital Accounts

		Taylor	Clarke			Taylor	Clarke
		£	£	*2001*		£	£
				Jan 1	Bank	2,000	6,000

Current Accounts

		Taylor	Clarke			Taylor	Clarke
2001		£	£	*2001*		£	£
Dec 31	Cash: Drawings	2,000	2,000	Dec 31	Interest on capital	100	300
31	Interest on drawings	50	100	31	Share of profits	2,550	1,700
31	Balances c/d	600	400	31	Salary		500
		2,650	2,500			2,650	2,500
				2002			
				Jan 1	Balances b/d	600	400

Fluctuating capital accounts

The distribution of profits would be credited to the capital account, and the drawings and interest on drawings debited. Therefore, the balance on the capital account will change each year, i.e. it will fluctuate.

If fluctuating capital accounts had been kept for Taylor and Clarke they would have appeared as:

Taylor

Dr			Capital Account			Cr
2001		£	*2001*			£
Dec 31	Cash: Drawings	2,000	Jan 1	Bank		2,000
31	Profit and loss		Dec 31	Profit and loss		
	appropriation account:			appropriation account:		
	Interest on drawings	50		Interest on capital		100
31	Balance c/d	2,600		Share of profits		2,550
		4,650				4,650
			2002			
			Jan 1	Balance b/d		2,600

Clarke

Dr			Capital Account			Cr
2001		£	*2001*			£
Dec 31	Cash: Drawings	2,000	Jan 1	Bank		6,000
31	Profit and loss		Dec 31	Profit and loss		
	appropriation account:			appropriation account:		
	Interest on drawings	100		Interest on capital		300
31	Balance c/d	6,400		Salary		500
				Share of profit		1,700
		8,500				8,500
			2002			
			Jan 1	Balance b/d		6,400

Fixed capital accounts preferred

The keeping of fixed capital accounts plus current accounts is considered preferable to fluctuating capital accounts. When partners are taking out greater amounts than the share of the profits they are entitled to, this is shown up by a debit balance on the current account and so acts as a warning.

20.9 Where no partnership agreement exists

Where no agreement exists, express or implied, Section 24 of the Partnership Act 1890 governs the situation. The accounting content of this section states:

1. Profits and losses are to be shared equally.
2. There is to be no interest allowed on capital.
3. No interest is to be charged on drawings.
4. Salaries are not allowed.

5. If a partner puts a sum of money into a firm in excess of the capital he has agreed to subscribe, he is entitled to interest at the rate of 5% per annum on such an advance.

This section applies where there is no agreement. There may be an agreement not by a partnership deed but in a letter, or it may be implied by conduct, for instance when a partner signs a balance sheet which shows profits shared in some other ratio than equally. Where a dispute arises as to whether agreement exists or not, and this cannot be resolved by the partners, only the courts will be competent to decide.

20.10 The balance sheet

The capital part of the balance sheet will appear as:

Balance Sheet as at 31 December 2001

			£	£
Capital accounts	Taylor		2,000	
	Clarke		6,000	
				8,000

Current accounts	Taylor	Clarke		
	£	£		
Interest on capital	100	300		
Share of profits	2,550	1,700		
Salary	–	500		
	2,650	2,500		
Less Drawings	(2,000)*	(2,000)		
Interest on drawings	(50)	(100)		
	(2,050)	(2,100)		
	600	400		
				1,000

 * Figures in brackets i.e. (2,000) is an accounting convention indicating a minus amount.

If one of the current accounts had finished in debit – for instance, if the current account of Clarke had finished up as £400 debit – the figure of £400 would appear in brackets and the balances would appear net in the totals column:

	Taylor	Clarke	
	£	£	£
Closing balance	600	(400)	200

If the net figure, e.g. the £200 just shown, turned out to be a debit figure then this would be deducted from the total of the fixed capital accounts.

20.11 A fully worked exercise

We can now look at a fully worked exercise covering nearly all the main points shown in this chapter.

Luty and Minchin are in partnership. They share profits in the ratio: Luty 3/5ths : Minchin 2/5ths. The following trial balance was extracted as at 31 March 2004:

	Dr £	Cr £
Office equipment at cost	6,500	
Motor vehicles at cost	9,200	
Provision for depreciation at 31.3.2003:		
Motor vehicles		3,680
Office equipment		1,950
Stock at 31 March 2003	24,970	
Debtors and creditors	20,960	16,275
Cash at bank	615	
Cash in hand	140	
Sales		90,370
Purchases	71,630	
Salaries	8,417	
Office expenses	1,370	
Discounts allowed	563	
Current accounts at 31.3.2003:		
Luty		1,379
Minchin		1,211
Capital accounts:		
Luty		27,000
Minchin		12,000
Drawings:		
Luty	5,500	
Minchin	4,000	
	153,865	153,865

A set of final accounts for the year ended 31 March 2004 for the partnership are to be drawn up. The following notes are applicable at 31 March 2004:

(a) Stock 31 March 2004 £27,340.

(b) Office expenses owing £110.

(c) Provide for depreciation: Motor vehicles 20% of cost, office equipment 10% of cost.

(d) Charge interest on capitals at 10%.

(e) Charge interest on drawings: Luty £180; Minchin £210.

(f) Charge £500 for salary for Minchin.

Luty and Minchin
Trading and Profit and Loss Account for the year ended 31 March 2004

	£	£	£
Sales			90,370
Less Cost of goods sold:			
Opening stock		24,970	
Add Purchases		71,630	
		96,600	
Less Closing stock		27,340	69,260
Gross profit			21,110

(continued)

Luty and Minchin
Trading and Profit and Loss Account for the year ended 31 March 2004

	£	£	£
Less Expenses:			
Salaries*		8,417	
Office expenses (1,370 + 110)		1,480	
Discounts allowed		563	
Depreciation: Motor vehicles	1,840		
Office equipment	650	2,490	12,950
Net profit			8,160
Add Interest on drawings: Luty		180	
Minchin		210	390
			8,550
Less Interest on capital: Luty	2,700		
Minchin	1,200	3,900	
Less Salary: Minchin		500	4,400
			4,150
Balance of profits shared: Luty 3/5ths		2,490	
Minchin 2/5ths		1,660	4,150

* *Does not include partner's salary.*

Luty and Minchin
Balance Sheet as at 31 March 2004

	Cost	Depreciation	NBV
Fixed assets	£	£	£
Office equipment	6,500	2,600	3,900
Motor vehicles	9,200	5,520	3,680
	15,700	8,120	7,580
Current assets			
Stock		27,340	
Debtors		20,960	
Bank		615	
Cash		140	
		49,055	
Less Current Liabilities			
Creditors	16,275		
Expenses owing	110	16,385	
Net Current assets			32,670
			40,250
Capitals			
Luty		27,000	
Minchin		12,000	39,000

Current accounts		Luty		Minchin	
Balances 1.4.2003		1,379		1,211	
Add Interest on capital		2,700		1,200	
Add Salary				500	
Add Share of profits		2,490		1,660	
		6,569		4,571	
Less Drawings	5,500		4,000		
Less Interest on drawings	180	5,680	210	4,210	
Balances 31.3.2004		889		361	1,250
					40,250

Fixed capital accounts Capital accounts which consist only of the original capital invested in the business.

Fluctuating capital accounts Capital accounts whose balances change from one period to the next.

Interest on capital An amount, at an agreed rate of interest, which is credited to a partner based on the amount of capital contributed by him/her.

Interest on drawings An amount, at an agreed rate of interest, which is based on the drawings taken out, and is debited to the partners.

Limited partner A partner whose liability is limited to the capital invested in the firm.

Partnerships Firms in which two or more people are working together to make profits.

Partnership agreement The contractual relationship, either written or verbal, between partners which usually covers details such as how profits or losses should be shared and the relevant responsibilities of the partners.

Partnership salaries Agreed amounts payable to partners in respect of duties undertaken by them.

Student Activities

20.1 Stead and Jackson are partners in a retail business in which they share profits and losses equally. The balance on the partners' capital and current accounts at the year end 31 December 2002 were as follows:

	Capital account £	Current account £
Stead	24,000	2,300 Cr
Jackson	16,000	3,500 Cr

During the year Stead had drawings amounting to £15,000 and Jackson £19,000. Jackson was to receive a partnership salary of £5,000 for extra duties undertaken.

The net profit of the partnership, before taking any of the above into account, was £45,000.

Required

(a) Draw up the appropriation account for the partnership for the year ended 31 December 2002.

(b) Show the partners' capital and current accounts.

20.2X Wain, Brown and Cairns own a garage and the partners share profits and losses in the ratio of Wain 50%, Brown 30% and Cairns 20%. Their financial year end is 31 March 2004 and the following details were extracted from their books on that date:

	Wain	Brown	Cairns
	£	£	£
Capital account balances	30,000	50,000	70,000
Current account balances	2,400 Cr	3,100 Cr	5,700 Cr
Partnership salaries	10,000	8,000	–
Drawings	12,000	15,050	14,980

The net profit for the year ended 31 March 2004 amounted to £60,000 before taking any of the above into account.

Required

(a) Prepare an appropriation account for the year ended 31 March 2004.

(b) Draw up the partners' capital and current accounts in columnar form for the year ended 31 March 2004.

20.3 King, Leigh and White are in partnership sharing profits and losses in the ratio 3 : 2 : 1 respectively. Interest is to be credited on the partners' capital accounts at 10% per annum. Leigh is to be credited with a salary of £2,000 per annum.

In the year to 31 December 2004 the net profit of the firm was £50,400. During the year the partners took drawings and were charged interest as follows:

	Drawings	Interest on drawings
	£	£
King	8,000	400
Leigh	7,200	360
White	4,800	240

The balances of the partners' accounts at 31 December 2003 were as follows:

	(All credit balances)	
	Capital accounts	Current accounts
	£	£
King	30,000	750
Leigh	28,000	1,340
White	16,000	220

Required

(a) Prepare the firm's profit and loss appropriation account for the year ended 31 December 2004.

(b) Show how the partners' capital and current accounts are to be displayed in the balance sheet as at 31 December 2004.

20.4X The following balances were extracted from the books of Bradford & Taylor as at 31 December 2007:

	£
Capital accounts	
Bradford	40,000
Taylor	30,000
Current accounts	
Bradford	3,450 Cr
Taylor	2,680 Dr
Drawings	
Bradford	8,000
Taylor	12,000
Net profit for the year	44,775

The following information is also available from their partnership agreement:

1. The partners are entitled to receive 5% interest on capital.
2. Taylor is to receive a partnership salary of £6,000.
3. Interest is to be charged on drawings as follows:

Bradford	£200
Taylor	£125

4. Bradford and Taylor are to share profits and losses in the ratio 3 : 2.

Required

(a) Show the profit and loss appropriation account for the year ended 31 December 2007.

(b) Show the partners' capital and current accounts for the year ended 31 December 2007.

(c) Show how the profits and losses would be distributed and how much each partner would receive if there was no partnership agreement.

20.5 Simpson and Young are in partnership sharing profits and losses in the ratio 3 : 2. At the close of business on 30 June 2003 the following trial balance was extracted from their books:

	Dr	Cr
	£	£
Premises at cost	28,000	
Motor vans (cost £16,000)	11,000	
Office equipment (cost £8,400)	5,600	
Stock 1 July 2002	18,000	
Purchases	184,980	
Sales		254,520
Wages and salaries	32,700	
Rent, rates and insurance	3,550	
Electricity	980	
Stationery and printing	420	
Motor expenses	3,480	
General office expenses	1,700	
Debtors and creditors	28,000	15,200
Capital accounts: Simpson		50,000
Young		20,000

		Dr £	Cr £
Drawings:	Simpson	10,000	
	Young	5,000	
Current accounts:	Simpson		640
	Young		300
Cash at bank		7,250	
		340,660	340,660

Notes

(i) Interest is to be allowed on capital accounts at the rate of 10% per annum, no interest is to be charged on drawings.

(ii) Rates prepaid at 30 June 2003 is £250.

(iii) Wages due at 30 June 2003 was £500.

(iv) Provide for depreciation as follows:

Motor van at 20% per annum on cost.
Office equipment at 10% using the reducing balance method.

(v) Stock 30 June 2003 was valued at £19,000.

Required Prepare the trading and profit and loss appropriation account for the year ended 30 June 2003, and a balance sheet as at that date.

 Kirkham and Keeling are in partnership sharing profits and losses in the ratio of 3 : 2. Their partnership agreement also provided for interest on capital to be given to the partners at 10% per annum, but no interest was to be charged on drawings. The following trial balance was drawn up at the end of the financial year:

Trial Balance of Kirkham & Keeling as at 30 June 2005

		£	£
Premises		59,200	
Motor vehicles (cost £30,000)		24,000	
Computer equipment (cost £12,000 at 1.7.2003)		8,000	
Cash at bank		12,500	
Debtors		56,000	
Creditors			30,400
Sales			509,040
Purchases		369,960	
Stock 1 July 2004		36,000	
Salaries		65,400	
Electricity		1,960	
Telephone		840	
Motor expenses		3,960	
Printing, stationery and advertising		3,000	
Rates and insurance		7,100	
General expenses		3,400	
Capital accounts:	Kirkham		100,000
	Keeling		40,000
Current accounts:	Kirkham		1,280
	Keeling		600
Drawings:	Kirkham	20,000	
	Keeling	10,000	
		681,320	681,320

Notes

   (i) The closing stock was valued at £38,000.

  (ii) Insurance paid in advance at 30 June 2005 amounted to £1,000.

 (iii) Motor expenses owing at 30 June 2005 amounted to £400.

 (iv) You are to provide for depreciation on the motor vehicles at 20% on cost. The computer equipment is expected to last three years from the date of purchase.

Required Prepare the trading and profit and loss appropriation account for the year ended 30 June 2005 and a balance sheet as at that date.

20.7 Mendez and Marshall are in partnership sharing profits and losses equally. The following is their trial balance as at 30 June 2006:

		Dr £	Cr £
Buildings (cost £75,000)		50,000	
Fixtures at cost		11,000	
Provision for depreciation: Fixtures			3,300
Debtors		16,243	
Creditors			11,150
Cash at bank		677	
Stock at 30 June 2005		41,979	
Sales			123,650
Purchases		85,416	
Carriage outwards		1,288	
Discounts allowed		115	
Loan interest: King		4,000	
Office expenses		2,416	
Salaries and wages		18,917	
Bad debts		503	
Provision for bad debts			400
Loan from J King			40,000
Capitals:	Mendez		35,000
	Marshall		29,500
Current accounts:	Mendez		1,306
	Marshall		298
Drawings:	Mendez	6,400	
	Marshall	5,650	
		244,604	244,604

Notes

   (i) Stock, 30 June 2006, £56,340.

  (ii) Expenses to be accrued: Office expenses £96; wages £200.

 (iii) Depreciate fixtures 10% on reducing balance basis, buildings £1,000.

 (iv) Reduce provision for bad debts to £320.

  (v) Partnership salary: £800 to Mendez. Not yet entered.

 (vi) Interest on drawings: Mendez £180; Marshall £120.

(vii) Interest on capital account balances at 10%.

Required Prepare a trading and profit and loss appropriation account for the year ended 30 June 2006, and a balance sheet as at that date.

CHAPTER 21

Manufacturing accounts

AIMS

- ■ **To be able to calculate prime cost and production cost of manufactured goods.**

- ■ **To be able to distinguish between stock of raw materials, work in progress and finished goods.**

- ■ **To draw up manufacturing accounts.**

- ■ **To be able to adjust the accounts in respect of work in progress.**

- ■ **To be able to make provision for unrealised profit.**

21.1 Introduction to manufacturing accounts

So far the accounts dealt with have related to retailing businesses; we will now consider firms which are manufacturers. For these firms a **manufacturing account** is prepared in addition to the trading and profit and loss account.

21.2 Divisions of costs

In a manufacturing firm the costs are divided into different types, which may be summarised in chart form as follows:

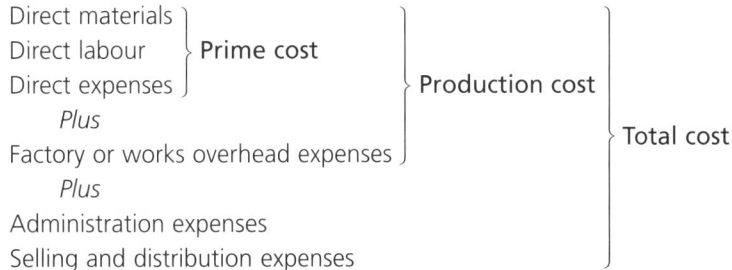

```
Direct materials  ⎤
Direct labour     ⎬ Prime cost        ⎤
Direct expenses   ⎦                   ⎬ Production cost   ⎤
      Plus                            ⎦                  ⎬ Total cost
Factory or works overhead expenses ⎦                     ⎪
      Plus                                               ⎪
Administration expenses                                  ⎪
Selling and distribution expenses                        ⎦
```

21.3 Direct and indirect costs

When you see the words **direct costs** you know that it has been possible to trace the costs of making an item being manufactured. If it cannot easily be traced to the item being manufactured, then it is an **indirect expense** and will be included under factory overhead expenses.

For example, the wages of a machine operator making a particular item will be direct labour. The wages of a foreman in charge of many men on different jobs will be indirect labour, and will be part of factory overhead expenses. Some other instances of direct costs are:

- Cost of direct materials, which will include carriage inwards on raw materials.
- Hire of special machinery for a job.

21.4 Factory overhead expenses

Factory overhead costs are all those costs which occur in the factory where production is being done, but which cannot easily be traced to the items being manufactured. Examples are:

- Wages of cleaners
- Wages of crane drivers
- Rent and rates of the factory
- Depreciation of plant and machinery
- Costs of operating fork-lift trucks
- Factory power
- Factory lighting.

21.5 Administration expenses

Administration expenses consist of such items as managers' salaries, legal and accountancy charges, the depreciation of accounting machinery and secretarial salaries.

21.6 Selling and distribution expenses

Selling and distribution expenses are items such as sales staff's salaries and commission, carriage outwards, depreciation of delivery vans, advertising and display expenses.

21.7 Format of final accounts

Manufacturing account section

This is debited with the production cost of goods completed during the accounting period. It contains costs of:

- Direct materials
- Direct labour
- Direct expenses
- Factory overhead expenses.

When completed this account will show the total of production cost. This figure will then be transferred down to the trading account.

Trading account section

This account includes:

- Production cost brought down from the manufacturing account.
- Opening and closing stocks of finished goods.
- Sales.

When completed this account will disclose the gross profit. This will then be carried down to the profit and loss account part.

The manufacturing account and the trading account can be shown in the form of a diagram:

Manufacturing Account

	£
Production costs for the period:	
Direct materials	xxx
Direct labour	xxx
Direct expenses	xxx
Factory overhead expenses	xxx
Production cost of goods completed c/d to trading account	xxx

Trading Account

		£	£
Sales			xxx
Less Production cost of goods sold:			
Opening stock of finished goods	(A)	xxx	
Add Production costs of goods completed b/d		xxx	
		xxx	
Less Closing stock of finished goods	(B)	xxx	xxx
Gross profit			xxx

(A) is production costs of goods unsold in previous period
(B) is production costs of goods unsold at end of the period

Profit and loss account section

This account includes:

- Gross profit brought down from the trading account.
- All administration expenses.
- All selling and distribution expenses.

When completed, this account will show the net profit.

21.8 A worked example of a manufacturing account

Exhibit 21.1 shows the necessary details for a manufacturing account. It has been assumed that there were no partly completed units (known as **work in progress**) at either the beginning or the end of the period.

Exhibit 21.1

Details of production cost for the year ended 31 December 2007:

	£
1 January 2007, stock of raw materials	500
31 December 2007, stock of raw materials	700
Raw materials purchased	8,000
Manufacturing (direct) wages	21,000
Royalties	150
Indirect wages	9,000
Rent of factory – excluding administration and selling and distribution blocks	440
Depreciation of plant and machinery in factory	400
General indirect expenses	310

Manufacturing Account for the year ended 31 December 2007

	£	£
Stock of raw materials 1.1.2007		500
Add Purchases		8,000
		8,500
Less Stock of raw materials 31.12.2007		700
Cost of raw materials consumed		7,800
Manufacturing wages		21,000
Royalties		150
Prime cost		28,950
Factory overhead expenses:		
Rent	440	
Indirect wages	9,000	
General expenses	310	
Depreciation of plant and machinery	400	10,150
Production cost of goods completed c/d		39,100

Sometimes, if a firm has produced less than the customers have demanded, then the firm may well have bought an outside supply of finished goods. In this case, the trading account will have both a figure for purchases and for production cost of goods completed.

21.9 Work in progress

The production cost to be carried down to the trading account is that of production cost of goods completed during the period. If items have not been completed, they cannot be sold. Therefore, they should not appear in the trading account.

For instance, if we have the following information, we can calculate the transfer to the trading account:

	£
Total production costs expended during the year	5,000
Production costs last year on goods not completed last year, but completed in this year (work in progress)	300
Production costs this year on goods which were not completed by the year end (work in progress)	440

The calculation is:

	£
Total production costs expended this year	5,000
Add Costs from last year, in respect of goods completed in this year (work in progress)	300
	5,300
Less Costs in this year, for goods to be completed next year (work in progress)	440
Production costs expended on goods completed this year	4,860

21.10 Another worked example of a manufacturing account

Exhibit 21.2

	£
1 January 2007, stock of raw materials	800
31 December 2007, stock of raw materials	1,050
1 January 2007, work in progress	350
31 December 2007, work in progress	420
Year to 31 December 2007:	
Wages: Direct	3,960
Indirect	2,550
Purchase of raw materials	8,700
Fuel and power	990
Direct expenses	140
Lubricants	300
Carriage inwards on raw materials	200
Rent of factory	720
Depreciation of factory plant and machinery	420
Internal transport expenses	180
Insurance of factory buildings and plant	150
General factory expenses	330

Manufacturing Account for the year ended 31 December 2007

	£	£
Stock of raw materials 1.1.2007		800
Add Purchases		8,700
Add Carriage inwards		200
		9,700
Less Stock of raw materials 31.12.2007		1,050
Cost of raw materials consumed		8,650
Direct wages		3,960
Direct expenses		140
Prime cost		12,750

Exhibit 4.4 (continued)

	£	£
Factory overhead expenses:		
Fuel and power	990	
Indirect wages	2,550	
Lubricants	300	
Rent	720	
Depreciation of plant	420	
Internal transport expenses	180	
Insurance	150	
General factory expenses	330	5,640
		18,390
Add Work in progress 1.1.2007		350
		18,740
Less Work in progress 31.12.2007		420
Production cost of goods completed c/d		18,320

The trading account is concerned with finished goods. If in the foregoing exhibit there had been £3,500 stock of finished goods at 1 January 2007 and £4,400 at 31 December 2007, and the sales of finished goods amounted to £25,000, then the trading account would appear as shown.

Trading account for the year 31 December 2007

	£	£
Sales		25,000
Less Cost of goods sold:		
Stock of finished goods 1.1.2007	3,500	
Add Production cost of goods completed b/d	18,320	
	21,820	
Less Stock of finished goods 31.12.2007	4,400	17,420
Gross profit c/d		7,580

The profit and loss account is then constructed in the normal way.

21.11 Apportionment of expenses

Quite often expenses will have to be split between:

- Factory overhead expenses: to be charged in the manufacturing account section

- Administration expenses: ⎫ to be charged in the profit and
- Selling and distribution expenses: ⎭ loss account section

An instance of this could be the rent expense. If the rent is paid separately for each part of the organisation, then it is easy to charge the rent to each sort of expense. However, only one figure of rent may be paid, without any indication as to how much is for the factory, how much is for the selling and distribution or for the administration buildings.

How the rent expense will be apportioned in the latter case will depend on circumstances, using the most equitable method. For instance, one of the following methods may be used:

- by floor area;
- by property valuations of each part of the buildings and land.

21.12 Full set of final accounts

A complete worked example is given below. Note that in the profit and loss account the expenses have been separated to show whether they are administration expenses, selling and distribution expenses, or financial charges.

The trial balance in Exhibit 21.3 has been extracted from the books of J Jarvis, Toy Manufacturer, as on 31 December 2007.

Exhibit 21.3

J Jarvis
Trial Balance as on 31 December 2007

	Dr £	Cr £
Stock of raw materials 1.1.2007	2,100	
Stock of finished goods 1.1.2007	3,890	
Work in progress 1.1.2007	1,350	
Wages (direct £18,000; factory indirect £14,500)	32,500	
Royalties	700	
Carriage inwards (on raw materials)	350	
Purchases of raw materials	37,000	
Productive machinery (cost £28,000)	23,000	
Accounting machinery (cost £2,000)	1,200	
General factory expenses	3,100	
Lighting	750	
Factory power	1,370	
Administrative salaries	4,400	
Salesmen's salaries	3,000	
Commission on sales	1,150	
Rent	1,200	
Insurance	420	
General administration expenses	1,340	
Bank charges	230	
Discounts allowed	480	
Carriage outwards	590	
Sales		100,000
Debtors and creditors	14,230	12,500
Bank	5,680	
Cash	150	
Drawings	2,000	
Capital as at 1.1.2007		29,680
	142,180	142,180

Notes at 31.12.2007

(i) Stock of raw materials £2,400, stock of finished goods £4,000, work in progress £1,500.

(ii) Lighting, rent and insurance are to be apportioned: factory 5/6ths, administration 1/6th.

(iii) Depreciation on productive and accounting machinery at 10% per annum on cost.

J Jarvis

Manufacturing, Trading and Profit and Loss Account for the year ended
31 December 2007

	£	£	£
Stock of raw materials 1.1.2007			2,100
Add Purchases			37,000
Add Carriage inwards			350
			39,450
Less Stock raw materials 31.12.2007			2,400
Cost of raw materials consumed			37,050
Direct labour			18,000
Royalties			700
Prime cost			55,750
Factory overhead expenses:			
General factory expenses		3,100	
Lighting 5/6ths		625	
Power		1,370	
Rent 5/6ths		1,000	
Insurance 5/6ths		350	
Depreciation of plant		2,800	
Indirect labour		14,500	23,745
			79,495
Add Work in progress 1.1.2007			1,350
			80,845
Less Work in progress 31.12.2007			1,500
Production cost of goods completed c/d			79,345
Sales			100,000
Less Cost of goods sold:			
Stock of finished goods 1.1.2007		3,890	
Add Production cost of goods completed		79,345	
		83,235	
Less Stock of finished goods 31.12.2007		4,000	79,235
Gross profit			20,765
Administration expenses:			
Administration salaries	4,400		
Rent 1/6th	200		
Insurance 1/6th	70		
General expenses	1,340		
Lighting 1/6th	125		
Depreciation of accounting machinery	200	6,335	
Selling and distribution expenses:			
Salesmen's salaries	3,000		
Commission on sales	1,150		
Carriage outwards	590	4,740	
Financial charges:			
Bank charges	230		
Discounts allowed	480	710	11,785
Net profit			8,980

J Jarvis
Balance Sheet as at 31 December 2007

Fixed assets	£	£
Productive machinery at cost	28,000	
Less Depreciation to date	7,800	20,200
Accounting machinery at cost	2,000	
Less Depreciation to date	1,000	1,000
		21,200
Current assets		
Stock:		
Raw materials	2,400	
Finished goods	4,000	
Work in progress	1,500	
Debtors	14,230	
Bank	5,680	
Cash	150	
	27,960	
Less Current liabilities		
Creditors	12,500	
Net current assets		15,460
		36,660
Financed by		
Capital		
Balance as at 1.1.2007		29,680
Add Net profit		8,980
		38,660
Less Drawings		2,000
		36,660

21.13   Market value of goods manufactured

The accounts of Jarvis, illustrated above, are subject to the limitation that the respective amounts of the gross profit which are attributable to the manufacturing side or to the selling side of the firm are not known. A technique is sometimes used to bring out this additional information. By this method the cost which would have been involved if the goods had been bought in their finished state instead of being manufactured by the firm is brought into account. This is credited to the manufacturing account and debited to the trading account in order to throw up two figures of gross profit instead of one. It should be pointed out that the net profit will remain unaffected. All that will have happened will be that the figure of £20,765 gross profit will be shown as two figures instead of one.

The accounts in summarised form will appear as shown.

J Jarvis
Manufacturing, Trading and Profit and Loss Account
for the year ended
31 December 2007

	£	£
Market value of goods completed c/d		95,000
Less Production cost of goods completed (as before)		79,345
Gross profit on manufacture c/d		15,655
Sales		100,000
Stock of finished goods 1.1.2007	3,890	
Add Market value of goods completed b/d	95,000	
	98,890	
Less Stock of finished goods 31.12.2007	4,000	94,890
Gross profit on trading c/d		5,110
Gross profit:		
On manufacturing	15,655	
On trading	5,110	20,765

21.14 Finished stocks at market price

SSAP 9 requires that the stocks should normally be valued at cost price if purchased, or cost of production if manufactured. However, if the net realisable value is lower than either of these then this valuation should be used instead.

If unsold finished stocks were valued at market price, and this was above the figure required by SSAP 9, then a provision for unrealised profit would have to be made. This provision would be debited to the trading account and credited to a provision account. In the balance sheet the provision would be deducted from the stock figures.

NEW TERMS

Direct costs   Costs that can be traced to the item being manufactured.

Factory overhead costs   Production costs in the factory which cannot be traced to the item being manufactured.

Manufacturing account   An account in which production cost is calculated.

Prime cost   Direct materials plus direct labour plus direct expenses.

Production cost   Prime cost plus factory overhead costs.

Total cost   Production cost plus administration, selling and distribution expenses.

Unrealised profit   The profit element of the year end valuation of factory finished goods.

Work-in-progress   Items not completed at the end of a period.

Student Activities

21.1   From the following information, prepare the manufacturing and trading account of E Chandler for the year ended 31 March 2008.

	£
Stocks at 1 April 2007:	
Finished goods	6,724
Raw materials	2,400
Work in progress	955
Carriage on purchases (raw materials)	321
Sales	69,830
Purchase of raw materials	21,340
Manufacturing wages	13,280
Factory power	6,220
Other manufacturing expenses	1,430
Factory rent and rates	2,300
Stocks at 31 March 2008:	
Raw materials	2,620
Work in progress	870
Finished goods	7,230

21.2X Draw up the manufacturing and trading account of W Stead for the year ended 31 August 2008 from the following:

	31.8.2007	31.8.2008
	£	£
Stock of raw materials	5,620	8,410
Finished goods stock	11,372	9,128
Work in progress	811	1,033
For the year		
Raw materials bought		22,200
Factory power		2,377
Sales		63,890
Manufacturing wages		14,522
Factory rent and rates		5,720
Other manufacturing expenses		3,879
Carriage on raw materials		610

21.3 Prepare manufacturing, trading and profit and loss accounts from the following balances of T Jackson for the year ended 31 December 2007.

	£
Stocks at 1 January 2007:	
Raw materials	18,450
Work in progress	23,600
Finished goods	17,470
Purchases: Raw materials	64,300
Carriage on raw materials	1,605
Direct labour	65,810
Office salaries	16,920
Rent	2,700
Office lighting and heating	5,760
Depreciation: Works machinery	8,300
Office equipment	1,950
Sales	200,600
Factory fuel and power	5,920

Rent is to be apportioned: Factory 2/3rds; office 1/3rd. Stocks at
31 December 2007 were: Raw materials £20,210; work in progress £17,390;
finished goods £21,485.

21.4 Chesterton & Son are manufacturers. At the end of their accounting year,
30 April 2001, the following information was available:

	£
Stocks, 1 May 2000:	
Raw materials	17,500
Finished goods	24,800
Work in progress	15,270
Wages and salaries:	
Factory direct	138,500
Factory indirect	27,200
Purchases of raw materials	95,600
Power and fuel (indirect)	18,260
Sales	410,400
Insurance	3,680
Returns inwards (finished goods)	5,200
Stocks, 30 April 2001:	
Raw materials	13,200
Finished goods	14,600
Work in progress	15,700

Notes

  (i) The partnership's machinery cost £82,000 and the provision for
       depreciation on 1 May 2000 was £27,000. Machinery is to be
       depreciated by 20% per annum using the reducing balance method.

 (ii) Fuel and power £390 is in arrears at 30 April 2001; at the same date
       insurance £240 is prepaid.

(iii) Insurance is to be allocated 5/8ths factory; 3/8ths administration.

Required For Chesterton & Son:

(a) A manufacturing account for the year ended 30 April 2001, showing
     clearly:

     (i)   Cost of raw materials consumed.
     (ii) Prime cost.
     (iii) Total cost of production.

(b) A trading account for the year ended 30 April 2001, showing clearly:

     (i)   Cost of sales of finished goods.
     (ii) Gross profit.

21.5X D Saunders is a manufacturer. His trial balance at 31 December 2006 is as
follows:

	£	£
Delivery van expenses	2,500	
Lighting and heating: Factory	2,859	
Office	1,110	
Manufacturing wages	45,470	
General expenses: Office	3,816	
Factory	5,640	
Salesmen: Commission	7,860	
Purchase of raw materials	39,054	
Rent: Factory	4,800	
Office	2,200	
Machinery (cost £50,000)	32,500	
Office equipment (cost £15,000)	11,000	
Office salaries	6,285	
Debtors	28,370	
Creditors		19,450
Bank	13,337	
Sales		136,500
Premises (cost £50,000)	40,000	
Stocks at 31 December 2005:		
Raw materials	8,565	
Finished goods	29,480	
Drawings	8,560	
Capital		137,456
	293,406	293,406

Prepare the manufacturing, trading and profit and loss accounts for the year
ended 31 December 2006 and a balance sheet as at that date. Take account
of the following adjustments:

1. Stocks at 31 December 2006: Raw materials £9,050; finished goods
   £31,200. There is no work in progress.

2. Depreciate machinery £2,000; office equipment £1,500; premises
   £1,000.

3. Manufacturing wages due but unpaid at 31 December 2006 £305, office
   rent prepaid £108.

21.6X The following data relate to Infortec Manufacturing, a new business,
manufacturing computers, which the owner, Phil Townsend, is proposing
to start with effect from 1 January 2002. He has produced the following
estimated figures for the year ended 31 December 2002 and has asked you
to help in preparing some information:

	£
Raw materials to be purchased	180,000
Production wages	41,750
Production supervisory wages	22,000
Other production overheads	15,170
Selling and distribution expenses	38,800

In order to set up the business, Phil Townsend would need to do the
following with effect from 1 January 2002:

- Open a new business bank account.
- Take out a business bank loan of £40,000. (Interest at 8% per annum to be paid out of the new business bank account).
- Place £50,000, which includes the £40,000 from the bank loan, into the new business bank account to cover future expenditure.
- Purchase, out of his own personal money, new production machinery and equipment costing £72,500. (Depreciation on this is to be calculated at 10% per annum on cost.)

On 31 December 2002:

	£
Closing stock of raw materials	15,600
Closing stock of work in progress	10,170
Closing stock of finished goods	20,400
Closing debtors estimated to be 1/12th of sales for the year.	
Closing creditors estimated to be 1/12th of raw materials purchased for the year.	

Notes

- The profit mark up is to be 20% on factory cost of sales.
- All payments and receipts to pass through the new business bank account.

Required

(i) Calculate the capital which would be invested by Phil Townsend in the business on 1 January 2002.

(ii) Calculate the prime cost of production of Infortec Manufacturing for the year ended 31 December 2002.

(iii) Calculate the total production cost of the finished goods to be made by Infortec Manufacturing during the year ended 31 December 2002.

(iv) Produce a statement showing the planned sales, factory cost of sales, gross profit and net profit of Infortec Manufacturing for the year ended 31 December 2002.

(v) Produce a summary of the business bank account for the year ended 31 December 2002 showing clearly the payments, the receipts and the closing balance.

(Association of Accounting Technicians)

Practice assessments

This section contains one practice assessment paper which is in the style of the AAT's Intermediate Level Assessment and one specimen examination type paper suitable for candidates studying for the ACCA's Certified Accounting Technician examination, in the unit 'Maintaining Financial Records and Preparing Accounts'.

The AAT's central assessment

The central assessment for 'Maintaining Financial Records and Preparing Accounts' consists of two sections. The case studies on which the sections are based will be unconnected. Both sections will contain three or four short answer questions.

The time allowed for the assessment will be 3 hours plus 15 minutes reading time; the time allocation for each section may not necessarily be equal, and students are reminded to read carefully the instructions on the assessment paper before commencing work.

The tasks involved will be based on a business or organisation using a manual system of accounting consisting of a cash book, general ledger, day books and sales and purchase ledgers. In Chapter 15, Sections 15.9 and 15.10, it can be seen that the view favoured by most examining bodies is that the sales ledger control account and the purchase ledger control account are maintained in the general ledger and are, therefore, part of the double entry system. The personal accounts of the debtors and creditors are classed as 'memorandum accounts'.

Section 1 includes exercises on the trial balance and extended trial balance. Also included will be tasks on identification and correction of errors, suspense accounts, bank reconciliation statement and control accounts.

Section 2 comprises practical exercises based on information and data given on manufacturing accounts, incomplete records for sold traders, partnership and club/society accounts.

Both sections will include short answer questions from across the standards of this unit.

The Certified Accounting Technician (CAT) examination paper

The examination for the above qualification, which covers the same standards as the AAT's central assessment, 'Maintaining Financial Records and Preparing Accounts', consists of three questions.

All three questions must be answered and the time allocation is 2 hours. The number of marks which each question, or part of a question, carries is shown at the end of the question.

PRACTICE ASSESSMENT (AAT STYLE)

The time allowed for this practice assessment is 3 hours plus 15 minutes reading time. The assessment is in two sections:

Section 1 This section contains two parts: Part A consists of an accounting exercise on the extended trial balance with adjustments and journal entries; and Part B consists of short answer questions.

Section 2 This section contains a practical exercise on club accounts plus short answer questions.

It is important to note that competence must be achieved in each section of the assessment; therefore, all tasks in each section must be attempted. All relevant workings must be shown.

SECTION 1 (Suggested time allocation for all tasks, 90 minutes)

Data

Martin Fisher is the proprietor of Martin Fisher & Co., a retail business in Cumbria.

- You are employed by Martin Fisher to assist with the book keeping.
- The business currently operates a manual accounting system consisting of a cash book, a general ledger, a sales ledger and a purchase ledger.
- Double entry takes place in the general ledger and the individual accounts of the debtors and creditors are therefore regarded as memorandum accounts.
- The business uses a purchases day book and a sales day book. The totals from these day books are transferred into the general ledger on a monthly basis.

The company's financial year end is 31 December 2003, on that date the balances were extracted from the general ledger and entered into a trial balance, as shown on page 306.

Task 1.1 Make appropriate entries in the adjustments columns of the extended trial balance. A blank form is provided on page 310, to take account of the following:

(a) The stock at 31 December 2003 was valued at £26,523 but this included some old stock that had previously been purchased for £960 but now has a net realisable value of only £330.

(b) Accruals at 31 December 2003: Lighting and heating £721; telephone £310.

(c) Prepayments at 31 December 2003: Insurance £230.

(d) The provision for bad debts is to be increased to £1,290.

(e) Provide for depreciation of the motor vehicles at 20% on cost and the fixtures at 15% using the reducing balance method.

Martin Fisher & Co.
Trial Balance as at 31 December 2003

Description	Ledger Balances	
	Dr	Cr
	£	£
Capital		60,375
Drawings	11,569	
Rent	14,956	
Purchases	415,027	
Sales		514,205
Salaries and wages	30,178	
Insurance	1,827	
Lighting and heating	2,332	
Printing and stationery	2,588	
Telephone	1,450	
Sundry expenses	2,171	
Motor vehicles	30,000	
Provision for depreciation of motor vehicles		18,000
Fixtures	23,420	
Provision for depreciation of fixtures		14,100
Balance at bank	23,881	
Petty cash	52	
VAT		9,174
Sales control account	47,330	
Purchases control account		30,219
Stock 1 January 2003	35,240	
Motor expenses	4,258	
Bad debts written off	794	
Provision for bad debts		1,000
	647,073	647,073

Task 1.2

Extend the figures into the extended trial balance columns for the profit and loss and balance sheet. Total all of the columns, transferring the balance of the profit or loss as appropriate.

Task 1.3

On completion of the final accounts for the year ended 31 December 2003 it was decided to change one of the two vehicles. Vehicle registration number N887 SDB was traded in at the local garage and a new estate car registration number V485 CDR was purchased.

Prepare the journal entries to record the disposal of the original vehicle and the purchase of the estate car from the details shown below. Narratives are not required.

(a) The original vehicle, N887 SDB, purchased on 1 January 2000, cost £15,000. It had been depreciated at 20% per annum since that date using the straight line method.

(b) On 3 January 2004, vehicle N887 SDB was traded in and replaced by V485 CDR. The trade-in allowance was £3,500.

(c) The new vehicle cost £18,800 and the balance due was paid by a cheque on 4 January 2004.

Task 1.4

Martin Fisher has decided to open another shop and is considering taking on a partner to assist him.

(a) Advise him of the advantages and disadvantages of forming a partnership.

(b) Martin also asks you how future profits would be shared among the partners. Advise him of the alternatives available for profit distribution.

Your answer should be written in the form of a memo to Martin.

Task 1.5

Martin Fisher asks you why you have not charged his drawings to the profit and loss account but instead shown them as a deduction from his capital account in the balance sheet, as these are surely his wages.

Explain to Martin the reasons for not charging the drawings in the profit and loss account.

Task 1.6

(a) Martin has heard that there are two methods of depreciation, namely the 'straight line method' and the 'reducing balance method'. Using the information shown below, compare the impact on yearly profits over a four-year period using:

(i) The straight line method of calculating depreciation.
(ii) The reducing balance method of calculating depreciation.

Illustrate your answer assuming that the fixed asset cost £16,000, has a life of four years and a residual value of £1,000. The reducing balance method rate of depreciation is 50%.

(b) Explain to Martin why charging depreciation does not provide the funds for the replacement of worn out or obsolete fixed assets.

SECTION 2 (Suggested time allocation 90 minutes for all tasks)

Laura Shaw is the treasurer of her local amateur dramatic society, the Whitefield Theatre Society. As the treasurer, she has asked you for your assistance in preparing some financial statements which she can present at the Society's Annual General Meeting. The Society's financial year end is 31 December 2003 and the following information is available:

Balances on 1 January 2003	£
Balance at bank	3,230
Subscriptions in arrears for 2002	175
Subscriptions received in advance for 2003	510
Scenery and costumes	1,800

In respect of the year to 31 December 2003, the following information is given to you:

	£
Subscriptions received (including 2002 arrears)	4,400
Scenery and costumes bought	1,700
Casual wages	1,000
Sale of theatre tickets	9,500
Printing, stationery and advertising	1,970
Hire of hall	5,050
Lighting and heating	1,500
Sale of refreshments	2,630
Cost of refreshments	1,220
Donations received	1,200
Sale of raffle tickets	1,370
Raffle prizes bought	580
Committee expenses	330

Notes

(a) The scenery and costumes are to be depreciated at 20% using the straight line method, items purchased during the year should also be included.

(b) At 31 December 2003, £200 was owing in respect of hire of the hall.

(c) Subscriptions in arrears as at 31 December 2003 were £440.

Task 2.1 Draw up the subscriptions account for the year ended 31 December 2003.

Task 2.2 Draw up the receipts and payments account for the year ended 31 December 2003.

Task 2.3 Prepare the income and expenditure account for the year ended 31 December 2003 to be presented to the members of the Whitefield Theatre Society.

Task 2.4 Comment briefly on the Society's financial progress during the year, making any recommendations to improve the financial position.

Task 2.5 Expenditure spent on pure research may be capitalised if an organisation so wishes.

(a) State whether you agree or disagree with the above statement.

(b) Discuss the reasons for your answer to (a) referring to the relevant statement of standard accounting practice.

Task 2.6 A business keeps the petty cash book using the imprest system. At the end of each period the petty cash book is balanced and the totals of the analysis columns posted to the relevant accounts in the general ledger and the imprest restored.

(a) What would the total of the VAT column represent?

(b) Where would the total of the VAT column be posted and would this be a debit or credit entry?

(c) If the petty cash float was £75 and the expenditure for the period totalled £60, what would be the double entry to restore the float?

Task 2.7

A joinery company is considering manufacturing bookcases since they feel there is demand for this product. The company estimates that in the first year of production they will make 10,000 bookcases with expected sales of 8,000. The following expenditure is expected to be incurred in the manufacture:

	£
Direct materials used	50,000
Direct labour used	20,000
Direct expenses	10,000
Selling and distribution expenses	4,000

(a) What is the prime cost of manufacture?

(b) How much is the cost of making one bookcase?

(c) If the mark-up on cost is 50%, what will be the selling price of each bookcase?

(d) What is the value of the closing stock of 2,000 units?

(e) If the company achieves its sales target of 8,000 bookcases in the first year, what will be the profit in the year?

Task 2.8

'How can my business possibly owe money to the bank since I have had a very profitable year?' Discuss this statement.

Extended trial balance

Description	Ledger Balances		Adjustments		Profit and Loss		Balance Sheet	
	Dr £	Cr £	Dr £	Cr £	Dr £	Cr £	Dr £	Cr £

SPECIMEN EXAMINATION PAPER NO. 1

(ACCA Accounting Technician style)

This specimen paper has been set by the authors of this book. It does not consist of past questions from the ACCA papers. Instead, it consists of questions set at the same standard as the real examinations, and also set using the same style of display and requirements.

Question 1 Please use the extended trial balance printed on page 315 to complete your answer.

(A) You have been asked by your principal in the accounting practice to prepare a set of accounts for a sole trader. The client is John Holden, a sole trader, and he is a wholesaler selling magazines to chemists. He does not have to charge value added tax on his sales.

A manual system of book keeping is in use, comprising the following items:

- A cash book.
- A general (or nominal) ledger. Besides the usual accounts there is also a sales ledger control account and a purchase ledger control account.
- Purchases and sales ledgers. These contain memorandum accounts for creditors and debtors, and are not regarded as part of the double entry system.

The accounts you are preparing are for the year ended 31 December 2003. John Holden has given you the following trial balance extracted from his books as at 31 December 2003:

	Dr £	Cr £
Sales		515,000
Returns inwards	1,575	
Purchases	327,500	
Returns outwards		2,168
Stock at 1.1.2003	72,400	
Wages	88,300	
Rent and rates	27,200	
Carriage inwards	550	
Packing materials	2,070	
Delivery expenses	6,840	
Electricity	2,340	
Bad debts written off	970	
Provision for bad debts at 1.1.2003		1,200
Fixed assets at cost		
Fixtures and equipment	55,000	
Motor vehicles	21,600	
Provision for depreciation at 1.1.2003		
Fixtures and equipment		22,000
Motor vehicles		10,000
Purchases ledger control account		29,270

	Dr £	Cr £
Sales ledger control account	51,640	
Bank account	17,520	
Cash in hand	305	
Capital account as at 1.1.2003		128,782
Drawings	32,888	
Suspense account		278
	708,698	708,698

On checking the accounts you find the following:

1. A refund of delivery expenses £416 on 15 July 2003 had been entered in the cash book but had not been posted anywhere else.

2. An item of returns inwards £114 on 31 October 2003 had been correctly entered in the customer's memorandum in the sales ledger but had not been entered in the sales ledger control account.

3. A payment of £252 on 16 December 2003 for electricity had been correctly entered in the cash book but had not been charged to the electricity account.

Required

(a) (i) Write up the journal entries necessary in respect of the information given in (1) to (3) above. Dates are not required, but you are required to show a narrative for each journal entry.

(9 marks)

(ii) Make the entries necessary on the extended trial balance provided.

(6 marks)

(b) (i) Give one way of confirming the balance on the sales ledger control account.

(2 marks)

(ii) State three reasons why the balance on an account maintained in the sales ledger may be different from that shown in the customer's own purchases ledger on the same date.

(6 marks)

(iii) For each of the reasons given by you to (ii) above, state whether or not a correcting entry is required in the general ledger.

(6 marks)

(B) On looking further at John Holden's books the following items are revealed to you:

1. Depreciation is to be provided on the following basis:
   - Fixtures and equipment: 15% per annum using the reducing balance method.
   - Motor vehicles: 25% per annum on the straight line basis giving one month's depreciation for each month's use. No vehicles had been sold during the year, but one had been bought for £7,200 on 1 June 2003.

2. Included in the figure for rent and rates is a payment for rent of £7,500 for four months for the period 1 October 2003 to 31 January 2004.

3. The bad debts provision is to be reduced to £1,060.

4. Stock at 31 December 2003 was calculated to be £91,750 at cost price. However, included in that are two items, the first cost £750 but will not be able to be sold for more than £400 less selling costs £50, and the other item, which cost £280 is badly damaged and is completely valueless.

5. A bill for carriage inwards still owing of £90 has not been entered in the books at all.

Required

(a) In respect of the information shown in (1) to (5) above you are to calculate the necessary adjustments.

(10 marks)

(b) Show the appropriate adjustments entered on the extended trial balance provided for you on page 315.

(5 marks)

(c) Extend the figures on the extended trial balance into the profit and loss account and balance sheet columns. Show the results for the year, stating whether it is a net profit or a net loss.

(16 marks)

(**TOTAL 60 marks**)

Question 2 T Mayall commenced business as a computer services consultant five years ago on 1 January 2001. His computers were purchased as follows:

	Date of purchase	Purchase cost
		£
Computer 1	1 January 2001	32,500
2	31 August 2001	35,000
3	7 May 2003	48,000
4	10 June 2004	42,500
5	11 October 2005	40,000

There were no computer disposals up to 31 December 2005. Mayall's financial year end is 31 December, and his normal practice has been to:

1. Use the straight line depreciation method assuming a residual value of nil and a computer life of five years.

2. Charge a full year's depreciation in the year of purchase on any computer bought in the first half of a financial year.

3. Charge no depreciation in the year of purchase on any computer bought in the second half of the financial year.

Required

(a) Calculate the summary net book value for computers that should appear on Mayall's balance sheet as at 31 December 2005. Show in the form of a table as follows:

Financial year ended 31 December	Depreciation per year 2001 2002 2003 2004 2005	Total	Net book value 31.12.2005
Cost £			
Computer 1 32,500			
Computer 2 35,000			
Computer 3 48,000			
Computer 4 42,500			
Computer 5 40,000			

(10 marks)

(b) Mayall wants to replace Computer 3 early in 2006. Show how the computer disposal account would appear if this computer were sold on 1 January 2006 for £16,250.

(5 marks)

(TOTAL 15 marks)

Question 3 The following is a summary of M Daley's bank account for the year ended 31 December 2007:

Bank Summary

	£		£
Balance at 1.1.2007	1,620	Payments to creditors for goods	117,948
Receipts from debtors	151,744	Rent	6,600
Balance at 31.12.2007	2,408	Rates	3,560
		Sundry expenses	1,500
		Drawings	26,164
	155,772		155,772

The following information is available:

Assets and liabilities:	31 Dec 2006 £	31 Dec 2007 £
Stock	55,448	60,576
Creditors	22,496	29,556
Debtors	36,124	34,496
Rates prepaid	840	900
Rent owing	600	–
Furniture and fittings, at valuation	10,000	9,000

All of the business takings have been paid into the bank with the exception of £38,520. Out of this, M Daley paid wages of £21,888, made drawings of £4,656 and purchased goods valued £11,976.

Required

(a) Calculate M Daley's opening capital as at 1 January 2007.

(b) Prepare the trading and profit and loss account for the year ended 31 December 2007 and a balance sheet as at that date.

(20 marks)

John Holden – Trial balance as at 31 December 2003

| | Balances per ledger | | Adjustments Question 1 Part (A) | | Adjustments Question 1 Part (B) | | Profit and loss account | | Balance sheet | |
| | | | | | Accrued | Prepaid | | | | |
	Dr £	Cr £	Dr £	Cr £	Dr £	Cr £	Dr £	Cr £	Dr £	Cr £
Sales		515,000								
Returns inwards	1,575									
Purchases	327,500									
Returns outwards		2,168								
Stock at 1.1.2003	72,400									
Wages	88,300									
Rent and rates	27,200									
Carriage inwards	550									
Packing materials	2,070									
Delivery expenses	6,840									
Electricity	2,340									
Bad debts	970									
Provision for bad debts 1.1.2003		1,200								
Fixtures and equipment	55,000									
Motor vehicles	21,600									
Provision for depreciation: Fixtures and equipment		22,000								
Provision for depreciation: Motor vehicles		10,000								
Purchases ledger control account		29,270								
Sales ledger control account	51,640									
Bank account	17,520									
Cash in hand	305									
Capital account		128,782								
Drawings	32,888									
Suspense account		278								
Closing stock										
Reduction: Provision for bad debts										
Prepayments: Rent										
Accruals										
Depreciation for the year: Fixtures and equipment										
Depreciation for the year: Motor vehicles										
Totals	708,698	708,698								
Profit for year										

Useful names and addresses

Association of Accounting Technicians (AAT)
154 Clerkenwell Road
London EC1R 5AD
Tel: 020 7837 8600   Fax: 020 7837 6970

Association of Chartered Certified Accountants (ACCA)
29 Lincoln's Inn Fields
London WC2A 3EE
Tel: 020 7242 6855   Fax: 020 7396 7070

Association of Taxation Technicians
12 Upper Belgrave Street
London SW1X 8BB
Tel: 020 7235 2544   Fax: 020 7235 2562

Chartered Institute of Management Accountants (CIMA)
63 Portland Place
London W1N 4AB
Tel: 020 7637 2311   Fax: 020 7631 5309

Chartered Institute of Public Finance and Accountancy (CIPFA)
3 Robert Street
London WC2N 6BH
Tel: 020 7543 5600   Fax: 020 7543 5700

Edexcel Foundation
BTEC
Stewart House
32 Russell Square
London WC1B 5DW
Tel: 0870 240 9800   Fax: 020 7758 6960

Institute of Chartered Accountants in England and Wales (ICAEW)
Chartered Accountant's Hall
PO Box 433 Moorgate Place
London EC2P 2BJ
Tel: 020 7920 8100   Fax: 020 7920 0547

Institute of Chartered Accountants in Ireland
11 Donegal Square South
Belfast BT1 5JE
Tel: 02890 321600   Fax: 02890 230071

Institute of Chartered Accountants in Scotland
27 Queen Street
Edinburgh EH2 1LA
Tel: 0131 347 0100   Fax: 0131 347 0105

Institute of Chartered Secretaries and Administrators
16 Park Crescent
London W1N 4AH
Tel: 020 7580 4741   Fax: 020 7323 1132

Pitman Qualifications
1 Giltspur Street
London EC1A 9DD
Tel: 020 7294 2469   Fax: 020 7294 2401

London Chamber of Commerce & Industry Examination Board (LCCI)
6 Graphite Street
London SE11 5EE
Tel: 020 7793 3850   Fax: 020 7582 1806

Oxford Cambridge and Royal (OCR)
Westwood Way
Coventry
CV4 8HS
Tel: 024 7647 0033   Fax: 024 7642 1944

Answers

Chapter 1 — Financial management of a business

1.1 Refer to text, Sections 1.1 and 1.4.
1.2 Refer to text, Section 1.3.
1.3 Refer to text, Section 1.5.
1.4 Refer to text, Section 1.6.

Chapter 2 — The accounting cycle

2.1 Refer to text, Section 2.2.
2.3 Refer to text, Section 2.6.
2.5 Refer to text, Section 2.8.
2.6 Refer to text, Section 2.9.
2.7 Refer to text, Section 2.9.
2.8 Refer to text, Section 2.9.

Chapter 3 — The trial balance

3.1 (a) C
　　(b) D
　　(c) D
　　(d)

Trial Balance

	Dr	Cr
Loan from father		6,000
Stock	11,865	
Bank overdraft		1,104
Debtors	9,276	
Motor car	16,500	
Cash in hand	363	
Creditors		8,298
Plant and machinery	11,700	
Capital		34,302
	49,704	49,704

Answer: C

　　(e) A

3.2 (a) Capital – credit
　　(b) Sales – credit
　　(c) Stationery – debit
　　(d) Bank overdraft – credit
　　(e) Day & Co. (creditor) – credit
　　(f) Machinery – debit

(g) Rent and rates – debit
(h) Drawings – debit
(i) Bank loan – credit
(j) Purchases – debit

3.3 (a) Error of principle
     (b) Error of commission
     (c) Error of omission
     (d) Error of original entry
     (e) Complete reversal of entries
     (f) Error of principle
     (g) Error of commission

3.5

J Jenkin's Books

Dr   Bank Account   **Cr**

Jan	1	Capital	10,000	Jan	2	Rent	500
	28	McGilvery Mfr.	64		8	Motor van	3,500
	28	Rogers & Brown	1,820		18	H Pickford & Son	320
	31	Cornerways & Co.	96		18	Plastic Ware Ltd	460
					30	Electricity	52
					31	Telephones	94
					31	Bailey's Ltd	1,200
					31	Balance c/d	5,854
			11,980				11,980
Feb	1	Balance b/d	5,854				

Dr   Cash Account   **Cr**

Jan	6	Sales	480	Jan 10	Stationery	45
	16	Sales	340		15	Wages	128
					29	Petrol	25
					30	Wages	320
					30	Stationery	92
					31	Balance c/d	210
			820				820
Feb	1	Balance b/d	210				

Dr   Sales Account   **Cr**

Jan 31	Balance c/d	3,615	Jan	6	Cash	480
				14	Cornerways & Co.	96
				14	McGilvery Mfr.	64
				14	Rogers & Brown	1,820
				16	Cash	340
				26	Cornerways & Co.	300
				26	Rogers & Brown	515
			3,615				3,615
				Fed	1	Balance b/d	3,615

Dr	Purchases Account				Cr
Jan 5	H Pickford & Son	320	Jan 31	Balance c/d	3,007
5	J Jackson Ltd	460			
5	Plastic Ware Ltd	980			
12	J Jackson Ltd	527			
25	Plastic Ware Ltd	720			
		3,007			3,007
Feb 1	Balance b/d	3,007			

Dr	Office Furniture Account				Cr
Jan 4	Bailey's Ltd	1,200			

Dr	Motor Van Account				Cr
Jan 8	Bank	3,500	Jan 31	Balance c/d	8,000
23	Park Car Sales	4,500			
		8,000			8,000
Feb 1	Balance b/d	8,000			

Dr	Rent Account				Cr
Jan 2	Bank	500			

Dr	Stationery Account				Cr
Jan 10	Cash	45	Jan 31	Balance c/d	137
30	Cash	92			
		137			137
Feb 1	Balance b/d	137			

Dr	Wages Account				Cr
Jan 15	Cash	128	Jan 31	Balance c/d	448
30	Cash	320			
		448			448
Feb 1	Balance b/d	448			

Dr	Motor Expenses Account				Cr
Jan 29	Cash	25			

Dr	Electricity Account				Cr
Jan 30	Bank	52			

Dr	Telephone Account				Cr
Jan 31	Bank	94			

Dr	Capital Account				Cr
			Jan 1	Bank	10,000

Dr		Cornerways & Co. Account				Cr
Jan 14	Sales	96	Jan 31	Bank		96
26	Sales	300	31	Balance c/d		300
		396				396
Feb 1	Balance b/d	300				

Dr		McGilvery Mfr. Account				Cr
Jan 14	Sales	64	Jan 28	Bank		64

Dr		Rogers & Brown Account				Cr
Jan 14	Sales	1,820	Jan 28	Bank		1,820
26	Sales	515	31	Balance c/d		515
		2,335				2,335
Feb 1	Balance b/d	515				

Dr		H Pickford & Son Account				Cr
Jan 18	Bank	320	Jan 5	Purchases		320

Dr		J Jackson Ltd Account				Cr
Jan 31	Balance c/d	987	Jan 5	Purchases		460
			12	Purchases		527
		987				987
			Feb 1	Balance b/d		987

Dr		Plastic Ware Account				Cr
Jan 18	Bank	460	Jan 5	Purchases		980
31	Balance c/d	1,240	25	Purchases		720
		1,700				1,700
			Jan 31	Balance b/d		1,240

Dr		Bailey's Ltd Account				Cr
Jan 31	Bank	1,200	Jan 4	Office furniture		1,200

Dr		Park Car Sales Account				Cr
			Jan 23	Motor van		4,500

J Jenkins
Trial Balance as at 31 January 2004

	Dr £	Cr £
Bank	5,854	
Cash	210	
Sales		3,615
Purchases	3.007	
Office furniture	1,200	
Motor van	8,000	
Rent	500	

(continued)

		Dr £	Cr £
Stationery		137	
Wages		448	
Motor expenses		25	
Electricity		52	
Telephone		94	
Capital			10,000
Cornerways & Co.		300	
Rogers & Brown		515	
J Jackson Ltd			987
Plastic Ware			1,240
Park Car Sales			4,500
		20,342	20,342

Chapter 4   Trading and profit and loss accounts: an introduction

4.1

C Rowlands
Trading and Profit and Loss Account
for the year ended 31 December 2006

	£	£
Sales		73,848
Less Cost of goods sold:		
Purchases	58,516	
Less Closing stock	10,192	48,324
Gross profit		25,524
Less Expenses:		
Wages	8,600	
Motor expenses	2,080	
Rates	2,680	
Insurance	444	
General expenses	420	14,224
Net profit		11,300

4.2

S Jennings
Trading and Profit and Loss Account
for the year ended 30 June 2004

	£	£
Sales		99,082
Less Cost of goods sold:		
Purchases	71,409	
Less Closing stock	11,498	59,911
Gross profit		39,171
Less Expenses:		
Wages	9,492	
Rates	2,000	
Printing and stationery	562	
Electricity	1,266	
Insurance	605	
Sundry expenses	1,518	
Motor expenses	3,109	18,552
Net profit		20,619

4.5

Mrs P Stewart

Trial Balance as at 31 March 2008

	Dr £	Cr £
Sales		24,765
Purchases	13,545	
Staff wages	2,100	
Drawings	5,500	
Rent and rates	1,580	
Electricity	565	
Motor expenses	845	
Insurance	345	
General expenses	245	
Cash in hand	135	
Cash at bank	2,675	
Creditors		3,285
Vehicle	5,875	
Fixtures and fittings	1,495	
Capital		6,855
	34,905	34,905

Closing stock £2,345

Mrs P Stewart

Trading and Profit and Loss Account

for the year ended 31 March 2008

	£	£
Sales		24,765
Less Cost of goods sold:		
Purchases	13,545	
Less Closing stock	2,345	
		11,200
Gross profit		13,565
Less Overheads:		
Staff wages	2,100	
Rent and rates	1,580	
Electricity	565	
Motor expenses	845	
Insurance	345	
General expenses	245	
		5,680
Net profit		7,885

 **Chapter 5**   Balance sheets

5.1

C Rowlands
Balance Sheet as at 31 December 2006

	£	£
Fixed assets		
Premises		20,000
Motor vehicle		12,000
		32,000
Current assets		
Stock	10,192	
Debtors	7,800	
Cash at bank	6,616	
Cash in hand	160	
	24,768	
Less Current liabilities		
Creditors	6,418	
Net current assets		18,350
		50,350
Financed by		
Cash introduced		48,000
Add Net profit for the year		11,300
		59,300
Less Drawings		8,950
		50,350

5.2

S Jennings
Balance Sheet as at 30 June 2004

	£	£
Fixed assets		
Premises		145,000
Computer equipment		8,000
Motor vehicle		16,500
		169,500
Current assets		
Stock	11,498	
Debtors	9,498	
Cash at bank	6,541	
Cash in hand	–	
	27,537	
Less Current liabilities		
Creditors	3,618	
Net current assets		23,919
		193,419
Financed by		
Capital introduced		185,000
Add Net profit for the year		20,619
		205,619
Less Drawings		12,200
		193,419

Mrs P Stewart
Balance Sheet as at 31 March 2008

	£	£	£
Fixed assets			
Fixtures and fittings			1,495
Motor car			5,875
			7,370
Current assets			
Stock	2,345		
Debtors	–		
Bank	2,675		
Cash	135	5,155	
Less Current liabilities			
Creditors	3,285	3,285	
Net current assets			1,870
Total net assets			9,240
Financed by			
Capital			6,855
Add Net profit			7,885
			14,740
Less Drawings			5,500
			9,240

Chapter 6 Trading and profit and loss accounts and balance sheets: further considerations

6.1

T Clarke
Trading Account for the year ended 31 December 2003

	£	£	£
Sales		38,742	
Less Returns in		890	37,852
Less Cost of goods sold:			
Purchases	33,333		
Less Returns out	495	32,838	
Add carriage inwards		670	
		33,508	
Less Closing stock		7,489	26,019
Gross profit			11,833

6.3

R Graham
Trading and Profit and Loss Account
for the year ended 30 September 2006

	£	£	£
Sales		18,600	
Less Returns in		205	18,395
Less Cost of goods sold:			
Opening stock		2,368	
Add Purchases	11,874		
Less Returns out	322	11,552	
Add carriage inwards		310	
		14,230	
Less Closing stock		2,946	11,284
Gross profit			7,111
Less Expenses			
Salaries and wages		3,862	
Rent and rates		304	
Carriage out		200	
Insurance		78	
Motor expenses		664	
Office expenses		216	
Lighting and heating		166	
General expenses		314	5,804
Net profit			1,307

Balance Sheet as at 30 September 2006

	£	£
Fixed assets		
Premises	5,000	
Fixtures	350	
Motor vehicles	1,800	7,150
Current assets		
Stock	2,946	
Debtors	3,896	
Bank	482	
	7,324	
Less Current liabilities		
Creditors	1,731	
Net current assets		5,593
		12,743
Financed by		
Capital		
Balance at 1.10.2005	12,636	
Add Net profit	1,307	
	13,943	
Less Drawings	1,200	12,743

6.4

B Jackson
Trading and Profit and Loss Account
for the year ended 30 April 2007

	£	£	£
Sales		18,600	
Less Returns in		440	18,160
Less Cost of goods sold			
Opening stock		3,776	
Add Purchases	11,556		
Less Returns out	355	11,201	
Add carriage inwards		234	
		15,211	
Less Closing stock		4,998	10,213
Gross profit			7,947
Less Expenses			
Salaries and wages		2,447	
Motor expenses		664	
Rent		576	
Carriage out		326	
Sundry expenses		1,202	5,215
Net profit			2,732

Balance Sheet as at 30 April 2007

	£	£
Fixed assets		
Fixtures	600	
Motors	2,400	3,000
Current assets		
Stock	4,998	
Debtors	4,577	
Bank	3,876	
Cash	120	
	13,571	
Less Current liabilities		
Creditors	3,045	
Net current assets		10,526
		13,526
Financed by		
Capital		
Balance as at 1.5.2006	12,844	
Add Net profit	2,732	
	15,576	
Less Drawings	2,050	13,526

Chapter 7   Accounting concepts and the regulatory framework of accounting

7.1   Objectivity is using a method that everyone can agree to, it is a fundamental principle of accounting which requires accounting information to be free from bias and be verifiable by an independent party. Refer to text Section 7.2 on page 61.

7.3 The prudence concept (see Section 7.4, page 63) would be used as the bases for your decision. Since the debt has been outstanding for a long time, has relatively low value and is unlikely to be collected, then it should be written off.

7.4 (a) The 'historical cost concept' (see Section 7.4, page 65) is an accounting convention whereby the assets of a business are recorded in the accounts at cost price.

(b) Advantages of using the cost method of valuation is that the assets can easily be verified since there will be an invoice available for checking the purchase price. Also, no valuations need be carried out on assets whose value may be subjective.

7.6 The role of the Accounting Standards Board, formed in 1990, was to replace the Statements of Standard Accounting Practice (SSAPs) and develop standards by issuing Financial Reporting Standards (FRSs). In November 1997 the ASB issued a third category of standard, the Financial Reporting Standard for Smaller Entities (FRSSEs). This was to give smaller companies the opportunity to use FRSSEs which contain less cumbersome rules than those contained in the SSAPs and FRSs. Smaller companies can choose whether to apply FRSSEs or continue to apply all the other accounting standards.

7.7 SSAP 5 – Accounting for Value Added Tax – the main aim of this standard is to obtain consistency of the accounting treatment and presentation of Value Added Tax (VAT) in the financial statement of a business. These requirements are as follows:

(i) Turnover shown in the profit and loss account should exclude VAT on taxable outputs (sales).

(ii) If VAT is paid on an item e.g. purchases, a fixed asset etc., and the firm cannot reclaim VAT, then VAT paid is included as part of the cost of the item.

(iii) Any amount due to, or from, Customs and Excise should be included in creditors or debtors, as appropriate and need not be disclosed as a separate item. Refer to Section 7.7 (page 68).

7.9 SSAP 13 Accounting for research and development requires that expenditure on pure (or basic) research is required to be shown as an expense in the profit and loss account. The reason for this is because the costs incurred are regarded as part of a continuing operation required to maintain the company's business and its competitive position and as such must be charged to the profit and loss account. Refer to Section 7.7 (page 72).

Chapter 8   Capital and revenue expenditure

8.1 (a) Refer to Sections 8.2 and 8.3 (pages 77 and 78).

(b) Capital: (i) Machinery; (ii) carriage on machinery; (v) drinks vending machine; (vii) wages for erection of office.
Revenue: (iii) Redecoration of premises; (iv) quarterly heating account.

8.3 Refer to Sections 8.2 and 8.3 (pages 77 and 78)
Capital:

(a) Building extension to factory is adding to the value of a fixed asset.

(b) Extra filing cabinets would be classified as capital expenditure since they are part of office furniture and are to be used in the business for several years.

(c) Legal fees in connection with a factory extension add to the cost of extension and are classed as capital expenditure.

T Taylor
Revised Profits Year to 31 December 2008

	£
Gross profit before corrections	95,620
Add (a) Purchases overstated	311
	95,931
Less (c) Sale of building	10,000
Revised gross profit	85,931
Net profit before corrections	28,910
Less Gross profit overstated (10,000 − 311)	9,689
	19,221
Add (d) Loan interest overstated	500
Revised net profit	19,721

Error (b) does not affect gross profit or net profit calculations.

Chapter 9 — Methods of depreciation and the acquisition of fixed assets

9.1 K Richardson

Straight Line

Cost	40,000
Year 1 Depreciation	7,000
	33,000
Year 2 Depreciation	7,000
	26,000
Year 3 Depreciation	7,000
	19,000
Year 4 Depreciation	7,000
	12,000
Year 5 Depreciation	7,000
	5,000

40,000 − 5,000 = 35,000 ÷ 5 = 7,000

Reducing Balance

Cost	40,000
Year 1 Depreciation 40% of 40,000	16,000
	24,000
Year 2 Depreciation 40% of 24,000	9,600
	14,400
Year 3 Depreciation 40% of 14,400	5,760
	8,640
Year 4 Depreciation 40% of 8,640	3,456
	5,184
Year 5 Depreciation 40% of 5,184	2,074
	3,110

9.2 (a)   *Straight Line*

Cost	37,500
Year 1 Depreciation	5,535
	31,965
Year 2 Depreciation	5,535
	26,430
Year 3 Depreciation	5,535
	20,895
Year 4 Depreciation	5,535
	15,360

$37,500 - 15,360 = 22,140 \div 4 = 5,535$

(b)   *Reducing Balance*

Cost	37,500
Year 1 Depreciation 20% of 37,500	7,500
	30,000
Year 2 Depreciation 20% of 30,000	6,000
	24,000
Year 3 Depreciation 20% of 24,000	4,800
	19,200
Year 4 Depreciation 20% of 19,200	3,840
	15,360

9.6 (a)   *Reducing Balance*

Dumper cost	6,000
Year 1 Depreciation 20%	1,200
	4,800
Year 2 Depreciation 20% of 4,800	960
	3,840
Year 3 Depreciation 20% of 3,840	768
	3,072

(b)   *Straight Line*

Dumper cost	6,000
Year 1 Depreciation	976*
	5,024
Year 2 Depreciation	976
	4,048
Year 3 Depreciation	976
	3,072

$* \ Calculation: \dfrac{6,000 - 3,072}{3} = \dfrac{2,928}{3} = 976$

9.9

Fixed Asset Register

Item No.   OF 27318
Description: Office Furniture
Purchase Date: 1 January 2001
Cost: £5,000
Estimated Life: 5 years   Location: Main Office

Purchase date	Cost (excl. VAT) £	Estimated life	Residual value £	Dep'n method SL or RB	% per annum	Dep'n for year £	Total dep'n to date £	Net book value £	Disposal proceeds (ex VAT) £	Profit/ loss on sale £
2001 1 Jan 31 Dec	5,000	6 years	500	RB	20%	1,000	1,000	4,000		
2002 31 Dec						800	1,800	3,200		
2003 31 Dec						640	2,440	2,560		
2004 31 Dec						512	2,952	2,048		

Fixed Asset Register

Item No: TL 34109
Description: Pressing Machine
Purchase Date: 1 July 2000
Cost: £25,000
Estimated Life: 4 years   Location: Machine Shop

Purchase date	Cost (excl. VAT) £	Estimated life	Residual value £	Dep'n method SL or RB	% per annum	Dep'n for year £	Total dep'n to date £	Net book value £	Disposal proceeds (ex VAT) £	Profit/ loss on sale £
2000 1 Jan 31 Dec	25,000	4 years	NIL	SL	25%	6,250	6,250	18,750		
2001 31 Dec						6,250	12,500	12,500		
2002 31 Dec						6,250	18,750	6,250		
2003 31 Dec						6,250	25,000	NIL		

9.10   The Moreland Machine Company

(i)   *Paying immediately for the purchase of vehicles*

Advantages:

- The vehicle belongs to the company immediately on payment.
- The company does not have to pay any interest charges.
- The company could negotiate on the purchase price with a view to obtaining a discount.

Disadvantages:

- Finding funds to finance the purchase of the vehicle.

(ii) *Buying the vehicles on hire purchase*

Advantages:

■ Obtain a new vehicle at a low initial outlay.

■ Pay for the vehicle by instalments which helps cash flow.

Disadvantages:

■ The vehicle does not belong to the company until the final payment is made.

■ Interest charges incurred.

■ If the company defaults in payment the vehicle could be repossessed.

Chapter 10 — Double entry records for depreciation and the disposal of assets

10.1

Dr		Motor Vans Account			Cr
2001		£	*2001*		£
Jan 1	Bank		Dec 31	Balance c/d	38,000
	(2 × £12,000)	24,000			
Jul 1	Bank	14,000			
		38,000			38,000
2002			*2002*		
Jan 1	Balance b/d	38,000	Dec 31	Balance c/d	38,000
2003					
Jan 1	Balance b/d	38,000			

Dr		Provision for Depreciation – Motor Vans Account			Cr
2001		£	*2001*		£
Dec 31	Balance c/d	6,200	Dec 31	Profit and loss	6,200
2002			*2002*		
Dec 31	Balance c/d	13,800	Jan 1	Balance b/d	6,200
			Dec 31	Profit and loss	7,600
		13,800			13,800
			2003		
			Jan 1	Balance b/d	13,800

Workings – Depreciation, motor vans (20% straight line)

	£
Year to 31 December 2001:	
(2 × 12,000 = 24,000) 20% of 24,000 for 1 year =	4,800
20% of 14,000 for 6 months =	1,400
Depreciation charge for year =	6,200
Year to 31 December 2002:	
20% of 38,000 for 1 year =	7,600

10.2   The Apex Production Company

Dr		Machinery Account			Cr
2003		£	*2003*		£
Jan 1	Bank	8,000	Dec 31	Balance c/d	8,000
2004			*2004*		
Jan 1	Balance b/d	8,000	Dec 31	Balance c/d	24,000
Jul 1	Bank (2 × £5,000)	10,000			
Oct 1	Bank	6,000			
		24,000			24,000

(continued)

Dr   Machinery Account   **Cr**

2005		£	2005		£
Jan 1	Balance b/d	24,000	Dec 31	Balance c/d	24,000
2006			2006		
Jan 1	Balance b/d	24,000	Dec 31	Balance c/d	26,000
Apr 1	Bank	2,000			
		26,000			26,000
2007					
Jan 1	Balance b/d	26,000			

Dr   Provision for Depreciation – Machinery Account   **Cr**

2003		£	2003		£
Dec 31	Balance c/d	1,600	Dec 31	Profit and loss	1,600
2004			2004		
Dec 31	Balance c/d	4,500	Jan 1	Balance b/d	1,600
			Dec 31	Profit and loss	2,900
		4,500			4,500
2005			2005		
Dec 31	Balance c/d	9,300	Jan 1	Balance b/d	4,500
			Dec 31	Profit and loss	4,800
		9,300			9,300
2006			2006		
Dec 31	Balance c/d	14,400	Jan 1	Balance b/d	9,300
			Dec 31	Profit and loss	5,100
		14,400			14,400
			2007		
			Jan 1	Balance b/d	14,400

Balance Sheet (extracts) as at 31 December

	Cost	Total depreciation	NBV
	£	£	£
2003			
Machinery	8,000	1,600	6,400
2004			
Machinery	24,000	4,500	19,500
2005			
Machinery	24,000	9,300	14,700
2006			
Machinery	26,000	14,400	11,600

Workings – Depreciation, motor vans (20% straight line)

2003	20% of 8,000 × 12 months = 1,600	1,600
2004	20% of 8,000 × 12 months = 1,600	
	20% of 10,000 × 6 months = 1,000	
	20% of 6,000 × 3 months = 300	2,900
2005	20% of 24,000 × 12 months = 4,800	4,800
2006	20% of 24,000 × 12 months = 4,800	
	20% of 2,000 × 9 months = 300	5,100

10.4 (a)

Dr   Computer Equipment Account   Cr

2002		£	*2002*		£
Apr 1	Bank	28,000	Dec 31	Balance c/d	28,000
2003			*2003*		
Jan 1	Balance b/d	28,000	Dec 31	Balance c/d	28,000
2004			*2004*		
Jan 1	Balance b/d	28,000	Dec 31	Balance c/d	28,000
2005			*2005*		
			Jul 1	Transfer computer equipment disposals account	28,000
Jan 1	Balance b/d	28,000			

Provision for Depreciation

Dr   Computer Equipment Account   Cr

2002		£	*2002*		£
Dec 31	Balance c/d	14,000	Dec 31	Profit and loss	14,000
2003			*2003*		
Dec 31	Balance c/d	21,000	Jan 1	Balance b/d	14,000
			Dec 31	Profit and loss	7,000
		21,000			21,000
2004			*2004*		
Dec 31	Balance c/d	24,500	Jan 1	Balance b/d	21,000
			Dec 31	Profit and loss	3,500
		24,500			24,500
2005			*2005*		
Jul 1	Transfer computer equipment disposals account	24,500	Jan 1	Balance b/d	24,500

Dr   Computer Equipment Disposals Account   Cr

2005		£	*2005*		£
Jul 1	Computer equipment	28,000	Jul 1	Transfer provision for depreciation computer equipment	24,500
1	Profit and loss (profit on disposal)	500	1	Bank	4,000
		28,500			28,500

Workings – Depreciation computer equipment (50% reducing balance)

2002	50% of 28,000 =	14,000
2003	50% of (28,000 – 14,000) =	7,000
2004	50% of (28,000 – 21,000) =	3,500

(b) Three from:

(i) Obsolescence/inadequacy
(ii) Depletion
(iii) Time factor
(iv) Wear and tear

Refer to text for description, Section 9.3.

10.6

Dr   Machinery Account   Cr

2009		£	2009		£
Jan 1	Balance b/d	52,590	Dec 31	Machinery disposals	2,800
Dec 31	Bank	2,480	31	Balance c/d	52,270
		55,070			55,070

Dr   Office Furniture Account   Cr

2009		£	2009		£
Jan 1	Balance b/d	2,860	Dec 31	Balance c/d	3,180
Dec 31	Bank	320			
		3,180			3,180

Dr   Provision for Depreciation: Machinery Account   Cr

2009		£	2009		£
Dec 31	Machinery disposals	1,120	Jan 1	Balance b/d	25,670
31	Balance c/d	29,777	Dec 31	Profit and loss	5,227
		30,897			30,897

Dr   Provision for Depreciation: Office Furniture Account   Cr

2009		£	2009		£
Dec 31	Balance c/d	1,649	Jan 1	Balance b/d	1,490
			Dec 31	Profit and loss	159
		1,649			1,649

Dr   Machinery Disposals Account   Cr

2009		£	2009		£
Dec 31	Machinery	2,800	Dec 31	Provision for depreciation	1,120
			31	Bank	800
			31	Profit and loss:	
				Loss on sale	880
		2,800			2,800

Balance Sheet as at 31 December 2009

	Cost	Total depreciation	NBV
	£	£	£
Machinery	52,270	29,777	22,493
Office furniture	3,180	1,649	1,531
	55,450	31,426	24,024

10.7 Jessop Printing Company

(a)

The Journal

Date	Details	Dr	Cr
2002		£	£
Apr 1	Computer equipment account	12,000	
	VAT account	2,100	
	Bank account		14,100
	Machinery account	20,000	
	VAT account	3,500	
	Bank account		23,500
Oct 1	Furniture and fittings account	8,000	
	VAT account	1,400	
	Bank account		9,400
2003			
Mar 31	Profit and loss account	6,000	
	Provision for depreciation – Computer equipment account		6,000
Mar 31	Profit and loss account	4,000	
	Provision for depreciation – Machinery account		4,000
Mar 31	Profit and loss account	800	
	Provision for depreciation – Fixtures and fittings account		800

(b)

Dr   **Computer Equipment Account**   Cr

2002		£	*2003*		£
Apr 1	Bank	12,000	Mar 31	Balance c/d	12,000
2003			*2004*		
Apr 1	Balance b/d	12,000	Mar 31	Balance c/d	12,000
2004					
Apr 1	Balance b/d	12,000			

Dr   **Machinery Account**   Cr

2002		£	*2003*		£
Apr 1	Bank	20,000	Mar 31	Balance c/d	20,000
2003			*2004*		
Apr 1	Balance b/d	20,000	Mar 31	Balance c/d	20,000
2004					
Apr 1	Balance b/d	20,000			

Dr   **Furniture and Fittings Account**   Cr

2002		£	*2003*		£
Oct 1	Bank	8,000	Mar 31	Balance c/d	8,000
2003			*2004*		
Apr 1	Balance b/d	8,000	Mar 31	Balance c/d	8,000
2004					
Apr 1	Balance b/d	8,000			

Dr — **VAT Account** — **Cr**

2002		£	2002		£
Apr 1	Bank (computer)	2,100	Oct 31	Balance c/d	7,000
1	Bank (machinery)	3,500			
Oct 1	Bank (furniture)	1,400			
		7,000			7,000
Nov 1	Balance b/d	7,000			

(e)

Provision for Depreciation
Dr — **Computer Equipment Account** — **Cr**

2003		£	2003		£
Mar 31	Balance c/d	6,000	Mar 31	Profit and loss	6,000
2004			2003		
Mar 31	Balance c/d	9,000	Apr 1	Balance b/d	6,000
			2004		
			Mar 31	Profit and loss	3,000
		9,000			9,000
			2004		
			Apr 1	Balance b/d	9,000

Provision for Depreciation
Dr — **Machinery Account** — **Cr**

2003		£	2003		£
Mar 31	Balance c/d	4,000	Mar 31	Profit and loss	4,000
2004			2003		
Mar 31	Balance c/d	8,000	Apr 1	Balance b/d	4,000
			2004		
			Mar 31	Profit and loss	4,000
		8,000			8,000
			2004		
			Apr 1	Balance b/d	8,000

Provision for Depreciation
Dr — **Furniture and Fittings Account** — **Cr**

2003		£	2003		£
Mar 31	Balance c/d	800	Mar 31	Profit and loss	800
2004			2003		
Mar 31	Balance c/d	2,400	Apr 1	Balance b/d	800
			2004		
			Mar 31	Profit and loss	1,600
		2,400			2,400
			2004		
			Apr 1	Balance b/d	2,400

(d)

Balance Sheet (extracts) as at 31 March

	Cost	Total depreciation	NBV
	£	£	£
2003			
Computer equipment	12,000	6,000	6,000
Machinery	20,000	4,000	16,000
Furniture and fittings	8,000	800	7,200
	40,000	10,800	29,200
2004			
Computer equipment	12,000	9,000	3,000
Machinery	20,000	8,000	12,000
Furniture and fittings	8,000	2,400	5,600
	40,000	19,400	20,600

Workings – Depreciation

Computer equipment – 50% reducing balance method

2003	Cost 12,000 (50% of 12,000) =	6,000
2004	50% of (12,000 – 6,000 = 6,000) =	3,000

Machinery – 20% straight line method

2003	20% of cost 20,000 =	4,000
2004	20% of cost 20,000 =	4,000

Furniture and fittings – 20% straight line method

2003	Cost 8,000 therefore 20% of 8,000 × 6 months =	800
2004	20% of 8,000	1,600

Chapter 11 — Bad debts and provision for bad debts

11.1 Data Computer Services

Dr		Bad Debts Account			Cr
2004		£	*2004*		£
Apr 30	H Gordon	1,110	Dec 31 Profit and loss		1,870
Aug 31	D Bellamy	640			
Oct 31	J Alderton	120			
		1,870			1,870

Dr	Provision for Bad Debts Account		Cr
		2004	
		Dec 31 Profit and loss	2,200

Profit and Loss Account
for the year ended 31 December 2004 (extracts)

Gross profit		xxx
Less Expenses:		
Bad debts written off	1,870	
Provision for bad debts	2,200	4,070

Balance Sheet as at 31 December 2004 (extract)

Debtors	68,500	
Less Provision for bad debts	2,200	66,300

11.2 (a)

Dr		Bad Debts Account			Cr
2003			*2003*		
Dec 31	Various debts	540	Dec 31	Profit and loss	540

(b)

Dr		Provision for Bad Debts Account			Cr
2003			*2003*		
Dec 31	Balance c/d	3,100	Jan 1	Balance b/f	2,600
			Dec 31	Profit and loss	500
		3,100			3,100
			2004		
			Jan 1	Balance b/d	3,100

(c)

Profit and Loss Account
for the year ended 31 December 2003 (extract)

Gross profit		xxx
Less Expenses:		
Bad debts written off	540	
Increase in provision for bad debts	500	1,040

(d)

Balance Sheet as at 31 December 2003 (extract)

Debtors	62,000	
Less Provision for bad debts	3,100	58,900

11.3 (i)

Dr		Bad Debts Account			Cr
2006			*2006*		
Aug 31	W Beet	85	Dec 31	Profit and loss	225
Sep 30	S Avon	140			
		225			225
2007			*2007*		
Feb 28	L J Friend	180	Dec 31	Profit and loss	490
Aug 31	N Kelly	60			
Nov 30	A Oliver	250			
		490			490

Dr		Provision for Bad Debts Account			Cr
2006			*2006*		
Dec 31	Balance c/d	550	Dec 31	Profit and loss	550
2007			*2007*		
Dec 31	Balance c/d	600	Jan 1	Balance b/d	550
			Dec 31	Profit and loss	50
		600			600

(ii)

Balance Sheet (extracts)

		2006		2007
Debtors		40,500		47,300
Less Provision for bad debts		550	39,950	600	46,700

11.5

Date *31 Dec*	Total *debtors*	Profit and *loss*	Dr/Cr	Final figure *for balance sheet*
2003	7,000	70	Dr	6,930 (net)
2004	8,000	10	Dr	7,920 (net)
2005	6,000	20	Cr	5,940 (net)
2006	7,000	10	Dr	6,930 (net)

11.7 (a) (i)

Dr			Provision for Bad Debts Account			Cr
2004			*2004*			
Dec 31	Balance c/d	3,000	Jan 1	Balance b/d	2,500	
			Dec 31	Profit and loss a/c	500	
		3,000			3,000	
2005			*2005*			
Dec 31	Profit and loss a/c	1,000	Jan 1	Balance b/d	3,000	
31	Balance c/d	2,000				
		3,000			3,000	
2006			*2006*			
Dec 31	Balance c/d	2,000	Jan 1	Balance b/d	2,000	
		2,000			2,000	
			2007			
			Jan 1	Balance b/d	2,000	

(a) (ii)

Profit and Loss Accounts
for the year ended 31 December (extracts)

2004	
Gross profit	xxx
Less Expenses:	
Increase in provision for bad debts	500
	xxx
2005	
Gross profit	xxx
Add Reduction in provision for bad debts	1,000
	xxx

2006
Gross profit
Since there is no change to the provision for bad debts
this year, no entry is required in the profit and loss account.

(a) (iii)

Balance Sheet as at 31 December (extracts)

2004		
Debtors	60,000	
Less Provision for bad debts	3,000	57,000
2005		
Debtors	40,000	
Less Provision for bad debts	2,000	38,000
2006		
Debtors	40,000	
Less Provision for bad debts	2,000	38,000

(b) When a debt is owed to a business and eventually it is evident that the debtor is unlikely to pay, then the business writes the debt off as bad. A provision for bad debts is an amount set aside as a provision for debts that are likely to remain unpaid by some of the firm's current debtors.

The provision is deducted from the debtors in the balance sheet to show the amount expected to be received from the debtors.

(c) Since many business transactions are carried out on a credit basis, then the risk of non-payment of some outstanding monies increases. Businesses have to accept this risk but in so doing often set aside a certain percentage of the outstanding debts in a "provision for bad debts account" to provide for any non-payment. The figure of debtors appearing in the balance sheet shows the figure of net debtors, after deduction of the provision. This therefore complies with the prudence concept.

11.8 (days and months omitted)

(a)

Bad Debts Account

2007	Debtors	1,200	*2007*	Profit and loss	1,200
2008	Debtors	1,600	*2008*	Profit and loss	1,600
2009	Debtors	2,350	*2009*	Profit and loss	2,350

(b)

Bad Debts Recovered Account

2008	Profit and loss	350	*2008*	Mrs P lles	350
2009	Profit and loss	150	*2009*	Debtor	150

(c)

Provision for Bad Debts Account

			2007	Profit and loss	2,000
2008	Balance c/d	2,800	*2008*	Profit and loss	800
		2,800			2,800
2009	Profit and loss	700	*2009*	Balance b/d	2,800
2009	Balance c/d	2,100			
		2,800			2,800

(d)

Profit and Loss Account (extracts)

2007		
Gross profit b/d		xxx
Less Expenses:		
Bad debts written off	1,200	
Provision for bad debts	2,000	3,200
2008		
Gross profit b/d		xxx
Add Bad debt recovered		350
		xxx
Less Expenses:		
Bad debts written off	1,600	
Increase in provision for bad debts	800	2,400
2009		
Gross profit b/d		xxx
Add Bad debt recovered		150
Reduction in provision for bad debts		700
		xxx
Less Bad debts written off	2,350	2,350

Chapter 12   Other adjustments for final accounts

12.1   C Homer

(a)

Rent Account

2008			2008		
Dec 31	Bank	1,600	Dec 31	Profit and loss	2,000
31	Owing c/d	400			
		2,000			2,000
			2009		
			Jan 1	Owing b/d	400

(b)

Insurance Account

2008			2008		
Dec 31	Bank	900	Dec 31	Profit and loss	635
			31	Prepaid c/d	265
		900			900
2008					
Jan 1	Prepaid b/d	265			

(c)

Motor Expenses Account

2008			2008		
Dec 31	Bank	7,215	Dec 31	Profit and loss	7,381
31	Owing c/d	166			
		7,381			7,381
			2009		
			Jan 1	Owing b/d	166

(d)

Rates Account

2008			2008		
Jan 1	Bank	750	Dec 31	Profit and loss	1,500
Jul 1	Bank	1,125	31	Prepaid c/d	375
		1,875			1,875
2009					
Jan 1	Prepaid b/d	375			

(e)

Rents Receivable Account

2008			2008		
Dec 31	Profit and loss	4,800	Apr 15	Bank	2,000
31	In advance c/d	1,600	Dec 15	Bank	4,400
		6,400			6,400
			2009		
			Jan 1	In advance b/d	1,600

12.2 H Saunders

(a)

Motor Expenses Account

2006			2006		
Dec 31	Cash and bank	744	Dec 31	Profit and loss	772
31	Owing c/d	28			
		772			772
			2007		
			Jan 1	Owing b/d	28

(b)

Insurance Account

2006			2006		
Dec 31	Cash and bank	420	Dec 31	Prepaid c/d	35
			31	Profit and loss	385
		420			420
2007					
Jan 1	Prepaid b/d	35			

(c)

Stationery Account

2006			2006		
Dec 31	Cash and bank	1,800	Jan 1	Owing b/f	250
31	Owing c/d	490	Dec 31	Profit and loss	2,040
		2,290			2,290
			2007		
			Jan 1	Owing b/d	490

(d)

Rates Account

2006			2006		
Jan 1	Prepaid b/f	220	Dec 31	Prepaid c/d	290
Dec 31	Cash and bank	950	31	Profit and loss	880
		1,170			1,170
2007					
Jan 1	Prepaid b/d	290			

(e)

Rent Received Account

2006			2006		
Jan 1	Owing b/f	180	Dec 31	Cash and bank	550
Dec 31	Profit and loss	580	31	Owing c/d	210
		760			760
2007					
Jan 1	Owing b/d	210			

12.5   M Baldock

Rates Account

2008			2008		
Jan 1	Balance b/d	104	Dec 31	Profit and loss	1,229
Dec 31	Bank	1,500	31	Prepaid c/d	375
		1,604			1,604

Packing Materials Account

2008			2008		
Jan 1	Balance b/d	629	Dec 31	Profit and loss	5,499
Dec 31	Bank	5,283	31	Cash: Scrap	172
31	Owing c/d	357	31	Stock c/d	598
		6,269			6,269

12.7

S Bayley
Trading and Profit and Loss Account
for the year ended 31 March 2007

	£	£
Sales		197,400
Less Cost of goods sold		
Opening stock	29,700	
Add Purchases	112,800	
	142,500	
Less Closing stock	35,100	107,400
Gross profit		90,000
Add Discounts received		3,600
		93,600
Less Expenses		
Wages and salaries (25,800 + 900)	26,700	
Rent (10,200 − 1,400)	8,800	
Discounts allowed	6,900	
Motor expenses (4,500 + 600)	5,100	
Bad debts written off	910	
Lighting and heating	1,550	
General expenses	5,640	
Increase in provision for bad debts	600	
Depreciation: Office equipment	1,800	
Motor vans	4,800	62,800
Net profit		30,800

S Bayley
Balance Sheet as at 31 March 2007

		Cost	Total depreciation	NBV
Fixed assets		£	£	£
Office equipment		14,400	1,800	12,600
Motor vans		24,000	4,800	19,200
		38,400	6,600	31,800
Current assets				
Stock		35,100		
Debtors	49,200			
Less Prov'n for bad debts	3,300	45,900		
Prepaid expenses		1,400		
Cash at bank		11,400		
Cash in hand		2,100	95,900	
Less Current liabilities				
Creditors		24,900		
Expenses owing		1,500	26,400	
Net current assets				69,500
				101,300
Financed by				
Capital				99,000
Add Net profit				30,800
				129,800
Less Drawings				28,500
				101,300

Chapter 13 ## Stock valuation

13.1 **(i)** FIFO Closing stock 20 × £40 = £800

(ii)

LIFO	Received	Issued	Stock after each transaction		
Jan	10 × £30		10 × £30	300	
Mar	10 × £34		10 × £30	300	
			10 × £34	340	640
Apr		8 × £34	10 × £30	300	
			2 × £34	68	368
Sep	20 × £40		10 × £30	300	
			2 × £34	68	
			20 × £40	800	1,168
Dec		12 × £40	10 × £30	300	
			2 × £34	68	
			8 × £40	320	688

(iii)

AVCO	Received	Issued	Average cost per unit stock held	No. of units in stock	Total value of stock
Jan	10 × £30		£30	10	£300
Mar	10 × £34		£32	20	£640
Apr		8	£32	12	£384
Sep	20 × £40		£37	32	£1,184
Dec		12	£37	20	£740

13.2

Trading Account for the year ended 31 December 2001

	FIFO	LIFO	AVCO			(All methods)	
Purchases	1,440	1,440	1,440	Sales	8 × £46	368	
Less Closing							
stock	800	688	740		12 × £56	672	1,040
Cost of goods							
sold	640	752	700				
Gross profit	400	288	340				
	1,040	1,040	1,040				1,040

13.5

D.C. Ltd
Stock Valuation as on 31 December 2008

				£
Value at 8.1.2009				50,850
Add	(a)	Error in calculation (1,600 − 160)	1,440	
	(b)	Sales at cost (500 − 100)	400	
	(d)	Casting error (4,299 − 2,499)	1,800	3,640
				54,490
Less	(c)	Reduce to N.R.V. (560 − 425)		135
Corrected value of stock at 31.12.2008				54,355

13.6 **(a)** **(i)** This year's profit would be overstated by £5,000.

(ii) Next year's profit would be understated by £5,000.

		£
(b)	Value of closing stock 30 June 2003	72,050
(i)	Reduction in value of videos to net realisable value 5 × £50	250
		71,800
(ii)	Music centre cost £500, repairs £100	100
		71,700

13.8 **(a)**

		£	£
(i)	Value of closing stock		43,795
	2 × £175 (cost price)	350	
	Net realisable value:		
	2 × £140	280	
	Less Repairs	35	245
	Therefore reduction in value of stock of 2 items		105
			43,690
			£
(ii)	Value of closing stock		107,300
	Less Reduction in value of stock (2,300 − 1,800)		500
			106,800

(b) **(i)** Decrease profit.

(ii) The concept of consistency.

Chapter 14

The journal

14.1

The Journal

Date	Details	Dr	Cr
2002		£	£
Jan 1	Computer	4,000	
	Data Systems Ltd		4,000
Jan 5	Drawings	120	
	Purchases		120
Jan 8	Bad debts	220	
	J Oddy		220
Jan 15	Motor vehicle	15,500	
	Smithy Garage		15,500
Jan 29	Office furniture and fittings	250	
	J Street		250

14.3 (i)

The Journal

		Dr	Cr
(a)	Suspense	3,000	
	Sales		3,000
	Correction of error sales day book undercast by £3,000		
(b)	Purchases	1,147	
	Dawson & Co.		1,147
	Goods purchased on credit from Dawson & Co.		
(c)	Motor repairs	585	
	Motor vehicles		585
	Motor repairs posted in error to motor vehicles account		
(d)	J Greenway	675	
	J Green		675
	Goods sold on credit to J Greenway posted in error to J Green's account		
(e)	Suspense	150	
	Electricity		150
	Payment of electricity account incorrectly debited £150 too much		
(f)	Suspense	2,250	
	Teape Ltd		2,250
	Payment of £2,250 received from Teape Ltd not credited to their account		

14.3 (ii)

Philip Hogan
Suspense Account

	£		£
Sales (a)	3,000	Balance b/d	5,400
Electricity (c)	150		
Teape Ltd (f)	2,250		
	5,400		5,400

Note that items (b), (c) and (d) do not pass through the suspense account, as they did not affect the balancing of the books.

	Dr £	Cr £
Drawings	2,800	
Stock	2,597	
Debtors (2,130 – 6)	2,124	
Furniture (1,750 + 120)	1,870	
Cash	1,020	
Returns inwards	85	
Business expenses	950	
Purchases (4,380 – 120)	4,260	
Discounts allowed	38	
Capital		5,500
Creditors (2,735 – 75)		2,660
Sales (7,430 + 108)		7,538
Discounts received		46
	15,744	15,744

14.5   **(i)** The Journal

		Dr	Cr
(a)	Returns inwards	100	
	Suspense		100
(b)	Drawings	80	
	Wages		80
(c)	Carriage inwards	75	
	Carriage outwards		75
(d)	Bank charges	270	
	Suspense		270
(e)	Sales ledger control (K Abbott)	385	
	Sales		385
(f)	Discounts allowed (2 × 218)	436	
	Suspense		436
(g)	Suspense	200	
	Rent		200
(h)	Purchases (24,897 – 24,798)	99	
	Suspense		99

(ii) Suspense Account

	£		£
Balance b/f	705	(a) Returns in	100
(g) Rent	200	(d) Bank charges	270
		(f) Discounts received	436
		(h) Purchases	99
	905		905

(iii)

Original incorrect gross profit				129,487
Add	(e)	Sales omitted		385
				129,872

Less	(a)	Returns in omitted	100	
	(c)	Carriage in understated	75	
	(h)	Purchases understated	99	274
				129,598

Original net profit			77,220
Add	Increase in gross profit, i.e. it also		
	increases net profit (129,598 – 129,487)		111
			77,331

Add	(b)	Wages overstated	80	
	(c)	Carriage outwards overstated	75	
	(g)	Rent rebate omitted	200	355
				77,686

Less	(d)	Bank charges omitted	270	
	(f)	Discounts allowed understated	436	706
Corrected figure of net profit				76,980

Chapter 15   Control accounts and reconciliation of ledger accounts

15.1

Sales Ledger Control Account

	£		£
Balances b/f	4,936	Returns inwards	1,139
Sales journal	49,916	Cheques and cash	46,490
		Discounts allowed	1,455
		Balances c/d	5,768
	54,852		54,852

15.3

Sales Ledger Control Account

2005		£	2005		£
May 1	Balances b/f	6,420	May 31	Cash and bank	10,370
31	Sales	12,800	31	Discounts allowed	395
31	Balances c/d	50	31	Set-offs:	
				Purchases ledger	145
			31	Balances c/d	8,360
		19,270			19,270

15.5

Purchases Ledger Control Account

	£		£
Returns outwards	2,648	Balances b/f	11,874
Bank	146,100	Purchases journal	154,562
Petty cash	78		
Discounts received	2,134		
Set-offs against sales ledger	1,036		
Balances c/d	14,530		
	*166,526		*166,436
* Difference between two sides	90		

Sales Ledger Control Account

	£		£
Balances b/f	19,744	Returns inwards	4,556
Sales journal	199,662	Bank and cash	185,960
		Discounts allowed	5,830
		Set-offs against purchase ledger	1,036
		Balances c/d	22,024
	219,406		219,406

Chapter 16   The extended trial balance

16.1

D Ford
Trial Balance as at 31 December 2003

	Dr £	Cr £
Sales		26,950
Purchases	20,300	
Rent	1,680	
Electricity	1,050	
Office equipment	3,500	
Debtors	4,760	
Creditors		6,300
Balance at bank	10,570	
Cash in hand	140	
Drawings	4,900	
Capital		14,000
Sundry expenses	350	
	47,250	47,250

16.3

G Brammer
Trial Balance as at 31 December 2002

	Dr £	Cr £
Capital		100,000
Premises	66,250	
Motor vehicle	17,000	
Office equipment	2,438	
Wages	19,637	
Purchases	37,455	
Sales		56,170
Commission received		1,050
Electricity	925	
Telephone	1,125	
Motor expenses	1,500	
Printing, stationery and advertising	2,050	
Creditors		8,500
Debtors	12,012	
General expenses	2,371	
Bank overdraft		3,505
Drawings	6,462	
	169,225	169,225

16.5 J Steadman – Extended trial balance as at 31 January 2003

	Description	Ledger Balances Dr £	Ledger Balances Cr £	Adjustments Dr £	Adjustments Cr £	Profit and Loss Dr £	Profit and Loss Cr £	Balance Sheet Dr £	Balance Sheet Cr £
BS	Capital		58,260						58,260
BS	Equipment	11,250						11,250	
BS	Furniture and fittings	6,000						6,000	
BS	Motor vehicles	17,370						17,370	
PL	Sales		96,030				96,030		
PL	Purchases	59,220				59,220			
BS	Cash at bank	750						750	
PL	General expenses	1,800				1,800			
PL	Wages	17,820		(a) 351		18,171			
PL	Rent, rates and insurance	7,650			(b) 600	7,050			
PL	Heating and lighting	2,100				2,100			
BS	Debtors	24,000						24,000	
BS	Creditors		10,800						10,800
PL	Stock 1 February 2002	17,130				17,130			
		165,090	165,090						
BS	Accrual – Wages				(a) 351				351
BS	Prepayment – Insurance			(b) 600				600	
BS	Stock – 31 January 2003			(c) 14,730				14,730	
PL	Stock – 31 January 2003				(c) 14,730		14,730		
				15,681	15,681				
	Net profit					5,289			5,289
						110,760	110,760	74,700	74,700

16.6 Rigby & Co. – Extended trial balance as at 31 July 2006

	Description	Ledger Balances Dr £	Ledger Balances Cr £	Adjustments Dr £	Adjustments Cr £	Profit and Loss Dr £	Profit and Loss Cr £	Balance Sheet Dr £	Balance Sheet Cr £
PL	Stock 1 August 2005	29,150				29,150			
PL	Purchases	243,800				243,800			
PL	Sales		509,450				509,450		
PL	Returns inwards	3,805				3,805			
PL	Returns outwards		2,655				2,655		
PL	Discounts allowed	6,620				6,620			
PL	Discounts received		5,750				5,750		
PL	Wages and salaries	76,500				76,500			
PL	Lighting and heating	9,250				9,250			
PL	Telephone, stationery and advertising	13,600				13,600			
PL	Motor expenses	10,500		(a) 200		10,700			
PL	General expenses	3,005				3,005			
PL	Rates and insurance	15,000			(b) 3,500	11,500			
BS	Motor vehicles (cost)	20,000						20,000	
BS	Accumulated depreciation		5,000		(d) 5,000				10,000
BS	Fixtures and fittings (cost)	22,100						22,100	
BS	Accumulated depreciation		9,945		(d) 3,315				13,260
BS	Creditors		21,900						21,900
BS	Debtors	31,700						31,700	
BS	Drawings	22,325						22,325	
BS	Cash in hand	995						995	
BS	Cash at bank	10,985						10,985	
BS	Capital		114,635						114,635
BS	Land and buildings	150,000						150,000	
		669,335	669,335						
BS	Accrual – Motor expenses				(a) 200				200
BS	Prepayment – Insurance			(b) 3,500				3,500	
BS	Stock – 31 July 2006			(c) 30,700				30,700	
PL	Stock – 31 July 2006				(c) 30,700		30,700		
PL	Depreciation – Motor vehicles			(d) 5,000		5,000			
PL	Depreciation – Fixtures and fittings			(d) 3,315		3,315			
				42,715	42,715				
	Net profit					132,310			132,310
						548,555	548,555	292,305	292,305

16.7 (i)   Workings

(a)   Rent: 1.5.2008 to 31.7.2008 = 3 months × 1,500 =   4,500
                1.8.2008 to 30.8.2009 = 9 months × 1,600 =   14,400
                                                                            18,900
          Rent paid during year   17,300
          Rent owing at 30.4.2009   1,600

(b)   Insurance paid in advance – 100

(c)   Depreciation:
          Motor vehicles = 20% SLM – 20% of £60,800 =   12,160
          Fixtures and fittings = 10% RBM = F & F cost   40,380
          Less Depreciation to date   21,600
          Net book value   18,780
          Therefore 10% of £18,780 =   1,878

(d)   Increase in provision for bad debts to 2% of debtors
                = 2% of £56,850 (new provision) =   1,137
          Less Old provision =   1,050
          Therefore increase =   87

(e)   Stock valuation 30.4.2009   £119,360
          Less Reduction in value of old stock
                3,660 – 2,060 =   1,600
          Less Badly damaged car door =   60   1,660
          New stock valuation 30.4.2009   £117,700

(f)   Debit – Creditors control   £235
          Credit – Purchases returns   £200
          Credit – VAT   £35

16.7(ii) Automania – Extended trial balance as at 30 April 2009

	Description	Ledger Balances Dr £	Ledger Balances Cr £	Adjustments Dr £	Adjustments Cr £	Profit and Loss Dr £	Profit and Loss Cr £	Balance Sheet Dr £	Balance Sheet Cr £
BS	Capital		135,000						135,000
BS	Drawings	42,150						42,150	
PL	Rent	17,300		1,600		18,900			
PL	Purchases	606,600				606,600			
PL	Sales		857,300				857,300		
PL	Sales returns	2,400				2,400			
PL	Purchases returns		1,260		200		1,460		
PL	Salaries and wages	136,970				136,970			
BS	Motor vehicles (MV) at cost	60,800						60,800	
BS	Provision for depreciation (MV)		16,740		12,160				28,900
	Fixtures and fittings (F & F) at cost	40,380						40,380	
	Provision for depreciation (F & F)		21,600		1,878				23,478
	Bank		3,170						3,170
	Cash	2,100						2,100	
	Lighting and heating	4,700				4,700			
	VAT		9,200		35				9,235
	Stock 1 May 2008	116,100				116,100			
	Bad debts	1,410				1,410			
	Provision for bad debts		1,050		87				1,137
	Debtors control account	56,850		*235				56,850	
	Creditors control account		50,550						50,315
	Sundry expenses	6,810				6,810			
	Insurance	1,300			100	1,200			
		1,095,870	1,095,870						
	Accruals				1,600				1,600
	Prepayments			100				100	
	Depreciation – Motor vehicles			12,160		12,160			
	Depreciation – Fixtures & fittings			1,878		1,878			
	Provision for bad debts – Adjustment			87		87			
	Closing stock – Profit and loss				117,700		117,700		
	Closing stock – Balance sheet			117,700				117,700	
				133,760	133,760				
	Net profit					67,245			67,245
						976,460	976,460	320,080	320,080

* Note: Made up of £200 purchases returns plus VAT £35 = £235

Chapter 17   Bank reconciliation statements

17.1

Dr			Cash Book			Cr
2009		£	*2009*			£
Mar 31	Balance b/d	9,740	Mar 31	Bank charges		70
31	Credit transfer:		31	Direct Debit:		
	E Mayall	473		Rent-Equip		138
			31	Balance c/d		10,005
		10,213				10,213
Apr 1	Balance b/d	10,005				

Bank Reconciliation Statement as at 31 March 2009

		£
Balance per cash book		10,005
Add Unpresented cheques:		
J Mason	92	
T Black	200	292
		10,297
Less Bankings not yet entered on bank statement		1,515
Balance per bank statement		8,782

17.2 (a)

Dr			Cash Book		Cr
		£			£
Dec 31	Balance b/d	9,155	Dec 31 Bank charges		110
31	Credit transfer:		31 Balance c/d		9,315
	P Todd	270			
		9,425			9,425
Jan 1	Balance b/d	9,315			

(b)

Bank Reconciliation Statement as at 31 December 2009

	£
Balance as per cash book	9,315
Add Unpresented cheque	575
	9,890
Less Bankings not yet on bank statement (945 + 300 + 890)	2,135
Balance per bank statement	7,755

OR

Bank Reconciliation Statement as at 31 December 2009

	£
Balance as per bank statement	7,755
Add Bankings not yet on bank statement (945 + 300 + 890)	2,135
	9,890
Less Unpresented cheque	575
Balance per cash book	9,315

17.4 (a)

Dr			Cash Book			Cr
		£				£
2006	(Totals so far)	737	2006	(Totals so far)		6,017
Mar 31	M Turnbull	57	Mar 31	BKS		49
31	Balance c/d	5,300	31	Bank charges		28
		6,094				6,094

(b) Bank Reconciliation Statement as at 31 March 2006

	£
Overdraft per cash book	5,300
Add Bankings not yet in bank statement	160
	5,460
Less Unpresented cheques	490
Overdraft per bank statement	4,970

17.6 (a) Reconciliation of Opening Balance

	£
Balance per cash book	1,620 O/D
Add Unpresented cheque: No. 351	279
	1,899
Less Credit received (already in cash book)	4,482
Overdraft per bank statement	2,583 O/D

(b)

Dr			Cash Book		Cr
2005		£	2005		£
Nov 8	BACS: Credit		Nov 30	Balance b/d	4,364
	Atlas Co.	270	24	S/O Grove Insurance	108
30	Balance c/d	4,402	29	Dishonoured cheque:	
				P Ash	57
			30	Bank charges	143
		4,672			4,672
			Dec 1	Balance b/d	4,402

(c) Bank Reconciliation Statement as at 30 November 2005

		£
Balance in hand as per cash book		4,402 O/D
Add Unpresented cheques:		
Cheque No. 421	1,092	
425	117	
427	758	
430	4,170	
431	137	
432	874	
433	1,947	9,095
		4,693
Less Cheques banked not yet		
entered on bank statement	864	
	1,260	2,124
Balance per bank statement		2,569

Chapter 18

Single entry and incomplete records

18.1

R Stubbs
Trading Account for the year ended 31 December 2009

		£	£
Sales			60,000
Less Cost of goods sold			
Stock 1.1.2009		9,872	
Add Purchases	(D)	50,748	
	(C)	60,620	
Less Stock 31.12.2009		12,620	
	(B)		48,000
Gross profit	(A)		12,000

Missing figures found in following order (A) to (D).

(A) Mark up is 25%. Therefore margin is 20%. Sales are 60,000 so margin is 20%
    × 60,000 = 12,000 gross profit.
(B) + (A) = 60,000. Therefore (B) + 12,000 = 60,000 and accordingly is 48,000.
(C) – 12,620 = 48,000. Therefore (C) is 60,620.
(D) + 9,872 = 60,620. Therefore (D) is 50,748.

18.3

B Arkwright
Statement of Affairs as at 31 December 2005

		£	£
Fixed assets			
Motor van at cost		2,800	
Less Depreciation		550	2,250
Current assets			
Stock		3,950	
Debtors		4,970	
Prepaid expenses		170	
Bank		2,564	
Cash		55	
		11,709	
Less Current liabilities			
Trade creditors	1,030		
Expenses owing	470	1,500	
Net current assets			10,209
Capital			12,459
Cash introduced			10,000
Add Net profit	(C)		
	(B)		
Less Drawings			5,673
	(A)		

Missing figures (A), (B) and (C) deduced in that order. (A) to balance is 12,459,
thus (B) has to be 18,132 and (C) becomes 8,132.

18.5 (a)

Dr			Total Debtors Account		Cr
2008		£	2009		£
Apr 1	Balances b/d	2,980	Mar 31	Cash	10,820
2009					
Mar 31	Sales	11,520	31	Balances	
				(difference) c/d	3,680
		14,500			14,500

Dr			Total Creditors Account		Cr
2009		£	2008		£
Mar 31	Cash	7,780	Apr 1	Balances b/d	1,880
31	Balances				
	(difference) c/d	2,220	2009		
			Mar 31	Purchases	8,120
		10,000			10,000

(b)

A Hanson
Calculation of Capital as at 31 March 2008
and 31 March 2009

	31.3.2008	31.3.2009
	£	£
Bank	1,460	1,740
Office furniture	600	500
Stock	2,320	2,620
Cash	60	80
Debtors	2,980	3,680
	7,420	8,620
Less Creditors	1,880	2,220
Capitals	5,540	6,400

(c)

		£
Capital 31.3.2008		5,540
Add Net profit	(B)	3,400
	(A)	8,940
Less Drawings		2,540
Capital as at 31.3.2009		6,400

By arithmetical deduction (A) is £8,940. Thus £5,540 + (B) = £8,940, i.e. (B) is £3,400.

18.7 Workings

Purchases Bank	29,487	*Sales* Banked	37,936
Cash	2,994	Cash	9,630
	32,481		47,566
− Creditors 31.12.2006	5,624	− Debtors 31.12.2006	9,031
	26,857		38,535
+ Creditors 31.12.2007	7,389	+ Debtors 31.12.2007	8,624
Purchases for 2007	34,246	Sales for 2007	47,159

Opening capital:	Bank	405	
	Stock	13,862	
	Debtors	9,031	
	Rates prepaid	210	
	Fixtures	2,500	26,008
	Less Creditors	5,624	
	Rent owing	150	5,774
			20,234

P Kelly
Trading and Profit and Loss Account
for the year ended 31 December 2007

	£	£
Sales		47,159
Less Cost of goods sold		
Opening stock	13,862	
Add Purchases	34,246	
	48,108	
Less Closing stock	15,144	32,964
Gross profit		14,195
Less Expenses		
Wages	5,472	
Rent (1,650 – 150)	1,500	
Rates (890 + 210 – 225)	875	
Sundry expenses	375	
Depreciation: Fixtures	250	8,472
Net profit		5,723

P Kelly
Balance Sheet as at 31 December 2007

Fixed assets		£	£
Fixtures at valuation		2,500	
Less Depreciation		250	2,250
Current assets			
Stock		15,144	
Debtors		8,624	
Prepayments		225	
		23,993	
Less Current liabilities			
Trade creditors	7,389		
Bank overdraft	602	7,991	
Net current assets			16,002
			18,252
Capital			
Balance at 1.1.2007			20,234
Add Net profit			5,723
			25,957
Less Drawings (1,164 + 6,541)			7,705
			18,252

18.9 (a)

Shelly Hamilton
Cash Book Summary year ended 31 December 2001

	Cash	Bank		Cash	Bank
	£	£		£	£
Capital		30,000	Trade creditors		32,250
Sales	72,240		Shop fixtures and fittings		10,500
Cash		72,006	Rent		5,500
			Salaries		12,900
			Electricity		1,823
			Insurance		1,800
			General expenses		936
			Travel agent's bill for holiday		1,140
			Drawings		12,000
			Telephone bill	84	
			Cleaning charges	150	
			Bank	72,006	
			Balance c/d		23,157
	72,240	102,006		72,240	102,006

(b)

Shelly Hamilton
Trading and Profit and Loss Account
for the year ended 31 December 2001

	£	£
Sales		72,240
Less Cost of sales		
Purchases (32,250 + 1,575)	33,825	
Less Closing stock	7,855	25,970
Gross profit		46,270
Less Expenses		
Rent (5,500 + 500)	6,000	
Salaries	12,900	
Electricity (1,823 + 234)	2,057	
Insurance (1,800 – 600)	1,200	
General expenses	936	
Telephone	84	
Cleaning	150	
Depreciation: Shop fixtures and fittings	1,050	24,377
Net profit		21,893

Shelly Hamilton
Balance Sheet as at 31 December 2001

	Cost	Total depreciation	NBV
	£	£	£
Fixed assets			
Shop fixtures and fittings	10,500	1,050	9,450
Current assets			
Stock	7,855		
Prepayment (insurance)	600		
Balance at bank	23,157	31,612	
Less Current liabilities			
Creditors	1,575		
Accruals (500 + 234)	734	2,309	
Net current assets			29,303
			38,753
Financed by			
Capital at 1.1.2002			30,000
Add Net profit			21,893
			51,893
Less Drawings (12,000 + 1,140)			13,140
			38,753

18.11 (a)   Calculation of opening capital

Jack Costagliola
Opening Statement of Affairs 1 October 2004

	Cost	Total depreciation	NBV
	£	£	£
Fixed assets			
Display equipment	10,600	1,590	9,010
Motor car	12,000	2,400	9,600
	22,600	3,990	18,610
Current assets			
Stock	10,000		
Bank	8,200		
Cash float	100	18,300	
Less Current liabilities			
Creditors	6,700	6,700	
Net current assets			11,600
			30,210
Less Long-term liability			
Loan from father			20,000
			10,210
Financed by			
Capital			10,210

(b) Calculation of bank balance as at 30 September 2005

	£
Bank balance 1 October 2004	8,200
Add Takings – Sales per (3)	112,000
	120,200
Less Payments per (1)	106,670
Bank balance 30 September 2005	13,530

(c) Cost of sales

	£
Sales	112,000
Profit margin (60% of £112,000)	67,200
Therefore cost of sales	44,800

(d)

Jack Costagliola
Trading and Profit and Loss Account
for the year ended 30 September 2005

	£	£
Sales		112,000
Less Cost of sales *(see (c))*		44,800
Gross profit		67,200
Less Expenses		
Wages	17,600	
Telephone (400 + 146)	546	
Electricity (1,250 + 96)	1,346	
Rent of shop premises	9,600	
Sundry expenses	720	
Motor expenses	1,340	
Loan interest (1,100 + 100)	1,200	
Rates and insurance	3,860	
Depreciation: Computer equipment	1,000	
Display equipment	1,590	
Motor car	2,400	41,202
Net profit		25,998

Jack Costagliola
Balance Sheet as at 30 September 2005

	Cost	Total depreciation	NBV
	£	£	£
Fixed assets			
Computer equipment	4,000	1,000	3,000
Display equipment	10,600	3,180	7,420
Motor car	12,000	4,800	7,200
	26,600	8,980	17,620
Current assets			
Stock	10,000		
Balance at bank	13,530		
Cash float	100	23,630	

Jack Costagliola
Balance Sheet as at 30 September 2005

	Cost	Total depreciation	NBV
	£	£	£
Less Current liabilities			
Creditors	1,000		
Accruals (96 + 146 + 100)	342	1,342	
Net current assets			22,288
			39,908
Less Long-term liability			
Loan from father			20,000
			19,908
Financed by			
Capital			10,210
Add Net profit			25,998
			36,208
Less Drawings (16,000 + 300)			16,300
			19,908

18.12

F Thomas
Trading Account for the period 1 January to 17 March 2002

		£	£
Sales			7,740
Less Cost of sales			
Opening stock		8,640	
Add Purchases		4,530	
		13,170	
Less Closing stock	(C)	6,720	
Cost of goods sold	(B)		6,450
Gross profit	(A)		1,290

Workings

Gross profit percentage last year $= \dfrac{4,500}{27,000} \times \dfrac{100}{1} = 16.66\%$ or 1/6

So (A) Gross profit = 1/6th of 7,740 = 1,290

(B) is therefore 7,740 − 1,290 = 6,450

(C) is therefore 13,170 − 6,450 = 6,720

Of the £6,720 stock owned by Thomas, £360 was in transit and thus not destroyed by fire.

Stock at cost lost in fire − £6,720 − 360 = £6,360

Chapter 19 Club and society accounts

19.1 (a) Accumulated fund as at 1 January 2004

	£
Equipment	500
Bank balance	186
	686

(b)

Uppertown Football Club
Income and Expenditure Account
for the year ended 31 December 2004

	£	£
Income		
Collections at matches		1,650
Profit on refreshments		315
		1,965
Less Expenditure		
Rent for pitch (300 − 60)	240	
Printing and stationery (65 + 33)	98	
Secretary's expenses	144	
Repairs to equipment	46	
Groundsman's wages	520	
Miscellaneous expenses	66	
Depreciation of equipment	125	1,239
Surplus of income over expenditure		726

(c)

Uppertown Football Club
Balance Sheet as at 31 December 2004

	Cost	Total depreciation	NBV
Fixed assets	£	£	£
Equipment (500 + 125)	625	125	500
Current assets			
Prepayment		60	
Cash		879	
		939	
Less Current liabilities			
Expenses owing		33	
Net current assets			906
			1,406
Financed by			
Accumulated Fund			
Balance at 1.1.2004 (500 + 180)			680
Add Surplus of income over expenditure			726
			1,406

19.3

Amateur Drama Society

Dr		Subscriptions Account		Cr

	£		£
In arrears b/d	235	In advance b/d	220
In advance c/d	140	Bank	2,600
Income and expenditure	2,630	In arrears c/d	185
	3,005		3,005
In arrears b/d	185	In advance b/d	140

19.4 **(a)** Subscriptions figure for income and expenditure – 420 members at £240 each = £100,800.

	£
(b) Subscriptions received 414 (420 − 6) members paying £240	99,360
Plus 8 members paying £250	2,000
Total receipts	101,360

19.5 (a)

Bradnop Golf Club
Bar Trading Account for the year ended 31 December 2008

	£	£
Sales		17,973
Less Cost of supplies sold		
Opening stock	1,764	
Add Purchases	11,658	
	13,422	
Less Closing stock	989	12,433
Gross profit		5,540
Less Wages of bar staff		2,809
Profit to income and expenditure account		2,731

(b)

Bradnop Golf Club
Income and Expenditure Account
for the year ended 31 December 2008

	£	£
Income		
Subscriptions (£18,760 − £180)		18,580
Profit on bar		2,731
Profits from raffles		4,980
		26,291
Less Expenditure		
Golf professional's salary	6,000	
Greenkeeper's wages	7,698	
General expenses	580	
Depreciation of equipment	760	15,038
Surplus of income over expenditure		11,253

Bradnop Golf Club
Balance Sheet as at 31 December 2008

	Cost	Total depreciation	NBV
	£	£	£
Fixed assets			
Clubhouse	21,000	–	21,000
Equipment	6,809	760	6,049
	27,809	760	27,049
Current assets			
Bar stocks		989	
Bank		1,570	
		2,559	
Less Current liabilities			
Subscriptions received in advance		180	
Net current assets			2,379
			29,428
Financed by			
Accumulated Fund			
Balance at 1.1.2008			18,175
Add Surplus of income over expenditure			11,253
			29,428

19.7 (a)

City Sports Club
Coffee Bar Trading Account for the year ended 31 December 2008

	£	£
Takings		2,798
Less Cost of supplies		
Opening stock	59	
Add Purchases	1,456	
	1,515	
Less Closing stock	103	1,412
Gross profit		1,386
Wages		650
Profit to income and expenditure		736

(b) Accumulated fund as at 1 January 2007

Equipment 2,788 + stock 59 + bank 1,298 = 4,145

(c)

City Sports Club
Income and Expenditure Account
for the year ended 31 December 2007

	£	£
Income		
Subscriptions (3,790 + 29)		3,819
Coffee bar profit		736
Profits from dances		186
Profit on exhibition		112
		4,853
Less Expenditure		
Wages (1,776 – 650)	1,126	
Rent of rooms	887	
Travelling expenses of teams	673	
Depreciation of equipment	279	
Loss on equipment sold	11	2,976
Surplus of income over expenditure		1,877

City Sports Club
Balance Sheet as at 31 December 2007

	£	£
Fixed assets		
Equipment (2,711 + 565)	3,276	
Less Depreciation	279	2,997
Current assets		
Coffee bar stock	103	
Debtors for subscriptions	29	
Bank	2,893	3,025
		6,022
Financed by		
Accumulated Fund		
Balance at 1 January 2007		4,145
Add Surplus for the year		1,877
		6,022

19.9 (a)

Carron Social Club
Calculation of accumulated fund as at 1 January 2005

	£
Equipment	16,000
Fixtures	2,400
Refreshment bar stocks	550
Subscriptions owing (24 × £50)	1,200
	20,150
Less Bank overdraft	1,650
	18,500

(b)

Receipts and Payments Account

Dr		**for the year ended 31 December 2005**	Cr

Receipts	£	*Payments*	£
Refreshment bar takings	8,960	Bank overdraft	1,650
Subscriptions received	30,100	Refreshment bar purchases	6,150
Donations	4,240	Rent	5,000
		Wages of bar staff	1,880
		New equipment	9,000
		Insurance	1,570
		Affiliation fees	360
		Transport expenses	7,140
		Wages of ground staff	9,370
		Balance c/d	1,180
	43,300		43,300

(c)

Dr		**Subscriptions Account**	Cr

	£		£
In arrears b/d	1,200	Bank	30,100
Income and expenditure*	30,000	In arrears** c/d	1,100
	31,200		31,200

* 600 members × £50 = £30,000
** Balancing figure

(d)

Carron Social Club
Refreshment Bar Trading Account
for the year ended 31 December 2005

	£	£
Takings		8,960
Less Cost of goods sold		
Opening bar stocks	550	
Add Purchases	6,150	
	6,700	
Less Closing bar stocks	940	5,760
		3,200
Less Expenses		
Staff wages	1,880	1,880
Net profit		1,320

(e)

Carron Social Club
Income and Expenditure Account
for the year ended 31 December 2005

	£	£
Income		
Subscriptions		30,000
Profit on bar		1,320
Donations		4,240
		35,560
Less Expenditure		
Rent (5,000 + 1,000)	6,000	
Insurance (1,570 − 210)	1,360	
Affiliation fees	360	
Transport expenses	7,140	
Wages of ground staff	9,370	
Depreciation: Equipment	5,800	
Fixtures	600	30,630
Surplus of income over expenditure		4,930

Carron Social Club
Balance Sheet as at 31 December 2005

	Cost £	Total depreciation £	NBV £
Fixed assets			
Equipment	20,000		
Add Additions	9,000	29,000	9,800	19,200
Fixtures		3,000	1,200	1,800
		32,000	11,000	21,000
Current assets			
Refreshment bar stocks	940		
Insurance paid in advance	210		
Subscriptions in arrears	1,100		
Bank	1,180	3,430	
Less Current liabilities			
Rent owing	1,000	1,000	
Net current assets			2,430
			23,430
Accumulated Fund			
Balance 1 January 2005			18,500
Add Surplus of income over expenditure			4,930
			23,430

Chapter 20 Partnerships

20.1 (a)

Stead and Jackson
Appropriation Account for the year ended 31 December 2002

		£
Net profit		45,000
Less Salary: Jackson		5,000
		40,000
Balance of profits shared:		
Stead 1/2	20,000	
Jackson 1/2	20,000	40,000

(b)

Capital Accounts

	Stead	Jackson			Stead	Jackson
	£	£	*2002*		£	£
			Dec 31 Balance b/d		24,000	16,000

Current Accounts

		Stead	Jackson			Stead	Jackson
2002		£	£	*2002*		£	£
Dec 31	Drawings	15,000	19,000	Dec 31	Balance b/d	2,300	3,500
31	Balances c/d	7,300	9,500	31	Salary		5,000
				31	Share of profits	20,000	20,000
		22,300	28,500	*2003*		22,300	28,500
				Jan 1	Balance b/d	7,300	9,500

20.3 (a)

King, Leigh and White
Appropriation Account for the year ended 31 December 2004

		£
Net profit		50,400
Add Interest on drawings:		
King	400	
Leigh	360	
White	240	1,000
		51,400
Less Interest on capital:		
King (10% of 30,000)	3,000	
Leigh (10% of 28,000)	2,800	
White (10% of 16,000)	1,600	7,400
		44,000
Less Salary: Leigh		2,000
		42,000
Balance of profits shared:		
King 3/6ths	21,000	
Leigh 2/6ths	14,000	
White 1/6th	7,000	42,000
		–

(b)

King, Leigh and White
Balance Sheet Extract as at 31 December 2004

				£	£
Capital Accounts					
King				30,000	
Leigh				28,000	
White				16,000	74,000
Current accounts	*King*	*Leigh*	*White*		
Balance b/d	750	1,340	220		
Interest on capital	3,000	2,800	1,600		
Share of profits	21,000	14,000	7,000		
Salary	–	2,000	–		
	24,750	20,140	8,820		
Less Drawings	(8,000)	(7,200)	(4,800)		
Less Interest on drawings	(400)	(360)	(240)		
	16,350	12,580	3,780		32,710

20.5

Simpson and Young
Trading and Profit and Loss Appropriation Account
for the year ended 30 June 2003

	£	£
Sales		254,520
Less Cost of sales		
Opening stock	18,000	
Add Purchases	184,980	
	202,980	
Less Closing stock	19,000	183,980
Gross profit		70,540
Less Expenses		
Wages and salaries (32,700 + 500)	33,200	
Rent, rates and insurance (3,550 – 250)	3,300	
Electricity	980	
Stationery and printing	420	
Motor expenses	3,480	
General office expenses	1,700	
Depreciation: Motor van (16,000 × 20%)	3,200	
Office equipment (5,600 × 10%)	560	46,840
Net profit		23,700
Less Interest on capital		
Simpson (50,000 × 10%)	5,000	
Young (20,000 × 10%)	2,000	7,000
		16,700
Share of profits		
Simpson 3/5ths	10,020	
Young 2/5ths	6,680	
		16,700

Simpson and Young
Balance Sheet as at 30 June 2003

	Cost	Accumulated depreciation		NBV
	£	£		£
Fixed assets				
Premises	28,000	–		28,000
Office equipment	8,400	3,360	(W1)	5,040
Motor vans	16,000	8,200	(W2)	7,800
	52,400	11,560		40,840
Current Assets				
Stock	19,000			
Debtors	28,000			
Prepayments	250			
Cash at bank	7,250	54,500		
Less Current liabilities				
Creditors	15,200			
Accruals	500	15,700		
Net current assets				38,800
				79,640

	Simpson	Young	Total
Financed by			
Capital accounts			
Balance b/f	50,000	20,000	70,000
Current accounts			
Balance b/f	640	300	
Add Share of profit	10,020	6,680	
Add Interest on capital	5,000	2,000	
	15,660	8,980	
Less Drawings	10,000	5,000	
	5,660	3,980	9,640
			79,640

(W1) Provision for depreciation on office equipment:
     8,400 − 5,600 + 560 = 3,360
(W2) Provision for depreciation on motor vans:
     16,000 − 11,000 + 3,200 = 8,200

20.7

Mendez and Marshall
Trading and Profit and Loss Account
for the year ended 30 June 2006

			£
Sales			123,650
Less Cost of goods sold:			
Opening stock		41,979	
Add Purchases		85,416	
		127,395	
Less Closing stock		56,340	71,055
Gross profit			52,595
Add Reduction in provision for bad debts			80
			52,675
Less Salaries and wages (18,917 + 200)		19,117	
Office expenses (2,416 + 96)		2,512	
Carriage outwards		1,288	
Discounts allowed		115	
Bad debts		503	
Loan interest		4,000	
Depreciation: Fixtures	770		
Buildings	1,000	1,770	29,305
Net profit			23,370
Add Interest on drawings: Mendez		180	
Marshall		120	300
			23,670
Less Interest on capitals: Mendez	3,500		
Marshall	2,950	6,450	
Salary: Mendez		800	7,250
			16,420
Balance of profits shared: Mendez		8,210	
Marshall		8,210	16,420

Mendez and Marshall
Balance Sheet as at 30 June 2006

	Cost £	Depreciation £	NBV £
Fixed assets			
Buildings	75,000	26,000	49,000
Fixtures	11,000	4,070	6,930
	86,000	30,070	55,930
Current assets			
Stock		56,340	
Debtors	16,243		
Less Provision for bad debts	320	15,923	
Bank		677	
		72,940	
Less Current liabilities			
Creditors	11,150		
Expenses owing	296	11,446	
Net current assets			61,494
			117,424

Mendez and Marshall
Balance Sheet as at 30 June 2006

	Cost £	Depreciation £	NBV £
Less Long-term liability			
Loan from J King			40,000
			77,424
Financed by			
Capitals			
Mendez		35,000	
Marshall		29,500	64,500

Current accounts	Mendez	Marshall	
Balance 1.7.2005	1,306	298	
Add Interest on capital	3,500	2,950	
Add Salary	800		
Add Balance of profit	8,210	8,210	
	13,816	11,458	
Less Drawings	6,400	5,650	
Less Interest on drawings	180	120	
	7,236	5,688	12,924
			77,424

Chapter 21   # Manufacturing accounts

21.1

E Chandler
Manufacturing and Trading Account
for the year ended 31 March 2008

	£	£
Stock of raw material 1.4.2007		2,400
Add Purchases		21,340
Carriage inwards		321
		24,061
Less Stock of raw materials 31.3.2008		2,620
Cost of raw materials consumed		21,441
Manufacturing wages		13,280
Prime cost		34,721
Factory overhead expenses		
Rent and rates	2,300	
Power	6,220	
Other expenses	1,430	9,950
		44,671
Add Work in progress 1.4.2007		955
		45,626
Less Work in progress 31.3.2008		870
Production cost of goods completed c/d		44,756
Sales		69,830
Less Cost of goods sold		
Stock of finished goods 1.4.2007	6,724	
Add Production cost of goods completed b/d	44,756	
	51,480	
Less Stock of finished goods 31.3.2008	7,230	44,250
Gross profit		25,580

21.3

T Jackson

Manufacturing, Trading and Profit and Loss Account

for the year ended 31 December 2007

	£	£
Stock of raw materials 1.1.2007		18,450
Add Purchases		64,300
Add Carriage inwards		1,605
		84,355
Less Stock of raw materials 31.12.2007		20,210
Cost of raw materials consumed		64,145
Direct labour		65,810
Prime cost		129,955
Factory overhead expenses		
Rent ²/₃	1,800	
Fuel and power	5,920	
Depreciation: Machinery	8,300	16,020
		145,975
Add Work in progress 1.1.2007		23,600
		169,575
Less work in progress 31.12.2007		17,390
Production cost of goods completed c/d		152,185
Sales		200,600
Less Cost of goods sold		
Stock finished goods 1.1.2007	17,470	
Add Production cost of goods completed b/d	152,185	
	169,655	
Less Stock finished goods 31.12.2007	21,485	148,170
Gross profit		52,430
Less Expenses		
Office salaries	16,920	
Rent 1/3	900	
Lighting and heating	5,760	
Depreciation: Office equipment	1,950	25,530
Net profit		26,900

21.4 (a)

Chesterton & Son
Manufacturing Account for the year ended 30 April 2001

		£	£
(i)	*Cost of raw materials consumed*		
	Opening stock	17,500	
	Add Purchases	95,600	
		113,100	
	Less Closing stock	13,200	99,900
	Direct wages and salaries		138,500
(ii)	Prime cost		238,400
	Factory overhead expenses:		
	Indirect wages and salaries	27,200	
	Power and fuel (18,260 + 390)	18,650	
	Insurance (5/8 × 3,440)	2,150	
	Depreciation	11,000	59,000
(iii)	Total cost of production		297,400
	Add Work in progress 1 May 2000		15,270
			312,670
	Less Work in progress 30 April 2001		15,700
	Production cost of goods completed to trading account		296,970

(b)

Trading Account for the year ended 30 April 2001

		£	£
	Sales	410,400	
	Less Returns inwards	5,200	405,200
(i)	*Less Cost of sales of finished goods*		
	Opening stock	24,800	
	Add Production cost of goods completed	296,970	
		321,770	
	Less Closing stock	14,600	307,170
(ii)	Gross profit		98,030

Index

Account
    control 178–90
    impersonal 13, 18
    memorandum 186–9, 192
    nominal 7, 13, 18
    personal 7, 13, 18
    real 7, 13, 18
    reconciliation with ledger accounts
        191
    suspense 165, 173
Accounting
    concepts and conventions 61–3
    cycle 4, 6, 17
    definition 1
    importance/need 2
    standards 60–73, 74
Accounting bases 64, 74
Accounting concepts 60–75
    accrual concept 62–3, 74
    business entity concept 64, 74
    consistency concept 62, 63, 74
    dual aspect concept 66, 74
    going concern concept 62, 75
    historical cost concept 65, 74
    matching concept 62, 75
    materiality concept 66
    money measurement concept 65,
        75
    prudence concept 62, 63, 75
    realisation concept 64–5, 75
    time interval concept 66, 75
    substance over form concept 66, 75
Accounting Policies 64, 74
Accounting Principles 74
Accounting Standards 60–73, 74
Accounting Standards Board (ASB) 3,
        61, 67, 74
Accounting Standards Committee (ASC)
        3, 61, 67, 74
Accrued expenses 130, 138, 199–200
Accumulated fund 258, 263
Amortisation 73, 74, 85
Answers to questions 318–75
Applied research (refer to SSAP 13) 73,
        74
Appreciation 86
Assessments
    central 303–10
    practice 303–15
    specimen examination paper 311–15
Assets 16, 17, 42
    current 16, 18, 43
    depletion 74, 86, 93
    fixed 16, 17, 42
Auditors 2, 4
Authorisation of assets 90, 93

Average stock valuation (AVCO) 71, 74,
        145, 150

Bad debts 117, 125, 168, 206
    provision for 117–25
    recovered 124, 125
Balance sheet 16, 17, 40–5
    definition 40
    horizontal layout 40, 43, 52
    model layout 56
    vertical layout 44, 53
Balancing off 13, 14, 17
Bank giro credits (refer to Credit
        transfer)
Bank lodgement 219, 225
Bank overdraft 220, 225
Bank paying-in slip 7, 8, 17
Bank reconciliation statements 217, 226
Books of original entry 9, 17, 154
Budget 3, 4

Capital 16, 17, 34, 43
Capital employed 137, 138
Capital expenditure 77, 80
Capital invested 136
Capital receipts 80
Carriage 48
    inwards 48, 54, 56
    outwards 48, 54, 56
Cash book 7, 9, 17, 217–25
Cash discounts 70
Casting 25, 26
Cheque counterfoil 7, 8, 18
Club and society accounts 257–63
    accumulated fund 258, 263
    donations 262, 263
    income and expenditure accounts
        258, 263
    life membership 263
    receipts and payments accounts 257,
        264
    subscriptions 260, 264
    treasurers' responsibilities 263
Confidentiality 73
Contra entries 184, 192
Control accounts 178–90
    advantages 185
    contra entries (set-offs) 184, 192
    purchases ledger control accounts
        179–90
    sales ledger control accounts 179–90
Credit note 7, 8, 18
Credit transfer 218, 226
Creditor 7, 13, 18
Current assets 16, 18, 43
Current liabilities 16, 18, 43

Day books 7, 9, 17, 19
    purchases 7, 9, 17, 19
    returns inwards 7, 9, 17, 19, 47
    returns outwards 7, 9, 17, 19, 46
    sales 7, 9, 17, 19
Debtor 7, 13, 18
Depletion 86, 93
Depreciation 72, 74, 93, 200–9
    (refer to SSAP 12) 4, 72, 90
    amortisation 73, 74, 85
    provision for depreciation 86–7, 89,
        90, 98–112
    reducing balance method 87, 93
    residual value 72, 75
    straight line method 87, 93
    useful economic life 72, 75
Development expenditure 73, 74
    (refer to SSAP 13) 4, 72–3
Direct costs 290, 298
Direct debit 220, 226
Dishonoured cheque 221, 226
Disposal of fixed assets 90, 91, 98–112
Donations 262, 263
Double entry book keeping 7, 9, 10, 18

Expenditure 77, 78, 80
Extended trial balance 196–211

Factoring 43, 45
Factory overhead costs 290, 298
Final accounts 15
    club and society 257–63
    incomplete records 233–48
    manufacturing 295–7
    model layout 54–6
    partnership 272–84
    sole trader 54–6, 129–38
Financial statements (refer to Final
        accounts) 2, 4
Financial Reporting Standards (FRSs) 3,
        4, 62, 67
Financial Reporting Standards for
        Smaller Entities (FRSSEs) 67
First-in-first-out (FIFO) 71, 75, 144,
        150
Fixed assets 16, 17, 43
    authorisation of 90, 93
    depreciation of 83
    disposal of 91, 93
    obsolescence 93
Fixed asset register 91, 93
Fixed capital accounts 278, 284
Fluctuating capital accounts 278, 284

General ledger 18
Goods for own use 136

Gross loss 15, 16, 18, 30
Gross profit 15, 16, 18, 30

Hire purchase 93

Impersonal accounts 13, 18
Income and expenditure accounts 258, 263
Incomplete records 233–48
    goods stolen or lost by fire 245
    missing figures 243–5
    statement of affairs 238–9, 248
Interest 79
    loan 79
Interest on capital 275, 284
Interest on drawings 275, 284
Invoice 18, 78

Journal 9, 18, 154–73
    entries on disposal of assets 103

Last-in-last-out (LIFO) 71, 75
Leasing 93
Ledgers 6, 7, 12, 13, 18
    general 7, 13, 18
    nominal (refer to general) 13, 18
    purchases 13, 19, 179, 182, 187
    sales 13, 19, 179, 182, 187
Liabilities 16, 18
    long-term 16, 18, 43
Limited company 3, 4
    private company 3, 4
    public company 3, 4
Limited partners 273, 284
Loan interest 79
Long-term liabilities 16, 18

Manufacturing accounts 29, 36, 289–98
    direct costs 290, 298
    factory overhead costs 290, 298
    finished stocks 298
    indirect costs 290
    prime cost 289, 298
    production cost 289, 298
    total cost 289, 298
    unrealised profit 298
    work-in-progress 292, 298
Margin 233–6, 248
Mark-up 233–6, 248
Memorandum accounts 186–9, 192

Net book value (NBV) 93, 99
Net loss 16, 18
Net profit 16, 18
Net realisable value 70, 75, 146
Nominal accounts 7, 13, 18
Non-trading organisations
    (refer to Club and society accounts)
    3, 4, 257–63

Objectivity 61, 75
Obsolescence 93

Partnership 3, 4, 272–84
    agreement 273–6, 284
    fixed capital accounts 278, 284
    fluctuating capital accounts 278, 284
    interest on capital 275, 284
    interest on drawings 275, 284
    limited partners 273, 284

no partnership agreement 280
    Partnership Act 1890 (s 24) 280
    profit and loss appropriation account 277
    salaries 276, 284
Partnership agreement 273, 274, 284
Partnership salaries 276, 284
Personal accounts 7, 13, 18
Petty cash book 7, 9, 18
Planning/decision making 2
Practice assessments 303–15
Prepaid expenses 131, 138, 199–200
Prime cost 289, 298
Production cost 289, 298
Profit and loss account
    (refer to Final Accounts)
Profit and loss appropriation account 277
Provision for bad debts 118, 125, 200, 202
Purchases day book 9, 19, 179–90
Purchase ledger 13, 19, 177–92
Purchase ledger control account 179–90
Purchase returns
    (refer to Returns outwards)
Pure basic research
    (refer to SSAP 13) 73, 75

Real accounts 19
Receipts 7, 8, 19, 80
    capital 80
    revenue 80
Receipts and payments account 257, 264
Reconciliation of ledger accounts 191–2
Reducing method of depreciation 89, 93
Regulatory accounting system 3, 60–75
Remittance advice 191, 192
Returns inwards 46–8, 56
    day book/journal 9, 17, 19, 47
Returns outwards 46–8, 56
    day book/journal 9, 17, 19, 46
Revenue expenditure 78, 80
Revenue receipts 80

Sales day book 9, 19
Sales ledger 13, 19, 177–92
Sales ledger control account 179–90
Sales returns
    (refer to Returns inwards)
Single entry 233–48
Skeleton trial balance 210
Sole trader 3, 4
Source document 7, 8, 19
Specimen examination paper 311–15
Standing order 220, 226
Statement of account 191, 192
Statement of affairs 238, 239, 248
Statements of Standard Accounting
    Practice (SSAPs) 3, 4, 62, 67
    SSAP 2 – Disclosure of accounting
        policies 4, 62–7
    SSAP 5 – Accounting for VAT
        4, 68–70
    SSAP 9 – Stocks and long-term
        contracts 4, 70–2, 146
    SSAP 12 – Accounting for
        depreciation 4, 72, 90
    SSAP 13 – Accounting for research
        and development 4, 72–3

Step-by-step guides
    depreciation in final accounts 112
    carriage inwards/outwards in final
        accounts 54
    extended trial balance 199–203
    incomplete records 247–8
    provision for bad debts in final
        accounts 125
    returns inwards/outwards in final
        accounts 54
Stock 4, 50–3, 70–2, 143–50, 200
    average cost (AVCO) 71, 74, 145, 150
    finished stocks 298
    first-in-first-out (FIFO) 71, 75, 144, 150
    last-in-last-out (LIFO) 71, 75, 144–5, 150
    net realisable value 70, 75, 146, 150
    sale or return 149, 150
    stock-taking 149
    work-in-progress 149
Straight line method of depreciation 87, 93
Subjectivity 61, 75
Subscriptions 260, 264
Suspense account 165, 173

Total cost 289, 298
Trial balance 14, 18, 20–6
    compensating error 24, 26, 161–2
    complete reversal of entries 24, 26, 162–4
    correction of errors 24, 25, 154–68
    definition 20
    errors of commission 24, 26, 158–9
    errors of omission 24, 26, 161
    errors of original entry 24, 26, 160–1
    error of principle 24, 26, 159–60
    extended trial balance 196–211
    skeleton trial balance 210
    uses 26
Trading and Profit and Loss Account 16, 18, 29, 46–56
    (refer to Final Accounts)
    model layout 54, 55
    horizontal style 30, 36, 52
    vertical style 30, 36, 53

Unpresented cheque 219, 226
Unrealised profit 298
Useful names and addresses 316–17

Value added tax (VAT) 4, 68–70, 75
    (refer to SSAP 5)
    accounting for VAT on fixed assets 110
    exempted firms 69, 74
    inputs 69, 75
    input tax 69, 75
    partly-exempt traders 69, 75
    output 69, 75
    output tax 69, 75
    rate 68
    taxable firms 68
    zero-rated firms 69

Work-in-progress 149, 292, 298
Working capital 137, 138
Written down value (WDV) 93, 99
    (refer to Net book value)

REDCAR & CLEVELAND BOROUGH COUNCIL
LIBRARY SERVICE